A TALE OF TWO AFRICAS:

NIGERIA AND SOUTH AFRICA AS CONTRASTING VISIONS

Published by
Adonis & Abbey Publishers Ltd
P.O. Box 43418
London
SE11 4XZ
http://www.adonis-abbey.com

First Edition January 2006

Copyright © Ali A. Mazrui 2006

British Library Cataloguing-in-Publication Data
A catalogue record for this book is available from the British Library

ISBN: 1-905068-29-8

Cover Design: MegaGraphix

Printed and bound in Great Britain by Lightning Source UK Ltd.

A TALE OF TWO AFRICAS:

NIGERIA AND SOUTH AFRICA AS CONTRASTING VISIONS

By Ali A. Mazrui

Edited by James N. Karioki

Adonis & Abbey
Publishers Ltd

Dedication

This book is dedicated to a very special Nigerian - my dearest wife,
Ejimah Pauline Maryam,
with much love.

ACKNOWLEDGEMENTS

In this volume we define a pivotal state as a state with outstanding qualifications for leadership based on size, location, population and resources. Four out of the five sub-regions of the African continent have an obvious pivotal state, a potential permanent member of a reformed Security Council of the African Union. Nigeria is the pivotal state for West Africa, South Africa for Southern Africa, Egypt for North Africa, and the Democratic Republic of the Congo is potentially pivotal for Central Africa. The fifth sub-region of Africa [Eastern Africa] does not have a clear-cut hegemonic state. Although Ethiopia has strong geographical and historical credentials for leadership in Eastern Africa, its status as "the first among equals" would not go unchallenged in its own sub-region of Eastern Africa.

In this book we are focusing on only two of the pivots: Nigeria and South Africa. Some of the chapters were written specially for this volume, while others are based on previous papers and lectures of mine.

I am deeply grateful to all those who had hosted those presentations in the past. More recently, I am especially grateful to my colleagues at the State University of New York at Binghamton; at Cornell University, Ithaca, New York; at the University of Jos in Nigeria; and at Jomo Kenyatta University of Agriculture and Technology in Kenya. In their discussions with me, these colleagues have stimulated new ideas.

Editorially, I am particularly grateful to my old friend and colleague, James N. Karioki who went through each chapter meticulously. He was often ruthless enough to delete some of my most favourite paragraphs from chapter to chapter! But I continue to believe that it was all ruthlessness of caring.

For bibliographical guidance and some excellent suggestions this book owes a lot to Thomas Uthup, a former academic colleague at Binghamton who has continued to render me sterling service in research and editing. Similarly, Amanda Wortmann at the African Institute of South Africa in Pretoria, South Africa, has been invaluable in making some insightful editorial comments and in the assembling of the bibliography.

Another former colleague, Amadu Jacky Kaba, has been a very valuable source of relevant social statistics and census figures, and has ably co-authored chapters 2 and 20 of this volume.

Much of my work on Nigeria has benefited from my being married to Pauline Uti, a Nigerian woman of great insight and dedication. My close friendship with the Nigerian scholar Jonah Isawa Elaigwu over the years has also greatly enriched my understanding of the politics of Nigeria.

My work on South Africa has benefited from two research institutes: the Africa Institute of South Africa (AISA) in Pretoria, and the Institute for Global Dialogue (IGD) in Johannesburg. Garth le Pere, the Executive Director of IGD in particular has always gone an extra mile in support of my scholarship in South Africa.

I have also been honoured and helped over the years by different South African universities, the South African media, Members of Parliament, government officials, religious leaders, businessmen and women, public intellectuals, writers and poets, and others. It has also been a great privilege to have known South Africa's first two Heads of State, Nelson Mandela and Thabo Mbeki, both before they became Presidents and during their years in office.

As Editor of this volume, James N. Karioki, a resident of Johannesburg, has kept me updated about news and trends in post-apartheid South Africa.

In all my travels to Nigeria, South Africa and other 'pivotal states,' I have benefited from my Administrative Assistant, Nancy Levis, who has become a genius in making complicated travel arrangements. When I am in Kenya these travel chores have been handled competently by my assistant at Jomo Kenyatta University, Michael Ngonyo Hindzano.

These chapters have had different typists at different stages, but I am especially grateful to AnnaMarie Palombaro, Barbara Tierno and Nancy Hall for the final stages of manuscript preparation.

Esther W. Githinji has been a tower of strength in James N. Karioki's editorial team. Bless them all!

Ali A. Mazrui
Binghamton University, Binghamton, New York and
University of Jos, Nigeria
December 2005

TABLE OF CONTENTS

Section IV: South Africa and the Multi-Racial Challenge

Section V: Comparative Leadership

PREFACE

COMPARATIVE EXCEPTIONALISM: NIGERIA AND SOUTH AFRICA

There is a sense in which every African country is unique in some special sense of its own. However, this book addresses more than that kind of particularism. The volume seeks to explore the particular ways in which Nigeria and South Africa are truly exceptional societies of the postcolonial era.

Every student of African affairs already knows that Nigeria is the largest country in Africa in population. But not many of us have taken note of the fact that the population of Nigeria is almost the equivalent of the populations of all the major European colonisers of Africa (the United Kingdom, France, Portugal and Belgium) added together.

Every student of African affairs may already know that South Africa is the most industrialized country on the African continent. But not every one realizes that in the 1960s South African surgeons were the first in the world to perform a successful heart transplant from one human being to another.[1] By 1990 South African technology (with the help of Israel)[2] had developed six nuclear weapons which were only dismantled in the 1990s because the era of political apartheid was coming to an end.[3]

We shall also indicate more clearly later not only the <u>comparative</u> exceptionalism of Nigeria and South Africa but also their <u>contrasting</u> models as alternative visions of Africa. Nigeria is indeed the Africa of human resources; South Africa is a land of mineral resources. Nigeria's climate and mosquito ridden habitation had repelled Europeans from settling there; South Africa's more moderate climate and spectacular natural endowments had, in contrast, attracted the largest concentration of white folks on the African continent. While Nigeria therefore remained a racially homogeneous country, (overwhelmingly Black), South Africa evolved into Africa's most multiracial society. Nigeria strongly illustrated the politics of religion in an African context, while South Africa manifested the politics of contending ideologies. After its civil war of 1967-70 Nigeria became Africa's largest exporter of oil. In the wake of its industrialization South Africa became Africa's greatest consumer of oil.

Nigeria has quite a few demographic surprises in addition to having a larger population than any European country apart from Russia. Nigeria also has more Muslims than any Arab country. Egypt is the most populous Arab country – but the Muslim percentage of Egypt's population (about 92% or about fifty five million) is still a little smaller than the sixty eight million Muslims of Nigeria in the year 2005.

This makes Nigeria the largest concentration of Muslims in the Black world, as well as being the largest Black country in population on this planet.

South Africa is the largest concentration of white people (Euro-extraction) outside the Western world (i.e. outside Europe and the Americas). In other words, South Africa has more Diaspora Europeans than any other country in the two largest continents of the world – Asia and Africa.

We hope to demonstrate in this book that Nigeria has produced the largest Black intelligentsia anywhere in the world. There are more people of Nigerian descent with advanced degrees than there are any other Black people with such degrees either in Africa or in the Diaspora.

South Africa's intelligentsia may be smaller than that of Nigeria, but South Africa has produced more Nobel laureates than any other African or Diaspora country in the world. Africa as a whole has won about a dozen Nobel prizes; half of those have been won by South Africans. South Africa has won four Nobel Prizes for peace, and two for literature.

But it is worth noting that the Nigerian, Wole Soyinka, was the very first African to win the Nobel Prize for literature. He won it in 1986.

Historically, the greatest African philosopher-king on the eve of European colonisation was Uthman Dan Fodio of Nigeria – an exceptionally learned Islamic reformer and jihadist conqueror. The greatest African warrior-king on the eve of European colonisation was Shaka Zulu of South Africa – an empire builder who has been compared with Napoleon Bonaparte. Nigeria had produced erudite and literary scholars before European colonialists overwhelmed the continent. South Africa had produced the greatest military hero of Africa's pre-colonial history – Shaka Zulu – while Nigeria experienced the scholarly legacy of the ruling house of Dan Fodio.

Nigeria's exceptionalism has also included a diversity of political systems in its history. Nigeria has combined monarchical systems (with Emirs, Obas, Onis, Ezes, Obis) with such republican or even stateless societies as the Tiv.

Nigeria has also experimented with both a secular federal level and the emerging Sharia (Islamic) systems of governance at the state level. Can a secular system at the national level be combined with theocracy at the provincial level?

Nigeria, unlike modern South Africa, has experienced both military rule and civilian governance. Indeed, Nigeria since independence has experienced more years under military rule than under civilian. In contrast, South Africa throughout the twentieth century and beyond has been under civilian governance.

South Africa's exceptionalism includes its being the most urbanized country in Africa south of the Sahara. The statistical part of chapter 2 should help to measure degrees of urbanization between South Africa and Nigeria.

Nigeria's exceptionalism includes the deep continuities of indigenous cultures. South Africa's exceptionalism has included the rapid pace of Westernisation. Two African countries -- deep in history, rich in culture, and diverse in demography -- have revealed comparative destinies of the African experience and contrasting visions of the African condition.

NOTES

[1] This heart transplant operation was performed by Christiaan Barnard and his team in December 1967. See Marais Malan, *Heart Transplant; The Story Of Barnard and the "Ultimate in Cardiac Surgery"* (Johannesburg: Voortrekkerpers, 1968) and Peter Hawthorne, *The Transplanted Heart; The Incredible Story of the Epic Heart Transplant Operations by Professor Christiaan Barnard and his Team* (Chicago: Rand McNally, 1968).

[2] The collabouration between the two states is described in David Fischer, "South Africa," in Mitchell Reiss and Robert S. Litwak, Eds., *Nuclear Proliferation After the Cold War* (Washington, DC: Woodrow Wilson Center Press and The Johns Hopkins University Press, 1994), pp. 209-213; Joel Peters, *Israel and Africa: The Problematic Friendship* (London: British Academic Press,

1992), pp. 159-161; and Benjamin M. Joseph, *Besieged Bedfellows: Israel and the Land of Apartheid* (New York: Greenwood Press, 1988), pp. 57-71.

[3] On South Africa's decision to give up nuclear weapons, see Joseph Cirincione, with Jon B. Wolfsthal and Miriam Rajkumar, *Deadly Arsenals : Tracking Weapons of Mass Destruction* (Washington, DC: Carnegie Endowment for International Peace, 2005), Second Edition, p. 407; Helen E. Purkitt and Stephen F. Burgess, *South Africa's Weapons of Mass Destruction* (Bloomington, IN: Indiana University Press, 2005), pp. 119-145; and Fischer, "South Africa," in Reiss and Litwak, Eds., *Nuclear Proliferation After the Cold War*, pp. 216-227.

SECTION I

SETTING THE STAGE

CHAPTER 1

NIGERIA AND SOUTH AFRICA AS CONTRASTING VISIONS: THEMES OF COMPARISON

(With James N. Karioki)

Almost exactly half a century separated the formal independence of South Africa in 1910 and the formal independence of Nigeria in 1960. These two countries have since become the most influential African countries between the River Niger and the Cape of Good Hope. Nigeria excels in human resources, since it has the largest population of any country in Africa. South Africa excels in mineral and material resources – ranging from gold to chrome, from diamonds to manganese, from platinum to iron-ore.

In much of the twentieth century, Africa had two types of European colonies: on the one hand, those which had attracted large numbers of white settlers and evolved a racial hierarchy, and, on the other, those African countries which were overwhelmingly indigenous and whose white populations consisted mainly of colonial administrators and temporary residents.

The most important example of the white-settler model of European colonisation was, of course, South Africa. On the eve of World War II, South Africa had indeed become the largest concentration of white people on the African continent. Extensive white settlement in an African country was good economic news for the economy and infrastructure, but bad political news for human relations. South Africa evolved into the most industrialized nation in Africa. But it also became the worst case of racism and apartheid.[1]

In contrast, the most important African country without a large European population was Nigeria. The absence of European enterprise and developmental skills deprived Nigeria of a more modern economic base and infrastructure. On the other hand, it also spared Nigeria the anguish of racial discrimination and the subsequent tensions of racial conflict.[2]

14

From Indirect Rule to Apartheid

In the first half of the twentieth century, the political policy which most shaped Nigeria's future was Lord Lugard's policy of Indirect Rule, seeking to decentralize power to local chiefs and Native authorities.[3]

In the second half of the twentieth century, the political policy which most shaped South Africa was the policy of apartheid, seeking to segregate the races socially and separate them territorially. What did Lord Lugard's policy of Indirect Rule in the first half of the twentieth century have in common with Verwoerd's policy of apartheid in the second half of that century?

At least in theory, both the policy of Indirect Rule in colonial Nigeria and the policy of apartheid in South Africa were based on a belief that Africans could best be ruled through their own indigenous institutions. In Nigeria the policy resulted in preserving such Native political institutions as the Emirates of Northern Nigeria. In South Africa the policy resulted in creating "Bantustans" with separate Native authorities.

Both Indirect Rule in Nigeria and apartheid in South Africa were based on a profound distrust of the potential for Westernisation of Africa. Theoretically, the doctrines aspired to protect the cultural authenticity of Africa. But on this issue Lord Lugard was more sincere than Prime Minister Verwoerd, the architect of apartheid. Lugard's Indirect Rule was genuinely based on the British cultural tradition of political gradualism. In the words of the British philosopher, Edmund Burke: *"Neither entirely nor at once depart from antiquity."*[4]

Britain's own domestic history illustrated the implementation of such gradualism. That is why Britain is still a monarchy and has a reformed House of Lords. The British policy of Indirect Rule was similarly premised on gradual rather than precipitate political change. As a consequence, Indirect Rule in Northern Nigeria slowed down such forces of Westernisation as Western education and popular political participation. The Sultan of Sokoto and the Emirs of other principalities in Nigeria retained considerable power under British sovereignty. The more artificial Native Authorities of Yorubaland and Igboland gained legitimacy and power from generation to generation and constituted a quest for cultural continuity.

Ostensibly, the apartheid ideology also valued cultural continuity and regarded Westernisation as a potentially disruptive force among Africans. Lord Lugard never used the term, *"separate development"*, in

15

relation to the Emirates of Northern Nigeria, but his policies did de facto result in Northern Nigeria's development in a different way from Southern Nigeria.[5]

On the other hand, Verwoerd and his successors never used the term *Indirect Rule* when referring to white control over the Bantu homelands, or the relationship between the central government in Pretoria and the rulers of the Bantustans. But in reality that relationship between white power and the Bantu homelands was indeed a form of "indirect rule".

However, Lord Lugard's motives were very different from the motives of the architects of apartheid. The designers of apartheid started from a lack of respect for Black people generally, while Lord Lugard respected the kings and princes of Nigeria within the confines of an imperial system. The architects of apartheid started with discrimination and segregation at the micro-level – racially separate lavatories, drinking fountains, schools, residential neighbourhoods. In essence, this was micro-apartheid.

But the ideology took a step further and attempted the territorial creation of separate racial homelands.[6]

In contrast, Lord Lugard believed in territorial amalgamation instead of territorial fragmentation. As Governor-General of colonial Nigeria, it was Lugard who united Southern Nigeria with Northern in 1914 – and thus created the most populous country in Africa. Lugard believed in relative cultural autonomy for the different ethnic groups of Nigeria – rather than territorial compartmentalization.[7]

On Politics and War

South Africa had two stages of sovereign independence – independence for white South Africans in 1910 and independence for all South Africans in 1994. Some of the worst conflicts in South Africa occurred before the attainment of full independence. Such conflicts ranged from the Anglo-Boer War of 1899-1902 to the struggle against apartheid from the 1960s onwards.

If South Africa's worst conflicts were before attainment of full independence, Nigeria's worst conflicts were after the end of colonial rule. This has included the Nigerian Civil War of 1967 to 1970,[8] the anti-Igbo pogrom of 1966 which helped to trigger the civil war, and the various communal and religious conflicts which have taken such a heavy toll over the years.

There had been conflicts in colonial Nigeria from time to time while the British were in power, but nothing compared with the carnage of the post-colonial civil war and its aftermath.

Another contrast between Nigeria and South Africa concerns the role of the military in politics. But let us place that issue in the wider context of trends in the rest of Africa. Throughout the second half of the twentieth century, Africa was divided between coup-prone countries and coup-proof states. Coup-prone countries experienced the sustained intervention of the military in politics – usually within the first decade of independence.[9] The first country to capitulate to a military coup in Anglophone Africa was indeed Nigeria with the Igbo-led coup of January 1966. The Nigerian coup was followed by the overthrow of Kwame Nkrumah in Ghana by soldiers in February 1966.

Coup-proof African countries, on the other hand, are those which have successfully avoided a military takeover of power through the second half of the twentieth century and beyond. Such countries include Senegal, Tanzania, Kenya, Zambia, Malawi, Morocco and others. Among the most coup-proof of all the African countries is the Republic of South Africa, equipped with armed forces which are particularly professional and well-trained. The South African military has been socialized into accepting civilian supremacy in the command structure.

Another puzzling aspect of the second half of the twentieth century is the fact that the overwhelming majority of military coups in Africa occurred north of the equator – and the equator cut Africa almost in half.

Coup-prone countries north of the equator in the second half of the last century were led by Nigeria.[10] Other coup-prone countries on the equator or north of it have included Ghana, Togo, Sierra Leone, the two Congo's, Sudan, Uganda, Rwanda, Burkina Faso, Ethiopia, Somalia and others.

Coup-proof countries south of the equator in the second half of the twentieth century were led by South Africa, but accompanied by Zimbabwe, Zambia, Swaziland, Botswana, Malawi and Tanzania. Mozambique and Angola had civil wars rather than military coups in the usual sense – and the civil wars were in part fuelled by apartheid South Africa. Little Lesotho did have a military coup – the exception that proved the rule.

What was it in the second half of the twentieth century which made Africa south of the equator disproportionately coup-proof and Africa north of the equator disproportionately coup-prone?

One theoretical explanation which might be advanced is chronologically based since most of Africa north of the equator attained independence earlier than Africa south of the equator, why was it surprising that military coups should also begin earlier north of the equator?

This chronological explanation will not work. Apart from Egypt, all the coup-prone countries north of the equator experienced their first coup within the first decade of independence. None of the African countries south of the equator experienced a military coup, even after a quarter of a century of independence.

Could another possible explanation for the military differences between north and south of the equator be climatic and ecological? There are indeed ecological variations between Africa south of the Sahara and Africa to the north. But it is almost impossible to identify their relevance as either triggers of military coups or inhibitors thereof.

Another scenario to explain differences in military behaviour between Africa south of the equator and Africa to the north would hinge on sociological variations between the two halves of the continent. Such sociological variables could include the deeper influence of white settlers in Southern Africa as an inhibitor to military coups. In reality, Southern Africa in the second half of the twentieth century was conflict-prone, even if it was not coup-prone. Southern Africa had disproportionate anti-colonial wars, but hardly any post-colonial military coups. Even though the Republic of South Africa had engaged in a variety of wars to defend apartheid – it had never experienced a military coup itself. Even today it is arguable that South Africa is conflict-prone, but not coup-prone. Post-colonial Nigeria, on the other hand, has been both conflict-prone and coup-prone. In South Africa the soldiers have been engaged in various clashes over the years, but the decisions to go to war were usually made by civilians.

In Nigeria, on the other hand, there have been both civilian-driven conflicts and militarily-sponsored conflagrations.[11] Moreover, Nigeria has experienced more post-colonial years under military rule than under civilian. On the other hand, South Africa since 1910 has not experienced any military take-over at all – though Prime Ministers like

Kruger and Smuts were [like Ike Eisenhower in the United States] initially soldiers before they became politicians and statesmen.

Between Ethnicity and Religion

Another major area of contrast between Nigeria and South Africa is the role of religion in their respective politics. The era of apartheid in South Africa was also the era of a <u>de facto</u> theocracy. The Dutch Reformed Church was virtually a state-religion, and much of the ideology of racial separation was legitimised in Biblical terms about the curse of Cain on Black people.[12]

Paradoxically, the first Christian winners of the Nobel Prize for Peace in Africa were Blacks of South Africa. The very first was Albert Luthuli, who was President of the African National Congress (1952-60) and was committed to Christian non-violence. He won the Nobel Prize for Peace in 1960, and was killed by a train n 1967.

The second African Nobel Peace Laureate was a professional cleric – a Bishop of the Church of England: Bishop (later Archbishop) Desmond Tutu won the Nobel Prize in 1984. The racial version of Christianity embodied in the doctrine of apartheid was rapidly outweighed by a more tolerant version of the Christian gospel.

We may conclude from this dichotomy that the major religious tensions of South Africa were not between Christians and believers of other faiths. The major tensions were between believers in one form of Christianity (right-wing Dutch Reformed Church) and believers in other versions of the message of Jesus (especially Anglicans and Catholics).[13]

In Nigeria, on the other hand, the most politicised religious cleavage since independence has been between Christians and Muslims. Almost all Hausa in Northern Nigeria are Muslims; almost all Igbo of Eastern Nigeria are Christians, while the Yoruba of Western Nigeria are split between Muslims and Christians.[14]

Every time Nigeria had a national election during the first three decades after independence, a Muslim-led government emerged. It began with the government of Abubakar Tafawa Balewa (1960-1966), which was overthrown in a military coup in January 1966. The next general election was in 1979, which produced another Muslim, Shehu Shagari, as President. He was re-elected four years later, only to be overthrown by fellow Muslims within months of the second term.

The third general election was in 1993, which produced yet another Muslim as the chosen Head of State – Chief Moshoola Abiola. Unfortunately, the military did not permit him to assume office. He subsequently died in prison.

During the first forty years of Nigeria's independence there were a number of communal conflicts – some ethnic ("tribal"), some sectarian (especially Christian versus Muslim) and several were both ethnic and sectarian at the same time. The worst was the anti-Igbo pogrom in Northern Nigeria in 1966 which was partly ethnic (Hausa versus Igbo) and partly religious (Muslim versus Christian) at the same time. The anti-Igbo riots set the stage for the Nigerian civil war of 1967-1970.

Northern Nigerians lost political control after the election of 1998 which elected Olusegun Obasanjo as President. Ironically, his fellow Yoruba voted against him in 1998, while the majority of Northern Muslim Hausa voters supported him. Obasanjo would not have ascended to power without considerable Muslim support – but his triumph marked the decline of Muslim political power in post-colonial Nigeria.

Partly in response to their political decline in the Federal Government, Northern Muslims turned to their culture and religion for a sense of autonomy. The pro-Sharia Islamic government gathered momentum. Although Nigeria as a whole was supposed to be a secular state, constituent parts of federal Nigeria began to opt for Islamic law as the provincial code. Starting with the state of Zamfara, a third of the states of federal Nigeria eventually went Islamic (twelve out of thirty-six states).[15]

Globally, the most controversial moment of this trend in Islamization came when an Islamic court in Northern Nigeria sentenced a pregnant woman, Amina Lawal, to death under Islamic law on charges of adultery. Fortunately, the international uproar (including protests from other African and Muslim countries) eventually helped to save Lawal's life, and prepared the way for her release.[16]

In South Africa religion had once impacted adversely inter-racial relations. In Nigeria religion continues to impact adversely "inter-tribal" relations. In South Africa, the worst religious tensions were between different denominations of Christians. In Nigeria the worst sectarian tensions continue to be between Christians and Muslims.

South Africa may be entering a phase of tension between different codes of morality rather than different sects of religion. In the post-apartheid era, South Africans have entered debates about domestic violence, same-sex marriages, gay rights and the probably link between sexual promiscuity and the spread of HIV-AIDS. The social aspects of morality are now more hotly debated than the racial politics of religion.

As for indigenous religions in both Nigeria and South Africa, they are less politicised than the Abrahamic religions of Christianity and Islam. But once again there is a marked contrast in the experiences of the two countries. In South Africa indigenous religions are under siege because of the heavy weight of Westernisation and capitalist transformation. But in much of Nigeria indigenous religions are still powerful, and often have a reverse impact on Christianity and Islam. In Nigeria the Abrahamic religions have not only changed indigenous culture; they, in turn, have been modified by ancestral Nigerian traditions. While South Africa has become a paragon of Westernisation, Nigeria continues to be a paradigm of indigenisation.

As for the economics of the two countries, they both have a heavy reliance on extractive industries. Nigeria is Africa's largest exporter of petroleum; South Africa is Africa's largest consumer of oil. The extractive industries of South Africa are of solids (platinum, gold, coal), rather than either liquid oil or natural gas, as in the case of Nigeria.

South Africa's mineral wealth has not only fuelled industrialization; it has also strengthened the agricultural sector with the revenue generated. Nigeria's oil wealth, on the other hand, has probably damaged Nigerian agriculture, reducing both the incomes of farmers and their motivation to remain in agriculture. The Nigerian elite has also changed some of their consumption patterns in favour of imported commodities like wheat and rice, rather than local root crops.

As for that insidious pathology of corruption, South Africa is still basically at a stage of elite and corporate corruption, rather than pervasive bribery, from grassroots to the pinnacles of society. Nigeria, on the other hand, has suffered a deeper malaise – and is sometimes internationally ranked among the three to five most corrupt countries in the world.[17]

Unfortunately, there is no guarantee that South Africa is not already experiencing the spread of the infection of corruption from the elite and the corporations to the wider ranks of society.[18] This may be one area of experience in which South Africa and Nigeria are not diverging as social contrasts, but converging into a shared social malaise. There is no room for complacency in either society. The struggle to transcend has to continue.

Conclusion

Nigeria and South Africa may be viewed as two contrasting paradigms of the African condition. In the period of European colonisation South Africa became a magnet for large scale European settlement, whereas Nigeria, as a British colony, was climatically and ecologically inhospitable for white settlement. This difference had momentous consequences for the two countries, both positive and negative. Large scale European settlement in a colony was normally good economic news for productivity and the infrastructure, but bad political news for human and race relations. Nigeria, on the other hand, was spared the woes of institutionalised racism, while being also denied the developmental skills of a white settler elite.

In the first half of the twentieth century Nigeria was shaped by Lord Lugard's policy of Indirect Rule, partly based on the belief that colonised people were best ruled through their own Native institutions. We have sought to demonstrate that the policy of apartheid in South Africa in the second half of the twentieth century was based on a similar principle of creating Native authorities for Africans in their Bantu homelands. But while Lord Lugard's motives were partly in a spirit of cultural tolerance, the architects of apartheid were motivated by a spirit of racial intolerance. The terms "Indirect Rule" and "Separate Development" were almost interchangeable between the two countries, but the motives were very different.

During the era of apartheid, religious tensions in South Africa were mainly between a racially based version of Christianity (the rightist Dutch Reformed Church) and the love-based gospel of Jesus (such as the Anglican and Catholic) churches. The love-based gospel won the Nobel Prize for Peace for Albert Luthuli and Bishop Desmond Tutu. Much later Nelson Mandela and F.W. DeKlerk won the Nobel Peace Prize together for reasons which were secular.

In Nigeria since independence, on the other hand, the sharpest religious tensions have been between Muslims and Christians. Sometimes these tensions exploded into communal riots, the worst of which were the anti-Igbo pogrom in Northern Nigeria in 1966. More recent political confrontations have resulted in Islamic movements among the Hausa which have culminated in the establishment of Islamic law (the Sharia) in a third of the states of Federal Nigeria.

In South Africa under apartheid religion conditioned inter-racial relations. In Nigeria since independence religion has conditioned "inter-tribal" relations. In post-apartheid South Africa sharper debates are between different codes of morality, rather than divergent sects of religion. Passions about domestic violence, gay rights and HIV/AIDS are in the process of replacing the older passions about the Biblical origins of racial differences.

In economic matters South Africa's mineral wealth has helped both industrialization and its highly productive agriculture. Nigeria's oil wealth, on the other hand, may have dampened the country's agricultural sector. The West African country's petro-wealth has enriched the urban elites, while often impoverishing the rural populations. Ironically, while Nigeria is Africa's largest exporter of oil, South Africa is Africa's largest consumer of oil.

South Africa is still at a stage of elite and corporate corruption, while Nigeria has descended to pervasive bribery from grassroots to the pinnacle of society. Unfortunately, there are signs that South Africa is moving in Nigeria's direction with regard to this social malaise. The two countries may need to learn from each other about how best to arrest social decomposition while accelerating economic development.

NOTES

[1] On South Africa's history, consult, for instance, Robert C. Cottrell, *South Africa: A State of Apartheid* (Philadephia, PA: Chelsea House, 2005); Nancy L. Clark and William H. Worger, *South Africa: The Rise and Fall of Apartheid* (Harlow, England and New York: Longman, 2004); and James Barber, *South Africa in the Twentieth Century: A Political History--In Search of a Nation State* (Oxford, UK and Malden, MA: Blackwell Publishers, 1999).

[2] On the history of Nigeria, see, for example, Toyin Falola, Ed., *Nigerian History, Politics and Affairs : The Collected Essays of Adiele Afigbo* (Trenton, NJ: Africa World Press, 2005); Richard A. Olaniyan, Ed. *The Amalgamation and its Enemies : An Interpretive History of Modern Nigeria* (Ile-Ife, Nigeria: Obafemi Awolowo University Press, 2003); Toyin Falola, *The History of Nigeria* (Westport, CT: Greenwood Press, 1999)

[3] For specific cases and analyses of "indirect rule" in Nigeria, see Toyin Falola, Ed., *Nigerian History, Politics and Affairs : the Collected Essays of Adiele*

Afigbo, (Trenton, NJ : Africa World Press, 2005), pp. 253-295; Olufemi Vaughan, *Nigerian Chiefs : Traditional Power in Modern Politics, 1890s-1990s* (Rochester, NY: University of Rochester Press, 2000), pp. 22-68; J. A. Atanda, *The New Oyo Empire: Indirect Rule and Change in Western Nigeria, 1894-1934* (London: Longman, 1973); and A. E. Afigbo, *The Warrant Chiefs: Indirect Rule in Southeastern Nigeria, 1891-1929* (New York: Humanities Press, 1972).

[4] Edmund Burke, *Reflections on the French Revolution*. The Harvard Classics, 1909-1914. Para 171. Accessed at <http://www.bartleby.com/24/3/7.html> (December 5, 2005).

[5] For an overview of this important figure in Nigerian history, consult Dame Margery F. Perham, *Lugard* (2 volumes), (London: Collins, 1956-60) as also Michael Crowder, "Lugard and Colonial Nigeria: Towards an Identity," *History Today* 36 (February 1986), pp. 23-29.

[6] Relatedly consult   Elaine Unterhalter, *Forced Removal : The Division, segregation and Control of the People of South Africa* (London: London : International Defence and Aid Fund for Southern Africa, 1987). For some general accounts, also see William Beinart and Saul DuBow, Eds., *Segregation And Apartheid In Twentieth-Century South Africa* (London and New York: Routledge, 1995); Philip Bonner, Peter Delius, Deborah Posel, Eds., *Apartheid's Genesis, 1935-1962* (Braamfontein and Johannesburg, South Africa: Ravan Press and Wits University Press, 1993); and Saul Dubow, *Racial Segregation and the Origins of Apartheid in South Africa, 1919-36* (Houndmills, Basingstoke, Hampshire, New York, and Oxford: MacMillan with St. Anthony's College, 1989).

[7] Documents relevant to this topic may be found in A. H. M. Kirk-Greene (Compiler and Editor), Lugard and the Amalgamation of Nigeria: A Documentary Record; Being a Reprint of the Report By Sir F. D. Lugard on the Amalgamation of Northern and Southern Nigeria and Administration 1912-1919; Together With Supplementary Unpublished Amalgamation Reports, and Other Relevant Documents (London: Cass, 1968) and for a selection, Olaniyan, Ed. *The Amalgamation and its Enemies*, pp. 209-237.

[8] Also known as the Biafra War; on this war, consult Herbert Ekwe-Ekwe, *The Biafra War : Nigeria and the Aftermath*, Lewiston, N.Y., USA : E. Mellen Press, 1990); Peter Schwab, Ed. *Biafra* (New York, Facts on File, 1971); and Zdenek Cervenka, *The Nigerian War, 1967-1970. History of the War; Selected Bibliography and Documents* (Frankfurt: Bernard & Graefe, 1971).

[9] The military role in African politics is described and analyzed in, for example, George Klay Kieh, Jr., and Pita Ogaba Agbese, Eds., *The Military and Politics in Africa : From Intervention to Democratic and Constitutional Control* (Aldershot, Hants, England ; Burlington, VT : Ashgate, 2004); Chuka Onwumechili, *African Democratisation and Military Coups* (Westport, CT: Praeger Publishers, 1998); and Ruth First, *The Barrel of a Gun: Political Power in Africa and the Coup* (London: Allen Lane, 1970).

[10]The coups in Nigeria are described in Onwumechili, *African Democratisation and Military Coups*, pp. 48-50.

[11] An overview of the North-South and other cleavages bedeviling Nigeria may be found in *The Economist* (January 15, 2000), pp. 14-15; also see *The Economist* (July 8, 2000), p. 47.

[12] On the Dutch Reformed Church's relationship with the apartheid state, see Tracy Kuperus, *State, Civil Society and Apartheid in South Africa : An Examination of Dutch Reformed Church-State Relations* (New York : St. Martin's Press, 1999).

[13] For discussions on the role of churches in South Africa under apartheid, see Douglas Johnston, "The Churches and Apartheid in South Africa," in Douglas Johnston and Cynthia Sampson, Ed., *Religion, The Missing Dimension of Statecraft* (New York: Oxford University Press, 1994), pp. 177-207, and Martin Prozesky, Ed., *Christianity Amidst Apartheid : Selected Perspectives on the Church in South Africa* (New York : St. Martin's Press, 1990).

[14] Analyses on earlier conflicts caused by religious differences may be found in Toyin Falola, *Violence in Nigeria: The Crisis of Religious Politics and Secular Ideologies* (Rochester, NY: University of Rochester Press, 1998), especially pp. 77-113; Simeon O. Ilesanmi, *Religious Pluralism and the Nigerian State* (Athens, OH: Ohio University Center for International Studies, 1997), pp. 174-207; M. H. Kukah and Toyin Falola, *Religious Militancy and Self-Assertion: Islam and Politics in Nigeria* (Aldershot, UK, and Brookfield, VT: Avebury Press, 1996), pp. 117-139; and Pat A. T. Williams, "Religion, Violence, and Displacement in Nigeria," *Journal of Asian and African Studies*, 32, 1-2 (June 1997), pp. 33-49.

[15] These states are listed in *Africa Research Bulletin* (September 22, 2000), Vol. 37, No. 8, p. 14077.

[16] Relatedly, consult O. U. Kalu, "Safiyya and Adamah: Punishing Adultery with Sharia Stones in Twenty-first Century Nigeria," *African Affairs* (2003), Volume 102, No. 408, pp. 389-408. It should be noted that the sentences of stoning have never been carried out. Even in the case of Amina Lawal, the case

against her was flawed and she may not have been in any danger of being executed at all, even under the Shariah. See the opinion piece by Helon Habila, "The Politics of Islamic Law: Shariah in Nigeria," *The International Herald Tribune*, (October 7, 2003).

[17] Nigerian leaders are believed to have stolen or misused $400 billion in government funds over the past four decades; for a representative story, see Lydia Polgreen, "As Nigeria Tries to Fight Graft, a New Sordid Tale," *The New York Times* (November 29, 2005).

[18] South Africa is still wrestling with the remnants of economic apartheid in the midst of new prosperity, as evinced by this report: Incompetence and greed are rife. In Ehlanzeni, a district of nearly a million people in Mpumalanga Province [in South Africa], 3 out of 4 residents have no trash collection, 6 out of 10 have no sanitation and 1 in 3 lack water - and the city manager makes more than Mr. Mbeki's $180,000 annual salary. Michael Wines, " Shantytown Dwellers in South Africa Protest Sluggish Pace of Change," *The New York Times* (December 25, 2005).

CHAPTER 2

NIGERIA AND SOUTH AFRICA: KEY FACTS AND STATISTICS

(With Amadu Jacky Kaba)

Nigeria and South Africa: The Birth and Adolescence of Two Pivotal States

Both South Africa and Nigeria are countries which were created by amalgamating two previously distinct territorial entities. In the case of South Africa, the amalgamation consisted of the Afrikaner (Boer) controlled republics of Transvaal and the Orange Free State, on one side, and the British colonies of the Cape and Natal, on the other.

The British had conquered the Boer republics in the Anglo-Boer War of 1899-1902.[1] In 1910 the British annexed the Afrikaner republics and united them with their own colonies in South Africa. The Union of South Africa was born consisting of elements which could otherwise have evolved into distinct sovereign states in the future.

Four years after the amalgamation of Boer and British South Africa, Lord Lugard amalgamated North and South Nigeria.[2] He was serving in Hong Kong when the British government in London offered him the opportunity of uniting the two parts of Nigeria. Because Northern Nigeria had clearer city-states and monarchical institutions than the South, Lord Lugard regarded Northerners as being at a more advanced stage of development and "civilisation". Yet Northern Nigeria, like Boer parts of South Africa at the beginning of the twentieth century, was marred by the institution of slavery. The two parts of Nigeria in that period were often described in terms like the following British imperial terms:

In the South were pagan tribes and in the north, historical Muslim city states and large walled cities whose emirs raided the tribal territories to the South for slaves....[Lugard's] policy was to support the native states and chieftainships, their laws and their courts, forbidding slave-raiding and cruel punishments and exercising control through native rulers.[3]

This was the policy which came to be known as "Indirect Rule" and which became one of the foundations of British colonial policy in Africa more generally.[4]

It worked best in those parts of Africa which had developed city-states or monarchies. Within Nigeria itself Indirect Rule was least successful in the Southeast "among the loosely organized societies of the Igbo and other southeastern tribes."[5]

The legacy of Lugard protected northern Nigeria from too much Christian missionary penetration and evangelising activism. However, that same Lugard legacy regarded Southern "pagan tribes" (so-called) as fair game for Christian missionary penetration and proselytism. The long-term consequences created a major cultural contradiction. The Southern "tribes" whom Lugard regarded as less "civilized and less developed" than the Hausa, responded to the stimulus of Western civilisation and Christian evangelisation, and attained higher levels of modernization than their northern compatriots.[6] The stage was being set for a major post-colonial regional cultural cleavage between North and South.

In South Africa, on the other hand, the union of Boer Republics with British colonies did eventually result in the relative unification of the Afrikaners and the English-speaking South Africans as white people – but at the expense of a deepening racial cleavage between Euro-South Africans, on one side, and Black, Indian and other South Africans of colour, on the other.

In both South Africa and Nigeria the Black population was led by a triad of vanguard "tribes". In Nigeria the three vanguard ethnic groups were the Hausa, the Yoruba and the Igbo – but with multiple smaller groups involved on the side. In South Africa the triad of Black "tribes" consisted of the Xhosa, the Zulu and the Sotho, who came to be collectively known as the Bantu in the era of apartheid.

The aftermath of World War II in Nigeria deepened even further the Westernisation of the Igbo and the Yoruba communities of the South as colonial policy became more committed to a policy of higher education. The first Western style university institution was established in Ibadan in the South. The overwhelming majority of students at what eventually became the University of Ibadan came from the Igbo, Yoruba and other Southern communities. Although the Hausa was the largest ethnic community in Nigeria, they were among the least represented among either the students and staff of Ibadan or among the Nigerians who went abroad for higher education.

In South Africa, the initial impact of World War II was to strengthen the trend towards Afrikaner nationalism and to reduce the national commitment to Western education for Black people. Increasing anti-British sentiment among the Afrikaners, and the rising obsession with the issue of race, resulted in the triumph of the Afrikaner-led National Party (NP) led by Daniel F. Malan. The NP captured power in 1948, with a manifesto in favour of reinforcing racial segregation under the "trusteeship and guardianship" of white South Africans. Under the leadership of Daniel Malan (1948-1957) and the even more imaginative and brilliant Hendrik F. Verwoerd (1958-1966), South Africa moved towards becoming the most institutionalised racist state in human history.[7]

And then came the year 1960 that marked, on the one hand, Nigeria's independence from British colonial rule, and on the other hand, also the year of the Sharpeville massacre in South Africa. Sovereign independence was a signal for euphoria and optimism from Lagos to Kano in Nigeria. The Sharpeville incident, on the other hand, was a catastrophe not only for the 69 unarmed African demonstrators killed by the South African police in the streets, but also for the reputation and standing of the South African apartheid regime in international diplomacy and world opinion.[8]

1960 was also the year when over fifteen other African countries became independent and joined the United Nations. Those who were previously ruled by Great Britain also joined the Commonwealth of Nations under the titular Headship of the Queen of England, Elizabeth II. South Africa had been a member of the Commonwealth since 1931 when it attained full sovereignty as a Dominion under white control.

But the convergence of two events in 1960 precipitated an agonizing reappraisal of South Africa's status in the Commonwealth. One trigger of the reappraisal was indeed the entry of new Black members into the Commonwealth, especially Nigeria which was potentially a real rival to South Africa in African affairs. The other trigger of the fundamental review of South Africa's place in the Commonwealth was indeed the Sharpeville massacre which could not have happened at a worse time from the prospective of the apartheid regime. South Africa was forced to withdraw from the Commonwealth and she became a republic on May 31, 1961. In other words, as the newly sovereign Nigeria entered the Commonwealth of Nations through the front door in 1960, South Africa had to exit from the Commonwealth from the rear door soon after.

While the year 1960 was a year of contrast between Nigeria's sovereign euphoria and South Africa's Sharpeville gloom, the year 1966 was a year of convergence between Nigeria and South Africa in violent episodes. Nigeria's experience was more overwhelming. Nigerian experienced its first military coup in January 1966.[9] It was a coup which was accompanied with the assassination of the Prime Minister, Abubakar Tafawa Balewa, and the murders of the Northern Sardauna of Sokoto and of some Yoruba leaders as well. The 1966 coup was Igbo-led with devastating consequences for the future of the country.[10]

In South Africa 1966 was also a year of assassination – the murder of Prime Minister Hendrik F. Verwoerd by a white man in the full glare of a parliamentary session. The assassination in South Africa did not lead to long-term instability. Prime Minister Balthahazar J. Vorster succeeded Verwoerd and continued his apartheid policies.

However, the assassinations of the Prime Minister in Nigeria and of the Sardauna of Sokoto prepared the ground for an anti-Igbo pogrom later in 1966 – which eventually exploded in the Nigerian civil war of 1967-1970.[11]

Since the civil war, Nigeria has experienced a continuous interplay between the politics of ethnicity and the politics of petroleum, Nigeria's most important natural resource.[12] In the Middle East the politics of oil have sometimes triggered conflict between states. In Nigeria the politics of oil have triggered conflict within states. Countries like Kuwait and Iraq have experienced petro-conquest. Nigeria, as a rentier dependent state, has experienced petro-capture. The interplay between the international oil companies, the enraged oil communities in the productive regions, the local elites, and vulnerable states under the curse of petroleum, have converged on the Nigerian civil society.[13]

South Africa's apartheid policies and white majority rule generated international coalition and opprobrium that helped to end the Afrikaner regime.[14] Under first Nelson Mandela and then Thabo Mbeki, the country has emerged as one of the more important democratic countries in Africa and the world. Nigeria too, after several military coups, has appeared to have made giant strides towards a democratic republic. Both countries are repositories of natural and human resources that make them pivotal states in Africa for the 21st century.

Let us look more closely at the facts and figures of the African condition as illustrated by Nigeria and the Republic of South Africa.

Nigeria and South Africa: Key Facts and Statistics[15]

Key Population Statistics (Table 1)

POPULATION	NIGERIA				SOUTH AFRICA	
	128,771,988 (July 2005 est.)				44,344,136 (July 2005 est.)	
Ethnic/Racial Groups (%)	Hausa-Fulani	29	Kanuri	4	Black[16]	79
	Yoruba	21	Ibibio	3.5	White	9.6
	Igbo (Ibo)	18	Tiv	2.5	Coloured	8.9
	Ijaw	10	Other	12	Indian/Asian	2.5
Males, By Age, (%)	65,111,516 (50.5)				21,514,224 (48.5)	
0-14 Years	27,466,766				6,760,137	
15-64 Years	35,770,593				13,860,727	
65 And Over	1,874,157				893,360	
Females, By Age, (Percent)	63,660,472 (49.5)				22,829,912 (51.5)	
0-14 Years	27,045,092				6,682,013	
15-64 Years	34,559,414				14,750,496	
65 And Over	2,055,966				1,397,403	
Average Life Expectancy	46.74				43.27	
Male Life Expectancy	46.21				43.47	
Female Life Expectancy	47.29				43.06	
Median Age	18.63				23.98	
Median Male Age	18.71				23.12	
Median Female Age	18.55				24.86	

Religious Diversity

As for Nigeria's religious breakdown, it is estimated that Muslims comprise 50 percent, Christian 40 percent, and indigenous beliefs 10 percent. In South Africa, the religious breakdown is: Zion Christian 11.1 percent, Pentecostal/Charismatic 8.2 percent, Catholic 7.1 percent, Methodist 6.8 percent, Dutch Reformed 6.7 percent, Anglican 3.8 percent, other Christian 36 percent, Islam 1.5 percent, other 2.3 percent, unspecified 1.4 percent, none 15.1 percent, according to the 2001 census.

Comparative Oil Statistics (Table 2)

	NIGERIA	SOUTH AFRICA
Oil Reserves	34 billion bbl[17]	7.84 million bbl[18]
Oil Production	2.356 million bbl/day[19]	196,200 bbl/day[20]
Oil Consumption	275,000 bbl/day[21]	460,000 bbl/day[22]

Comparative armed forces and military

NIGERIA

Military manpower - military age and obligation: 18 years of age for voluntary military service (2001)

Military manpower - availability: *males age 18-49:* 26,804,314 (2005 est.)

Military manpower - fit for military service: *males age 18-49:* 15,053,936 (2005 est.)

Military manpower - reaching military age annually: *males:* 1,353,161 (2005 est.)

Military expenditures - dollar figure: $544.6 million (2004)

Military expenditures - percent of GDP: 0.8% (2004)

SOUTH AFRICA

Military branches: South African National Defence Force (SANDF): Army, Navy, Air Force, Joint Operations, Joint Support, Military Intelligence, Military Health Service (2004)

Military manpower - military age and obligation: 18 years of age for voluntary military service; women have a long history of military service in non-combat roles - dating back to World War I (2004)

Military manpower - availability: *males age 18-49:* 10,354,769 (2005 est.)

Military manpower - fit for military service: *males age 18-49:* 4,927,757 (2005 est.)

Military manpower - reaching military age annually: *males:* 512,407 (2005 est.)

Military expenditures - dollar figure: $3.172 billion (2004)

Military expenditures - percent of GDP: 1.5% (2004)

Military - note: with the end of apartheid and the establishment of majority rule, former military, black homelands forces, and ex-opposition forces were integrated into the South African National

Defence Force (SANDF); as of 2003 the integration process was considered complete.

Key Economic Indicators

NIGERIA

GDP: purchasing power parity - $125.7 billion (2004 est.)

GDP - real growth rate: 6.2% (2004 est.)

GDP - per capita: purchasing power parity - $1,000 (2004 est.)

Industries: crude oil, coal, tin, columbite, palm oil, peanuts, cotton, rubber, wood, hides and skins, textiles, cement and other construction materials, food products, footwear, chemicals, fertilizer, printing, ceramics, steel, small commercial ship construction and repair.

SOUTH AFRICA

GDP: purchasing power parity - $491.4 billion (2004 est.)

GDP - real growth rate: 3.5% (2004 est.)

GDP - per capita: purchasing power parity - $11,100 (2004 est.)

Industries: mining (world's largest producer of platinum, gold, chromium), automobile assembly, metalworking, machinery, textile, iron and steel, chemicals, fertilizer, foodstuffs, commercial ship repair.

Comparative urbanization in Nigeria & South Africa

NIGERIA

The urban population in Nigeria (as % of total) in 1975 was 23.4%; in 2003, 46.6%; and projected to be 55.5% in 2015.

SOUTH AFRICA

The urban population in South Africa (as % of total) in 1975 was 48%; in 2003, 56.9%; and projected to be 62.7% in 2015.[23]

NOTES

[1] On the Boer War, see Denis Judd and Keith Judd, *The Boer War* (London: John Murray, 2002) and John Camaroff, Ed., with Brian William and Andrew Reed, *Mafeking Diary: A Black Man's View of a White Man's War*, by Sol T. Plaatje (Cambridge, UK; Athens, OH: Meridor Press in association with J. Currey and Ohio University Press, 1990).

[2] Relevant documents on the amalgamation in Nigeria may be found in A. H. M. Kirk-Greene (Compiler and Editor), *Lugard and the Amalgamation of Nigeria: A Documentary Record; Being a Reprint of the Report By Sir F. D. Lugard on the Amalgamation of Northern and Southern Nigeria and Administration 1912-1919; Together With Supplementary Unpublished Amalgamation Reports, and Other Relevant Documents* (London: Cass, 1968) and for a selection, consult Richard A. Olaniyan, Ed. *The Amalgamation and its Enemies : an Interpretive History of Modern Nigeria* (Ile-Ife, Nigeria : Obafemi Awolowo University Press, 2003) , pp. 209-237.

[3] See, for example, the entry on Lugard, *The New Encyclopedia Britannica* (Micropedia), Vol. 7, 15th Edition [London and Chicago, 1986 reprint], pp. 549-550.

[4] For specific cases and analyses of "indirect rule" in Nigeria, see Toyin Falola, Ed., *Nigerian History, Politics and Affairs : the Collected Essays of Adiele Afigbo*, (Trenton, NJ : Africa World Press, 2005), pp. 253-295; Olufemi Vaughan, *Nigerian Chiefs : Traditional Power in Modern Politics, 1890s-1990s* (Rochester, NY: University of Rochester Press, 2000), pp. 22-68; J. A. Atanda, *The New Oyo Empire: Indirect Rule and Change in Western Nigeria, 1894-1934* (London: Longman, 1973); and A. E. Afigbo, *The Warrant Chiefs: Indirect Rule in Southeastern Nigeria, 1891-1929* (New York: Humanities Press, 1972).

[5] The New Encyclopedia Britannica, pp. 550.

[6] An analysis of Lugard's papers by one researcher concluded that although the northern emirs tried to have schooling open to all, these efforts were not successful because the British Colonial Office was afraid that educated people would be harder to rule; see Peter K. Tibenderana, "The Emirs and the Spread of Western Education in Northern Nigeria, 1910-1946," *Journal of African History* (1983), 24, 4, pp. 517-534.

[7] Relatedly, see William Beinart and Saul DuBow, Eds., *Segregation And Apartheid In Twentieth-Century South Africa* (London and New York: Routledge, 1995).

[8] On the Sharpeville massacre and consequences, see, for instance, James Barber, *South Africa in the Twentieth Century: A Political History--In Search of a Nation State* (Oxford, UK and Malden, MA: Blackwell Publishers, 1999), pp. 164-165.

[9] This of course launched a pattern of coups in Nigeria; for an overview, see Chuka Onwumechili, *African Democratisation and Military Coups* (Westport, CT: Praeger Publishers, 1998), pp. 48-50.

[10] For an account of this coup, see Henry E. Nwigwe, *Nigeria – The Fall of the First Republic* (London: Motorchild Press, 1972).

[11] Consult Herbert Ekwe-Ekwe, *The Biafra War : Nigeria and the Aftermath* (Lewiston, N.Y., USA : E. Mellen Press, 1990); Peter Schwab, Ed. *Biafra* (New York, Facts on File, 1971); and Zdenek Cervenka, *The Nigerian War, 1967-1970. History of the War; Selected Bibliography and Documents* (Frankfurt: Bernard & Graefe, 1971).

[12] For one example, see Abdul-Rasheed Na'Allah, Ed., *Ogoni's Agonies : Ken Saro-Wiwa and the Crisis in Nigeria* (Trenton, NJ : Africa World Press, c1998).

[13] On the impact of oil on the Nigerian economy, consult Kelechi Amihe Kalu, *Economic Development and Nigerian Foreign Policy* (Lewiston, NY: Edwin Mellen Press, 2000), pp. 64-72.

[14] International reactions to the apartheid regime are surveyed in Adrian Guelke, *Rethinking the Rise and Fall of Apartheid: South Africa and World* Politics (Houndmills, Basingstoke, Hampshire and New York: Palgrave MacMillan, 2005); Audie J. Klotz, *Norms in International Relations:The Struggle Against Apartheid* (Ithaca, NY: Cornell University Press, 1995); and Kenneth W. Grundy, *South Africa: Domestic Crisis and Global Challenge* (Boulder, CO: Westview Press, 1991).

[15] Unless otherwise noted, all the statistics below are compiled and computed based on data in the 2005 Central Intelligence Agency World Factbook. <http://www.odci.gov/cia/publications/factbook/index.html>. October 11, 2005.

[16] These figures are derived from the 2001 South African census.

[17] This figure is as of 2004.

[18] This figure is as of January 1, 2002.

[19] This figure is as of 2004.

[20] This figure is a 2001 estimate,

[21] This figure is for 2001.

[22]This figure is a 2001 estimate.

[23] This is derived from United Nations, *World Urbanization Prospects: The 2003 Revision Database* (Department of Economic and Social Affairs, Population Division. New York, 2004) available at <http://hdr.undp.org/statistics/data/ indicators.cfm?x=42&y=1&z=1>. November 16, 2005.

SECTION II

THE AFRICAN CONTEXT

CHAPTER 3

THE AFRICAN STATE AS A POLITICAL REFUGEE

P artly because of the end of the Cold War, the African state and the political refugees its failures are creating, share a number of characteristics. In global terms the African state has got increasingly marginalised, being pushed into the ghetto of the world-system. Like Africa's refugees, many African states were already living, at least partly, on handouts before the 1990s. Since then, the situation has become worse. Francophone economies have lost the financial asylum they used to enjoy from the French franc. Just as a disproportionate number of the refugees of the world are in Africa, a disproportionate number of disabled and impoverished states are also in Africa.

Both disabled African states and displaced African people invite donor-fatigue. The ears of the international community have become weary of appeals for further charity. The end of the Cold War has also been diverting Western investment and aid not only towards the former members of the Warsaw Pact but also towards the newly liberalizing economies of China, Vietnam and India. The new priorities of the post-Cold War era are, to some extent, bad news both for disabled African states and for displaced African people.

The metaphor of the African state as a political refugee also arises out of the reality of institutional collapse, psychic bewilderment and human dislocation. Just as individual refugees are in need of humane intervention and sanctuary, so the African state in places like Rwanda, Liberia, Somalia and Angola must either be rescued by international action or be destroyed by the monumental forces bearing down upon such doomed states.

An individual refugee needs moral space within which to recover his or her own human sense of balance. A failed state also needs moral space within which to recover its own sense of purpose. An individual refugee sometimes tries to survive by devouring the rivals on the run, refugee "eating" refugee, the cannibalism of the dispossessed. The failed state tries to survive by devouring its own citizens, the rage of the castrated.

Individual refugees can cross borders and seek safety and asylum in other lands. If the failed state is replaced by a government created by the rebel army, it is theoretically possible for the failed state to also go into exile. For example, if the Rwandese Patriotic Front (RPF) had formed the government of Rwanda, it is conceivable for the failed state to have sought political asylum in the Democratic Republic of the Congo and become Rwanda's Hutu government-in-exile in Kinshasa. Thus the African state can conceivably be a literal refugee and not merely a metaphorical one if the remnants of the Hutu-state in Rwanda were to be granted institutional asylum as a government-in-exile next door.

But what is involved in this process of state-failure in the first place? What are the historical significance, as well as the political meaning, of what we have been observing from Monrovia to Maputo, from Kigali to Kismayu?

Birth Pangs or Death Pains?

Let us begin with an overarching issue. We used to think that decolonisation consisted of the nationalist struggle against colonialism and the final granting of independence and substitution of national flags and national anthems. Colonially-educated members of the African elite like Jomo Kenyatta and Julius Nyerere came to the fore and spoke up; some of them, including Kwame Nkrumah and Léopold Sédar Senghor, actually inherited the reins from their colonial masters and ruled the colonial state.

The question that has arisen especially since the 1990s is whether decolonisation brought formal independence or the collapse of the colonial state instead. It is not the changing of the guards on Independence Day, raising the new flag and singing the new national anthem, while leaving the old structures intact. Rather, it is the much more cruel and bloody disintegration of colonial structures. Decolonisation need no longer be equated with liberation.

Have Somalia, Rwanda, Liberia, Angola, and Burundi been experiencing the death pangs of an old order dying and groaning for refuge? Or are we witnessing the birth pangs of a real but devastating birth of a genuinely post-colonial order?

Is the old slate of the colonial order being washed clean with buckets of blood? Or is the blood in fact spilling in the maternity ward of history as a new Africa is trying to *breathe* amidst the mess of convulsive birth pangs? Are the desperate refugees victims of the horrors of their dying order or brutalized witnesses to a rebirth?

Until we know whether that it is the birth pangs of a truly decolonised Africa, we cannot celebrate. In any case, who can celebrate in the midst of all this blood and carnage? Who can celebrate amid the displaced and the dispossessed?

But whether the colonial state is dying or not, we do need to understand what constitutes state-failure, as opposed to what represents political-collapse.

The State in Six Functions

Before we can assess if and when the state has failed and moaning to be rescued, we need to clarify in our minds what are the basic functions of the state. Six state-functions seem to be particularly crucial.

First, sovereign control over *territory*; second, sovereign oversight and supervision (though not necessarily ownership) of the *nation's resources*; third, effective and rational *revenue extraction* from people, mines and corporations; fourth, capacity to build and maintain an *adequate national infrastructure* (roads, postal services, telephone system, railways and the like); fifth, capacity to render *basic services* such as sanitation, education, housing, fire brigade, hospitals and clinics, immunization facilities; and sixth, *capacity for effective governance* and maintenance of law and order.

When we are observing a state in the process of failing, let us not limit ourselves just to the sixth function - "*effective* governance and maintenance of law and order". We may get a longer notice of a state in decay if we worked out indicators of performance in all six areas - control over territory, resources, infrastructure, revenue collection, social services as well as governance, law and order. Long before the African state has been reduced to a political refugee, it may already show other signs of desperation.

Until the year 2000, the government of Angola had clearly lost sovereign control over a large proportion of the territory of the country - with consequences for control of resources, infrastructure, revenue, social services and governance. Needless to say, a lot of people have also been displaced.

First, on the issue of sovereignty, do governments sometimes lose control at night and regain it during the day? Certain foreign reports claim that specific suburbs of Algerian cities are under the control of the authorities during daytime and under the control of the Islamic militants at night.

Second, regarding sovereign oversight over the nation's resources, it is arguable that very few African states have effective controlling jurisdiction over their country's resources. Mining companies, oil companies, distant controllers of coffee and cocoa prices and rampant local corruption have all drastically diluted the concept of *resource-sovereignty* in Africa. Long before the African state failed to govern, it failed to control its resources.[1]

Sovereignty over resources is not of course to be confused with the actual ownership of resources, which may be in private or corporate hands. The democratic state in South Africa is too young to have failed in anything much. But has it not already failed in providing for the democratic transfer of resources? Political apartheid may be dead, but economic apartheid is alive and well so far.[2] Most of the best land and the mineral wealth are owned by whites, local or foreign. How temporary is this situation?

Does state-failure begin in resource-impotence? Is the failure of the Democratic Republic of Congo (DRC) state due to its impotence in overseeing the immense resources of the country? Is the DRC state already trying to be rescued? Is this state already a political refugee?

Third, failure to *extract revenue* is often directly related to inadequate control over resources. The tax system is in shambles in one African country after another. A state without a capacity for a rational collection of revenue from citizens or for delivery of goods and services is a state heading for ever deepening decay. It is also a state ever looking for handouts from foreign donors. Revenue collection and rational allocation can be one of the major ways of learning economic rationality. African states are denying themselves that learning process.

Fifth, there is the state's role in providing essential services such as roads, sanitation, postal services, educational infrastructure, and (in Africa) also government hospitals and clinics. A state which lags further and further behind in providing such services is heading for massive popular discontent and either regime-failure or state-collapse.

Finally, there is the sixth and, quite often, most catastrophic stage in state failure: serious *failure in governance,* sometimes leading to an entire collapse of law and order. Clouds of death and displacement appear ominously. Both the people and the state are on the verge of seeking political asylum.

This is the ominous stage when the state is no longer able *either* to monopolize the legitimate use of violence or to set the rules of when the citizens may legitimately use violence.

It is to this sixth stage of state failure that we must now turn in detail.

Between Tyranny and Anarchy

Every African government has continued to walk that tight rope between too much government and too little government. At some stage an excess of government becomes tyranny; at some other stage too little government becomes anarchy. Either trend can lead to the failed state. Indeed, either trend may lead to the collapse of the state, to death and to large-scale displacement.

Somalia under Siad Barre was a case of tyranny finally leading to the collapse of the state; the Congo (Leopoldville), or what is now the DRC, in 1960 was a case of *anarchy* nearly destroying the new post-colonial state. It was saved by the United Nations' (until the 1990s) largest peacekeeping operation (ONUC).[3]

A major unresolved dilemma lies in civil-military relations. Perhaps in everybody's experience military rule often leads to too much government, almost by definition. On the other hand, civilian rule in countries like Nigeria and Sudan has sometimes meant too little government, with politicians squabbling among themselves and sometimes plundering the nation's resources. If military regimes have too much power, and civilian regimes have too little control, countries like Nigeria and Sudan have to find solutions for the future. Otherwise destruction and displacement loom threateningly.

Nnamdi Azikiwe, the first president of independent Nigeria, once proposed a constitutional sharing of power between the military and civilians. It was called *diarchy*, a kind of dual sovereignty. At the time that Azikiwe proposed the dual sovereignty idea (part military, part civilian) in 1972, he was roundly denounced, especially by intellectuals and academics who were against military rule. But the dilemma has still persisted in Azikiwe's own country, Nigeria, and elsewhere in Africa: how to bridge the gap between the ethic of representative government and the power of the military.

Has Egypt quietly evolved a diarchy since the 1952 revolution, a system of government of dual sovereignty between civilians and soldiers? Has Azikiwe's dream found fulfilment in Egypt, however imperfectly? Or is the Egyptian system still in the process of becoming a diarchy but has not yet arrived there? Starting as a military-led system in 1952, has it become increasingly *civilianised*, yet still in the process of change towards full power-sharing?

Another dilemma concerning too much government versus too little hinges on *the party system*. There is little doubt that one-party states tend towards too much government. This has been the case in most of Africa.

On the other hand, multiparty systems in Africa have often degenerated into ethnic or sectarian rivalries resulting in too little control. This tendency was illustrated by Ghana under Hilla Limann, Nigeria under Shehu Shagari and the Sudan under Sadiq El-Mahdi in the 1980s. The state was losing effective control in all three cases. Ghana has since improved; Nigeria and Sudan declined further.

If one solution to the civil-military dilemma is diarchy (the dual sovereignty), what is the solution to the dilemma between the one-party state and the multi-party system?

Uganda once felt its way towards one solution to the dilemma: a *no-party* state. Concerned that a multiparty system would only lead to a reactivation of Uganda's ethnic and sectarian rivalries, President Yoweri Museveni put the weight of his name, office and prestige to this principle of a Uganda without political parties for at least five years. In an election held in March 1994 to choose members of a Constituent Assembly, candidates in favour of a no-party Uganda seemed to have won a majority of the seats. Since then Uganda has moved closer to a multi-party state.

Under both Idi Amin (1971-1979) and the second administration of Milton Obote (1980-1985) Uganda experienced some of the worst excesses of both tyranny and anarchy at the same time. Although the state did not actually collapse, each government lost control over large parts of the territory and was unable to perform many of the basic functions of the state. Thousands of people were displaced or escaped into exile. Champions of a 'Uganda without political parties' hoped that their new party-less approach to politics would avert the type of situation that brought Idi Amin into power in the first place.

There are other possible solutions to the dilemma between multiparty anarchy and one-party tyranny. One possibility is a *no-party presidency* and a *multiparty parliament*. This could give a country a strong executive with extensive constitutional powers, but one who is elected in a contest between *individuals* and not between party-candidates. Parliament or the legislature, on the other hand, could remain multiparty. The president would *not be allowed* to belong to any political party.

It is true that a system of a presidency without a political party may indeed give undue advantage to Africa's millionaires, the '*Black Ross Perots*' or other '*M.K.O. Abiolas.*' That may be the price to pay for a no-party presidency in a multi-party society.

All of the above are situations where the state succeeds or fails in relation to the nature of the political institutions (military or civilian, multiparty or one party or other).

But in reality a state succeeds or fails in relation to wider societal configurations as well. In post-colonial Africa ethnicity continues to be a major factor conditioning success or failure of the state.[4] Yet here too mother Africa presents its contradictions. The road to state-collapse or state-displacement could be either through having too many groups in the process - or, paradoxically, too few.

Previous failures of the state in Uganda were partly due to the very ethnic richness of the society - the striking diversity of Bantu, Nilotic, Sudanic and other groups, each of which was itself internally diverse. The political system was not yet ready to sustain the immense pressures of competing ethno-cultural claims. Lives were lost, thousands were displaced.

Ethiopia under Mengistu Haile-Mariam also drifted towards state-failure partly because the system was unable to accommodate its rich cultural and ethnic diversity. Mengistu's tyranny did not foster free negotiations, or compromise, or coalition-building among ethnic groups. Lives were lost, thousands were again displaced.

But how can a state fail or collapse because it had too *few* ethnic groups? At first glance it looks as if Somalia has been such a case.

George Bernard Shaw used to say that the British and the Americans were a people divided by the *same language*.[5] It may be truer and more poignant to say that the Somali are a people divided by the *same culture*. The culture legitimises the clans which are among the central bases of discord. The culture legitimises a macho response to inter-clan stalemates. The culture legitimises inter-clan feuds.

Inter-clan rivalries among the Somali would decline if the Somali themselves were confronting the competition of other ethnic groups within some kind of plural society. The Somali themselves would close ranks if they were facing the rivalry of the Amhara and the Tigre in a new plural society. It is in that sense that even a culturally homogenous society can have major areas of schism if wise answers are not found for them.

In any case, Somalia even on its own could be studied as a *plural* society of many *clans* rather than of many "tribes". The single culture of the Somali people may be a misleading indicator. The pluralism of Somalia is at the level of *sub-ethnicity* rather than ethnicity.

That disguised pluralism of Somalia was exploited by Siad Barre to play off one clan against another. Siad Barre's tyranny lasted from 1969 into the 1990s. It turned out to be the high road to the destruction of the Somali state. The Somali became more than nomads: many became refugees.

The real contrast to the *plural* society as a threat to the state is the *dual* society. The plural society endangers the state by having more sociological diversity than the political process can accommodate. Paradoxically, the dual society endangers the state by having less sociological differentiation than is needed for the politics of compromise.

It is to this under-studied and even unrecognised category of the dual society that we now turn.

The Dual Society and Political Tension

As we grapple with new levels of conflict in Africa, from Kigali to Kismayu, from Maputo to Monrovia, we ought at least to try and identify which socio-political situations are particularly conflict-prone.

Quite a good deal of work has been done on the plural society in Africa - the type of society like Kenya or Tanzania which has a multiplicity of ethnic groups and plurality of political allegiances. What has yet to be explored adequately is the phenomenon of *the dual society*: a country whose fundamental divide is between two groups or two geographical areas. The state in a dual society is vulnerable in a different way from the state in a plural society. In a dual society two ethnic groups may account for more than three quarters of the population.

Rwanda is a dual society. So is the Sudan. But they are dual societies in very different senses. Rwanda is an *ethnically* dual society whose fatal cleavage is between the majority Hutu and the minority Tutsi. Burundi is similarly bifurcated between majority Hutu and minority Tutsi.

Sudan is a *regionally* dual society divided between a more Arabised northern Sudan and a Christian-led Southern Sudan. But although the Sudan is regionally dual, it is *ethnically* plural. Both northern and southern Sudan are culturally diverse within themselves.

Cyprus is both regionally and ethnically dual between Greeks and Turks. There is a stalemate hovering between partition and confederation, with the United Nations still trying to mediate. Czechoslovakia was also both ethnically and regionally dual between Czechs and Slovaks. In the post-communist era, the country has indeed partitioned itself into separate Czech and Slovak Republics. In effect the state of the old Czechoslovakia has collapsed and split into two.[6]

The most risky situations are *not* those involving a convergence of ethnic duality and regional (territorial) duality, as in Cyprus or Czechoslovakia. It is true that when the two ethnic groups are concentrated in separate regions, it increases the risk of territorial or political separatism and secession. But, in human terms, that may not be the worst scenario.

The most risky form of duality is that of pure ethnic differentiation without territorial differentiation. It means that there is no prospect of a Cyprus stalemate, keeping the ethnic groups separate but peaceful. It also means that there is no prospect of Czechoslovakia's 'gracious parting of the ways,' creating separate countries. Rather, the two groups are so intermingled in neighbourhoods, at times so intermarried, that a soured ethnic relationship is an explosive relationship.

Rwanda and Burundi fall into that category of ethnic duality without regional duality. The two groups are intermingled from village to village, certainly from street to street. Rwanda also happens to be the most densely populated country on the African continent (estimated at 210 persons per square kilometre in the 1980s - or, about 540 persons per square mile).

Ethnic duality without regional separation can be a prescription for hate at close quarters. Rwanda's and Burundi's tragedies are a combination of ethnic duality, population density, geographic intermingling and the legacies of colonial and pre-colonial relationships.

Northern Ireland is also a case of ethno-religious duality (Protestant and Catholic) with considerable intermingling within the north. There is no question of partitioning the north itself into a Catholic sector to be united with the Irish Republic and a Protestant section loyal to the United Kingdom. A second Irish partition is not in the cards, not least because the population of the north is too geographically intermingled for another partition. Intra-communal hate is therefore immediate and at close range.

Is Sri Lanka in the Indian Ocean also a dual society, with the two biggest groups being the majority Sinhalese and the minority Tamils? The population is intermingled to a substantial extent, but the Tamil Tigers rebel groups are fighting for a separate Tamil homeland in predominantly Tamil areas. Militarily the country still faces a stalemate.

Ethnically dual societies are vulnerable to the risk of polarization. The absence of potential mediating coalitions through other groups makes the Rwandas and Burundis of this world more vulnerable than ever to periodic ethnic convulsions. Cultural frontiers without territorial frontiers: a dual identity within a single country, a society at war with itself.

Sudan is also a country at war with itself, but its duality is regional rather than ethnic. As we indicated, both northern and southern Sudan is multi-ethnic, but the South is distinctive by being culturally more indigenous, less Islamised, and led in the main by Christianised Sudanese.

There was a civil war in the Sudan between the two regions between 1955 and 1972, ending with the Addis Ababa accords of the latter year.[7] In 1983, a second Sudanese civil war broke out, and raged until 2005. Both civil wars created hundreds of thousands of refugees and displaced persons.

The first civil war (1955-1972) was more clearly secessionist. The Southern rebels wanted to pull out of Sudan and form a separate country (the Czechoslovakia style solution of later years.) The second Sudanese civil war has been more ambivalent about secession. Indeed, until his untimely death in a helicopter clash in 2005, the Southern military leader, Colonel John Garang, emphasized that he stood for a democratisation of the whole of the Sudan rather than for southern secession.

There is indeed some nation-wide intermingling between southerners and northerners, but on a modest scale. The real divide is region-specific and can be demarcated territorially, unlike the division between Hutu and Tutsi in Rwanda.

The speed of killing in Rwanda in April and May 1994 was much faster than almost anything witnessed in the Sudanese civil war - some two hundred thousand people were killed in Rwanda within barely a two-week period. "There are no devils left in Hell", declared the cover title to one of the May 1994 issues of the American news magazine's *Time*, "They are all in Rwanda".[8] More were killed later. A third of the population of the country was subsequently displaced or dislocated.

Of course, the state has not collapsed in Khartoum though it has had no control over some parts of the South. Secondly, unlike the Rwandan national army, the Khartoum national army has not been seeking out helpless civilians for slaughter, from refugee camps to hospitals. However, over the long run, both civil wars have indeed been costly in human lives and human suffering. The Sudan has yet to find a definitive solution to its violent dualism. Its split cultural personality between the North and the South has so far been more divisive than its split ethnic personality among diverse "tribes" and clans.

The dual society continues to cast its shadow over plural Africa, from Zimbabwe (Shona versus Ndebele) to Algeria (Arab versus Berber), from Nigeria (North versus South) to the tensions of Kigali and Khartoum. While Czechoslovakia was a case of *both* ethnic and territorial dualism (Czech versus Slovak) and Burundi as well as Rwanda are cases of ethnic dualism (Tutsi versus Hutu) without territorial dualism, Yemen has been a case of territorial dualism (north versus south) without significant ethnic dualism.

Is the distinction between the self-styled Republic of Somaliland and the rest of Somalia a case of territorial dualism without ethnic dualism (as in the case of Yemen)? Or is there sub-ethnic dualism between the two parts of Somalia which make it more like the case of Cyprus (Greek-Cypriot versus Turkish-Cypriot), both ethnically distinct and territorially differentiated? Alternatively the two parts of Somalia may be an *intermediate* category of dualism, equally prone to internecine conflict. Displacement is less of a problem in the Republic of Somaliland than in the rest of Somalia.

The United Republic of Tanzania is a more artificial case of dualism between the much smaller member, Zanzibar, and the mainland of the old Tanganyika. Arab refugees from the 1960s are beginning to return to Zanzibar. There have indeed been heated political disputes between the two parts of the United Republic - with separatist sentiments sometimes manifested on the island of Zanzibar and sometimes, paradoxically, manifested among mainlanders. Are there ominous ethno-religious warning signs in Tanzania which we ought to monitor?

Statehood: The Tragedy of Peaceful Neighbours

It is one of Africa's glories that in spite of artificial borders which have split ethnic groups, there have been very few border clashes or military confrontations between African countries. But it is also a terrible fact to acknowledge that one of the tragedies of the African state is that there has not been enough tension and conflict *between* states.

The balance between external conflict and internal conflict has tilted too far on the side of the internal. And as human history has repeated time and time again, civil wars often leave deeper scars, are often more indiscriminate and more ruthless, than are inter-state conflicts short of either a world war or a nuclear war. The United States, for example, lost more people in its own civil war in the 1860s than in any other single war in its 200-year history, including Vietnam and the two world wars.[9]

Additionally, the history of the nation-state in Europe reveals a persistent tendency of the European state to externalise conflict and thus help promote greater unity at home. A sense of nationhood within each European country was partly fostered by a sense of rivalry and occasional conflict with its neighbours. And the consolidation of the European state as a sovereign state was also partly forged in the fire of inter-European conflicts. The Peace of Westphalia of 1648, which has often been credited with being the original formal launching of the nation-state system, was signed after thirty years of yet further inter-state European conflicts.[10]

What ought to be remembered therefore is that the state-system which Africa has inherited from Europe was originally nurtured on the bosom of conflict and war. It can even be argued that just as 'one cannot make an omelette without breaking eggs,' one cannot build and strengthen statehood and nationhood without the stimulus of conflict. The only question is whether the conflict is with outsiders or with the state's own citizens. Post-colonial Africa is disproportionately burdened with internalised conflict. This is, at least in the short run, detrimental to both the consolidation of statehood and to the promotion of a shared sense of nationhood in the population.

The people displaced by internal conflict are also vulnerable in a different sense. Usually, their adversaries are *not* enemy planes about whose approach they can be forewarned by the sound of the siren. On the contrary, their enemies may be literally their next-door neighbours with whom they sat down at sunset and chatted about the harvest or the children, or with whom they shared a meal, only the day before. At its worst the blood letting in Rwanda, Burundi, Somalia, and Liberia has sometimes been from house to house, in pitiless intimacy.

A related problem of people displaced by a civil war concerns their eventual repatriation and resettlement. To many of them, returning home becomes a psychic nightmare even after peace is ostensibly restored. The most recent memory of their village is the horror of neighbour murdering neighbour in the presence of their own children, children who once used to play together with their own. For many refugees home is not "Sweet Home." On the contrary, 'Home' is a synonym for 'hell,' and 'neighbour' is another word for 'nemesis.'

One of Africa's post-colonial tragedies continues to be, paradoxically, that there have been no external wars for which to plan and for which to invoke a sense of national purpose. And where there was a semblance of inter-African state conflict - as in the case of Ethiopia and Somalia in the 1970s and early 1980s - the regional conflict was almost overshadowed by the wider superpower rivalry between the Soviet Union and the United States. Excessive external participation in the conflict between Ethiopia and Somalia deprived the regional confrontation of any compensating value as a unifying force for either Ethiopia or Somalia. On the contrary, Somalia's defeat in the Ogaden struggle was the *coup de grace* which helped to precipitate Somalia's descent into anarchy without saving the Ethiopian government of Mengistu Haile-Mariam from military and political collapse.

In other words, when an inter-state African conflict is excessively a reflection of some wider rivalry between big powers, the inter-state conflict loses the compensating advantages of either consolidating local statehood or unifying a local sense of nationhood. Neither Ethiopia nor Somalia gained from their own conflicts of the 1970s and 1980s.

On the one hand, the politico-military disagreements between Nigeria and Cameroon in the 1990s about disputed islands are potentially unifying for both Nigeria and Cameroon. On the Nigerian side, the unifying potential would have increased if French troops were disproportionately visible in apparent defence of Cameroonian interests. On the other hand, Tanzania's invading troops in Uganda in 1979 were welcomed by most Ugandans as liberators from the tyranny of Idi Amin.

Conclusion

What are Africa's options in reducing the heavy tilt on the side of civil wars instead of external conflicts? Clearly manufacturing state-wars against each other just for the sake of national integration or state-formation is unthinkable. Even Rwanda and Burundi cannot be encouraged to go to war against each other as an alternative to Hutu versus Tutsi civil wars in each of them separately. Inter-state wars should have some semblance of credibility and not be entirely artificial. Wars between Rwanda and Burundi are more likely to exacerbate brutality between Hutus and Tutsis rather than to unite the two *states* internally. At least for the foreseeable future the Hutu and Tutsi are condemned to having periodic inter-ethnic wars rather than inter-state wars, although every ethnic conflagration in one of the countries has always risked the ignition of another next door.

In the circumstances, one solution to a civil war is indeed to take sides. The state-borders are entirely artificial, and the intermediate rules of the game are basically externally imposed. Should Africa be entirely governed by the external rules? Or are there other moral rules which, in certain circumstances should be equally compelling?

One yardstick is which side in a civil war is the side of the majority. Another yardstick is which side in a civil war is likely to save more lives. In the civil war in Rwanda in 1994 the government side represented the majority Hutu in the country. On the other hand, the Rwandese Patriotic Front (RPF) as a military force (Tutsi-led) was more disciplined and seemed likely to be more concerned about saving lives.

In the absence of external conflicts confronting African states, one casualty might well be *neutrality in a civil war*. Sides might well have to be taken in civil conflicts in the face of carnage and anarchy. The

51

international partisanship is bound to play havoc with the interests of the refugees, but refugees are always pawns in the equilibrium of power in any case.

In Rwanda the choice in May 1994 was between the rudiments of the Hutu state (ethnically majoritarian but recklessly destructive) and the Rwandese Patriotic Front (led by the minority Tutsi but significantly more disciplined and seemingly capable even of self-criticism). The Hutu state was on the verge of being accused of systematic genocide. The Rwandese Patriotic Front seemed to be the only credible corrective to such majoritarian genocide.

Since almost all African countries are unstable in varying degrees, we must not assume that they are unstable for the same reasons. Put differently, because all patients in a hospital are sick in varying degrees, we do not assume that they suffer from the same disease.

Conflict prevention requires greater and greater sophistication in diagnosing conflict-prone situations. Unfortunately Africa is full of contradictions - conflict generated by too much government versus conflict generated by too little; conflict generated by too many ethnic groups, as distinct from conflict ignited by too few ethnic groups. It is dark outside. Africa is waiting for her real dawn. It is to be hoped that the wait is not too long.

What is the solution in situations of acute state-failure or political collapse? Before total collapse, the state maybe the equivalent of a political refugee: desperate, bewildered, sometimes destructive, but fundamentally moaning to be rescued from a nightmare which may in part be of its own making.

One option is *unilateral intervention by a single neighbouring* power in order to restore order. There is the precedent of Tanzania's invasion of Uganda in 1979, with troops marching all the way to Kampala. Tanzania then put Uganda virtually under military occupation for a couple of years. The Ugandan state was temporarily a refugee camp. Tanzania's intervention was very similar to Vietnam's intervention in Cambodia to overthrow Pol Pot, except that the Vietnamese stayed on in Cambodia much longer. The question arises whether Yoweri Museveni's Uganda should have intervened in Rwanda in April 1994 the way that Julius Nyerere's Tanzania intervened in Uganda fifteen years earlier.

Another scenario of intervention is that *by a single power but with the blessings of a regional organization.* There is no real African precedent but there is an Arab one: Syria's intervention in the Lebanese civil war with the blessings of the League of Arab States. *De facto*, the Lebanese state was a refugee camp with Syria as a sentry.

A third scenario of intervention is inter-African *colonisation and annexation*. In a sense this is a kind of *self-colonisation*. One precedent is Tanganyika's annexation of Zanzibar in 1964, partly under pressure from US President Lyndon B. Johnson and Sir Alec Douglas-Home of Great Britain. The West wanted to avert the danger of a Marxist 'Cuba' on the clove island off the East African coast. Nyerere was persuaded that an unstable or subversive Zanzibar would be a threat to the mainland. He got the dictator of Zanzibar at the time, Abeid Karume, to agree to a treaty of union - very much like the British used to convince African chiefs to "accept" treaties by which they ceased to be sovereign. Nobody held a referendum in Zanzibar to check if the people in the country wanted to cease being a separate independent nation. But the annexation of Zanzibar was the most daring case of what became, de facto, *Pax Tanzaniana*.

The fourth scenario as a solution to political collapse is *regional integration*. This is when the state as a political refugee is integrated with its host country. In the longer run, one solution to Rwanda and Burundi may well be a federation with Tanzania so that Hutus and Tutsis stop having *de facto* ethnic armies of their own, but have those soldiers retrained as part of the federal army of the United Republic of Tanzania. A union of the three countries is not entirely a new idea. German colonialism before World War I had leaned towards treating Tanganyika and Rwanda-Urundi as one single area of jurisdiction.

Union with Tanzania for Rwanda and Burundi would, in the short run, be safer than union with the DRC in spite of the shared Belgian connection with the Congo and the link of the French language. Tanzania is a more stable and less vulnerable society than the DRC, and a safer haven for Hutus and Tutsis. It is indeed significant that Hutus and Tutsis on the run are more likely to flee to Tanzania than to the DRC in spite of ethnic ties across the border with the latter. Moreover, Hutus and Tutsis are getting partially Swahilised linguistically and should be able to get on well with "fellow" Tanzanian citizens. As citizens they would be assimilated in due course; their former refugee state would be subsumed and integrated.

A fifth scenario for conflict-resolution is the establishment of an *African Security Council*, complete with permanent members in the style of the United Nations Security Council. The permanent members could be Egypt from North Africa, Nigeria from West Africa, Ethiopia from eastern Africa, and the Republic of South Africa from Southern Africa. There should be some non-permanent members, ranging from three to five. The principle of permanent members would be reviewed every thirty years. For example, in thirty years it may be necessary to add the Democratic Republic of Congo as a permanent member to represent Central Africa. In times of crisis should the African Security Council meet at the level of African heads of state? Should each permanent member have a veto or not? These issues would also have to be addressed. The African Union has taken some tentative steps towards a nascent Security Council.

The sixth scenario of conflict-resolution in times of political collapse is the *establishment of a Pan-African Emergency force* - a fire brigade to put out fires from one collapsed state or civil war to another, and teach Africans the art of a Pax Africana. Should this Pan-African Emergency force be independently recruited and trained in a specialized manner? Or should it be drawn from units of the armed forces of member states? And how are the training, maintenance and deployment of the Emergency Force to be paid for? Certainly the successes and failures of ECOMOG in Liberia should be studied carefully in preparation for this new venture. The emergency force should be trained to use minimum violence.

One minimum solution is a High Commissioner for Refugees and Displaced Africans under the African Union. Since Africa has become the biggest concentration of displaced persons in the world, it is increasingly imperative that Africans should assume responsibility for at least some of the functions of refugee relief. A continent of one tenth of the world's population is rapidly becoming a region of half of the displaced people of the world. What is demanded is not merely Africa's participation in refugee-relief; it is Africa's leadership which is needed. An A.U. High Commissioner for Refugees and Displaced Africans would be a start, equipped with the necessary resources to coordinate with the United Nations High Commission for Refugees (UNHCR).

The eighth scenario of conflict management would consist of *ad hoc* solutions from crisis to crisis more in the tradition of mediation and search for solutions than in the tradition of the use of force. Such *ad hoc* efforts are definitely much better than nothing, and could constitute a major part of Africa's search for *Pax Africana*, an African peace established and maintained by Africans themselves.

In this more modest tradition of intervention was the Organization of African Unity's Mechanism on Conflict Prevention, Management and Resolution of the 1990s, which for the first time gave the continental inter-governmental organization a more active role in internal civil conflicts. Modest as the mechanism was, it signified a qualitative shift in the orientation of African heads of state.

But behind all the scenarios and the entire search for solutions, behind the pain and the anguish, is the paramount question: *Are we facing birth pangs or death-pangs in the present crises? Are we witnessing the real bloody forces of decolonisation - as the colonial structures are decaying or collapsing? Is the colonial slate being washed clean with the blood of victims, villains and martyrs? Are the refugees victims of a dying order, or are they traumatized witnesses to an epoch- making rebirth?*

Is this blood from the womb of history giving painful birth to a new order?

> The blood of experience meanders on
> In the vast expanse of the valley of time
> The new is come and the old is gone
> And time abides a changing clime

NOTES

[1] See, for example Robert H. Jackson and Carl G. Roseberg, "Why Africa's Weak States Persist: The Empirical and the Juridical in Statehood", in Atul Kohli Ed., *The State and Development in the Third World* (Princeton, NJ: Princeton University Press, 1986) pp. 259-282.

[2] See, "South Africa: Sharing Power", *Africa Confidential* Vol. 35 No. 10 (20 May 1994) pp. 1-5 and "South Africa: The Mandate for Mandela", *Africa Confidential* Vol. 35 No. 9 (6 May 1994) pp. 1-5.

[3] See for example, A. LeRoy Bennett, *International Organizations: Principles and Issues* (Englewood Cliffs, NJ: Prentice Hall, 1991) 5th ed.

[4] See, for example, Naomi Chazan, et al *Politics and Society in Contemporary Africa* (Boulder, CO: Lynne Rienner, 1988) especially pp. 101-125.

[5] Cited in Susan Ratcliffe, Ed., *The Oxford Dictionary of Quotations* (Oxford and New York: Oxford University Press, 1994) p. 188.

[6] See for example, Arthur S. Banks (ed.) *Political Handbook of the World 1993* (Binghamton, NY: CSA Publications, 1994) pp. 211-6 and pp. 735-8.

[7] See, for example, Dunstan M. Wai, *The African-Arab Conflict in the Sudan* (New York and London: Africana Publishing Co, 1981) and M.O. Beshir, *The Southern Sudan: Background to Conflict* (New York and London: C. Hurst and Company, 1968).

[8] This was a quote from a Christian missionary who witnessed the carnage in the Central African country which *Time* decided to use over a picture of a Rwandese mother holding its baby at a refugee camp near Ngara, Tanzania. See *Time* Vol. 143 No. 20 May 16, 1994, cover page and pp. 56-63. See also "Rwanda: Civilian Slaughter" *Africa Confidential* Vol. 35 No. 9 (6 May 1994) pp. 5-6 and "Rwanda: A Double Agenda" *Africa Confidential* Vol. 35 No. 10 (20 May 1994) p. 8 and "Rwanda: From Coup to Carnage", *Africa Confidential*, Vol. 35 No. 8 (15 April 1994) p. 8 and, "Streets of Slaughter" *Time* Vol. 143 No. 17 (April 25, 1994) pp. 45-6 and, "Rwanda: All the Hatred in the World", *Time* Vol. 143 No. 24 (June 13, 1994) pp. 36-7. For example on June 9, 1994 the RPF announced that the Roman Catholic Archbishop of Kigali and several other priests had been murdered by four of its own troops and that the RPF would see to it that the perpetrators would be brought to justice.

[9] During the American Civil War there were battles that claimed thousands of lives on a single day (such as the Battle of Antietam, which claimed 4,800 lives on a single day), and the war itself claimed 623,000 lives; see Philip S. Paludan, *A People's Contest: the Union and Civil War, 1861-1865*, Second Edition, (Lawrence, KS: University of Kansas Press, 1996), p. 316 for a comparative casualty count of major US wars.

[10] The Westphalian compact also led to mores against international intervention in territories covered by a state's sovereignty but internal excesses and state failure may be testing these mores; relatedly, consult Gene M. Lyons and Michael Mastanutono, Eds. *Beyond Westphalia? State Sovereignty and International Intervention* (Baltimore, MD: Johns Hopkins University Press, 1995).

CHAPTER 4

BETWEEN RACIAL APARTHEID AND LINGUISTIC APARTHEID: CHALLENGES FOR FRANCOPHONIE, SOUTH AFRICA AND THE AFRICAN RENAISSANCE

What was unique about Francophonie until the 1990s was that it was the only international and intergovernmental club based on <u>linguistic apartheid</u>. In concept, Francophonie was based on a vision that the world consisted of two kinds of nations - French-speaking and the "outer aliens". No other community of nations was conceived in such stark linguistic terms.

On the other hand, South Africa until the 1990s was a country based on <u>racial apartheid</u>. The underlying vision was that humanity consisted of a hierarchy of races with whites at the top, blacks at the very bottom, and other races such as Indians and mixed ethnicity in-between. From 1948 onwards no other country in the world conceived itself in such stark racially segregationist terms.[1]

What has happened with Francophonie in the 1990s is that linguistic criteria of admission to the club have been considerably loosened. Indeed has the principle of linguistic apartheid been abandoned altogether?

What has happened in South Africa is the demise of the political aspects of racial apartheid combined with the continuing resilience of the economic aspects of apartheid.[2]

The central politics of Francophonie has been the politics of language. The central politics of the African Renaissance has been the politics of race. The Commonwealth has been caught up in the politics of race and civil liberties.

Francophonie and the Commonwealth

If Francophonie was linguistic apartheid based on the French language, why was the Commonwealth not a similar apartheid system based on the English language?

Although English is indeed the official language of the Commonwealth (as it is one of the six official languages of the United

57

Nations), the main qualification for Commonwealth membership was until the 1990s historic rather than linguistic. Members of the Commonwealth had to have directly shared the experience of British imperial history (Britain as the former imperial power and the other as former colonies).[3] There were no linguistic credentials needed, either de jure or de facto. Indeed, when India became a member in 1947, Hindi was intended to replace English in India in stages. When Tanganyika (now Tanzania) became independent in 1961, Julius K. Nyerere was committed to increasing Swahilisation. And when Cyprus became independent in 1961, Greek and Turkish languages did replace English as the official languages.

In its earlier phases Francophonie also seemed to be based on qualifications of shared history. But the shared language was always important for France. The earlier membership consisted almost entirely of France and its former empire, but linguistic solidarity mattered. As membership expanded, the qualifications of shared language superseded the qualifications of shared imperial history. In Africa, the former Belgian dependencies of Congo (Kinshasa), Rwanda and Burundi were next for incorporation into the fraternity of Francophonie. The official language of the former Belgian colonies was of course French.

The Commonwealth was born long before most of Africa became independent. [4] Ironically, the first full African member of the Commonwealth was South Africa under white-rule, going back to Commonwealth origins under the Statute of Westminster enacted by the British Parliament in 1931. White-ruled Southern Rhodesia (now Zimbabwe) subsequently became an associate member of the Commonwealth long before Ghana was admitted as the first Black-led member in 1957.[5]

A minimum of democratic culture was one of the qualifications of continuing membership of the Commonwealth - as distinct from a minimum of the French language as a credential for continuing association with Francophonie.

From 1936 to 1961 the minimum of democratic culture in the Commonwealth was sometimes limited to the white electorate of a particular member-country. This was certainly true of the Union of South Africa and, in a different sense, to Australia at one time. It was also true of the white electorate of the associate member of Southern

Rhodesia. Parliamentary democracy was practised, but within racial limits.

In 1947, India and Pakistan provided the first non-white governments admitted to membership of the Commonwealth, and in 1957 Ghana became the first Black government. But South Africa was still a member, with parliamentary democracy still confined mainly to the white electorate.

It was not until 1961, when South Africa was forced to withdraw from the Commonwealth, that respect for racial equality became a qualification for remaining in the Commonwealth. Ironically parliamentary democracy was already under severe stress in the new non-white Commonwealth. In Pakistan the military was already exercising disproportionate power. And in Ghana and Tanzania theories were soon to emerge justifying single-party democracies.[6]

1961 had brought commitment to racial equality as a qualification for membership of the Commonwealth. For a while this new principle seemed to overshadow the older principle of commitment to democracy. Before long the Commonwealth's most passionate foreign policy crusade became the struggle against apartheid in South Africa. Summit meeting after Summit meeting of the Commonwealth was dominated by the issue of apartheid. During the years of Margaret Thatcher in power there was a persistent cleavage between her government (reluctant to impose sanctions on South Africa) and much of the rest of the Commonwealth.[7]

There was a time when South Africa seemed destined to experience one of the bloodiest examples of *primary* civil wars - an actual racial war appeared inevitable. After all, everywhere else in Africa where there had been a large white minority there had been severe bloodshed before full majority rule was realized. Kenya experienced the Mau Mau war (1952 - 1960); Algeria experienced its war of independence (1954-1962); Rhodesia and Angola had their equivalent conflicts. Since South Africa had the largest white minority of them all, how could South Africa possibly avert the same bloodstained fate?

But one particular difference turned out to be more relevant than many people imagined. The whites of South Africa identified themselves with Africa but not with the Africans. The Afrikaners especially were passionately loyal to the African soil (the land) but not loyal to the African blood (the indigenous people).[8]

In contrast, the whites of colonial Algeria were nascent Francophonie. They were loyal neither to Africa nor to the Africans. Their loyalty was to France. They owed no special allegiance to the soil of Africa except as a means of livelihood. They certainly owed no loyalty to the blood of the indigenous peoples. They attempted to turn African into an extension of France through a military coup.[9] Was this Francophonie gone anti-African?

Similarly the whites of Angola attempted to turn their part of Africa into an extension of Portugal. This is in contrast to those whites of South Africa who identified themselves with the African soil so much that they called themselves Afrikaners, and even attempted to monopolise the word "Africans" for themselves.

Actually Anglophone whites were only marginally better than Francophone whites in their loyalty to Africa. White Rhodesians were simply too British, many of them enjoying dual citizenship right through Ian Smith's Unilateral Declaration of Independence (U.D.I.). Of all the whites of Africa perhaps only the *Afrikaners* had evolved a mystical relationship to the African land. The Afrikaners mixed their sweat mystically with the African soil, but did not mix their blood spiritually with the African people.

How did South Africa avert a racial war in the twentieth century? One reason was indeed cultural. This was the simple fact that the Afrikaners were halfway towards Africanisation through a marriage between the Afrikaner soul and the African soil. They avoided the white colonial Algerian sin of identifying both the soul and the Algerian soil with France.

A second reason why South Africa has averted a racial war in the twentieth century is essentially a division of labour between Black political power and white economic privilege. The white man said to the Black man: "You take the crown, and I will keep the jewels."

The Black man was to acquire the political crown, while the white man retained the economic jewels. In many ways, while political apartheid has ended, economic apartheid is still intact. The best land, the best mines, the best jobs, the best shops and commercial opportunities, are still overwhelmingly in white hands or under white control. The challenge for the post-Mandela South Africa is how to dismantle economic apartheid without causing widespread economic and social havoc. Perhaps this is the supreme challenge of the African Renaissance in Southern Africa.[10]

While most people are convinced that South Africa has indeed averted a primary civil war in the twentieth century (White versus Black), can we be complacent about averting it in the twenty-first century if economic apartheid remained intact? Twenty-first century South Africa may not have the moral leadership of the rank of Nelson Mandela.[11] It may still have the valuable resource of the marriage between the Afrikaner soul and the African soil.

But this brings us to the third reason why South Africa has averted a racial war in the twentieth century. This concerns Africa's short memory of hate. Cultures vary considerably in their hate-retention. The Irish have long retention of memories of atrocities perpetrated by the English. The Armenians have long memories about atrocities committed against them by the Turks in the Ottoman Empire. The Jews have long memories about their martyrdom in history.

On the other hand, Jomo Kenyatta proceeded to forgive his British tormentors very fast after being released from unjust imprisonment. He even published a book entitled *Suffering without Bitterness*.[12]

Where but in Africa could somebody like Ian Smith who had unleashed a war which killed many thousands of Black people remain free after Black majority rule to torment his Black successors in power whose policies had killed far fewer people than Ian Smith's policies had done?[13]

Is a short memory of hate a precondition for the African Renaissance? Nelson Mandela lost twenty-seven of the best years of his life. Yet on being released he was not only in favour of reconciliation between Blacks and Whites. He went to appeal to white terrorists who were fasting unto death not to do so. He went out of his way to go and pay his respects to Mrs. Verwoerd, the widow of the architect of apartheid.[14] Is Africa's short memory of hate sometimes "too short?" Is it nevertheless necessary for the African Renaissance?

What saved South Africa from a primary racial war in the twentieth century? It was mainly a convergence of those three forces -- the mystical relationship between the Afrikaner soul and the African soil, the black African's short memory of hate, and the historic bargain which conceded the political crown to Blacks and kept the economic jewels to Whites at least this century.

Was there a fourth reason why South Africa avoided a racial war? Was the fourth reason the international sanctions against South Africa? In this case it was not the <u>soul</u> of the Commonwealth, but its <u>conscience</u>

which served as the vanguard of international action against apartheid in South Africa.

From Eurafrica to Francophonie

France invented the concept of "Eurafrica" - suggesting an organic relationship between Europe and Africa, deep enough to transform the two continents into a single integrated international sub-system. How does this concept relate to the French language? How does this concept relate to Francophonie?

Eurafrica became the core of Francophonie. The majority of French-speaking people in the world are in the Western world - mainly in France itself. However, the majority of French-speaking states are in Africa. Over twenty members of the Organization of African Unity are French-speaking in the sense of having adopted French as an official language. These are Algeria, Benin, Burundi, Chad, Cameroon, Central African Republic, Comoros, Congo, Coté d'Ivoire, Djibouti, Burkina Faso, Gabon, Guinea, Malagasy, Mali, Mauritania, Morocco, Niger, Rwanda, Senegal, Réunion, Togo, Tunisia and the Democratic Republic of Congo (formerly Zaire).[15]

Without Africa the French language would be almost a provincial language. The Democratic Republic of Congo (DR Congo) is the largest French-speaking country after France in population - and destined to be the largest absolutely fairly early in the twenty-first century.[16] If the Congo succeeds in stabilizing itself, and in assuming effective control over its resources, it may become France's rival in influence and power in French-speaking Africa as a whole. Indeed, one day DR Congo (Kinshasa) could become a major force in Francophonie as a whole.[17]

When we look at this global scene, the French language is declining in influence as a language. On the other hand, Francophonie as a fraternity of states is expanding in membership and purpose. Let us take each of these propositions in turn. Why is French declining in Europe and the North as a whole? Why is Francophonie as a club expanding?

The most important challenge to the French language in the Northern hemisphere has been caused by the vast expansion of American influence in the twentieth century. The American language has of course been English. While the spread of the English language in Africa has been mainly due to the impact of imperial Britain, the spread of the English language in east and south-east Asia and in

Europe, and its expanding role in international affairs, has been largely due to the new American hegemony in the world. The triumph of the English language globally has ranged from increasing usage in diplomacy to its pre-eminent role as the supreme language of aviation and air-control.[18]

A related reason for the shrinkage of French in world affairs concerns the computer revolution and the Internet. The amount of information circulating in English is so much greater than what is transmitted in French that English is gaining the ascendancy even further. The old adage that "nothing succeeds like success" has now been computerized. The global influence of American computer firms like IBM and Microsoft has reinforced this Anglo-computer revolution. Even French scientists are not passionate supporters of efforts to impose French language on the French Internet.[19]

At the other end of social concerns is the decline of the cultural influence of the upper classes in Europe. Royal houses in continental Europe as a whole had once preferred to use the French language extensively. In the aftermath of the Russian revolution in 1917 and the subsequent development of social egalitarianism in Europe as a whole, linguistic snobbery declined, and linguistic pragmatism became the norm. Aristocratic linguistic snobbery had once favoured French; egalitarian linguistic pragmatism in continental Europe was later to favour the English language.[20]

The fourth factor behind the decline of French especially in the Northern hemisphere was Britain's entry into the European Economic Community (later European Union). [21] This made English more decisively one of the official languages of the community. The new language became increasingly influential in the affairs of the European Union, both written and oral. Smaller members of the Union have more frequently turned to English rather than French in the post-Gaullist era of European affairs.[22]

The fifth factor behind the decline of French in the Northern hemisphere is linked to the decline of the power of the French-speaking Walloons in Belgium. The days of French pre-eminence in Belgium were coming to an end in the 1980s, although francophone Brussels still remained the capital of the country. Belgium moved towards a neo-federal structure, rooted in the principle of linguistic parity between French and Flemish.[23]

It is arguable that in North America the French language has made some gains as a result of greater recognition of bilingualism in the whole federation of Canada. On the other hand, there has been a decline of linguistic nationalism in Quebec since the old militancy of the 1960s. And the French of Quebec has got increasingly contaminated by Anglocisms. The Quebec language is genuinely under siege.[24]

The decline of the role of German in Europe has also tended to favour English rather than French. When the Scandinavian countries regarded German as virtually their first foreign language, there was a tendency to invest in the French language as well for a sense of balance. But when Scandinavians turned more decisively to the English language as their first foreign tongue, it was not just German which suffered; it was also French. Since English was in any case of wider international utility than German, its adoption by Scandinavians as the premier foreign language reduced the need to "balance" it with French.

Of course, Scandinavians are greater linguists than average in any case. Their schools are still sensitised to the importance of French and German as well as English. But linguistic priorities have indeed changed in the Nordic syllabuses and curricula - and in class enrolments. The English language has definitely been the main beneficiary of the decline of German - and the French language has also sustained a decline in educational emphasis.

Japan too has experienced shifts in emphasis, which have demoted German and French - and raised the role of English in educational and linguistic priorities. Between the Meiji Restoration in 1868 and Japan's defeat in World War II in 1945, Japan's main Western role models were indeed Germany and France. This Franco-German orientation affected not only Japan's curricula and syllabi. It also profoundly influenced its legal system and civil code.

It was the American occupation of Japan (1945-1952) which decisively shifted Japan from a Franco-German role model to the Anglo-Saxon alternative. The United States' continuing special relationship with Japan after the post-war occupation consolidated Japan's cultural re-orientation. While the Americans under Douglas MacArthur imposed upon Japan in 1947 a national constitution basically drawn from continental European experience, much of the rest of the Westernisation of Japan has been a case of cultural Americanisation -- from Japanese introduction to baseball to Japanese enthusiasm for American pop-stars. The very economy of Japan has interlocked itself with the American economy. The confirmation of the English language as Japan's first Western language in the post-war era has been part of this American phase of Japan's transformation. The decline of French and German languages in Japanese priorities was an inevitable consequence of the Americanisation of Japan.[25]

A particularly surprising development was the decision of the Socialist Party of Japan to adopt a campaign anthem written in the English language in the election campaign for the Lower House in 1989-1990. It marked the beginning of a new role for English in Japanese politics.

In the Great Lakes area of Africa the French language has also sustained setbacks in the 1990s. Political leadership in Rwanda was captured by Anglophone Tutsi who had grown up and been educated in Uganda. English had a new political role in Rwanda. So did Kiswahili in the post-Mobutu Congo.

If these have been the main factors which have resulted in the decline of the French language in the Northern hemisphere, which factors have contributed to the simultaneous expansion and consolidation of Francophonie? What indeed is Francophonie?

Twenty-one French-speaking countries coalesced as an intergovernmental organization for cooperation and created Francophonie in March 1970. The initial official name of the organization was *l'Agence de Cooperation Culturelle et Technique (ACCT)* [Agency for Cultural and Technical Cooperation]. Current membership includes 49 member countries, four countries with the status of associate - Albania, Greece, Macedonia, and Andorra – and ten observer countries such as the Czech and Slovak Republics, Slovenia, Croatia and Poland.[26]

Major institutional reforms were decided during the Hanoi summit (14-16 November 1996). Following these reforms, ACCT became **l'Agence de la Francophonie** (Agency of the Francophonie). The old purely administrative Secretariat General under ACCT was elevated to a more visible and political status, and it is now called the **Secretariat General de la Francophonie** (General Secretariat of the Francophonie) reporting directly to the Conference of Heads of States and Governments, and the Ministerial Conference.

The *Agence de la Francophonie* is headed by an *Administrateur Général* (General Administrator) appointed by the General Conference for 4 years, renewable. The Administrator runs the programs and day-to-day operations of the Agency. The first appointed General Administrator under the new formula is <u>Roger Dehaybe</u>, from Belgium.

The *Secrétariat Général de la Francophonie* has as head a Secretary General who is the political spokesman and official representative of the Francophonie at the international level. Former United Nations Secretary General <u>Boutros Boutros-Ghali</u>, an Egyptian, was elected at the Hanoi summit as the first Secretary General of the *Francophonie*.[27] Former Senegalese President Abdou Diouf succeeded him at a Beirut summit in 2002.[28] There is no official indication that the General Administrator must come from the North and the Secretary General from the South. But non-official sources, such as the media, have suggested that sort of division of labour.

What must be emphasized in the first instance is that the Southern expansion of Francophonie is particularly strong in Africa. On the whole the distribution of the French language is *bi-continental* - large number of French-speaking *individuals* in *Europe,* and large number of French-speaking *states* in *Africa.* Europe and Africa are by far the primary constituencies of Francophonie.

Of course there are smaller francophone constituencies in Quebec, Lebanon, Syria, Indo-china and elsewhere. But these are peripheries of the Francophone world. The main theatre of action is in Europe and Africa.

The historical factors which have favoured expansion in Africa have included the type of states which French and Belgian imperialism had created during the colonial period. These were often multi-ethnic countries which needed a lingua franca. Colonial policy had chosen the French language as the lingua franca - and the entire educational system and domestic political process consolidated that linguistic choice.[29]

A related factor was the assimilationist policy of France as an imperial power. This created an elite mesmerized by French culture and civilisation. A surprising number still retained dual citizenship with France even after independence. If President Bokassa was anything to go by, some African Heads of State may secretly still be citizens of France. As an aspect of the cultural lifestyle of Francophonie, annual holidays in France continue to be part of the elite culture of Francophone West and North Africa.

With some subsidies and technical assistance, the French language is also featuring more and more in class rooms in <u>Commonwealth</u>

Africa. Before independence British educational policy-makers were more committed to the promotion of indigenous African languages than to the promotion of the rival French legacy in British colonies. Nor were French offers of language teachers for schools in British colonies welcome.

The global French fraternity of Francophonie now has, as we indicated, a Secretariat in Paris partly headed by an African, Boutros Boutros-Ghali. There is a parallel administrative agency headed by somebody else. Membership of the Francophonie club now enlists countries which have not adopted French as a national language, but which can be persuaded to teach more French in their schools.

The difference which Africa's independence has made partly consists in greater readiness on the part of Anglophone governments to accept France's offers of teachers of the French language. Many an African university in the Commonwealth has been the beneficiary of technical assistance and cultural subsidies from the local French Embassy or directly from France. Portuguese-speaking Africa is even more responsive to the attractions of Francophonie.

France's policy in Africa is consolidated partly through an aggressive cultural diplomacy. Considerable amounts of money are spent on French-style syllabi and curricula in African schools, and on the provision of French teachers, advisors and reading materials. A residual French economic and administrative presence in most former French colonies has deepened Africa's orientation towards Paris.

In addition, every French President since Charles de Gaulle has attempted to cultivate special personal relations with at least some of the African leaders. There is little doubt that French-speaking African Presidents have greater and more personalized access to the French President than their Anglophone counterparts have had to either the British Prime Minister or the British Head of State, the Queen, in spite of Commonwealth conferences.

Here again is a case of reciprocal conquest. In spite of the global decline of French, there is little doubt that the French language and culture have conquered large parts of Africa. Many decisions about the future of Africa are being made by people deeply imbued by French values and perspectives.

Indeed, Francophonie is expanding its constituency in Africa, at least outside Algeria. It is true that the post-colonial policy of re-Arabisation in Algeria is designed to increase the role of Arabic in schools and public affairs at the expense of the pre-eminent colonial role of the French language. The rise of Islamic militancy in Algeria may pose new problems to aspects of French culture. It is also true the late Mobutu Sese Seko's policy of promoting regional languages in the old Zaire (Lingala, Kikongo, Tshiluba and Kiswahili) was partly at the expense of French in Zairean (now Congolese) curricula. We also mentioned how from 1994 French has also suffered a setback in Rwanda, led by Anglophone Tutsi originally educated in Uganda. But such setbacks for French in Africa are compatible with the expansion of Francophonie as a club of states. On the whole French is still a major presence in Africa, though the pace of its expansion has drastically declined.

However, when all is said and done, France's aspiration to remain a global power requires a cultural constituency as well as an economic one. It seems likely that this era will continue to signify a change in France's *economic* priorities in favour of the new pan-European opportunities and against the older investments in Africa. But it seems equally certain that a more open Europe after the end of the Cold War will favour the English language at the expense of the French language even within France itself. As custodian of the fortunes of French civilisation, France could not afford to abandon the cultural constituency of Francophonie entirely in favour of the more open Europe. The collapse of the Soviet Empire has been a further gain for the English language. France may need Africa more *culturally*, but less *economically*.

Its cultural constituency in Europe has been declining; its cultural constituency in Africa becomes more valuable than ever as the centrepiece of Francophonie. A remarkable interdependence has emerged - still imperfect and uneven, but real enough to make Africa indispensable for the recognition of France as a truly global power and the acceptance of the French language as a credible <u>world</u> language. <u>Eurafrica</u> as a concept gets part of its meaningfulness in the destiny of Francophonie. As a language French may be in decline; but as an international cultural club Francophonie is expanding and getting more institutionalised.

From the point of view of Francophonie and the Commonwealth, Egypt has been almost unique. This is a country which was only briefly occupied by the French following Napoleon's invasion of 1798. On the other hand, Egypt was occupied by Great Britain for a much longer period, beginning in 1882 until formal independence in 1923 - and then partially controlled by Britain in one way or another until the Egyptian revolution of 1952.[30]

And yet Egypt today is a member of Francophonie (in spite of the brevity of French rule) and <u>not</u> a member of the Commonwealth (in spite of more than half a century of British control).

In a sense it is easier to see why no Arab country previously ruled by Britain chose to join the Commonwealth than to explain why Egypt subsequently chose to join Francophonie. Most Arab leaders regarded the Commonwealth as a continuation of the British Empire, and therefore the face of neo-colonialism. Many Arabs also blamed the British (the Mandated power in Palestine) for not trying harder to prevent the partition of Palestine and the creation of the State of Israel. And when Egypt was under a revolutionary Nasserite regime from 1952 to 1970, it was more remote than ever that Egypt would want to have anything to do with the Commonwealth.

Under Gamal Abdel Nasser, Egypt did not want to be much associated with France either - not in the wake of the Suez invasion of 1956 and the Algerian war of independence of 1954 - 1962.

But in the wider social elite of Egypt there was always a fascination with France - what might be called the Napolean-De Lesseps-Aida complex. DeLesseps was the French engineer who designed the Suez Canal. It was opened in 1869 by the Empress Eugénie, consort of Napoleon III. The Khedive of Egypt, to celebrate the opening of the Canal, commissioned Giusseppe Verdi to compose an opera. The masterpiece was <u>Aida</u>, produced in Cairo in 1871, a glittering French-Italian-Ottoman occasion. Although <u>Aida</u> as an opera was Italian, its link with the opening of the Suez Canal Gallicised it in the Egyptian imagination.

It was this triple complex - the mystique of Napoleon's brief occupation of Egypt, the French role in the building of the Suez Canal, and the superb opera which was created to celebrate the opening of the Canal - which contributed to keep alive among some sectors of the Egyptian elite an enduring fascination with France. Schools based on the French language have continued to the present-day; so have aspects of the Napoleonic code in the Egyptian legal system.[31]

All this goes part of the way towards explaining why Egypt in the last quarter of the twentieth century was at last ready to join

Francophonie - although Egypt has never seriously considered joining the Commonwealth.

The Origins of the African Renaissance

But when did the African Renaissance begin? One important date is Africa's recapture of the Suez Canal in 1956. Gamal Abdel Nasser nationalized the waterway which had been built not just by a French engineer called De Lesseps, but also by hundreds of Egyptian workers, many of whom lost their lives.

In Francophone Africa the genesis of the African Renaissance was courageous in a different way. It was the vote for independence by the people of Guinea (Conakry) in 1958, defying the massive French pressure to vote the other way. The people of Guinea stood alone in their preference for sovereignty, although their leader Sékou Touré later let them down by becoming a tyrant.[32]

For Commonwealth Africa the African Renaissance began when Nigeria demonstrated Africa could be plunged into a civil war and have a one-man "Truth and Reconciliation Commission" - Yakubu Gowon.

Although Gowon presided over the Nigerian civil war, he was more than Africa's Abraham Lincoln. He was constantly worried during the conflict about civilian casualties on both sides, though modern war has that propensity. He constantly discouraged the Federal propaganda machine from describing Biafrans as "the enemy". And when the war ended he insisted that there were to be no reprisals, no Nuremberg trials, and no victimisation of the vanquished. By an ironic twist of fate, General Gowon after the war became a hero to many Igbos, the former Biafran secessionists.[33]

If there is an African Renaissance we should also be impressed by what Gowon did when he was overthrown in a military coup in 1975. Former Heads of State who have the humility to go back to school should be part of the African Renaissance. Gowon went to become a university undergraduate. The same man who had been honoured by Cambridge University in England as Head of State with an honourary doctorate was standing in a cafeteria line at Warwick University a few years later as an undergraduate. I first met him in his undergraduate but post-presidential days. He continued his studies at Warwick right up to the Ph.D. Gowon had qualities worthy of the African Renaissance. He was truly a one-man "Truth and Reconciliation Commission."

And if General Dr. Gowon had seen something in others worth saluting, it was mainly because there was so much greatness in Gowon himself. As the poet said:

When the high heart we magnify
And the sure vision celebrate
And worship greatness passing by
Ourselves are great[34]

The only Nigerian Head of State who first came to power as a military ruler and was later freely elected is another soldier, General Olusegun Obasanjo. Is such a transition from military ruler to a freely elected civilian ruler a kind of renaissance?

That is arguable. But Obasanjo's earlier moral claims were more compelling. They were established in 1979.

What has the African Renaissance got to learn from General Obasanjo himself? "Giving up political power voluntarily" is the answer. This was exactly twenty years before Nelson Mandela did the same thing.

Within less than a week of each other, Obasanjo and Jerry Rawlings of Ghana were the first African military rulers to hand over power voluntarily to elected civilian administrations. Obasanjo was the first Nigerian Head of State of any kind to voluntarily relinquish power – and, at that, to somebody not of his own choosing. Both Leopold Senghor of Senegal and Julius K. Nyerere of Tanzania were subsequently to hand over power to people who had needed their prior approval as heirs.

But in Nigeria it has been argued that the 1979 elections over which General Obasanjo presided were the only free elections held in the country between independence in 1960 and 1999. Obasanjo, a Yoruba man, presided over elections which brought into power the Hausa dignitary, Shehu Shagari. Many fellow Yoruba continued to blame Obasanjo for not playing the ethnic card and handing over power to Chief Obafemi Awolowo.

African renaissance should encourage Heads of State to follow Obasanjo's example in his first Administration in the 1970s -- and bow out gracefully without unfairly playing the ethnic card. Obasanjo bowed out after less than four years. Leopold Senghor in Senegal bowed out gracefully soon after -- but after 20 years in power. Normally Heads of State should bow out after 10 years, and only in exceptional circumstances after 15 years. Obasanjo's second Administration from 1999 should also emulate the spirit of Obasanjo's first regime a quarter of a century earlier.

When the high heart we magnify,
And the sure vision celebrate,
And worship greatness passing by,
Ourselves are great.

The African Renaissance should strengthen the links between the Academy and the media as two systems of information and knowledge. We might call this concept ACA-MEDIA (as distinct from ACADEMIA) -- linking the world of scholars with the world of reporters and journalists. The new South Africa may be moving in that direction.

The links between scholarship and other modes of information and communication are bound to deepen. The African Renaissance needs to respond constructively to the merging ACA-MEDIA, alongside the more traditional respect for ACADEMIA.

The African Renaissance should always pursue South-South cooperation, and pay special attention to Africa's friends in India, Malaysia, Pakistan, China, of course Africa's more immediate neighbours in the Arab world, and in many other countries elsewhere.

What is AFRENAISSANCE?

In 1994 I was invited to a conference at the Central State University in Wilberforce, Ohio. There was one major condition imposed on paper-writers for this conference. No papers which were *pessimistic* about the African condition would be admitted. This was a conference for *Afro-optimists* -- not for Afro-pessimists. I accepted the condition. I wrote a paper entitled "AFRENAISSANCE' (one word). If I had known that the term "African Renaissance" was going to be so popular in Southern Africa a few years later, I would have insisted on the immediate publication of my paper.

Unfortunately I gave the English language rights of my paper to Central State University who have been in negotiations with Stanford University Press about publishing the whole proceedings. They are taking their time. Until today the main published proof that I had written such a paper was in *German*. A German publication had translated my paper and published it in 1996.[35]

The Renaissance in the history of Europe was a return to the Greco-Roman Classics. The European Renaissance was partly a liberation from the heavy hand of Christianity (imported from the Middle East) and an attempt to recover the spontaneity of ancient Greece at its best. *Afrenaissance* or the Renaissance in Africa must also be in part a return to the classics. And what is a return to the African classics? It must involve a partial return to African culture and civilisation. The African Renaissance must in part involve the *re-Africanisation* of Africa based on seven principles. Let me discuss these principles briefly.

The Seven Pillars of AFRENAISSANCE

1) A new systematic recognition of the probable authenticity of African oral history (The History Imperative);

2) A new respect for African languages and oral literatures (The Language Imperative);

3) A readiness to train, encourage and use African talent in all fields of human endeavour, from forestry to medicine, from business to nuclear physics (The Talent Imperative);

4) A recognition of Africanity as one dignified face of humanity (The Dignity Imperative);

5) A sustained capacity for self-reliance and self-development among African peoples (The Imperative of Self-Reliance);

6) A reactivated will for humane self-rule and clean governance in spite of massive pressures to the contrary (the imperative of humane self-rule). Even soldiers like Gowon and Obasanjo could contribute to that spirit, let alone more saintly figures like Nelson Mandela and Archbishop Tutu;

7) A creative African response to a world of globalisation and historic trends (the imperative of creative accommodation to globalisation). Africa may have to teach the world the culture of a short memory of hate and speedy reconciliation.

The third principle of encouraging talent at all ages becomes important in its wider consequences in the arts and the sciences, in literature and philosophy, and in practical skills. In 1998, the Modern Library Board of the United States issued its list of the 100 best novels published in the 20th century in the English language.[36] Was this a kind of linguistic apartheid based on English? The Modern Library Board (Random House) also *ranked* those novels. ULYSSES by James Joyce was ranked first and foremost. And THE MAGNIFICENT AMBERSONS by Booth Tarkington was ranked No. 100. The majority of the books were from the Commonwealth and almost all the rest from the United States.

No African novel in the English language made the first 100 -- not even Chinua Achebe's work or the work of Nobel Laureates Wole Soyinka and Nadine Gordimer. Was this linguistic apartheid combined with racial apartheid? Not quite. While Africa was completely out of the league, the African Diaspora did make it. Ralph Ellison's *INVISIBLE MAN* made it for No. 19, Richard Wright's *NATIVE SON* made it as No. 20 and James Baldwin's *GO TELL IT ON THE MOUNTAIN* made it for No. 39.

Muslims were relieved that the list did not include Salman Rushdie's *SATANIC VERSES*, but the list did include Salman Rushdie's *MIDNIGHT'S CHILDREN* (No. 90). Books about Africa by non-Africans which made the list include Joseph Conrad's *HEART OF DARKNESS* (No. 67) and V.S. Naipaul's *A BEND IN THE RIVER* (No. 83), both of which also feature in Commonwealth literature.

Should we be alarmed that none of the great African writers have made the list of the top 100? It would have been nice if Chinua Achebe's novel *THINGS FALL APART* (1958) was included in the list of the 100 top novels of the 20th century. It certainly deserved to be. Other Achebe enthusiasts might vote for *ARROW OF GOD* (1964) as Achebe's most profound novel. But none of his works made the list. Was linguistic apartheid verging on the racial?

There is a consolation. The only authors who made the list of the top-100 of the century whose mother tongue was *not* English were Joseph Conrad, Vladimir Nabokov and Salman Rushdie. All the rest were *native* products of Anglo-Saxon linguistic culture in one degree or another. This includes V.S. Naipaul. They were native speakers of English.

This means one of two things: *either* writing in English when English is not one's native language is a far bigger handicap than we all assumed *or* that the judges of the top 100 novels of the 20th century were simply too Anglo-Saxonic themselves. On balance I prefer the *latter* explanation. The judges were probably too *Anglo-Saxonic* in their prejudices, even if some judges were from the Commonwealth.

As part of the African Renaissance, it was appropriate that the year 2002 saw, at the Zimbabwe International Book Fair, an announcement of the twelve best and the 100 best African books of the 20th century in any language, indigenous or European. Books were selected in three categories: Creative Writing, Literature for Children, and Scholarship/ Non-Fiction.[37] But we should also select ten best major *poems* in any indigenous African language, ten best *plays* in any European or indigenous African language, and the ten best books *for* or *by* children from Africa in any language.

> *When the little heart we magnify*
> *And the sure vision celebrate*
> *And worship mini-greatness passing by*
> *Ourselves are great.*

In a hundred years would we be able select a hundred works under each category rather than ten/twelve of each? There is a certain neatness in the Swahili concept of <u>mia kwa mia</u> ("a hundred by hundred"). The competition of <u>ten</u> best novels in a hundred years would of course be ten times more severe than a competition for a hundred novels in a hundred years. But in either case Africa would be celebrating a convergence of high hearts, a constellation of sure visions. This would be the <u>aesthetic</u> side of the African Renaissance. To paraphrase inversely another poet:

> *Deign on the passing genius to turn thine eyes,*
> *And lean awhile on art to be wise.*[38]

If Francophonie had started as <u>linguistic apartheid</u> based on the French language, the Modern Library Board of the United States had drifted towards a form of <u>linguistic apartheid</u> based on the English language. The African Renaissance aspires to transcend the apartheid of language, as well as of race. Ultimately the Renaissance celebrates the high heart not in individual heroes but in the African continent, as a whole; it magnifies the sure vision not from citizen to citizen, but in the mighty will of the African people collectively.

NOTES

[1]A guide to the complex laws governing race relations in South Africa under apartheid may be found in Muriel Horrell, *Laws Affecting Race Relations in South Africa* (Johannesburg, South Africa: South African Institute of Race Relations, 1978); for a general survey, see Harold Wolpe, *Race, Class, and the Apartheid State* (London: Currey, 1988).

[2] Between 1995 and 2000 in the post-apartheid South Africa, according to one estimate, average income of black households fell by 19 percent while white household incomes rose by 15 percent; see Richard Morin, "Despite Deep Woes, Democracy Instills Hope," *Washington Post* (March 31, 2004).

[3] However, in 1995, Mozambique was granted membership -- although it was not a British colony, and its official language was Portuguese; see Arthur S. Banks and Thomas C. Muller, eds., *Political Handbook of the World, 1998* (Binghamton, NY: CSA Publications, 1998), p. 1081.

[4] For one history of the British Commonwealth, see Nicholas Mansergh, *The Commonwealth Experience, Volumes I and II* (Toronto and Buffalo, NY: University of Toronto Press, 1983).

[5] Dates of membership of Commonwealth countries may found in Banks et al, *Political Handbook of the World, 1998*, p. 1080.

[6] See Mansergh, *The Commonwealth Experience*, pp. 166-187.

[7] For an account of one such confrontation, consult, for example, Norman Gelb, "Thatcher Takes on the Commonwealth: Staving Off Sanctions," *New Leader* 69 (July 14/28, 1986), pp. 6-7.

[8] The Afrikaner's quasi-religious attachment to the land, similar to that of Zionists to areas of Palestine and modern-day Israel and that of the Protestants in Ireland to Ulster, is detailed in Donald H. Akenson, *God's People: Covenant and Land in South Africa, Israel, and Ulster* (Ithaca and London: Cornell University Press, 1992), p. 63.

[9] See, for example, G. A. Kelly, *Lost Soldiers: The French Army and Empire in Crisis, 1947-1962* (Cambridge, MA: MIT Press, 1965).

[10] After more than a decade, the economic divide between black and white South Africans continues; see Morin, "Despite Deep Woes, Democracy Instills Hope," *Washington Post* (March 31, 2004).

[11] See Suzanne Daley, "His Beloved Country Repays Mandela in Kind," *New York Times* (March 23, 1999).

[12] Jomo Kenyatta, *Suffering Without Bitterness* (Nairobi and Chicago: East African Publishing House and Northwestern University Press, 1968).

[13] For an overview of the transition from the minority white rule to the majority black rule in Zimbabwe, consult Anthony Parsons, "From Southern

Rhodesia to Zimbabwe, 1965-1985," *International Affairs* Vol. 9, No. 4, (November 1988), pp. 353-361. More recently, Zimbabwe has seen the harsh treatment of legitimate black opposition by its ruler and former liberation leader Robert Mugabe; see, for instance, Craig Timberg, "Mugabe Gains Expanded Powers: Zimbabwe's Parliament Votes to Restrict Travel, Limit Appeals on Land Seizures," *Washington Post* (August 31, 2005).

[14] See Richard Morin, "A World Apart: A Decade After the Fall of Apartheid in South Africa, An Isolated White Community Clings to Its Past," *Washington Post* (March 31, 2004).

[15] This list is drawn from Banks and Muller, eds., *Political Handbook of the World*, and David Crystal, ed., *The Cambridge Encyclopedia of Language* (Cambridge: Cambridge University Press, 1997).

[16] See the map in Dennis Ager, *Identity, Insecurity and Image: France and Language* (London: Multilingual Matters, 1997), p. 157.

[17] Even French public policy accepts that the demographic future of French rests in Africa; see Agers, *Identity, Insecurity, and Image*, p. 175.

[18] A report in *The Economist* (December 20, 1986) entitled "The New English Empire," pp. 127-131, describes this new dominance of the English language. For a fascinating history of the world's languages, see Nicholas Ostler, *Empires of the Word : A Language History of the World* (New York: HarperCollins, 2005), and for a comparative study of English and French, also see Ronald Wardhaugh, *Languages in Competition : Dominance, Diversity, and Decline* (Oxford, UK; New York; and London, England: B. Blackwell and A. Deutsch, 1987)

[19] Agers, Identity, Insecurity, and Image, p. 167.

[20] For the Russian example, see the discussion in J. N. Westwood, *Endurance and Endeavor: Russian History, 1812-1992* (Oxford: Oxford University Press, 1993), p. 12.

[21] A fascinating account of the EEC's dealings with the first British application to join the EEC in 1961 is drawn in N. Piers Ludlow, *Dealing With Britain: The Six and the First UK Application to the EEC,* (Cambridge and New York: Cambridge University Press, 1997).

[22] The European Union has three working languages -- English, French, and German, necessitating the use of the largest translation staff in the world, numbering more than 1500 people. See *The Economist* (August 29, 1998), p. 50.

[23] Belgium's path toward relative amity between the regions is detailed in Lisbeth Hooghe, "Belgium: Hollowing the Center," in Ugo M. Amoretti and Nancy Bermeo, Eds., *Federalism and Territorial Cleavages* (Baltimore, MD: Johns Hopkins University Press, 2004), pp. 55-92 and Rolf Falter, "Belgium's Peculiar Way to Federalism," in Kas Deprez and Louis Vos, Eds., *Nationalism in Belgium: Shifting Identities, 1780-1995* (Houndmills, Basingstoke, Hampshire and New York, NY: Macmillan Press & St. Martin's Press, 1998), pp. 177-197. For an overview of Belgian regional cleavages, see John Fitzmaurice, *The Politics of Belgium: Crisis and Compromise in a Plural Society* (New York: St. Martin's Press, 1983) and also consult Alexander B. Murphy, *Regional Dynamics and Cultural Differentiation in Belgium: A Study in Cultural Political Geography* (Chicago: University of Chicago Committee on Geographical Studies, 1988).

[24] The tensions between Quebec and Canada are detailed in Kenneth McRoberts, *Misconceiving Canada: The Struggle for National Unity* (Toronto, New York, and Oxford: Oxford University Press, 1997).

[25] The two periods of Japanese transformation are detailed in Anne Waswo, *Modern Japanese Society, 1848-1994* (Oxford: Oxford University Press, 1996).

[26] For details on this organization, see Ager, pp. 185-190 and the list of current members is available at <http://www.francophonie.org/membres/etats/> (November 15, 2005).

[27] See Craig R. Whitney, "French Speakers Meet Where Few Will Hear,"*New York Times* (November 17, 1997).

[28] Reported on the web-site <http://www.francophonie.org/secretaire/presentation/> (November 15, 2005).

[29] For a portrait of French colonialism in Africa in the early part of the 20th century, see Jean Suret-Canale, *French Colonialism in Tropical Africa, 1900-1945* (London: C. Hurst, 1971).

[30] However, Egypt was never a formal Crown Colony; see Alan Warwick Palmer, *Dictionary of the British Empire and Commonwealth* (London: Murray, 1996), pp. 112-113.

[31] See Arthur Goldschmidt, Jr., *Modern Egypt: The Formation of a Nation State* (Westport, CT: Westview Press, 1988), p. 45.

[32] The evolution of Toure's ideology is described in, for example, R. W. Johnson, "Sekou Toure and the Guinean Revolution," *African Affairs* (October 1970), Volume 69, No. 277, pp. 350-365.

[33] Consult John D. Clarke, *Yakubu Gowon: Faith in a United Nigeria* (London and Totowa, NJ: F. Cass, 1987).

[34] These lines are from John Drinkwater's play *Abraham Lincoln*, (Boston: Houghton and Mifflin, 1919), available as a Project Gutenberg publication at <http://www.gutenberg.org/files/11172/11172-h/11172-h.htm> (November 17, 2005).

[35] The German journal was *International Politik* (Bonn), which published my paper in Volume 51, No. 9, 1996, pp. 11-18. The German version became an entry in a bibliography compiled by Abdul S. Bemath, *The Mazruiana Collection* (New Delhi: Sterling Publishers, and Johannesburg: Foundation for Global Dialogue, 1998).

[36] Paul Lewis, "'Ulysses' at Top As Panel Picks 100 Best Novels," *New York Times*, (July 20, 1998).

[37] The complete list of books may be found at the web-site <http://www.zibf.org.zw/awards/100bestbooks.html> (November 16, 2005)

[38] These lines are stimulated by Samuel Johnson's poem, "The Vanity of Human Wishes," (London, 1749); see J. D. Fleeman, ed., *Samuel Johnson: The Complete English Poems* (New Haven and London: Yale University Press, 1971).

CHAPTER 5

AFRICA'S TRIPLE HERITAGE: THE SPLIT SOUL OF A CONTINUENT

Three civilisations have shaped contemporary Africa: Africa's own inheritance, Islam, and Western traditions. The interplay of these three civilisations is the essence of Africa's triple heritage. The three civilisations offer various values that compete for African allegiance. In every African country today, the triple forces of indigenous culture, Islam, and Westernisation vie for dominance.

This contest for supremacy can lead to open conflicts, as was the case with the Nigerian 2002 Miss World Beauty Pageant. While its organizers saw it as a healthy exercise, it was resisted by Islamic groups that saw it as an importation of undesirable western values bordering on the prurient and debasement of women. The ensuing demonstrations against the organisers of the pageant resulted in loss of life and property. Ultimately the event was relocated from Abuja to London.[1] Even a simple exercise such as conducting a census can easily cause misunderstanding in African situations of mixed cultures.

Africa is indeed a competitive territory with imported Islamic and western values contending with indigenous African values and customs. This competition has often led to stymied development, as much energy is dissipated in resolving conflicts. On the other hand, 'three civilisations forged into one' can sometimes be enriching.

Communication has played mediating roles in the management of the interrelationships among the elements of the triple heritage. But because communication is embedded in the elements, it has not always been a neutral channel. It can be an active progenitor purposively fuelling change, or deliberately slowing down some new ideas. The slow pace of development in many African countries can be attributed to the (mis) management of communication in the context of the triple heritage. There is an incipient crisis in the interrelationship among the elements of Africa's triple heritage, and the results of this crisis can be seen all around us. Governments are unstable, national economies are under strain, infrastructures are undeveloped or unmanaged and the continent's abundant natural resources are wasted or misappropriated. And yet the triple heritage presents <u>a paradox in communication</u>. African languages as media of communication have been immensely enriched by contact with Arabic, European Languages and Islam. Hausa, Kiswahili, Wolof and Somali are inconceivable without Islam.[2]

Going by the number of cellular phones, transistor radios, video recorders, television sets, and satellite receivers in African cities, it is obvious that many Africans are enamoured of new communication technology, very often for all the wrong reasons. The euphoria about the new technology is "an illusion of modernity, a mirage of progress, a facade of advancement. The reality behind the facade continues to be grim and devastating."[3] Without proper incorporation of indigenous African values in the equation for the use of the communication infrastructure, genuine development will continue to elude Africa.

It is useful for us to distinguish between *modernization* and *development*. By modernization is meant "innovative change based on more advanced knowledge and leading to wider social horizons. We define development as modernization minus dependency, the promotion of innovative change and broadening of social horizons without excessive reliance on others."[4]

In many African countries, the mismanagement of the triple heritage has resulted in serious dislocations which make even the degree of dependent modernization impossible to maintain. It is as if previous achievements in national growth are being reversed today, and the continent is in the process of disintegration and social decay. Instead of growing economies, increasing per capita incomes, closer integration among countries, and increasing political freedom, Africa's collective experience seems to be characterized by decreasing competence and social capital. It is as if the ancestors of Africa are angry with the present generation, and have placed a curse on us. Our sin is attempting to ignore the value of indigenous African wisdom in the management of contemporary African problems. We are turning our backs on previous centuries and attempting to modernize without consulting cultural continuities. For instance, we embrace foreign influences as panaceas for our inadequacies, and disregard the pivotal role of Africanity.

Even before Islam came to Africa there was an older triple heritage in the continent—an interplay between African culture, Semitic culture,

81

and the legacy of Greece and Rome. This ancient triple heritage is best illustrated in Ethiopia, where Christianity has flourished since the fourth century, the impact of Judaism is captured in local versions of the legend of Solomon and Sheba, and the Greco-Roman legacy is manifest in both social traditions and brick and mortar.[5] This ancient triple heritage evolved when the Semitic element (which was once both Hebraic and Arabian) narrowed to become mainly Islamic. On the other hand, the Greco-Roman legacy expanded to become the impact of modern Western civilisation as a whole on African life and culture.

Grandiose or Simple Past?

But what is the African strand in these legacies? How much of an indigenous civilisation did Africa have before the arrival of Islam and the West? One African school of interpretation emphasizes that Africa had indeed produced great kings, grand empires, and elabourate technological skills before the aliens colonised her. The evidence is from the remains of Great Zimbabwe to the bronze culture of West Africa.[6] Indeed, ancient Egypt was itself an African miracle and, in part, a 'Negro' civilisation. This perspective prefers to emphasize the glorious moments in Africa's history and the grand civilisations it produced.

In contrast, there is the perspective of romantic primitivism. Here the idea is not to emphasize past grandeur, but to validate simplicity and give respectability to Africa's non-technical traditions. This historical perspective takes pride in precisely those traditions that European arrogance would seem to despise. In the words of the Martiniqan poet Aime Cesaire, who invented the word *Negritude*,

> Hooray to:
> Those who have invented neither powder nor compass
> Those who have tamed neither gas nor electricity
> Those who have explored neither the seas nor the skies . . .
> My negritude is neither a tower nor a cathedral;
> It plunges into the red flesh of the soil.
> Hooray for joy,
> Hooray for love,
> Hooray for the pain of incarnate tears.[7]

As Jean –Paul Sartre once pointed out, this African revelling in not having invented either powder or the compass, this proud claim of nontechnicalness, is a reversal of the usual cultural situation. "What would pass as a deficiency becomes a positive source of wealth."[8] There is a sense in which not to have is to be wealthy, in a different sense of "wealth."

Now let us juxtapose these two African perspectives. While proponents of Africa's glorious past look to the pyramids as a validation of Africa's dignity, take pride in the ruins of ancient Zimbabwe, and turn to the ancient empires of Ghana, Mali, and Malawi for official names of modern republics, those who prefer romantic primitivism, on the other hand, seek solace in stateless societies, find dignity in village life, and adulate the cultural validity of traditions and beliefs of rural folks.

What both types of African society have shared is nearness to nature. For centuries the continent has had abundant animal life and vegetation, and the indigenous religions have fused God, man, and nature. Islam and Western Christianity have challenged this fusion. Only man alone is supposed to have been created in the image of God. This is contrary to indigenous African beliefs in which the image of God takes many forms. Among God's creatures only man is, according to Islam and Western Christianity, close to sacredness, in possession of a soul, and destined for spiritual immortality.[9] This is contrary to indigenous African religions, which allow other creatures to share in sacredness and sometimes endow mountains and springs with a holiness of their own.[10]

The coming of Islam and especially of Westernism, has disrupted the African's ancient relationship with nature. The impact of the West has been particularly harmful. Capitalism and the cash economy have resulted in the rape or prostitution of Africa's environment, often by Africans themselves. Under the impact of the profit motive which came with the West, the African no longer holds nature in awe; he holds it in avarice and greed. Traditionally, Christianity has neither sacred nor profane animals, and has been largely a prisoner of its anthropocentric views.[11] Islamic doctrine includes profane animals(especially the pig and the dog) but no sacred ones. Indigenous African religions have always had room for both sacred and profane fellow creatures. By taking the animal kingdom outside the moral realm, the Western impact on Africa has reduced animals to their economic worth.

Gender Relations

In the final analysis, Africa's triple heritage is a social complexity rather than merely an ecological doctrine. The triple heritage is about human relationship not only with nature, not only with God, but also with humanity. Fundamentally, it is also about man's relationship with woman. Has Africa's triple heritage complicated the role of women in society or has it improved prospects for the female of the species?

Islam gives women more economic rights (e.g. the right to inherit land) than they enjoy under some indigenous "tribal" laws. On the other hand, Islam gives women narrower economic roles (e.g. cultivating the land or marketing the produce) than women pursue under indigenous traditions. There is a conflict here between formal rights (better protected by Islam) and practical roles (better promoted by indigenous culture).[12]

A similar dilemma can be detected in the Western impact on Africa. Semi-educated or non-Westernised African women in the countryside are often at the core of agricultural production: tilling the land and sometimes marketing the produce. But with Western education, women move from the productive sector to the service sector. They learn a European language and other verbal and literary skills, only to leave the soil in preference to the office. Western education turns African women into clerks and secretaries instead of cultivators. This is a case of functional marginalisation.

It may be true that the West's impact upon Africa may have raised the legal status of women, but it has narrowed the economic functions of women. Women's rights are better protected in the post-colonial era, but the role of women is less fundamental to the society than it was before. In short, the African woman is confronted with expanding rights and a shrinking role in the post-colonial state.[13]

But African problems are not merely between men and women. There are also problems between men and men in the political arena and economic domain. Africa's triple heritage is at the centre not only of the conflict between indigenous and imported cultures but between tradition and modernity. The triple heritage has also affected the other basic conflicts within the African condition: the tensions between city and countryside, between soldiers and politicians, between the elite and the masses, between ethnic groups and social classes, between the religious and the secular, between a longing for autonomy and the shackles of dependency.

African Predicament

Given the dilemmas of the African predicament, there are searches for new ways of understanding its problems and a quest for a new science to solve them. Western economists have in the past focused on theories of economic growth and economic development. In the case of post-colonial Africa, should we be looking for a theory of economic decay?[14] Western aid donors have increasingly turned their consciences to those African countries which have always been poverty-stricken or the least developed, and may always remain seriously deprived. But a country like Ghana was once well-endowed and has since declined.[15] So were Mali, Ethiopia, and Uganda. Are these more deserving or less? Are their worsening under-development and relentless decay a warning signal for Africa as a whole?

Ivory Coast, once regarded as a bastion of political stability is suddenly facing internal strife and rebellion by a section of the armed forces.[16] The notorious internal crises in Sudan, Sierra Leone, Liberia and the Democratic Republic of the Congo (DRC, formerly Zaire) are continuing with varying degrees of intensity. Perhaps the only African countries that can be judged immune to the pervasive internal conflicts which are so common in the continent include countries like Lesotho, Senegal, and Namibia.

Explaining Africa's Predicament

The problem of societal decay can be measured by diminishing productivity, declining stability, and the erosion of public morality. Dependency theories do not really explain decay. Taiwan and Singapore may be very dependent but, unlike Kenya, Nigeria, and the DRC, their economies are booming rather than decaying. So why is Africa faced with the danger of decay?

We may already have theories of economic "take-off."[17] We now need a theory of crash-prevention. But it is arguable that a country like Kenya had already "taken off" economically when it became politically independent in 1963. Why has the craft of state been losing altitude so dangerously? How can Kenya start ascending again? How much of a lesson to the rest of Africa is the whole story of countries like Kenya, Nigeria, and the DRC? And what has the triple heritage got to do with these dilemmas between development and decay, between a capacity for self-help and a weakness for dependency? What is the role of communication, in all its ramifications of interpersonal, intercultural, mass mediated, and diplomatic, in better management of Africa's rich resources? The soul of Africa is presently split three ways, and is in search of its own inner peace. The split soul of a continent is what the triple heritage is all about.

Environment: In Touch With Nature

Since Africa is the most tropical of all continents (split almost in half by the Equator,) Africa's history and culture are pre-eminently products of Africa's geography and of the African genius for adaptation under harsh conditions. For centuries the most immediate neighbours of African peoples were the animals with whom they shared the continent. Africa's location has brought in more human neighbours (Arabs and Europeans) but sometimes at the expense of older animal neighbours in the African environment. Africa's climate is a mixed blessing, generating a wide range of natural phenomena, from jungle to desert, from abundant life to deadly diseases. Post-colonial Africa is witnessing expanding human population, diminishing numbers of wild beasts, and a continuing struggle between man and the elements.[18]

Religion: New Gods

Christianity had two entries in Africa. Its first influence emerged through Egypt and Ethiopia early in the Christian era (as part of the ancient triple heritage of African, Semitic, and Greco-Roman influences). Its second arrival was through European colonialism (as part of the modern triple heritage of Africanism, Islam, and Westernisation). This new European religious thrust found older gods in the continent. Indigenous religions were still alive and strong. Islam arrived in Africa during the seventh century. Today, Africa is witnessing increasing evangelisation from foreign religions, which are enfeebling indigenous African religions.[19]

Technology: New Tools

Today, different historical stages of technology co-exist at the same time within Africa—the "tribal" spear coexists with the modern missile, the ironsmith with the steel mill, the talking drum with satellite broadcasting, witchcraft with nuclear physics, herbal medicine with advanced surgery. Both Islam and Westernism helped to introduce new tools of production (cultivation and manufacture), of construction (building both states and bridges), of communication (vehicles and verbs), of rehabilitation (different forms of medicine), and of destruction (from the Arab sword to the Western machine gun). This is quite apart from the rich heritage of skills independently evolved in Africa over the centuries.[20]

The West has been better at transferring its tools of destruction than its tools of production. Postcolonial Africa is becoming militarily more sophisticated but industrially less effective. The religious strands of the Semitic and Western legacies have been particularly successful in transmitting the tools of construction—from the churches and synagogues of Ethiopia to the mosques of the Sahel. Islamic tools of communication range from the role of languages like Arabic, Hausa, and Kiswahili to the historic functions of dhows (boats) in East Africa and camels across the Sahara. The new tools are not being successfully adapted to fit into the indigenous milieu, and thus some of them introduce problems and new conflicts, instead of serving as solutions.

Tension: New Conflicts

In many African societies guns came with the trans-Atlantic slave trade. Africa has in fact experienced a triple heritage of slavery: indigenous, Islamic, and Western-oriented. Indigenous slavery was the least commercialised and basically the most humane.[21] With regard to Islamic slavery, why do we not hear of black Arab rebellions and riots the way we hear of black American riots? A major reason is that over the centuries Islamic culture and lineage have permitted both cultural assimilation and interracial marriages.[22] If the father is Arab and free, then the child is Arab and free, even if the mother was originally an African slave.

The trans-Atlantic slave trade was the most race-conscious, the largest in scale, and the most resistant to assimilation.[23] But at least the West generated its own abolitionist movement—while simultaneously generating new empire-builders. England, the leading abolitionist power in the nineteenth century, was simultaneously the leading imperialist power.[24] Additional conflicts afflicted Africa—imperial wars of conquest, primary African resistance, Africa's involvement in other people's wars (World War I and II, the Cold War and the French War in Vietnam), and modern liberation wars against colonial rule and white minority regimes. And now Africa is being drawn into the war between Western militarism and Middle Eastern terror.[25]

Post-colonial Africa has also experienced conflicts arising from artificial colonial borders (e.g. the Biafran War and the Somali, Eritrean and Ethiopian conflicts), from limited resources (e.g. rice riots in Liberia and water riots in Ibadan), from entrenched conservative institutions (e.g. the Ethiopian revolution), from new fragile institutions (e.g. the series of military coups all over in Africa), from ethno-sectarian differences (e.g. the Sudanese civil war) and from emerging class differences (e.g. labour unrest, etc.). The new triple heritage has given Africa the warrior tradition from indigenous culture, the jihad tradition from Islam, and the guerrilla tradition from revolutionary radicalism. This is quite apart from the tradition of the colonial army which sometimes inherited the post-colonial state.[26] African countries are plagued by incessant internal conflicts that make state governments unstable, and foreign direct investments unattractive. Many of the conflicts in Africa have defied easy solutions due to the intricate interrelationships among the elements of the continent's triple heritage. Yet there are now fewer military regimes than there were in the 1980s, significantly more multi-party experiments and fewer single-party regimes in Africa.[27]

Stability: Uneasy Lies the Head

All societies have political systems, but not all political systems are states. Traditional Africa consisted of both states and stateless societies. The states were often in the tradition of "romantic gloriana" – a glorious view of the past. The states in Africa (as everywhere) attained stability through instruments of coercion. The stateless societies attained stability through traditions of consensus. Both Islam and Westernism are state-building civilisations. Africa's stateless heritage has been endangered first by Islam and its state-building jihads and later by Westernism and its obsession with boundaries and standing armies. Africa's stateless societies ("tribes without rulers") are an endangered species- almost doomed to extinction. But meanwhile, 'tribes' which were stateless in pre-colonial times, like the Langi of Uganda or even the Ewe of Ghana, have sometimes captured the post-colonial state.

But what is the fate of the post-colonial state? It is subject to two negative pulls: the pull of tyranny (entailing centralized violence) and the pull of anarchy (involving decentralized violence). A major reason for the dialectic between tyranny and anarchy is the fragility of the institutions inherited from the colonial era.

Politically, Africa is caught between two or more traditions. There is a culture gap between the new institutions from the West and the ancient cultures of Africa and Islam. The elder tradition gave special legitimacy to Jomo Kenyatta's rule. The sage tradition was manifested in Mwalimu (Teacher) Julius Nyerere and in (Poet) Leopold Senghor. The Islamic sage tradition (the "mullah") is perpetuated among the marabouts and maallems of Africa. The monarchical tendency in Africa made the former president of the Ivory Coast, Felix Houphouët-Boigny, construct his own Ivorian 'Palace of Versailles' in his hometown, Yamoussoukro.

New political developments in the twenty-first century will introduce new criteria of qualifications. A former journalist (Benjamin Mkapa) is president in Tanzania, and Sierra Leone elected a former international civil servant (Alhaji Tijan Kabba). Nigeria and Ghana elected former military rulers. Liberia has elected Ellen Johnson-Sirleaf, a former economist, as Africa's first elected female head of state.[28] It is too early to discern a continental pattern, though it is tempting to expect more professionals to aspire to political leadership, as western education spreads more widely, and ordinary people get disenchanted with career politicians and ex-dictators.

All over Africa the political arena shows many gaps in the representation of various groups. African politics is still largely male-dominated. The question has arisen whether androgynisation of politics would help to moderate the scale of violence which has characterized the contradictory tendencies of anarchy and tyranny.[29] Other political gaps which Africa has to narrow are the gaps between soldiers and politicians, between ethnicity and nationhood, between rich and poor, between the indigenous and the foreign elements of political culture, and between the religious and the secular.

The search for solutions has included the experimental one-party state, the search for new ideologies, the use of a national language for national integration, the search for better leadership, and the use of external troops for internal stability (like the use of Cuban troops in Angola and Ethiopia and the French troops in her former territories in Ivory Coast). As they say, the struggle continues—and uneasy still lies the head that wears an African crown. African political development must find ways to accord greater significance to indigenous African values of justice, fairness, equity, rewards, and punishment, without which the endemic conflicts of our triple heritage will continue to undermine our development efforts.

Culture: The Restless Soul

Another element of the triple heritage is seen from the perspective of searching for a cultural synthesis. Africa's values are in conflict. The struggle continues for a new morality. For instance, maybe Africa should not be trying to resolve the conflict between the ethic of monogamy and the ethic of polygamy. It should recognize both monogamy and polygamy— provided all parties confirm their consent under oath. Perhaps polyandry should also be admissible— provided all parties consent under oath. Perhaps issues like tribal nepotism and corruption are more serious morally than the numbers of wives or husbands that a single citizen may have. Africa is already debating issues like integrated legal codes, indigenised ideologies, the role of art in religion, and other dimensions of cultural synthesis.

Global Africa: The Battle of Ideas

The West intended Africa to be a passive factor on the world scene- more acted upon than acting. Africa has frustrated that goal by the grand transformation of a people from objects in the designs of others into an active force in global history. Africans as a people are scattered around the world. One out of every five people of African ancestry lives outside the parent continent. Africa is a net exporter of high-level human resources.[30]

According to the December 2002 US Census report of the 400,000 African immigrant workers aged 16 and older in the United States, 36.5 percent are in managerial and professional specialities. For native-born Americans, the equivalent figure is 30.9 percent. Whereas Nigerian universities and the civil service are overburdened by the poor quality of resources, about six out of every ten Nigerians aged 18 and older in the US has one or more university degrees. It is estimated that there may be as many as 250,000 Nigerians in the US, and that about half the members of major Nigeria associations in the US have master's and/or doctorate degrees.[31]

A recent report from the US Census report, among African immigrants who were 25 years or older, nearly half (49.3 percent) had at least a bachelor's degree. The comparative rate for Asian immigrants of the same age was 44.9 percent. For native-born Americans, the rate was 25.6 percent. The US Census results show clearly that "immigrant Africans to the United States have become more recently the best-educated category of all residents of the country, immigrant or native born."[32] A combination of push-pull factors are throwing an increasing number of Africans into voluntary exile in western countries and international organisations, as a new form of human dispersal.

The Jews called their dispersal around the world "the Diaspora." Africa has two Diasporas—that created by the slave trade (especially blacks in the Americas) and that created by the disruptions of colonialism (including Africans in Europe). The Diaspora of slavery in America attempted to dis-Africanise the imported sons and daughters of the "black" continent.[33] American history addressed the following commands to the African-American:

Forget your ancestry, remember what you look like,
Forget who you are, remember your skin colour,
Forget you are African, remember you are Black.

In the second half of the twentieth century, African-Americans have been faced by three theoretical options:

- being partially re-Africanised in culture and allegiance.

- being more fully Americanised and integrated into mainstream USA.

- going separate as "blacks," distinct from both Africa and white America.

From Africa's point of view the best solution would be if African-Americans were re-Africanised enough to care about what happens to Africa and Americanised enough to influence U.S. policy towards Africa. Renewed interest in their ancestry—travel to Africa and contact with Africans—is the beginning of re-Africanisation. As long as African-Americans are disproportionately in America's inner cities and ghettos, their domestic influence on U.S. policy will be thin. But if the temple of privilege is pulled down, work could start on the shrine of equality. The civil rights movement initiated the process. But by definition that was a struggle for rights. The second phase is a struggle for power. At the moment it is taking the form of running for elections and trying to penetrate the citadels of authority. One American city after another has elected a black mayor. And when Jesse Jackson in the

1980s made a bid for the presidential nomination of the Democratic party, the unthinkable at last became mentionable: a black effort to reach the very pinnacle of American power.[34]

The Black Power movement of the 1960s was characterized by marches; its equivalent today is strategic migration of African Americans into high political office and the top levels of corporate life. General Colin Powell as Secretary of State, and Condoleeza Rice as National Security Adviser—subsequently Secretary of State-- to President George W. Bush are providing visible role models for a new generation of African Americans, less accustomed to open/blatant racism.

But while the Diaspora of slavery in America is experiencing less and less racism, the Diaspora of colonialism in Europe is confronting more and more discrimination. North Africans in France are vulnerable, as are large numbers of African and Caribbean asylum seekers in Germany, Britain, and other European cities. There are different variations of Euro-racism, depending on the peculiar circumstances of the European countries' experience with coloured people. French racism is partly cultural rather than based on colour. There seems to be less hostility to black Africans in France than to lighter skinned North Africans. The fact that Arabs are perceived more clearly as "Muslims" than are Senegalese may be part of the explanation. The French are more culturally prejudiced than the British, but have less colour prejudice than either the British or the white Americans.[35]

To some extent a culture war is taking place in France between French civilisation and Islam. The conflict includes moral tensions—Islamic prudishness versus French sexual libertarianism. Will France become more prudish as Muslims become more influential in French society? Or will Islam in France succumb to the temptations of French indulgence? For better or worse, the latter is more likely than the former.[36] Islam is less likely to change French culture than Africa changed French politics.

By fighting for their independence, Algerians changed the course of European history as a whole. The stresses of the Algerian war tore down the French Fourth Republic, brought Charles de Gaulle back to power, resulted in a more stable constitution in France (the Fifth Republic) and helped to transform both the North Atlantic Treaty Organization (NATO) and the European Economic Community (EEC) under the influence of Gaullist designs. The success stories of NATO and the European Union have not provided learning lessons for African countries, which still lack a regional military force and a viable supra-regional integration agency. The African Union, which is a replacement for the Organization of African Union, has the promise of promoting closer integration if it can overcome structural handicaps.[37] It also needs a visionary – a role which Libyan leader Muammar Qaddafi has been working on for decades. Qaddafi is prepared to use his country's wealth to promote Arab, African, and Muslim solidarity, giving a new twist to triple heritage.

Qaddafi regards oil as a historic opportunity for present day Muslims to ensure an influential role for Islam in world affairs. But over the years Qaddafi's nationalism has become partially secular. He does share the late President Nasser's ambition of leading the three worlds of Islam, the Arabs, and the Africans. But at his most ambitious Qaddafi adds a fourth and more comprehensive constituency: the tricontinental world of Africa, Asia, and Latin America.[38] The universe of exploited societies is to be represented by Libya in North-South confrontations, in Qaddafi's view.

The West has often supported or subsidized dissident movements within the Third World—like Reagan's support for UNITA in Angola and the contras in Nicaragua. Qaddafi has argued that if it is all right for the West to destabilize the Third World, it must be all right for the Third World to destabilize the West. Why are US dollars for Nicaraguan and Angolan rebels morally different from Qaddafi's dollars for anti-West dissidents? The double standards are glaring. Since September 11, 2001, the US Government has been working tirelessly at building global coalitions in its war with terrorisms. The groundswell of global public opinion has been managed to make it hard not to support the current war on terrorism – as defined by the US administration. And yet is America now emerging as a new kind of Empire, the hegemon of the twenty-first century?[39]

Though Qaddafi is not the most popular African leader, his use of economic resources for global political purposes may be a lesson addressed to fellow Africans and other Third World societies. While Western investors "make a killing" in stock exchanges, African producers are often too passive. Many international development arrangements are made to be favourable to only Western countries, to the detriment of African countries. African media have been too willing to present international news in typical Western perspectives, and have not provided enough Africa-oriented interpretations to enlighten African publics. [40] African governments are only just beginning to challenge the passive role that Western capitalism had intended for them.

Many individual African countries or regional blocs of countries can hold some Western mineral stock exchanges at ransom by the sheer size of their mineral resources. But because they hardly flex their mineral muscles, and are ever so willing to go along with Western guidelines, their collective wealth promotes the development of other countries abroad, and leaves their own economies pitifully stagnant. It is time for African countries to be real and influential actors in global economic affairs.

Afro Power

There are two additional forms of power that Africa has dreamed about as instruments of global participation-the power of traditional sorcery and the power of modern science. What relevance has "voodoo" for international affairs? The answer lies in the story of the city of Berlin: as a symbol of the partition of Africa in the nineteenth century and a symbol of the division of Europe in the twentieth. From this city European statesmen worked the rules of the scramble and eventual fragmentation of Africa. Did Africa's ancestors proclaim a curse upon Europe?

The curse of Africa's ancestors may have befallen Europe's descendants. And the wall of Berlin did bear tragic testimony to the role of nemesis in modern history, the possible relevance of "voodoo" in global statecraft. Though the Berlin wall came crashing following the end of communism, the wounds it inflicted have not yet healed, and the differences in the economic fortunes of the two sides may take a long time to nullify. So there may still be something to be said about Afro power in this respect.

But sorcery need not be an alternative to science. It can be its reinforcement. And the most secret of all sciences by Western rules is nuclear technology. Should Africa break the conspiracy of nuclear silence and acquire nuclear know-how itself? The West is saying, "Nuclear weapons are not suitable for Africans and children under sixteen." Can Africa afford to be so marginalised? Though the United States is vehemently opposed to the development of nuclear capabilities by Iraq, Iran, and North Korea, there is no consensus on what qualifies a country to be a nuclear power. There is room for a new kind of black power in the millennium. The present nuclear club is too exclusive to be sustainable for long.

In fact, two sets of blacks will be the vanguard of the black world in the twenty-first century—black Americans, by the power of sheer numbers which qualify them as a vital voting bloc in the United States, and Black South Africans, heirs to both mineral wealth and industrial pre-eminence in Africa. The shift from Afro passivity to activism is climbing to a new plateau of leverage and influence. But in the final analysis the battle of ideas must continue—Africa not just a learner, but also a teacher; not just an imitator of others but a model in her own right. The most important of all lessons, when all is said and done, is a transition from a traditional belief that "my tribe is the world" to a new globalist vision: "the world is my tribe; the human race my family."

Conclusion

In the interaction between Africa and the twin forces of Islam and Western civilisation, African culture has fluctuated in impact. Indigenous African institutions have suffered more than African culture in this unequal exchange of influence. The colonialists tried to supplant indigenous African institutions with bogus European imports which have not fitted well with aspects of African culture. The resulting tension between new imported structures and old resilient indigenous culture is part of the post-colonial war which has been waging incessantly in Africa.

African schools have adopted foreign curricula, which are delivered in the languages of the colonial powers. Different countries have adopted foreign political systems of elections, campaigns, and political patronage, much of which has no semblance to indigenous African politics. Some of the results have been rampant corruption, pervasive underdevelopment, and disconnection with the African soul. Genuine development has eluded many African countries because of the mismanagement of the interrelationship among the elements of the triple heritage. Two strands of solutions are appropriate in addressing the development problems of the continent.

The first strand is the imperative of looking inwards towards our ancestry, laying due emphasis on our native intelligence, collective wisdom, and the true essence of Africanity. This requires recognition of the value of our innate and traditional resources, which made our ancestors survive waves of onslaughts from foreign enemies and natural hazards. Although our languages have been greatly enriched by the Triple Heritage, our communicators have not lived up to our expectations in the area of popularising indigenous African values and resources, which are often positioned as inferior to foreign ideas. Our rich tradition of performing arts, pedagogical apparatus, and socialization tools should be marshalled to facilitate the purposive development of the totality of the African environment. In spite of the prevalence of modern communication technology in Africa, much weight needs to be given to indigenous communication, especially the power of the oral tradition. This inward imperative "requires a more systematic investigation into the cultural preconditions of the success of each project, of each piece of legislation, of each system of government." [41]

Africa is not an isolated island, and must exercise its rightful roles in an increasingly global world community. The second strand is an imperative of looking outwards to the wider world, which is the origin of the two foreign elements of the triple heritage. As Africa matures in its relationship with other world regions, it must stand ready to selectively borrow, adapt, and creatively formulate its strategies for planned development. Africa's contribution to the pool of immigrant human capital in the United States and Brazil is higher than that from other world regions. This should not be a one-way exchange, and so African countries ought to devise strategies to tap into the global pool of human capital for development. In the final analysis, genuine development of the continent is possible and sustainable only when we can reconcile with our ancestors and also forge new relationships with the wider world, with mutual respect and full dignity. Our triple heritage of indigenous, Islamic and Western forces can serve as catalysts for growth and development, if we find the right communicative environment. Africa is the most resilient of all the continents. After all, the Africans are a people of the day before yesterday and a people of the day after tomorrow. Destiny has spread Africans so widely that the sun never sets on the descendants of Africa. If the world is a village today, it began as an African village in the mists of antiquity.

NOTES

[1] The objections resulted in a move from Nigeria to London. For one report, see "Miss Turkey wins Miss World," BBC News (December 7, 2002), <http://news.bbc.co.uk/2/hi/uk_news/england/2552593.stm> December 7, 2005.

[2] For an example of Islamic influence – and subsequent secularization -- see Ali A. Mazrui and Pio Zirimu, "The Secularization of An Afro-Islamic Language," *Journal of Islamic Studies* 1, 1 (1990), pp. 23-35.

[3] Ali A. Mazrui, *The Africans: A Triple Heritage* (London: BBC Publications, 1986), p. 201.

[4] Ibid.

[5] On the history of Ethiopia, consult, for instance, Richard Pankhurst, *The Ethiopians : A History* (Oxford, UK and Malden, MA: Blackwell Publishers, 2001).

[6] A guide to these ancient civilisations may be found in Vivian V. Gordon, comp. *Kemet and Other African Civilisations: Selected References* (Chicago, IL: Third World Press, 1991).

[7] These lines are from his poem, "Journal of a Homecoming," (Cahier d'un retour au pays Natal); for commentary, see Gregson Davis, *Aimé Cesaire* (Cambridge, New York and Melbourne: Cambridge University Press, 1997), pp. 20-61.

[8] See J. P. Sartre, "Black Orpheus," in Robert Bernasconi, Ed., *Race* (Malden, MA: Blackwell Publishers, 2001), p. 130.

[9] Indeed, according to one scholar, "Especially in its Western form, Christianity is the most anthropocentric religion in the world." See Lynn White, Jr., "The Historical Roots of Our Ecologic Crisis," in Francis A. Schaeffer, Ed., *Pollution and the Death of Man: The Christian View of Ecology* (Wheaton, IL: Tyndale Publishing House, 1970), p. 107.

[10] Consult Bertus Haverkort, Katrien van t Hooft and Wim Hiemstra, Eds., *Ancient Roots, New Shoots : Endogenous Development in Practice* (Leusden, The Netherlands; London ; New York : : ETC/Compass in association with Zed Books and Palgrave, 2003), pp. 141-142.

[11] See Paul Waldau, *The Specter of Speciesism: Buddhist and Christian Views of Animals* (Oxford and New York: Oxford University Press, 2002), p. 202.

[12] Of course, there is a problem between what is theoretically available to Muslim women, and the actual application of appropriate rights in Muslim societies. For a guide to this state of affairs, see Shaheen Sardar Ali, *Gender and Human Rights in Islam and International Law: Equal Before Allah, Unequal Before Man?* (The Hague and Boston: Kluwer Law International, 2000); and for a case study, Annelies Moors, *Women, Property, and Islam: Palestinian Experience, 1920-1990* (New York: Cambridge University Press, 1995).

[13] For some general overviews of the changing roles and status of women in Africa, consult Peter N. Stearns, *Gender in World History* (London and New York: Routledge, 2000), pp. 93-96; Catherine Coquery-Vidrovitch, *African Women: A Modern History*, trans. Beth Gillian (Boulder, CO: Westview Press, 1997); and for specific case studies, consult Wolfgang Benedek, Esther M. Kisaakye and Gerd Oberleitner, Eds., *The Human Rights of Women: International Instruments and African Experiences* (London ; New York : Zed Books in association with World University Service and Palgrave, 2002), pp. 229-316.

[14] For one analysis - although somewhat dated, -- see Patrick Chabal, "The African Crisis: Context and Interpretation," in Richard Werbner and Terence Ranger, Eds., *Postcolonial Identities in Africa* (London and Atlantic Highlands, NJ: Zed Books, 1996), pp. 29-54.

[15] A number of fascinating but depressing comparisons between Ghanian and South Korean progress are made by Herbert H. Werlin in his "Ghana and South Korea: Explaining Development Disparities," *Journal of African and Asian Studies* Volume 29, Numbers 3-4 (July/October 1994), pp. 205-225.

[16] See Norimitsu Onishi, "Dictator Gone: Ivory Coast Splits into Ethnic and Political Violence," *The New York Times* (Oct 27, 2000).

[17] The take-off theory is most famously associated with W. W. Rostow, *The Economics of Take-Off Into Sustained Growth* (New York: St. Martin's Press, 1963, 1964).

[18] For examples and discussions, see Michael Darkoh and Apollo Rwomire, Eds., *Human Impact on Environment and Sustainable Development in Africa* (Aldershot, Hampshire, England and Burlington, VT: Ashgate, 2003) and Raymond Bonner, *At the Hand of Man: Peril and Hope for Africa's Wildlife* (New York: Knopf, 1993).

[19] For descriptions of this evangelization efforts and impact, consult Steve Brouwer, Paul Gifford, Susan D. Rose, *Exporting the American Gospel: Global Christian Fundamentalism* (New York: Routledge, 1996), pp. 151-178.

[20] After all, one of the early humans orginating in Africa was termed "Homo Habilis" or "Handy Man" for the tools used by them; see Graham Connah, *Forgotten Africa: An Introduction to its Archaeology* (London and New York: Routledge, 2004), pp. 7-12.

[21] See Paul Lovejoy, *Transformations in Slavery: A History of Slavery in Africa* (Cambridge and New York: Cambridge University Press, 2000), p. 13.

[22] Lovejoy, Transformations in Slavery, pp. 17-18.

[23] A comprehensive analysis of the slave trade may be found in Joseph E. Inikori and Stanley L. Engerman, Eds., *The Atlantic Slave Trade: Effects on Economies and Peoples in Africa, the Americas, and Europe* (Durham, NC: Duke University Press, 1992).

[24] See Judith Jennings, *The Business of Abolishing the British Slave Trade, 1783-1807* (London and Portland, OR: Frank Cass, 1997) and Dale H. Porter, *The Abolition of the Slave Trade in England, 1784-1807* (Hamden, CT: Archon Books, 1970).

[25] For a report lamenting the end of the African "safe haven," see *New African*, 367 (October 1998), pp. 16-17.

[26] Coups and military takeovers were rampant in the first few decades after independence in many African countries. For descriptions and analyses, see George Klay Kieh, Jr., and Pita Ogaba Agbese, Eds., *The Military and Politics in Africa: From Intervention to Democratic and Constitutional Control* (Aldershot, Hants, England ; Burlington, VT : Ashgate, 2004).

[27] For an assessment of freedom in African countries, see Adrian Karatnycky, "Freedom in the World 2005: Civic Power and Electoral Politics," <http://www.freedomhouse.org/research/freeworld/2005/essay2005.pdf>, December 4, 2005.

[28] See Lane Hartill, "President in Waiting Stays Cool in Liberia: Johnson-Sirleaf Unruffled by Fraud Claims," *The Washington Post* (November 14, 2005).

[29] Reports and analyses of women and politics in Africa with particular attention to Liberial may be found in Hartill, "President in Waiting Stays Cool in Liberia," *The Washington Post* (November 14, 2005); Hartill, "Liberia's 'Iron Lady' Goes for Gold: Election Would Mark a First for Africa, "*The Washington Post* (October 5, 2005); and Lydia Polgreen, "Many Liberian Women See the Ballot Box as a Step Up," *The New York Times* (October 19, 2005).

[30] A 2005 World Bank study pointed out that a quarter to almost half of the college educated citizens of African countries like Ghana, Mozambique, Kenya, Uganda lived abroad in an O.E.C.D. country; for a report, see Celia W. Dugger, "Developing Lands Hit Hardest by 'Brain Drain'," *The New York Times* (October 25, 2005).

[31] Consult Ali A. Mazrui, "Brain Drain between Counter-terrorism and Globalisation" *African Issues* (2002), Vol. 30, No. 1.

[32] Mazrui, "Brain Drain between Counter-terrorism and Globalisation" *African Issues* (2002), Vol. 30, No. 1., p. 89.

[33] Descriptions and analyses of the various African Diasporas may be found, for example, in the following: Joseph E. Harris, Ed. *Global Dimensions of the African Diaspora* (Washington, DC: Howard University Press, 2003), 2nd ed.; Shihan de Silva Jayasuriya and Richard Pankhurst, Eds., *The African Diaspora in the Indian Ocean* (Trenton, NJ: Africa World Press, 2003); Erna Brodber, *The Continent of Black Consciousness: On the History of the African Diaspora From Slavery to the Present Day* (London: New Beacon Books, 2003); John Hunwick and Eve T. Powell, *The African Diaspora in the Mediterranean Lands of Islam* (Princeton, NJ : Markus Wiener Publishers, 2002); Darlene Clark Hine and Jacqueline McLeod., Eds., *Crossing Boundaries: Comparative History of Black People in Diaspora* (Bloomington, IN: Indiana University Press, 1999); E.L. Bute, *The Black Handbook: The People, History and Politics of Africa and the African Diaspora* (London and Washington: Cassell, 1997); Alusine Jalloh and Stephen E. Maizlish, Eds., *The African Diaspora* (College Station, TX: Texas A&M University Press, 1996); Michael L. Coniff, *Africans in the Americas: A History of the Black Diaspora* (New York: St. Martin's Press, 1994); and Edward Scobie, *Global African Presence*, (Brooklyn, NY: A & B Books, 1994).

[34] For accounts of Jackson's bid for the Presidency in 1988, see, for instance, Elizabeth O. Colton, *The Jackson Phenomenon : The Man, The Power, The Message* (New York: Doubleday, 1989) and Penn Kimball, *Keep Hope Alive! : Super Tuesday and Jesse Jackson's 1988 Campaign for the Presidency* (Washington, DC and Lanham, MD: Joint Center for Political and Economic Studies Press and National Book Network, 1992).

[35] Residual racism and suspicion between racial minorities led to large-scale riots in many African cities; for some reports and analyses from an American perspective, see Molly Moore, "France Beefs Up Response to Riots: Plan Includes Curfews, More Police Officers, *"The Washington Post* (November 8, 2005) and Keith Richburg, "The Other France, Separate and Unhappy," *The Washington Post* (November 13, 2005) and for some French perspectives, see

op-eds by Oliver Roy, "Get French or Die Trying," *The New York Times* (November 9, 2005); Antoine Audouard, "The Revolt of Ennui," *The New York Times* (November 9, 2005)

[36] In some cases, French government and society may force changes on Muslims in France, as illustrated by the head-scarves ban. See Keith Richburg, "French President Urges Ban On Head Scarves in Schools: Chirac Confronts Spread of Islam," *The Washington Post* (December 18, 2003).

[37] Some of the legal and political issues in the creation of the African Union are explored in Thomas K. Tieku, "Explaining The Clash And Accomodation Of Interests Of Major Actors In The Creation Of The African Union," *African Affairs* (Apr2004), Vol. 103, Issue 411, pp. 249-267, and Corinne A. A. Packer and Donald Rukare, "The New African Union And Its Constitutive Act," *American Journal of International Law*," (April 2002), Vol. 96, Issue 2, pp. 365-379.

[38] On Libya's outreach to Africa, see René Lemarchand, ed., *The Green and the Black: Qadhafi's Policies in Africa* (Bloomington, IN: Indiana University Press, 1988). This orientation of Qaddafi has been a few years in the making; see, for example, "Qaddafi Turns to Africa," *The Economist* (April 24, 1999), p. 43 and "Qaddafi, Ruler of Africa?" *The Economist* (September 16, 2000), p. 53.

[39] Americans are not always willing to admit that the United States is an imperial power; consult Dimitri K. Simes, "America's Imperial Dilemma," *Foreign Affairs* (November-December 2003), Vol. 82, No. 6, p. 93. For some negative consequences of the US as an imperial power, see, for instance, Chalmers Johnson, *Blowback: The Costs and Consequences of American Empire* (New York: Henry Holt, 2001, 1st Owl Books ed.) and Michael Parenti, *Against Empire* (San Francisco, CA: City Lights Books, 1995).

[40] Al-Jazeera, for instance, has begun to challenge the Western perspective and near-monopoly in reporting on Middle East issues. Consult Hugh Miles, *Al-Jazeera: The Inside Story of the Arab News Channel that is Challenging the West* (New York: Grove Press, 2005 and Mohammed el-Nawawy and Adel Iskandar, *Al-Jazeera : How The Free Arab News Network Scooped The World and Changed the Middle East* (Cambridge, MA : Westview Press, 2002)

[41] Mazrui, *The Africans: A Triple Heritage*, p. 21.

CHAPTER 6

THE EROSION OF THE STATE AND THE DECLINE OF RACE

T wo great streams of global change that are reaching a new turning point in our own day are, firstly, the rise and decline of the *state*; and secondly the rise and decline of *race* as a basis of human relations. From Africa's point of view, the foundations of the colonial state can be traced back to the Berlin Conference which was convened by Otto von Bismarck in 1884-5 and helped to set the stage for the partition of Africa. The recent erosion of the state in Africa has ranged from its total collapse in countries like Somalia and Rwanda to the forces of political decentralization like those in KwaZulu, Ethiopia and Southern Sudan.

In the painful erosion of the state in Africa, the United Nations and its agencies are increasingly involved either as peacemakers, peacekeepers or as caregivers for refugees. Elsewhere in the world the credibility of the United Nations is severely in question, but in Africa the United Nations is helping to deal with some of the most severe consequences of Otto von Bismarck. Meanwhile, Africans themselves are seeking to be more effective as continental actors in tandem with efforts of the world body.

We have named this first transition of the rise and decline of the state in Africa 'From Bismarck to Boutros,' culminating with Boutros Boutros-Ghali, the sixth Secretary-General of the world body and the first African to hold this position.

The second grand theme is the rise and decline of *race* as a mover of history. Here too we could have chosen a period of about a century, and discussed race from the beginning of social Darwinism to the ideology of apartheid. But Western racism affected Africa much earlier than did Western colonialism. We have thus chosen to address the issue of race partly from a cultural perspective, from Shakespeare's *Othello* to the predicament of O. J. Simpson.

From Bismarck to Boutros

One of the great paradoxes about Otto von Bismarck was that he united the Germans and helped to divide Africa. He helped to unite the Germans both by territorial unification and through social welfare policies which pacified large sections of the population at a period of social unrest. He united the Germans partly through war, and partly through welfare.

There was a duality in Bismarck's role in Africa. He divided Africa partly because of his role as the convener of the 1884-5 Berlin Conference which worked out the ground rules for the Europeans in their scramble for Africa. Bismarck also helped to divide Africa by being among those scrambling colonialists grabbing for territory.

During his incumbency, Otto von Bismarck was perhaps the most influential statesman of the Western world. Boutros Boutros-Ghali was arguably one of the most influential statesmen of the world during his tenure as the Secretary-General of the United Nations a century later. The Black world as a whole was profoundly affected in the great transition from the age of Bismarck to the era of Boutros-Ghali. Let us juxtapose these two leaders more closely.

Since this chapter is partly about the rise and decline of the state, it is worth remembering that Bismarck re-invented the state in Europe. He was a pioneer of the welfare state and one of the architects of the socially engaged system of governance.

Prince Otto von Bismarck lived from 1815 to 1898. To his 'credit' were three European wars which helped to foster German unification. The wars were with Denmark (1864), Austria (Seven Years' war, ending in 1866), and France (1870-1). He was made Prince von Bismarck on March 21, 1871 and appointed Chancellor of the German Empire in that same year. He then proceeded to govern the German Empire from January 1871 to 1890. In the military sense, Bismarck united the Germans and helped to divide Africa.

Bismarck was also responsible for introducing state insurance in his country: for sickness in 1883, for accident in 1884, and for old age in 1889. He united Germans through social healing in this manner. He was an innovator in the history of the Welfare state. It is in this sense that Bismarck re-invented the European state. It has been suggested that, "These measures of state socialism appear now as precursors of the modern welfare state... Despite this policy, Bismarck was opposed to any regulation of working hours or working conditions."[1]

It has also been argued:

The tragedy of Bismarck's career was that he himself created in united Germany the monarchical-military power which first overthrew him and then in the fateful years of 1914-1918 destroyed his empire.[2]

But before that Bismarck had carved out his place in African history. In 1884, he quarrelled with Britain and within the course of a single year obtained the Cameroons, South-West Africa (now Namibia), East Africa (Tanganyika, Rwanda and Burundi) and part of New Guinea. In 1889, Bismarck declared, 'I am not a colonial man.' Yet, he brought Germany closer to a colonial role than any other modern figure, with the exception of Adolf Hitler. A.J.P. Taylor cites the gem regarding Bismarck: [British statesman] Gladstone said of Bismarck. "He made Germany great and Germans small."[3]

But why would one choose the period from Bismarck to Boutros? Let us look at the case of juxtaposition. To some degree, the link gives us a century of relations between the West and the African world. Prince Otto von Bismarck was in power in Germany in the 1880s, busy re-inventing the state. By the 1990s Africa had experienced a century of Western colonisation, emerged from old style colonial state, and had produced the first African Secretary-General of the United Nations.

It was Bismarck who convened the Conference of Berlin, a meeting of Western powers designed to set down the rules of the game in Europe's scramble for Africa. The conference closed in 1885. In 1945 the United Nations was born. In 1960 more than 15 newly independent African states became members of it. By 1995 the United Nations was knee-deep in some of the problems of those states, including salvage operations for collapsed states.

Some regard Cambodia as a United Nations' triumph in peace-making; many regard Somalia as a failure of both the United Nations and the United States. Bosnia is a sore in the body politic of the world community, for in Bosnia the United Nations was semi-impotent. Bosnia was a mockery of issues of statehood and sovereignty.

Many would accuse the United Nations of criminal negligence over Rwanda in 1994. More could have been done to reduce, if not avert, the catastrophe.[4] Yet, the collapse was part of the wider decline of the state in Africa

Is the UN under-utilizing *preventive diplomacy* in pursuit of peace? Is the UN too cautious in pursuing *peace enforcement*? Will it be forced to engage in Nigeria in the days ahead? Did the UN do enough to avert catastrophe in Burundi? All these are difficult questions. They merely illustrate that, while we have indeed averted a world war in the second half of the 20th century, we have multiplied regional, local and ethnic conflicts and escalated their human cost.[5]

Should regions like Africa look for alternative peacekeeping arrangements? The UN wants to keep the peace once somebody else has made it. Who is to make peace in Africa? Who is to enforce it? If the state is in decline, where are the transitional arrangements for *Pax Africana?*

Some African countries may simply need to be temporarily controlled by other African countries. Inevitably, some dysfunctional countries may need to submit to trusteeship and even tutelage for a while, as Zanzibar did when it was annexed by Tanganyika in 1964 to form Tanzania.

Although the world body bears the name "the United Nations", some of its members are among the most fragmented states in human history.[6] In Africa, the UN is a peacekeeper but not often a peacemaker and certainly not a peace-enforcer. Africa needs alternative solutions.

Regional integration is one solution in some cases. Should Tanzania, Burundi and Rwanda be persuaded to form one federation? Certainly if Burundi and Rwanda had been united into a large state, where the balance between Tutsi and Hutu would have been part of a more diverse population, the savagery of 1994 could have been averted.[7] If Hutu and Tutsi became part of the United Republic of Tanzania, they might well discover what they have in common and unite politically against other Tanzanians.

This is a safer solution than uniting Rwanda and Burundi with Uganda. The latter would simply destabilize Uganda by seriously altering the ethnic balance between the Baganda and the ethnic compatriots of Ankole, and any residual balance between North and the South in Uganda. But even a federation of Rwanda, Burundi and Tanzania would need to be financed by the international community. Incentives would be needed, especially to persuade Tanzania.

If *recolonisation* or *self-colonisation* is the path that lies ahead for Africa, there must be a continental authority to ensure that such an order does not merely mask base aims of exploitation. Collective responsibility should be morally restrained.[8] If the UN does not want to enforce peace, can Africa create a machinery for *Pax Africana?*

The state in Africa may be in decline and in crisis but the wider international system is still state-based. One longer term solution to problems exposed by today's crises is the establishment of an African Security Council composed of five pivotal regional states, or potential pivotal regional states, which would oversee the continent. This council would have a Pan African Emergency Force, an army for intervention and peacekeeping, at its disposal. And there would also be an African High Commissioner for Refugees linked to the UN's High Commission.

While Africa accounts for one-tenth of the world's population, it sometimes accounts for nearly one half of the world's refugees and displaced persons. It is time Africa took a leading role in organizing the relief of its own refugees.

Temporarily, should Pan-Africanism mould itself in the image of the UN? The African Security Council that should be formed over the coming decades would be anchored in the North by *Egypt* and in the South by South Africa. Although Nigeria has experienced troubling times in recent years, it would be the pivotal state in West Africa. Its size and resources could give it the equivalent weight of India in South Asia, if it can find political stability.

In East Africa, the pivotal country is still in doubt. *Ethiopia*, among the fragile of the largest African states today, is the most likely anchor because of its size. Although Kenya is more stable, it is far smaller. In Central Africa, the presumed regional power of the future, *Zaire*, is currently itself in need of trusteeship. If Zaire can avoid collapse into chaos in the near future, it will be one of the major actors in Africa in the 21st Century. Zaire has the population and resources to play a major role. In the twenty-first century it will even surpass France as the largest French-speaking nation in the world.

As permanent members of an African Security Council, these five states would co-ordinate among each other and with the UN. Regional integration is the order of the day in Europe, North America, East Asia and even, tentatively, of course, in the Middle East. If Africa, too, does not follow this path, lack of stability and economic growth will push the entire continent further into the desperate margins of the global society.

In tandem with the efforts of UN to establish a peaceful world order, Africans need an African peace enforced by Africans, from

Angola to Algeria. Africans need to be collectively responsible for the fate of Africa in the post-colonial age.

These are no doubt frightening ideas for proud peoples who spilled so much blood and spent so much political will freeing themselves from the onslaught of European powers which was unleashed by Otto von Bismarck. To be sure, self-colonisation, if we can manage it, is better than resurrecting Bismarck and re-establishing colonisation by outsiders. Better still would be self-conquest. But that implies an African capacity for self-control and self-discipline rarely seen since before the curse of Otto von Bismarck, colonialism.

Such discipline will have to be found in the 21st century if Africa is to undertake successful social engineering and build resilient and solid foundations for the post-state age of the future.

The African Condition and the State of the World

The end of the Cold War has diminished Africa's influence in the United Nations.[9] But the same post-Cold War era has contributed to the expansion of the United Nations' role in Africa. The African leverage on the UN has declined; the UN's leverage upon Africa has expanded.[10] Let us take each of these propositions in turn.

With the end of the Cold War Africa has lost a major constituency for Third World causes in the United Nations, the old Socialist bloc. On most issues of African concern the members of the old Warsaw Pact could be relied upon to vote with those forces in Africa which were eager for change. East European socialists were often allies of Africa in world affairs.[11]

The collapse of official communism in Eastern Europe, and the disintegration of the USSR and the dismantling of the Warsaw Pact have produced an Eastern Europe far more likely to listen to the wishes of Washington, DC, than to the yearnings of the Third World.[12] Africa's voting base in the United Nations has shrunk dramatically. The state has declined in power in the former Warsaw Pact also, and Africa is among the losers.

The disintegration of the USSR and Yugoslavia, and the split of Czechoslovakia into two separate countries, has also been part of the decline of the state. The result is more than 15 additional non-African members to the total membership of the United Nations. Thus Africa has lost not only its Socialist allies but also its status as one third of the total membership of the United Nations. Its percentage in the voting statistics of the world body has shrunk further, with additional damage to its self-confidence. After all, Africa's main strength had been in number of votes.

The end of the Cold War has also weakened Africa in the United Nations by undermining the old checks-and-balances of the former two superpowers. Small countries are no longer in the envious position of playing off one imperial power against another. Competitive imperialism is better than monopolistic imperialism precisely because big power rivalry of the kind characterized by the Cold War was sometimes to the advantage of weak regions like Africa.[13]

The end of the Cold War has also shaken the self-confidence of those African countries and leaders that once thought that there were alternatives to capitalism in the quest for development. All of a sudden many of these leaders and countries see themselves as being so vulnerable to Western economic power that they have given up trying to have an independent foreign policy. Even former radical leaders in countries like Tanzania, Ghana, Zimbabwe and the African Nation Congress of South Africa have permitted themselves to mellow and acquiesce in the face of Western triumphalism after the Cold War. Old African warriors of self-reliance became the new implementers of Western-sponsored policies of structural adjustment. [14] The wider economic fears of African leaders at home make them cautious collabourators at the United Nations. Africa is enfeebled by the consequences of the end of the Cold War. As the state declines worldwide, Africa is marginalised further.

And yet, just when Africa is losing influence in the United Nations, the world body is increasing its influence in Africa. One reason is the political collapse of a number of African states, especially Somalia, Rwanda and Liberia, in order of degree of United Nations' involvement.

A related factor is the aftermath of the messy withdrawal of Portugal from her African colonies, leaving behind a civil war in Angola and conceding independence without preceding multi-party elections in Mozambique. The mess cost hundreds of thousands of lives in the following twenty years. The United Nations inherited part of the mess. Fortunately, the UN has made real progress towards a solution in Mozambique and even in Angola, though the latter is more modest.

A third factor behind increasing UN involvement in Africa is that the world body has had its first and second African Secretary-Generals, Boutros Boutros-Ghali and Kofi Annan. At first sight one would have thought that Boutros-Ghali's role would have been to reduce the enfeeblement of Africa in the United Nations. To some extent it did strengthen Africa. But Boutros-Ghali also viewed Africa as being in special need of United Nations' intervention. His own convictions on this matter were one of the factors behind the nature of the United Nations' intervention in Somalia while it lasted.[15]

Even with the best intentions in the world, Boutros Boutros-Ghali felt that it was more important that the United Nations exercised more power in Africa than that Africa exercised more influence in the United Nations. Quite understandably, the Secretary-General felt that Africa needed the United Nations' help more than the United Nations needed Africa's help. But perhaps that is where we should stop and pause.

The United Nations' role as a peacekeeping actor may stand or fall according to whether it can make a success of its African responsibilities. The problems in Africa are already horrendous and are likely to get worse. Even mere peace-keeping (as distinct from peace-enforcing) has many risks.[16] As the African state fragments, political violence is often let loose.

For the next five years the United Nations should have a moratorium on any *new* peacekeeping role outside Africa. The UN should not undertake any *new direct* peacekeeping role outside Africa. But the UN should keep the option of persuading some of its members to assume responsibilities on its behalf elsewhere. Why Africa?

First, the UN can make a much bigger difference in Africa than elsewhere. Even the so-called failed enterprise in Somalia probably saved more lives than the United Nations' so-called success story in Cambodia. Certainly the United Nations and the United States together in Somalia might have saved more lives from starvation than have UN missions in Cyprus, Lebanon, Croatia and elsewhere combined.[17] The stakes in terms of human lives in Africa can be truly high.

Second, during 1994 the Angolan civil war sometimes witnessed the destruction of at least one thousand lives a week. Helping to end such a war has a much bigger human return for UN efforts than have some of its peacekeeping efforts elsewhere.[18]

Third, peacekeeping *within* a country is almost the lowest denominator in governance. Some African countries are pretty close to the lowest denominator in governance. What the UN might be trying to do in such a country and what the country's rudimentary government might be trying to do could be pretty close. In Africa both the UN and African governments could be jointly learning the skills and ethics of governance, sometimes in unison.

Fourth, we do need to choose a criterion for limiting the UN peacekeeping operations. How about a *geographic* limitation for the next five years? A moratorium on all new peacekeeping projects *outside* Africa: There should be no such new projects before the year 2010. The UN should use Africa as its only school for learning the dynamics of ethnicity and security in world affairs for the next *five* years.

Fifth, during the five years of Afrocentric peacekeeping, the UN and the African Union should explore ways of institutionalising self-policing by African states themselves, including the creation of a Pan-African Emergency Force and an African Security Council composed of 5 pivotal states.

Sixth, the UN may also have to learn in Africa about a future world with a reduced role for the state. Some African countries are in retreat from the state - Somalia, Rwanda, Liberia, (not by design) and Ethiopia (by design). Somalia is back to a kind of a pre-state condition; Western Europe through regional integration may be moving towards a *post-state condition* long after Bismarck, but not necessarily after Boutros-Ghali. The UN may have to adjust itself to a post-state age, conceivably in the late 21st century. The UN can be educated about *pre-statehood* and *post-statehood* partly by engagement in Africa.[19]

But there has been another great stream of global change apart from the rise and decline of the state. This second momentous global stream has been the rise and decline of race as a basis of human relations and racism as a historical force. The impact of this racial force upon the fortunes of the African people is even older than the impact of the colonial state has been.

We shall approach this second great global stream from a *cultural* perspective. If the decline of the state in Africa can be captured by the title 'From Bismarck to Boutros,' the decline of race in the Black experience as a whole can be captured in the heading 'From Shakespeare's Othello to the trial of O. J. Simpson.' South Africa has been caught in the tumultuous interplay between both global streams of change.

From Shakespeare's Othello to O. J. Simpson

Othello, the Moor of Venice was written by William Shakespeare at a time when colour-based racism in Europe was in the process of being *born* for the first time. The tragedy of O.J. Simpson and Nicole Brown, on the other hand, took place at a time when *overt* colour-based racism was in decline. The two tragedies together, Othello and Desdemona and O.J. Simpson and Nicole, bracket together the golden age of overt racial prejudice in Western history.

Shakespeare's life covered the period of April 1564 to April 1616. When Shakespeare was writing, religious prejudice was still significantly stronger than colour prejudice. That is why *The Merchant of Venice* as a play is more anti-Semitic than *Othello* is anti-Black. Although Shakespeare gives him great egalitarian lines, Shylock in *The Merchant of Venice* is ultimately an unsympathetic figure, and his demands for his pound of flesh panders to some of the most persistent Western stereotypes about the so-called 'Semitic avarice' or Jewish greed.[20]

The play *Othello* includes a range of anti-Black statements, but the play is on the side of the Black Moor on that issue, and against the racists.[21] The most racist character in the play is perhaps Iago who also happens to be 'Viciousness Incarnate,' a symbol of evil in the play.

The play is about a white woman falling in love with a Black man, ready to abandon herself to him. He marries her. There are a number of references to his making love to her. All this is about a subject which was later going to be at the heart of Western racism - cross-colour sexuality. And yet Shakespeare is on the side of the lovers - Othello and Desdemona. The absolute villain in the play is the white man, Iago. European pigmentational racism was still underdeveloped in Shakespeare's day.

This period is followed by the escalation of skin-based racism. Before long this new evil of 'racism' is more firmly married to an ancient evil called 'slavery' to produce the most racist system of slavery in history, *the trans-Atlantic slave trade and slavery*. Othello's racial compatriots in Africa enter a long period of hardship and humiliation - and O.J. Simpson's ancestors are deeply affected by the traumatic disruptions of enslavement.

By the time O.J. Simpson ascends to national prominence in the America of the 20th century, a fundamental change is under way. The colour-based racism which was born when *Othello* was being staged in London, or when it was published in 1662, had first risen to dazzling heights of enslavement and colonisation, but was now allowing Black men to become millionaire sporting heroes of racially mixed games.

There was a time in recent U.S. history when a Black man sometimes risked his life by winking at a white woman. Until 1969 it was an offence in some American states for a Black man to marry a white woman, let alone to murder her.[22] But O.J. Simpson could marry Nicole Brown without violating some anti-miscegenation law since overt racism was declining.

In another sense, a more direct military analogy to Othello is Colin Powell, whose poverty-stricken parents had come from Jamaica. A Colin Powell who had helped to win wars for white-led America, and who had risen to become Chairman of the United States' Joint Chiefs of Staff and Secretary of State. If Desdemona was a senator's daughter, Colin Powell, as Othello could probably become a senator himself, or Vice President of the United States of America.[23]

In young Nicole Brown and young Desdemona there was not only the attraction of racial and class contrasts in relation to the men they fell in love with. There was also the fatal attraction of hero-worship. Othello was the great military hero of the battlefield; O.J. Simpson was the great sporting hero of the football field. And both Othello and Simpson had a physical presence that was almost larger than life.

The similarities between warfare and competitive sports has intrigued sociologists. And I myself once wrote a serious academic article on "Boxer Muhammed Ali and Soldier Idi Amin as International Political Symbols."[24] Moreover, both war and competitive sports like football and boxing have been pre-eminently masculine.

Desdemona's hero-worship lasted to the end. She fell in love with Othello when listening to his stories about heroic deeds in his life, moments of triumph. She little knew that before long Othello would be a danger to her, that he would cause her pain, and that there was no ultimate triumph for either.

On the issue of Desdemona's love through hero-worship Othello put it best:

> She loved me for the dangers I had passed,
> And I loved her that she did pity them,
> This only is the witchcraft I have used.[25]

Desdemona listened in awe to the Black man's autobiographical tales of adventure, pathos, pain and victory. She once feared his appearance. She fell in love with the Black experience personified. She fell in love with his life-story.

We shall never know how much of Nicole's early hero-worship was because of O.J. Simpson's sporting triumphs and how much of the heroism lay in O.J.'s status as a celebrity. Was there also the pull of masculinity writ large? Nicole knew little about football at the time.

Somewhere between Othello and Desdemona lies Paul Robeson, the astonishingly versatile African American who dazzled the world early in the first half of the twentieth century. On Broadway in 1943, Paul Robeson played the part of *Othello* and the production lasted longer than any other Shakespearean play (nearly 300 performances). His second New York production of *Othello* was staged soon after World War II. He saw the play as a tragedy of the *outsider*, citing the analogy of a Black American soldier trying to court a Japanese woman in Japan.

Othello was not only dark-skinned, he was also not of Venetian society, a stranger in Venice. Paul Robeson preferred the paradigm of the outsider rather than the paradigm of race. He became increasingly convinced that the most enduring and most lasting divide in society is not racial but class.

For radically different reasons O.J. Simpson had also become a class-oriented citizen rather than a race-oriented citizen. By the time he married Nicole Brown, O.J. Simpson was marrying 'below his station in life.' Othello, on the other hand, was to some extent marrying within his class. Desdemona was a *Senator's* daughter; Othello as a general was almost in the same class but for his status as an outsider.

The re-Africanisation of O.J. Simpson is a consequence of the double-murder trial. Some are born African, some *become* African and some have Africanity thrust upon them. It might even be true that some are born 'black,' some become 'black' and some have 'blackness' thrust upon them. It took a monumental tragedy for O.J. Simpson to combine class identity with a racial identity.

Does the culture of warfare affect a general's relationship with his spouse? Does the culture of competitive sports affect a sportsman's relationship with his wife? Does the general or the seasoned sportsman manifest the *discipline* side of warfare and sport? Or are they affected more by the *confrontational* aspects of war and competitive sport?

In war, political infidelity is treason. In a World Cup Soccer match kicking a ball into your own goal net could cost you your life! In Latin

America that can be literal. In both war and competitive sport infidelity is a form of treachery. The question which arises is whether the soldier in Othello and the footballer in O.J. Simpson were fertile breeding ground for what Iago calls "jealousy...the green-eyed monster which doth mock the meat it feeds on."[26]

The character Othello does have a personal philosophy which links his military style with his decisiveness in love. He thinks that both in love and war it is important to respond *decisively* and act *swiftly*.

> To be once in doubt
> Is once to be resolved....
> I'll see before I doubt; when I doubt, prove;
> And on the proof, there is no more but this:
> Away at once with love or jealousy[27]

Commenting on this Susan Snyder has said, "What works for the soldier is tragic for the husband; it pushes him past the doubt he cannot tolerate to an act of closure that is irrevocable."[28]

We do not know if O.J. Simpson was in any way involved in the murder of Nicole. But there are witnesses who can testify to spouse-abuse. How much of the abuse was aroused by "jealousy...the green-eyed monster"? And is this degree of physical jealousy affected by the sub-culture of competitive football, the way Othello's jealousy was affected by the sub-culture of the military? "When it was too late, and 'the green eyed monster' had destroyed Desdemona, Othello uttered his immortal lament:

> Then must you speak
> Of one that loved not wisely, but too well[29]

Leopold Senghor, founder President of Senegal, created the supreme irony of being a prophet of negritude and the husband of a white woman, the paradox of his 'bigamy'--married to a philosophy of Blackness and to a partnership with whiteness. Senghor sings of the Black woman:

> Naked woman, dusky woman!
> Ripe fruit with firm flesh,
> dark ecstasy of Black wine,
> mouth which makes mine lyrical...
> Naked woman, dusky woman.

The Ghanaian poetess, Efua Morgue, refuses to submit to the socio-cultural and racial prejudices which are threatening her love for a white man:

Tradition, race,
Political snares,
They formed a horrid cluster
Us to part in twain
To tear us bodily.

In a poem apparently written before another African writer was himself married to a white woman, and published in an article thirty years later, the poet writes about "Eden" (presumably meaning "the forbidden fruit" of inter-racial sex of the colonial era):

All the shadows that night
Failed to hide that sight
Of her body, all white
As I held her.

I emerged from my gown,
And she sensed I was brown
As I pulled her down
To embrace her.

Through the branches moonlight
Came, and the pond to the right
Reflected with delight
As I loved her.

With Bessie Head of South Africa, the Desdemona was her own mother whose fate was at least as tragic as that of Nicole Brown Simpson or Shakespeare's original Desdemona. Her mother belonged to an upper class wealthy white family. When the mother got pregnant with a Black man out of wedlock, the family succeeded in classifying her as insane. Bessie Head was therefore born in a Pietermaritzburg Mental Hospital. Her father had been a 'stable boy' looking after the horses. He and the white woman got attracted to each other. A different version of a real-life Othello and Desdemona tragedy, although we know far more about the offspring than about either parent.

In Southern Africa there is of course an immense corpus of literature addressing the problem of apartheid and the socio-cultural pathologies of racism and McCarthyism. In South Africa itself this does include the literature of new Desdemonas, like Peter Abraham's *Path of Thunder*.[30] A coloured man, Larry Swartz, and an Afrikaner woman, Sarie Villiers, had a love affair. All the absurdities of apartheid are caught up in this Othello-and-Desdemona affair. As one of Peter Abrahams' characters says:

> The tragedy is not in Swartz and this girl. The tragedy is in the land and in our time. You must be a native or a half-caste or a Jew or an Arab or an Englishman or Chinaman or a Greek: that is the tragedy. You cannot become a human being....For that reason Swartz and this girl who have now become human beings will suffer.

On October 24, 1818, the following announcement was made at the Cape of Good Hope:

ENGLISH THEATRICALS:

Under the sanction of His Excellency, The Governor .... This Evening the amateur company will perform the Tragedy of <u>Othello</u>

With the musical farce of *The Poor Soldier*.

These were the lighter moments of European colonisation of Africa. But for that very reason they were the most pregnant with meaning. The white man was now in Africa, not merely with his ship anchored in the harbour, not merely with his guns, not merely with his technology of production, but also with his culture and his art.

The play was given in Dutch for the first time on May 28, 1836, 'Othello, of De Jaloersche Zwart' ('Othello or the Jealous Black.')[31] But the play continued to be quite popular against the background of 'illicit' interracial intimacy in South Africa. Dutch-speaking South Africans had been among the most vociferous opponents of racially mixed marriages and mixed sex; and yet the great majority of the Cape coloured population of South Africa (people of mixed origin) are Afrikaans-speaking. Many include some Afrikaner ancestry in their genealogy.

In March 1837, a Dutch-speaking society, *Voor Vlyt en Kunst* (For Diligence and Art), attempted another production of *Othello*, with Iago played by 'a gentleman lately arrived from India.'

The nearness of tragedy to comedy is sometimes emphasized in situations of anxiety. Even in the nineteenth century, South Africa was in such a situation. <u>Othello</u> was sometimes produced as a comedy, with white men taking the part of both Othello and Desdemona, and making the most of "Desdemona's little endearments towards her black 'hobby.' That production, apparently hilarious, was given again a few days letter.

On December 30, 1854, Gustavus V. Brook, from the Theatre Royal of Liverpool, arrived at the Cape and announced he would stage *Othello*. Sometimes alterations were made to spare combined Calvinist and Victorian sensibilities, but on balance *Othello* continued to be to white South Africans "a play better understood here than any other of Shakespeare's works. Its hero (a *coloured* man) who had wooed and won a *white* lady, ships, bay soldiers, a castle and a governor, being all-familiar in the colonist's ear."[32]

The literary historian, Eric Rosenthal, has shown that by the end of the nineteenth century, few towns in South Africa had failed at some or another time to witness at least an amateur performance of Shakespeare. And because of the real racial predicament, the most popular play was Othello. More than a century later, I received an invitation to give a series of lectures at the University of Cape Town. Ali Mazrui was no Othello, but he was at the time married to a white woman.[33]

In general, I did share the belief that South Africa should be isolated diplomatically, economically, militarily, but I had mixed feelings about isolating South Africa intellectually. I was never sure whether South Africa should indeed be insulated from the flow of more rational ideas. Would my going to South Africa have broken the political isolation that I favoured? Or would it have been a case of preventing intellectual isolation, which I did not favour?

I therefore wrote to the University of Cape Town to indicate that I would consider the invitation if the following conditions were agreed to in advance: first, that I should be able to say whatever I wanted; second, that I should be able to address racially mixed audiences; and third, that I should be able to come with my wife. The last condition was a deliberate test of the system at its most sensitive point.

Of course, my colleagues at the universities of Cape Town and Witwatersrand were not responsible for the laws of the country, but their response can be paraphrased as follows:

We have been in consultation with our lawyers. That you should want to say whatever you want -- we can risk; that you should want to address racially mixed audiences -- we can virtually guarantee; but that you should want to come with your wife -- we are afraid that is impossible. You would immediately be liable to prosecution on arrival under the immorality laws and would therefore be subject at the very minimum to considerable embarrassment, and at the maximum to actual imprisonment.

A few years later I cited this anecdote in a lecture entitled "Academic Freedom in Africa". I sought to demonstrate that academic freedom sometimes depended upon wider freedoms in a given society including freedom to mate across racial lines.

Not long after publication of my talk, I received the following letter from J. Weilbach, private secretary to the then prime minister of South Africa, Mr. Jon Vorster.

Dear Professor Mazrui,

I have been instructed by the Honourable Prime Minister to inform you that he has just read your article in the August/September 1975 edition of Commonwealth under the heading: Academic Freedom in Africa.

In the article concerned you are reported as writing that your colleagues at the University of Capetown advised you that it was impossible for you to bring your English wife to South Africa because you would "immediately be liable to prosecution upon arrival under the immorality laws.

This of course is not so and whoever gave you that advice misled you because the act is not at all applicable to you or your wife and neither of you could have been arrested or prosecuted.

I was puzzled. Did Prime Minister Vorster mean that I was exempt from the laws as an act of executive dispensation? Breyten Breytenbach had after all been permitted more recently to go to South Africa with his Vietnamese wife. Similarly, the minister of information of the Ivory Coast was permitted to go to South Africa with his Swedish wife. I wrote to the private secretary of the prime minister to ask the following:

Is the Prime Minister's reassurance to me concerned with the recent easing of "petty apartheid" in the wake of experimentation in detente? Or am I to interpret your letter as a categorical denial that the immorality laws were ever intended to apply to black foreigners with their white wives?

The reply from Mr. Vorster's office was even more startling.

I have been instructed by the Honourable Prime Minister . . . to reiterate that should you come to South Africa, you would not be liable to prosecution under South Africa law on account of your English wife . . . . In fact, there has never been a period in the South African history in which you or your wife could have been so charged because it has never been an offence for a husband and wife whatever their races, to live together in this country provided they are lawfully married . . . .It may be mentioned that in the State Law Advisers confirmed the views expressed therein.

The Prime Minister is, therefore, of the opinion that whoever advised you of the legal position misled you either wilfully or through appalling lack of knowledge. You are at liberty to use this letter in any way you may see fit.

I assume the last sentence was partly to give me the option to use the letter for a visa which would enable my wife and me to go to South Africa. The letter would itself in turn provide protection once we were in South Africa.

But what did Vorster really mean in the assertion that never in the history of South Africa were there laws to prevent the marriage of an Othello to a Desdemona? It has been suggested that the prime minister at the time had chosen to be strictly legalistic, first by taking advantage of the fact that I had not distinguished in my original London speech between the immorality laws and the laws against mixed marriages. Secondly, while my marriage would not have been lawful had it taken place in South Africa originally, the fact that it was a marriage under the laws of another country gave it independent legitimacy. In reality, none of these shades of distinction had been permitted to any significant extent until the 1970s after international pressure.

Prime Minister Vorster, however, unjustly reprimanded the officers of the University of Cape Town for 'misleading foreign scholars.' The officers of the university had just done their duty in the light of South African tradition until the 1970s. South Africa clearly and emphatically had enjoyed Othello on the stage, and its social correlative in secret hotel rooms on weekends in neighbouring Lesotho and Swaziland. But within the territory of apartheid proper, mixed marriages had to be prevented by the bigger tragedy of the systematic separation of the races in almost all domains of human activity.

Were the laws to prevent the marriage of an Othello to a Desdemona really wrong? After all, *Othello* was a tragedy. The black man murdered his devoted white wife. And yet *Othello* is not really a tragedy of racial incompatibility, but a tragedy of *subversion*. The evil factor in <u>Othello</u> is the force which seeks to separate black from white: the harbinger of hate, Iago. And whatever the producers at Cape Town might have done when they made Iago an Indian in the nineteenth century, William Shakespeare in his wisdom made the evil Iago well and truly white.

Iago might therefore be seen as racism itself: constantly seeking to cultivate jealousies in human beings otherwise destined to live together. The spirit of subversion is in Iago. What feeds Iago's hate are two forces familiar in the history of racism. On one side is occupational insecurity and jealousy, and on the other, sexual insecurity and jealousy. In Shakespeare's character, both forces feed Iago's venomous villainy. As Iago confessed:

> . . .Now I do love her too;
> Not out of absolute lust, though peradventure
> I stand accountant for as great a sin
> But partly led to diet my revenge,
> For that I do suspect the lusty Moor
> Hath leap'd into my seat; the thought whereof
> Doth, like a poisonous mineral, gnaw my inwards
> And nothing can or shall content my soul
> Till I am even'd with him, wife for wife:
> Or failing so, yet that I put the Moor
> At least into a jealousy so strong
> That judgement cannot cure.[34]

Shakespeare's Iago was the philosophy of apartheid incarnate. The question which arose was whether the philosophy would drive in the end the blacks of South Africa to rise against the whites. Both sides deeply loved the land. Yet, unless the pernicious Iago of hate in their midst was exorcised in time, one patriot from either side might one day have been forced to say when it was too late:

> When you shall these unlucky deeds relate,
> Speak of me as I am, nothing extenuate.
> Nor set down aught in malice: then must you speak
> Of one that loved not wisely, but too well.[35]

In South Africa the play could be seen as an allegory of contradictions. The Blacks were falling in love with white culture but not with white people. The whites loved Africa, the land, but not Africans, the people. Subversive white racism called Iago could have made Blacks rise against whites, and then self-destruct, like Othello. Has South Africa's Othello been rescued in time before being driven to murder Desdemona by the white racism called Iago? Let us hope the worst has been permanently averted.

Conclusion

If in the days of Shakespeare's *Othello* the religious divide was more important than the racial divide (as illustrated by *The Merchant of Venice*), is the class divide becoming more important in the days of O.J. Simpson, Colin Powell and Condoleeza Rice? When religious prejudice declined after Shakespeare, colour prejudice intensified. Now that colour prejudice is in decline, is it being replaced by *class struggle,* or by a *resurrection of religious prejudice*?

New anti-Jewish plays like *The Merchant of Venice* are unlikely in mainstream Western civilisation. But Muslim equivalents of Shylocks are already being invented. *The Merchant of Venice* may be a thing of the past, but *The Thief of Baghdad* is back as a revised Western stereotype of Muslim villainy. Not the 'Noble Moor' but 'the Terrorist Arab' is the new image.

Have we come full circle? Are we now seeing race prejudice decline and religious prejudice rise after centuries of a reverse equation? Or are both race and religion giving way to two entirely different confrontations: *class struggle* (rich Black O.J., poor white Nicole) and *the war of the sexes* (which gender is abusing which?)

The full answer lies in the womb of the 21st Century. But I am convinced that the theatrical tragedy of Othello and Desdemona at the end of the sixteenth century and the real-life tragedy of O.J. Simpson and Nicole Brown towards the end of the twentieth century bracket together the golden age of colour-conscious racism in Western civilisation. Othello and Desdemona were at the beginning of colour-conscious Western racism; O.J. Simpson and Nicole were caught up in the contradictions of the decline of racism.

There are still many racial battles to be fought; many struggles against religious bigotry to be engaged. But when all is said and done, racial conflict will eventually give way to class struggle; religious conflict will be overwhelmed by the gender re-definitions of the future. In the final analysis, the only cliché that continues to make powerful sense is the proposition that <u>the</u> *struggle continues.* As Desdemona reminded us:

Men's natures wrangle with inferior things,
Though great ones are their object. 'Tis even so.
For let our finger ache, and it endues
Our healthful members even to a sense
Of pain.[36]

Yes, even today the doors have been closing racially. Racism, anti-Semitism and chauvinism have been rising in the 1990s in Bismarck's old country, the newly re-united Germany, and in Shakespeare's land, 'that sceptred isle, demi-paradise.' History is playing out its contradictions.

Bismarck helped to set the stage of the West's penetration of Africa. The Conference of Berlin of 1884-5 helped to define the rules of annexation. O.J. Simpson's land, the United States, was similarly ambivalent. Germany and the United States lived to become colonially peripheral, but capitalistically central. The two countries built relatively small territorial empires, but against the background of considerable domestic development. Both countries touched the destiny of the Black world. The United States was a major factor in the history of slavery and O.J. Simpson's ancestors. Germany was a major factor in the history of imperialism at different stages.

It just so happens that the last colony to celebrate independence in Africa was, in a sense, Bismarck's colony, Namibia or South West Africa. Once a German colony following the Conference of Berlin, it became a Mandate of the League of Nations after World War I, and was administered by South Africa for more than sixty years.

Partly under United Nations auspices, the United States under Ronald Reagan and George Bush helped facilitate Namibia's independence. History has indulged her ironic sense of humour again. The last European colony on the African continent in the 20th century was among the first of Bismarck's colonies in the last century. And O.J. Simpson's country was cast by destiny to help liberate Bismarck's last surviving Black dependency.

What is the connecting link between the erosion of the state and the decline of race? A central cause is the continuing expansion and globalisation of capitalism. As has been pointed out repeatedly, capitalism has been eroding the exclusivity of state-sovereignty. The global market-place is dictating its own terms to governments and to the nation-state. Phenomena like the European Union are, in addition, illustrations of enlargement of political scale within which individual nations lose control over movement of labour, goods, services and capital in relation to their neighbours. Is the European Union a potential state writ-large? Or is it a post-state formation? The evidence would seem to favour the latter scenario. Capitalism is a major cause behind this decline of the state.

Political apartheid in South Africa was killed as much by the logic of capitalism as by the forces of African nationalism and struggle. Overt compartmentalized racial discrimination was inimical to market forces. In time, among the greatest opponents of apartheid were the great capitalistic and pro-market forces in the country. Racism had become an antiquated chain restraining the pursuit of profit and the maximization of returns. So the decline of racism was also, in part, a response to the logic of global capitalism.

But as capitalism was weakening the state and race, it was inadvertently releasing other cultural forces as the twentieth century approached its close. Consciousness of class and relative deprivation had begun to take new forms, potentially transformative.

There had also been the rise of the new consciousness of ancestry, ethnicity and tribal origins, ranging from the ethnic convulsions in Bosnia to the demands for political decentralization for KwaZulu and for the Kenya Coast. The new Ethiopian constitution seeks to devolve power to ethno-cultural regions. The rightwing militias in the United States are a special kind of tribalism.

Thirdly, the erosion of the state and the decline of race have helped to give a new lease of life to primordial forces of religion, ranging from Islamic militancy in Iran and Algeria to Hindu militancy in India, and from right-wing Christian movements in the United States to the Buddhist factor in the Sri Lankan civil war.[37]

The question which has now arisen is whether capitalism has inadvertently released forces which will in time check its own seemingly relentless expansion. Capitalism may have succeeded in cutting the state down to size. It may have succeeded in cutting down race and racism down to size. But in so doing capitalism has released once again the ancient forces of ethnicity, ancestry, tribality, religion and cultural nationalism.

Are these the human forces which will one day arrest the once relentless expansion of capitalism? Are these the human forces which will one day cut down to size capitalism itself?

The question is wide open, and South Africa might well be one of the global labouratories of such momentous social changes.

NOTES

[1]Ralph Haswell Lutz, *Collier's Encyclopedia* (New York: Macmillan Education Corporation and P.F. Collier Inc., Volume 4 of 24 volumes, 1980) pp. 224-5.

[2] Lutz, *Collier's Encyclopedia*, p. 224.

[3] *Encyclopedia Britannica*, Vol. 2 out of 30 volumes, 15th edition, 1974.

[4] Saadia Touval, "Why the UN Fails", in *Foreign Affairs* (Sept/Oct 1994), Vol. 73, No. 5, pp. 44-57.

[5] See James N. Rosenau, *The United Nations in a Turbulent World* (Boulder, CO and London: Lynne Rienner Publishers, 1992).

[6]Thomas George Weiss, David P Forsythe, Roger A Coate, *The United Nations and Changing World Politics* (Boulder, CO: Westview Press, 1994), pp. 83-100.

[7]See Stephen D. Goose and Frank Smyth, "Arming Genocide in Rwanda", *Foreign Affairs* (Sept/Oct 1994), Vol. 73, No. 5, pp. 86-96.

[8] See, Ali A. Mazrui, "Decaying Parts of Africa Need Benign Colonisation," *International Herald Tribune* (4 August 1994), and William Pfaff, "A New Colonialism? Europe Must Go Back into Africa," *Foreign Affairs* (Jan/Feb 1995), Vol. 74 No. 1, pp. 2-6.

[9] For a historical perspective, consult Edmond Kwam Kouassi, "Africa and the United Nations since 1945", chapter in Ali A. Mazrui Ed., *Africa Since 1935 General History of Africa Vol. VIII* (London and Berkeley, CA: Heinemann and University of California Press, 1993) pp. 829-904.

[10] See Larry A. Swatuk, "Review Essay: Dead-End to Development? Post-Cold War Africa in the New International Division of Labour", *African Studies Review* (April 1995), Vol. 38, No. 1, pp. 103-117.

[11] This has borrowed from Mazrui, "The United Nations and Four Ethical Revolutions of the Twentieth Century", presented at the international

conference to mark the 50th anniversary of the United Nations, sponsored by La Trobe University, Victoria, Australia, July 2-6, 1995.

[12] Consult Zbigniew Brzezinski, "A Plan for Europe" *Foreign Affairs* (Jan/Feb 1995), Vol. 74, No. 1, pp. 26-42.

[13] Relatedly, John Lewis Gaddis has observed in a recent book, *The Cold War: A New History*:

> The international system appeared to be one of bipolarity in which, like iron filings attracted by magnets, all power gravitated to Moscow and Washington. In fact, though, the superpowers were finding it increasingly difficult to manage the smaller powers, whether allies or neutrals in the cold war, while at the same time they were losing the authority they had once taken for granted at home.

William Grimes "If You Must Have a War, Make Sure It's a Cold One," *The New York Times* (December 28, 2005).

[14] See World Bank, *Sub-Saharan Africa: From Crisis to Sustainable Development* (Washington D.C.: The World Bank, 1989) pp. 63-88.

[15] See John Gerard Ruggie, "Wandering the Void: Charting the UN's New Strategic Role", *Foreign Affairs* (Nov/Dec 1993), Vol. 72, No. 5, pp. 26-31.

[16] See William J. Durch Ed., *The Evolution of UN Peacekeeping: Case-studies and Comparative Analysis* (New York: St. Martin's Press, 1993).

[17] Chester A. Crocker, "The Lessons of Somalia", *Foreign Affairs* (May/June 1995), Vol. 74, No. 3 , pp. 2-8.

[18] See assorted issues of *Africa Confidential* (London) 1994-95.

[19] Henry Grunwald, "When Peacekeeping Doesn't Work," *Time* (26 June 1995), p. 82.

[20] On anti-semitism in Shakespeare's plays consult Thomas Cartelli, "Shakespeare's Merchant, Marlowe's Jew: The Problem Of Cultural Difference," *Shakespeare Studies* (1988), Vol. 20, pp 255-260; and Marion D. Perret, "Shakespeare's Jew: Preconception and performance," *Shakespeare Studies* (1988), Vol. 20, pp. 261-268.)

[21] Discussions on Shakespear's treatment of the racial aspects of Othello include J. Adelman, "Iago's Alter Ego: Race as Projection in 'Othello'," *Shakespeare Quarterly* (Summer 1997), Volume 48, Number 2, pp. 125-144, and

M. Neill, "Unproper Beds: Race, Adultery and the Hideous in 'Othello'," *Shakespeare Quarterly* (Winter 1989), Volume 40, Number 4, pp. 383-412.

[22] In 1969, the Supreme Court decision in *Loving V.* State of Virginia had made it possible for racial intermarriage. For an overview of this case, see David Allyn, *Make Love, Not War: The Sexual Revolution, An Unfettered History* (Boston: Little, Brown, 2000), pp. 85-92. Excerpts from the decision may be found in Abraham L. Davis and Barbara Luck Graham, *The Supreme Court, Race, and Civil Rights* (Thousand Oaks, CA: Sage Publications, 1995), pp. 214-216.

[23] Preliminary thoughts on this question were presented as "O.J. Simpson and Shakespeare's Othello" at the annual meeting of the African Heritage Studies Association, Philadelphia, March 30-April 2, 1995.

[24] Ali A. Mazrui, "Boxer Muhammed Ali and Soldier Idi Amin as International Political Symbols: The Bioeconomics of Sport and War," in *Comparative Studies in Society and History* (April 1977) Vol. 19, No. 2, pp. 189-215.

[25] *Othello*, Act I, Scene 3, lines 181-183.

[26] *Othello*, Act 3, Scene 3, Lines 189-191.

[27] *Othello*, Act 3, Scene 3, Lines 204-205, 215-217.

[28] Susan Snyder, "Othello: A Modern Perspective" in The New Folger Library edition of *Othello* edited by Barbara Mowat and Paul Werstine (New York and London: Washington Square Press, Pocket Books) 1993, p. 292.

[29] *Othello*, Act 5, Scene 2, lines 389-390.

[30] Peter Abrahams, *Path of Thunder* (New York: Harper, 1948).

[31]Cited by Eric Rosenthal, "Early Shakespeare Productions in South Africa", *English Studies in Africa*, (Sept. 1964), Vol. 7, No. 2, p. 210. I am greatly indebted to Rosenthal's research for these insights into early productions of Othello in Shaka's land.

[32]Cited by Rosenthal, "Early Shakespeare Productions in South Africa", pp. 212-13.

[33] Consult Ali A. Mazrui, "Through the Prism of the Humanities: Eurafrafrican Lessons from Shakespeare, Shaka, Puccini and Senghor", Robert

W. July and Peter Benson, Eds. *African Cultural and Intellectual Leaders and the New African Nations* (New York and Ibadan: Rockefeller Foundation and Ibadan University Press, August 1982).

[34] *Othello*, Act 5, sc, 2, lines 300-311.

[35] *Othello*, Act 5, sc. 2, lines 341-344.

[36] *Othello*, Act 3, Scene 4, lines 161-165.

[37] The clash between race and culture has for the time being resulted in the threat of global apartheid. See Ali A. Mazrui, "Global Apartheid? Race and Religion in the New World Order", chapter commissioned by the Nobel Foundation (Oslo, Norway) in Geir Lundestad and Odd Arne Westad, Eds., *Beyond the Cold War: New Dimensions in International Relations,* (Stockholm: Scandinavian University Press, 1993) pp. 85-98.

Section III

MULTI-ETHNIC AND MULTI-RELIGIOUS NIGERIA

CHAPTER 7

MEGA-NIGERIA FROM LUGARD TO GOWON: BETWEEN EXCEPTIONALISM AND TYPICALITY

T he cohesion of the United States as one country rests on the roles of two personalities – George Washington and Abraham Lincoln. Paradoxically, the survival of Nigeria as one country also rests on two personalities – Lord Lugard and General Yakubu Gowon. George Washington was a rebel against British rule, but laid the foundations of post-colonial American unification. Lord Lugard was a representative of the British colonial order, but served the destiny of amalgamating Northern and Southern Nigeria into one country in 1914.[1] This event launched *Mega-Nigeria*, an enlargement of political scale.

When George Washington's achievement was threatened by separatism and secession in the 1860s, Abraham Lincoln came to the rescue and saved the Union. When Lord Lugard's amalgamation of North and South was threatened by separatism and secession in the 1960s, Yakubu Gowon came to the rescue and helped to save the Union and to preserve Mega-Nigeria.[2]

From World War I to the Biafra War

The year 2004 marked the 90th anniversary of the amalgamation of Northern Nigeria with Southern. In 1914 Lord Lugard, the British Administrator, had unified what could have been two separate countries, each destined to have at least 50 million people by the end of the 20th century. It is an open question which of the two halves of the country would finally have retained *Nigeria* as its name.

But because Lugard amalgamated the two halves into one entity, Nigeria developed into a country of more than 120 million people by the beginning of this millennium.[3]

It is a surprise of historic proportions that the amalgamation has survived these ninety years. It has survived the vagaries of differentiated colonial policies when the North was governed differently from the South.[4]

Nigeria's amalgamation has survived Northern separatism after World War II when Northern Nigeria wanted to attain independence as a separate country from the South. Kwame Nkrumah, the Ghanaian leader, described Northern separatism at that time as a form of '*Pakistanism*' – with the goal of religiously inspired partition. Yakubu Gowon was at the time a mere child and a Christian and was not involved in Muslim separatism.

Nigeria's amalgamation survived Eastern separatism in the first decade of independence when the Eastern region attempted to invent Biafra and helped to unleash a civil war from 1967 to 1970.[5] At this time, Yakubu Gowon was a grown man and he was called upon to play his supreme historical role, that of saving the Union of a singular Mega-Nigeria.

As Governor-General of Nigeria during the period of World War I, Lord Lugard had contradictory effects on the future of Nigeria's unity. Lugard was the architect of Nigeria's national amalgamation, but his policies were detrimental to Nigeria's national integration. Amalgamation broadened the national boundaries and merged north and south into one country. National integration was supposed to be the process by which ethnic and religious divisions would be softened or ameliorated as the people acquired a sense of shared citizenship and national consciousness.

Lord Lugard virtually invented the British policy of Indirect Rule in Africa, which attempted to govern Africans through their own "native authorities." Indirect rule was particularly successful in Nigeria, leaving the Emirates of the north virtually intact and especially strong.[6] As a colonial policy which respected indigenous institutions, Indirect Rule was more humane than the assimilation policies pursued by France and Portugal. But by helping to preserve indigenous cultures and native institutions, Indirect Rule also helped to sustain "tribal identities" in Nigeria, and thus made national integration more difficult. It might, therefore, be said that while Lord Lugard was a hero of national amalgamation, he was inadvertently an adversary of national integration.

At independence amalgamation had given Nigeria an ethnically mixed single national army. But inadequate national integration had made ethnic consciousness a little too strong within the armed forces.[7] Amalgamation had made the Nigerian army strong enough to control both halves of the country, North and South. But ethnic divisions within the armed forces turned Nigeria's first military coup in January 1966 into an ethnic bloodbath (essentially in favour of the Igbo).[8] The counter-coup which followed a few months later deepened the ethnic and regional divide. The country remained amalgamated, but not adequately integrated. Onto this stressful national stage stepped young Yakubu Gowon, then in his early thirties.[9] His twin tasks were first to prevent the break-up of Nigeria's amalgamation and, secondly, to try to promote greater national integration.

A major set-back to both ambitions was the anti-Igbo pogrom which broke out in northern Nigeria in September-October 1966, killing many people and triggering off large-scale migration of the Igbo back to the Eastern region.[10] Igbo separatism entered a new phase. The break up of Nigeria's amalgamation was ominously on the horizon.

One solution was a looser federation, what was described as confederation at the Aburi meeting in Ghana between Yakubu Gowon and the Igbo leader, Colonel Emeka Odumegwu Ojukwu. Gowon failed to persuade Ojukwu to drop his secessionist aspirations and Ojukwu declared the separation of Biafra from Nigeria.[11] Ojukwu hoped that the Yoruba of the Western region would join him and also secede, thus ending the legacy of 1914.

General Gowon made a shrewd and brilliant move. He abolished the old regions of Nigeria and divided the country into twelve new states.[12] This helped to diffuse fear of Northern domination among the Yoruba and other groups, and encouraged Eastern minorities to turn against Igbo leadership and pray for a Federal victory.

Weakening the original political regions of post-colonial Nigeria helped the cause of national integration. But what about saving the Union which had been created in 1914? General Gowon succeeded in keeping the Yoruba and other groups within the Nigerian Federation. By July 1967 Gowon was ready to declare "police action" to stop the secession.[13]

But Yakubu Gowon was constantly aware that saving the territorial integrity of Nigeria was useless without simultaneously pursuing the national integration of its people. He was emphatic about a 'code of conduct' and sensitive rules of engagement. He insisted that so-called Biafrans should not be called 'enemies,' but should be regarded as fellow Nigerians who needed to be won back into the national fold. He was a benign war leader who was against the so-called "quick kill".[14] He could have made the illegal night-flying to Biafra dangerous for the aircraft. But for almost a year and a half he shut a blind eye to these night-flights of relief supplies to Biafra.

131

Yakubu Gowon triumphed in saving the Union, but he still needed to promote greater national integration. His leadership helped to avert another anti-Igbo bloodbath in the wake of Biafra's defeat. He permitted mercy missions to be rushed to the former Biafra. Within a single year, the agonies of widespread disease and starvation were reversed in the Eastern region.

On the tenth anniversary of Nigeria's independence he declared plans for new elections, a new constitution and a new population census. He said military rule would be needed until 1976. He wanted time to consolidate civil reconstruction as part of the process of national integration. He later made the mistake of asking for even more time at a moment in history when the country was impatient for a return to civilian rule. His fellow soldiers, led by Murtala Muhammed, overthrew him in July 1975.[15]

Like Abraham Lincoln, Yakubu Gowon had saved the Union of his country. Like Lincoln, Gowon's tenure of office was ended by force. But while Lincoln was assassinated, Yakubu Gowon went into exile for at least a decade.

Our main focus in this chapter is, of course, Nigeria rather than the United States, but we hope to conclude with a discussion of whether Nigeria is a future African equivalent of the United States, and whether Yakubu Gowon is Africa's equivalent of Abraham Lincoln.

Between Exceptionalism and Typicality

There are indeed certain attributes which make Nigeria strikingly unique in Africa - setting it apart in configuration from all other African countries. This aspect might be called *Nigeria's exceptionalism*. Many of those attributes are a consequence of the policies of Lord Lugard, on one side, and General Gowon, on the other.

There are other attributes, however, which make Nigeria a mirror of the African experience as a whole, making Nigeria a good illustration of what the whole of Africa is all about. This side of Nigeria might be called *Nigeria's typicality*. Some particular ups-and-downs of the *country* may be typical of the entire *continent*. To understand Nigeria is to comprehend this dialectic between the exceptionalism of Nigeria in the African configuration and the typicality of Nigeria as a mirror of the continent.

The exceptionalism of Nigeria includes of course the huge size of its population in relation to its neighbours. It is by far the most populous country in Africa. This is a central aspect of the 1914 amalgamation. The next country in size on the African continent is Egypt, and yet Egypt is only a little more than half of Nigeria's population.[16] When ECOWAS was formed in 1975 upon the initiative of Nigeria and Togo; its population is close to 150 million people from *sixteen* countries. More than half of ECOWAS' total population were Nigerians.[17] The Gross National Product of ECOWAS in 1975 was US 79.9 billion dollars; the bulk of that came from Nigeria.[18] General Yakubu Gowon was a major architect of this ambitious African regional organization. He was strengthened by the legacy of enlargement from 1914.

Nigeria's exceptionalism also includes the combination of immense human resources (youthful and potentially gifted population) with immense natural resources (led by oil and gas). In 1914 Lord Lugard knew about Nigeria's palm oil. Nigeria's other oil – petroleum – had yet to reveal itself.

Towards a Pax Nigeriana

Almost from independence Nigeria's exceptionalism included a potential leadership role to help keep the peace in West Africa - a kind of Pax Nigeriana.[19] For better or for worse, Nigeria's regional rival in this peacekeeping role has not been another West African country. It has in fact been France.[20] It has been France, combined with Nigeria's own internal problems, which have prevented Pax Nigeriana from fulfilling its regional mission to the full.

Opinion is divided within France in this new millennium as to whether to continue Paris's historic role in Africa or whether to find a new mission for French destiny in the newly emerging countries of Eastern and Central Europe.[21] If France is beginning to withdraw from Africa (as the devaluation of the C.F.A. franc portended) the so-called regional "vacuum" left behind is likely to be increasingly filled by Pax Nigeriana.

On the evidence so far, Pax Nigeriana - keeping the peace in West Africa under Nigeria's auspices – is better fulfilled when Nigeria is under military rule than when it is under the politicians. The most spectacular exercises in Pax Nigeriana occurred in the 1990s when Nigeria led the forces of ECOWAS (the ECOMOG troops) into Liberia first to restore peace and then to help re-start electoral democracy. The final result were elections in Liberia in 1997 which returned Charles Taylor to power for a while.[22]

In 1998 Nigeria more unilaterally took on the army in Sierra Leone which had overthrown the elected government of President Ahmad Kabbah. Nigeria reversed the military takeover and restored the constitutionally elected government.[23] But what had made it possible for Nigeria to play this role of "Big Brother" in West Africa? Mega-Nigeria's enlargement of scale went straight back to the unification of 1914 and to the preservation of the Nigerian Union under the leadership of Yakubu Gowon.

For most of the 1990s, Nigeria paradoxically became a force for democracy away from home but remained a dictatorship at home. Nigerian forces helped to restore relative freedom to the peoples of Liberia and Sierra Leone - but the Nigerian forces were slow to extend freedom to the Nigerian people at home.

This does not mean that Nigeria should not have helped to re-democratise Liberia and Sierra Leone. General Sani Abacha's regional role was one of the positive aspects of Pax Nigeriana. But doing good abroad is no excuse for not doing better at home. Fortunately, there were indications that the military government after Abacha wanted a honourable way towards re-civilisation. The last elections of the end of the 20th century brought a former soldier to head the new democracy – General Olusegun Obasanjo.

It is arguable that one of the first exercises of Pax Nigeriana occurred in Tanzania in 1964. Army mutinies in Uganda, Kenya and Tanganyika had forced the three governments to invite British troops to return to East Africa and disarm their own mutinous soldiers.

President Julius K. Nyerere understandably disbanded the whole mutinous army once order was restored. But who was going to keep the peace in a Tanganyika without an army? Julius Nyerere called upon fraternal troops from Nigeria to fill the vacuum while Nyerere set about creating an alternate indigenous security force. It is arguable that the beginnings of Pax Nigeriana lie in a voluntary partnership between Nigeria and what later became Tanzania. Nigerians helped Tanzanians keep the peace in their own country in 1964. Ironically, this marked the 50th anniversary of the amalgamation of Nigeria into one country.

Nigerian Politics: Between the Sublime and the Theatrical

Perhaps it is also part of Nigeria's exceptionalism that it has not just one pivotal ethnic group in a national configuration but three. Uganda has one pivotal group - the Baganda. Kenya has in reality two outstanding pivotal groups - the Luo and Kikuyu. Senegal's outstanding pivotal group are the Wolof.

Is Nigeria <u>exceptional</u> in having three very large pivotal ethnic groups, each with a dazzling record of achievement? The Hausa, the Yoruba and the Igbo-Nigeria would not have had such a triad of vanguard ethnic groups if the 1914 amalgamation had not occurred, and if it had not been preserved by Yakubu Gowon's government. Ironically, it took a member of a minority group to save the union vanguard ethnic groups. [24] Yakubu Gowon illustrates what great vanguard <u>individuals</u> can be produced by <u>non-vanguard</u> ethnic groups.

The Hausa are by far the largest linguistic group not only in Nigeria but also in West Africa as a whole. Within Nigeria itself the Hausa also have a long record of *skills of governance* from precolonial days, right through colonialism until postcolonial days.[25]

The Yoruba have in many ways the most complex indigenous culture of them all. The Yoruba impact on global Africa and the rest of the Black world is less about the Yoruba language and more about the Yoruba religion and culture. Yoruba religious rites are to be witnessed in countries as diverse as Brazil, Jamaica, Haiti, Surinam, Nigeria, Dahomey (now Republic of Benin) and the United States.[26]

The Igbo were the great technologists of Nigeria in the second half of the twentieth century. Their triumph in economic skills in Northern Nigeria in the 1950s and 1960s contributed to their vulnerability as a people in 1966. During the Nigerian civil war the Igbo's innovativeness also produced Africa's first locally made gun-vehicles. During the Civil War the Igbo displayed levels of innovative daring unknown in postcolonial African history. The Igbo created rough-and-ready armed militarised vehicles as well as the beginnings of Africa's industrial revolution.[27] This renaissance was aborted by the oil bonanza from the 1970s onwards.

During the Biafra war Nigeria was more internally innovative than externally prosperous. The Nigerian Civil War produced some of the high points of Nigeria's experience with technological innovation. The Nigerian oil bonanza after the 1973 OPEC price escalation created disincentives to Nigerian enterprise.[28]

135

War had brought out both the best and the worst of Nigeria in human terms. But <u>technologically</u> the power of spilt blood in Nigeria produced greater innovation than the power of sprouting petroleum. The pain of Biafra was technologically more fruitful than the profit of OPEC. While Commander-in-Chief Yakubu Gowon was mobilizing the Federal forces, Colonel Emeka Ojukwu was inspiring and motivating Igbo innovation.

Nigeria's exceptionalism in 1998 included the extraordinary phenomenon of five political parties choosing the same man as their Presidential candidate - Sani Abacha - even when Abacha was not even a member of any of these parties.[29] This was unprecedented anywhere in the world. At one level this showed political opportunism at its most glaring, and was not a credit to the complex size of Nigeria. But at another level this could have been a defensible constitutional experiment if it had been presented as such.

When Africa had one-party states (as in Kenya, Zambia, Tanzania and the Ivory Coast), the real choice for voters involved elections to the legislature. The choice of the Head of State was never in doubt in those African one-party states. The legislative choice was between *individual* candidates within the same party.

What Nigeria might have evolved in 1998 was a system a little more pluralistic than the one-party state but a little *less* pluralistic than a system of full-blown electoral competition at all levels. At the presidential level, the people of Nigeria would have no more choice than the electorates of Africa's one-party states had before the 1990s. But at the level of *legislative* elections the people of Nigeria could choose between *parties* and not simply between *individuals*. At least theoretically the people of Nigeria would have had more choice in 1998 than the people of one-party Kenya had before 1992. However, the Nigerian voter was not impressed. And Abacha did not live long enough to be the Head of five political parties.

Let us now shift from Nigeria's exceptionalism, its uniqueness, to Nigeria's typicality in the African context.

Ideologies: The Cultural and the Economic

Nigeria's *typicality* includes the fact that Nigerians are more strongly moved by socio-cultural ideologies than by socio-economic ideologies. Socio-cultural ideologies appeal to such cultural forces as ethnicity, religion, nationalism, race-consciousness and regional allegiance.

Socio-economic ideologies try to appeal to such economic interests as class, economic equity, trade union rights and the like. Marxism, ujamaa and most other forms of socialism are socio-economic ideologies. Ethnicity, nationalism and regional allegiance are socio-cultural ideologies.

In Nigeria, as in most other parts of Africa, ethno-cultural ideologies are much stronger than ethno-economic ones. A classic Nigerian example was Obafemi Awolowo's effort to move Nigeria a little to the left. When he looked to see who was following him, it was not the dispossessed of all ethnic groups of Nigeria who followed; it was his fellow Yoruba of all social classes and levels of income.

Another example from Kenya was Oginga Odinga's modest attempt to move Kenyans a little to the left. When Oginga looked to see who was following him, once again it was not the dispossessed of Kenya of all ethnic groups. It was his fellow Luo of all social classes and levels of income.

Africa is a continent of surplus passion but deficit power. Nigerians as Africans feel strongly about many aspirations. In the controversial words of a highly distinguished African philosopher, -- ex-president, a kind of philosopher king -- Leopold Senghor of Senegal, 'Emotion is black.... Reason is Greek.'[30]

Nigeria is typical of Africa also because of the swings between *tyranny* (too much government) and *anarchy* (too little government). When under military rule, Nigeria leans towards tyranny (too much government). When under civilian administration, Nigeria leans towards anarchy (too little government). In spite of the fact the country was at war from 1967 to 1970, military rule under Yakubu Gowon was more benign than military rule either before the Gowon regime or subsequent to it.

Nigeria's triple heritage is a convergence of indigenous African values, Islamic culture, and the impact of the West (both secular and Christian). In one sense, this convergence of the three legacies is part of Nigeria's *typicality*.[31]

But Nigeria is *exceptional* in having those three civilisations (Africanity, Islam and the West) almost equal in power.

Can we measure political development by the yardstick of declining scale of political violence? Let us try with Nigeria. The first two decades of Nigeria's independence were the age of <u>regicide</u> and primary violence. The killing of the King or Head Executive as a trend was regicide. Of the eight supreme leaders of Nigeria in the first 20 years, four had been assassinated.[32]

The eight supreme leaders were Azikiwe, Balewa, Ahmadu Bello, Ironsi, Gowon, Murtala, Obasanjo and Shagari. The 50% who were assassinated were of course <u>Balewa</u>, <u>Ahmadu Bello</u>, <u>Ironsi</u> and <u>Murtala Muhammed</u>. Regicide was at a 50% rate - a high rate indeed. Ahmadu Bello was technically a regional leader but with immense federal and national power. In all, three Northern leaders were killed, as compared with one Southern.

The next 20 years of Nigeria's independence (1980 to the year 2000) were to be of militarism and constitutional experimentation.[33] Things were still rough, but governing Nigeria had become less fatal for the incumbents! These were the last years of Shagari, those of Buhari, those of Babangida and his immediate successors, and the emergence of Sani Abacha. The most promising experiment was the Babangida transition which collapsed ignominiously with the aborted election of June 1993.[34] That transition would apparently have brought M.K.O. Abiola into power. It would have been a remarkable stage in the electoral amalgamation of the two halves of Nigeria. For the first time a <u>Southern</u> Muslim would have presided over Nigeria.

Under Abacha the years of militarism and constitutional experimentation could have continued, on the other hand, with a new concept of presidential recycling from military ruler to elected Head of State. If Abacha had lived and run for the Presidency, he would have been partially following the precedent of Jerry Rawlings who captured power twice by the barrel of the gun and later gained legitimacy through the ballot box and the electoral process.[35] But Abacha died in June 1998 before that scenario could be attempted in Nigeria. The experiment in North-South amalgamation was inconclusive and was still subject to ups and downs.

Is Nigeria a Reincarnation of the United States?

As we now leave what Nigeria has in common with the rest of Africa, we may need to take into account what Nigeria has in common with the United States. We will not permit the Atlantic to divide us.

How much do Nigeria and the United States have in common? Is Nigeria a potential future reincarnation of the United States? That question is much bigger than is often assumed. Of all the countries of Africa Nigeria is the closest approximation to the United States. There is a love-hate relationship between the two countries - and yet no African country can more accurately be described as the United States in the making than Nigeria. Liberia is an approximation of the African American experience, rather than a potential reincarnation of the United States.

The United States is the colossus of the Western hemisphere. Nigeria is the colossus of West Africa. Thanks to the legacy of 1914, Nigeria's population outnumbers the populations of the rest of the fifteen original members of ECOWAS combined, as we indicated.

The United States issued the Monroe Doctrine in 1823 which eventually became a legitimisation of *Pax Americana* in the Western hemisphere. In addition to barring Europe from the New World, the Monroe Doctrine legitimised American intervention in Latin American countries in pursuit of either democracy or the free market for American business.[36]

Nigeria under Abacha evolved not the Monroe Doctrine but the *Monrovia Doctrine* legitimising intervention in West Africa by troops led by Nigeria. Instead of *Pax Americana*, we began to witness the birth and development of *Pax Nigeriana*: the right of Nigeria to "pacify" any unruly neighbours. Abacha may have started something of long-term duration. In the West African region, it began in Monrovia, Liberia. It has since also been implemented in Sierra Leone. Nigeria as the "Big Brother" of West Africa is a direct descendant of the unification of 1914.

Nigeria is virtually the only African country which has consistently tried to maintain a *federal system of government* similar to the U.S.. It is true that federalism and military rule make very strange bedfellows. Nigerian federalism has been distorted by militarism.

Nevertheless, while the very word "federalism" was almost anathema all over the rest of Africa, in Nigeria terms like "the federal character" of Nigeria have added new forms of legitimacy to localized autonomies. Federalism in the USA is alive and well. Federalism in Nigeria is alive, but not well.[37] But that is more than can be said for federalism in the rest of Africa. Nigeria's exceptional need for federalism is partly because of the enlargement of scale initiated by the amalgamation of 1914. When Gowon abolished the original sub-regions, he invented a new federalism.

Like the United States in the 1860s, Nigeria in the 1960s fought a civil war to save the union and save the boundaries of their respective federations. On the union or federal side in both civil wars, the leadership was in the hands of remarkably humane personalities - Abraham Lincoln in the American civil war, Yakubu Gowon in the case of the Nigerian conflict.

In the case of the assassination of the top leader, the Nigerian case skipped one leader. It was not Yakubu Gowon who was assassinated - as was the case with Abraham Lincoln. It was the leader who replaced Gowon, Murtala Muhammed. The assassination missed a beat in the Nigerian case.

It is one of the ironies of history that the United States and Nigeria produced their most compassionate leaders in conditions of a civil war. Abraham Lincoln sought to teach his compatriots that a nation could not long endure half slave and half free. He also bequeathed to the lexicon of global democracy the concept of "government of the people, by the people, for the people."

Yakubu Gowon had no major speech like the Gettysburg Address to be remembered by, but he had a remarkable life to be celebrated for. Lincoln ascended the pinnacle of power from a log cabin to the White House. Yakubu Gowon reversed the direction from State House as a presidential resident to the classroom and cafeteria as an undergraduate. Lincoln went up the ladder of privilege to the Presidency, and then death intervened before he could fall from grace. Gowon ascended to the top, but then lived to face the challenge of a fall from the pinnacle. Instead of resentment, he embraced his new circumstances. He said, "I on my part have accepted the change and pledge my full loyalty to the nation, to my country and to the government." He was in Kampala, Uganda, when he was overthrown.[38]

He eventually entered Warwick University in England, initially as an undergraduate in political studies, often seen in the cafeteria with other students. The man who as Head of State had previously been honoured by Cambridge University in England with a Doctor of Laws, honouris causa, found the humility to pursue a bachelor's degree at Warwick afterwards. Even more than Abraham Lincoln, Yakubu Gowon had been challenged to the test of humility after ascending to ultimate power. Yakubu Gowon passed that test of ultimate humility.

But in Gowon's case, humility had its rewards. He found a new ladder of upward social mobility. After his bachelor's degree he pursued a Doctorate of Philosophy (Ph.D.) in political studies.[39] He eventually became a Research Professor at the University of Jos for a while.

In the United States Woodrow Wilson had experienced a transition from being a Professor to becoming President of the United States. That was at about the time of Lord Lugard's amalgamation of Nigeria during World War I. Yakubu Gowon reversed Wilson's trajectory. Gowon followed a transition from being Head of State of Nigeria to becoming a Professor. But it was Abraham Lincoln, rather than Woodrow Wilson, who was closest to Yakubu Gowon in moral stature.

The question arises whether more than forty years after independence Nigeria's political culture is like that of the American frontier, rough and ready, with high anarchic tendencies. Are Nigerians themselves, by African standards, rugged individualists operating in pursuit of self-interest? Leaders from Murtala to Abacha tried to curb that individualism but failed to destroy it.

Nigeria's combination of a large population with great natural resources is another comparison with the United States. In the case of Nigeria, petro-power is not yet at ease with human power - but the potential is unmistakable.

There are no 'Red Indians' in Nigeria, natives to be hunted down and exterminated as they were in the USA. But are there 'cowboys' in Nigeria by another name, conducting *economic duels* with each other with relentless aggrandizement? Is there a *frontier culture* in post-colonial Nigeria which is eroding ancient African standards of restraint? These Nigerian 'cowboys without Indians' have indeed tarnished the country's name in Africa and around the world.[40]

Language is both a medium of national integration and a badge of national identity

Americans in the frontier evolved their own version of the *English language*. Nigerians also evolved their own version of English, not just pidgin-- although that is rich enough-- but also innovative phrases in standard English, such as the phrase 'go slow' to mean 'traffic congestion' and the question mark 'not so?' to serve all kinds of purposes.[41]

141

Nigerians also are evolving their own pronunciations. University professors pronounce the word 'Senate' as 'Sinate'; and the word 'peasant' as 'pisant.' And since they are speaking Nigerian standard English, who is to say they are wrong? One of these days Nigerians may also evolve their own way of spelling English words just as Americans have done. Pidgin English has gone further than the American English in domesticating the English language.[42]

Nigerians have bought one half of the American dream but not yet the other half. Nigerians have bought economic liberalism and pro-market ideologies. Socialist reformers in Nigeria have had a hard time winning converts. Nigerians like the idea of the economic individual as a moneymaker. Is such rabid individualism good or bad for national integration? In the West it has been good. In Nigeria it remains to be seen.

The other side of the American dream - *political* pluralism and liberal democracy - Nigeria has yet to sustain it for any length of time. Both civilian politicians and soldiers in Nigeria have played havoc with liberal values and democratic disciplines. In Africa there is sometimes tension between the process of democratisation and the trend towards national integration.

On *corruption*, does Nigeria reflect an earlier America or a continuing American reality? Mike Wallace was once interviewing Louis Farrakhan on the CBS TV program "60 Minutes".[43] Mike Wallace (a white American interviewer) chided Farrakhan for visiting Nigeria, already ranked as the most corrupt country in the world in some Western publications. Farrakhan said to Wallace "I won't accept your describing Nigeria as the most corrupt country."

Wallace challenged Farrakhan: "Tell me which country is more corrupt than Nigeria." Farrakhan responded, "I live in one," meaning the United States was more corrupt than Nigeria. This was long before the exposure of American corporate corruption like Enron and Halliburton. In both Nigeria and the United States, neither democracy nor national integration has been able to eliminate corruption.

There is no doubt that earlier this century the United States was even more corrupt. But has it made progress? On *nepotism* it has. No US President is ever again likely to nominate his brother as Attorney General of the USA, as John F. Kennedy appointed his younger brother, Robert Kennedy.

On *violence*, both Nigeria and the United States are (by absolute standards) quite violent societies. The USA has excessive individually-focused violence, (mugging, youth homicide, disproportionate street violence.) Nigeria has excessive group-focused violence (ethnic-focused, religion-focused, regionalist-focused). Inter-group violence in Nigeria is a greater threat to national integration than is inter-individual violence in the U.S.A.

The *elite* of Nigeria has become disproportionately American-trained in part. It began with the first president of Nigeria, Nnamdi Azikiwe. The proportion of Nigerians educated in the United States has been increasing all the time since Zik was head of state. Is this Americo-homogenisation of higher education in Nigeria helpful or harmful to national integration? Unfortunately the brain drain <u>from</u> Nigeria has also been disproportionately finding its way to the United States.

American universities are teaching the Hausa language, the Yoruba religion, and the Igbo political experience. Lincoln University in Pennsylvania inaugurated a series of annual conferences named after Nnamdi Azikiwe. The first conference was attended by former President Shehu Shagari of Nigeria, former President Julius K. Nyerere of Tanzania, Professor Adebayo Adedeji, Professor J. Isawa Elaigwu, Professor Jacob Ade Ajayi and a host of other distinguished Nigerians and their friends.

Nigerian universities are showing signs of partial Americanisation. We now have the concept of *semester*, and the concept of *semester-long courses*. This used to be totally alien from the original British tradition of our colonial masters. In Nigeria we now have the title 'Associate Professor,' which is really American and was alien to the original British paradigm of Lecturer, Senior Lecturer, Reader and full Professor. The American equivalent is Lecturer, Instructor, Assistant Professor, Associate Professor and professor. Is this academic homogenisation an asset to the unification of the Nigerian elite?

Nigerian universities participate in such American academic schemes as the 50-year old *Fulbright scheme*. Nigerians also deal with American foundations like Ford, Rockefeller, MacArthur, Carnegie and U.S. Federal Government schemes.

The United States may be Nigeria writ large. It may be Nigeria writ richer, it may be Nigeria writ more modern. But if Nigeria survives in its modern boundaries, Mega-Nigeria may indeed become a reincarnate of the American experience in West Africa - for better or for worse. That may be Nigeria's ultimate exceptionalism, reinforced by the enlargement of 1914.

If Nigerians do not like the prospect of becoming the United States of West Africa, the time to act is *now*. How can we *abort* the reincarnation of the United States in the new Nigeria of tomorrow? Or is that American version of *exceptionalism* worth pursing? Nigerians are bound to be deeply divided on such issues. A Nigerian chorus of conflicting views would constitute their ultimate *typicality*. Echoes of 1914 are reverberating.

Conclusion

The Nigerian experience continues to be a rich mine of potential lessons for Africa. Some are lessons of what to avoid, some are about what to emulate, and still others are a declaration that what is relevant in one society is not necessarily pertinent for another. But there are occasions when the wider African experience holds the key towards helping Nigerians to realize some of their own ideals. The giant of petroleum needs to listen to the voices of the powerless.

Out of the interaction between Nigerians and other Africans we hope to understand *Global Africa* as a whole, including the African Diaspora. After all, thanks to Lugard and Gowon, Nigeria is the largest concentration of Black people under one government in the history of the world. Never before in history have more than 120 million Blacks been under one government.

Yet Nigeria became independent in 1960 as part of a crowd of new states. Over fifteen African countries were admitted to the United Nations that year as new sovereign members. Nigeria was only one of them. And yet the population of Nigeria outnumbered the populations of almost all the other new African states added together. This was a legacy of the 1914 amalgamation. That dialectic between being "part of the African crowd" and being unique has continued to be the essence of the Nigerian predicament ever since. It is the challenge of Nigeria's *exceptionalism*, on one side, and Nigeria as a *mirror of the African condition* on the other. The legacy of Lugard's amalgamation of 1914 has transformed the Black experience as a whole.

We have reached a stage when we can affirm that over two thirds of the news from Africa is good - but it is not adequately being reported. Economies are beginning to take a turn for the better. One-party states have given way to legalized opposition parties; the number of military regimes has declined significantly; corruption is being discussed more openly though it is not yet under control; political apartheid has been substantially dismantled though economic apartheid is still alive and well; the demographic transition in population growth has begun to occur, and population growth rates are declining.

While HIV-AIDS is a new killer in Africa, civil wars are fewer in number and are no longer being artificially prolonged by cynical Cold War rivalries. The United Nations has had two African Secretaries-General in succession, Boutros Boutros-Ghali and Kofi Annan; the Commonwealth has its first African Secretary-General Elezar Emeka Anyaoku; African states are assuming regional security responsibilities in such situations as ending the civil war in Liberia or ending a military take-over in Sierra Leone and addressing the conflicts in Darfur, Congo and Burundi. African women are raising their political aspirations to the level of becoming presidential candidates in countries like Kenya and Liberia. South Africa already has a sitting female Deputy President.[44]

Meanwhile, the contradictions of Nigeria persist. Is it a microcosm of Africa or is it a microcosm of America? Is Nigeria unique or is it a mirror of the African condition? And what other paradoxes does Nigeria embody?

Thanks to Lord Lugard and General Gowon, Nigeria is the largest concentration of educated Africans in one country, and yet learned Nigerians are more efficient and productive outside Nigeria than within. Why is the home environment less conducive to maximum creative performance by its citizens than exile has been?

Now the question has arisen as to whether Nigeria's amalgamation will survive the politics of Shariacracy in the North, the new nationalism of the Yoruba, and the tensions of politicised petroleum.

In the course of these ninety years of amalgamation, Nigeria has developed a dialectic between its own uniqueness and what it shares with the rest of Africa. There are certain aspects of Nigeria which continue to make it exceptional and other aspects which make Nigeria typical of the African experience. Let us explore this dialectic between Nigeria's exceptionalism and Nigeria's typicality. The phenomenon of Mega-Nigeria continues to bestride the African world like a Colossus.

Nigeria's paradoxes go beyond exceptionalism vs. typicality. Nigeria has had more years under military rule than any other English-speaking country in Africa, and yet Nigeria has helped restore democracy in Liberia and Sierra Leone. A major producer of oil has often some of the longest lines for petrol in Africa. Nigeria has more Muslims than any Arab country including Egypt, and as many Christians as the rest of West Africa added together. Nigeria produced the first African winner of the Nobel Prize for Literature, the first African Secretary-General of the Commonwealth, the first African football team to win the Olympic gold medal, the first African experimental motor-car locally invented, and the biggest national constellation of gifted novelists, poets, historians, playwrights and philosophers of any one African country. And, thanks to Lugard and Gowon, Nigeria is indeed the largest concentration of Black people under one government in human history – more than 120 million Black citizens. Whither Nigeria? Whither Africa? And how will the tension between exceptionalism and typicality play out?

It is ninety years since the unification of Northern and Southern Nigeria. Let us understand Mega-Nigeria better by knowing more about the African condition. It is over thirty years since Yakubu Gowon helped to save the Union. Let us get new insights about Africa by digging further into the Nigerian predicament. After all, deeper than the wells of petroleum are the inner recesses of the African mind. Let us challenge that mind more creatively in preparation for the next ninety years of the fundamental singularity of Nigeria which the government of Yakubu Gowon helped to save.

NOTES

[1] For an extensive collection of relevant documents, see A. H. M. Kirk-Greene (Compiler and Editor), Lugard and the Amalgamation of Nigeria: A Documentary Record; Being a Reprint of the Report By Sir F. D. Lugard on the Amalgamation of Northern and Southern Nigeria and Administration 1912-1919; Together With Supplementary Unpublished Amalgamation Reports, and Other Relevant Documents (London: Cass, 1968) and for a selection, consult Richard A. Olaniyan, Ed. *The Amalgamation and its Enemies : an Interpretive History of Modern Nigeria* (Ile-Ife, Nigeria : Obafemi Awolowo University Press, 2003) , pp. 209-237.

[2] Indeed, General Yakubu Gowon's last name has been indicative of the desire for unity in Nigeria. Gowon is an acronym for "Go On With One Nigeria," as pointed out by Vincent O. Nmehielle, "Sharia Law in the Northern States of Nigeria: To Implement or Not to Implement, the Constitutionality is the Question, *Human Rights Quarterly* (August 2004), Volume 26, No. 3, p. 757.

[3] It was estimated that Nigeria's population was at 126 million in 2004; see "Muslim Mobs, Seeking Vengeance, Attack Christians in Nigeria," *New York Times* (May 13, 2004).

[4] A critical view of the amalgamation is provided by Adiele E. Afigbo, "The Amalgamation: Myths, Howlers and Heresies," in Olaniyan, Ed. *The Amalgamation and its Enemies*, pp. 45-57.

[5] On the Biafra War, consult Herbert Ekwe-Ekwe, *The Biafra War : Nigeria and the Aftermath*, Lewiston, N.Y., USA : E. Mellen Press, 1990); Peter Schwab, Ed. *Biafra* (New York, Facts on File, 1971); and Zdenek Cervenka, *The Nigerian War, 1967-1970. History of the War*; Selected Bibliography and Documents (Frankfurt: Bernard & Graefe, 1971).

[6] For specific cases and analyses of "indirect rule" in Nigeria, see Toyin Falola, Ed., *Nigerian History, Politics and Affairs : the Collected Essays of Adiele Afigbo*, (Trenton, NJ : Africa World Press, 2005), pp. 253-295; Olufemi Vaughan, *Nigerian Chiefs : Traditional Power in Modern Politics, 1890s-1990s* (Rochester, NY : University of Rochester Press, 2000), pp. 22-68; J. A. Atanda, *The New Oyo Empire: Indirect Rule and Change in Western Nigeria, 1894-1934* (London: Longman, 1973); and A. E. Afigbo, *The Warrant Chiefs: Indirect Rule in Southeastern Nigeria, 1891-1929* (New York: Humanities Press, 1972).

[7] Indigenization and promotion in the armed forces became subject to ethnic and political machinations; see Toyin Falola, *A History of Nigeria* (Westport, CT: Greenwood Press, 1999), p. 116.

[8] A. Oyewole, *Historical Dictionary of Nigeria* (Metuchen, NJ: Scarecrow Press, 1987), pp. 143-144.

[9] Gowon, born October 19, 1934, was then thirty-one years old; see Paul E. Lovejoy, "Historical Setting," in Helen C. Metz, Ed. *Nigeria : a Country Study* (Washington, DC:U.S. G.P.O., 1992), p. 57

[10] Ekwe-Ekwe, *The Biafra War*, pp. 63-67.

[11] Ekwe-Ekwe, *The Biafra War*, pp. 68-69.

[12] Ekwe-Ekwe, *The Biafra War*, p. 69.

[13] Lovejoy, "Historical Setting," p. 59; Falola, *A History of Nigeria* , p. 123.

[14] Lovejoy, "Historical Setting," p. 61; Ekwe-Ekwe, *The Biafra War*, pp. 115-116.

[15] Oyewole, *Historical Dictionary of Nigeria,* p. 144.

[16] According to the on-line *CIA World Factbook*, while the population of Nigeria is estimated at 128 million, that of Egypt's is estimated at 77 million; these statistics were accessed on April 30, 2005 at <http://www.odci.gov/cia/publications/factbook/rankorder/2119rank.html>

[17] See Uka Ezenwe, *ECOWAS and the Economic Integration of West Africa* (New York : St. Martin's Press, 1983), p. 151.

[18]The Nigerian GNP was about 55 billion; see A.B. Akinyemi, S.B. Falegan, and I.A. Aluko, *Readings and Documents on ECOWAS : Selected Papers and Discussions from the 1976 Economic Community of West African States Conference* (Lagos and Ibadan : Nigerian Institute of International Affairs : Macmillan Nigeria, 1984) p. 15

[19] This role has been enhanced by its position in ECOWAS, and for a description of the evolution of ECOWAS from a group formed for economic purposes to its current political and military activities, see Emmanuel I. Udogu, "Economic Community of West African States: From an Economic Union to a Peacekeeping Mission," *The Review of Black Political Economy* (Spring 1999), 26, 4 . pp. 57-74.

[20]A list of French military interventions in Africa may be found in Gordon Cumming, *Aid toAfrica: French and British policies from the Cold War to the New Millennium* (Aldershot, Hampshire, England and Burlington, VT: Ashgate, 2001), p. 410.

[21] For some discussions on the history and future of France in Africa, see essays by Chris Alden, "From Policy Autonomy to Policy Integration: The Evolution of France's Role in Africa," pp. 11-25; Jean-Francois Bayart, "End-Game South of the Sahara? France's Africa Policy," pp. 26-41; Emeka Nwokedi, "France, The New World Order, and the Francophone West African States: Towards a Reconceptualization of Privileged Relations, pp. 195-217; all in Chris Alden and Jean-Pascal Daloz, Eds., *Paris, Pretoria, and the African Continent : The International Relations of States and Societies in Transition* (Houndmills,

Basingstoke, Hampshire and New York, N.Y: Macmillan Press ; St. Martin's Press, 1996).

[22]The Liberian case is analyzed in Jibrin Ibrahim, *Democratic Transition in Anglophone West Africa* (Dakar, Senegal: CODESRIA, 2003), pp. 43-48; Adekeye Adebajo, *Building Peace in West Africa : Liberia, Sierra Leone, and Guinea-Bissau* (Boulder, CO: Lynne Rienner Publishers, 2002), pp. 43-78; Robert Mortimer, "ECOMOG, Liberia, and Regional Security in West Africa," in Edmond J. Keller & Donald Rothchild, Eds., *Africa in the New International Order : Rethinking State Sovereignty And Regional Security* (Boulder, CO: Lynne Rienner Publishers, 1996), pp. 149-164; and Ademola Adeleke "The Politics and Diplomacy of Peacekeeping in West Africa: The ECOWAS Operation in Liberia," *The Journal of Modern African Studies*, Vol. 33, No. 4. (Dec., 1995), pp. 569-593.

[23] On the Sierra Leonean case, see Ibrahim, *Democratic Transition In Anglophone West Africa*, pp. 49-54; Adebajo, *Building Peace in West Africa : Liberia, Sierra Leone, and Guinea-Bissau*, pp. 79-109; and Abiodun Alao, *Sierra Leone: Tracing the Genesis of A Controversy* (London: Royal Institute of International Affairs, June 1998).

[24] Gowon belonged to the Anga group in the Middle Belt; see Lovejoy, "Historical Setting," p. 57.

[25] On the Hausa, see Ibrahim Khaleel, "The Hausa," in Marcellina Ulunma Okehie-Offoha and Matthew N.O. Sadiku, Eds., *Ethnic & Cultural Diversity In Nigeria* (Trenton, NJ: Africa World Press, 1996), pp. 37-62

[26] An overview of the Yorubas may be found in Mathew Sadiku, "The Yoruba," in Okehie-Offoha and Sadiku, Eds., Ethnic & Cultural Diversity In Nigeria, pp. 125-147.

[27] See C. B. Nwachuku and Aja Akpuru-Ajo, "The Igbo in the Political Economy of Nigeria," in U. D. Anyanwu and J.C.U. Aguwa, *The Igbo and the Tradition of Politics*, (Enugu, Nigeria : Fourth Dimension Publishing, 1993), pp. 188-198.

[28] On the impact of oil on the Nigerian economy, consult Kelechi Amihe Kalu, *Economic Development and Nigerian Foreign Policy* (Lewiston, NY: Edwin Mellen Press, 2000), pp. 64-72.

[29] As Falola has noted, this was not entirely due to Abacha's popularity; see Falola, *A History of Nigeria*, p. 203.

[30] For a listing of Senghor's many works and a short overview of this influential African's life, see <http://www.au-senegal.com/decouvrir_en/senghor.htm> (March 15, 2004).

[31] Relatedly, see Ali A. Mazrui, *The Africans: A Triple Heritage* (Boston: Little, Brown, 1986).

[32] According to one analysis, this corresponds (but as is typical of the African colossus in the case of Nigeria, exceeded) to a general African pattern where deaths of incumbent heads of state in the case of coups peaked in the 1960s and declined or remained steady in subsequent decades; see George K. Kieh, Jr., "Military Engagement in Politics in Africa," in George Klay Kieh, Jr., and Pita Ogaba Agbese, Eds., *The Military and Politics in Africa : From Intervention to Democratic and Constitutional Control* (Aldershot, Hants, England ; Burlington, VT : Ashgate, 2004), p. 46.

[33] For an overview of coups in Nigeria, see Chuka Onwumechili, *African Democratisation and Military Coups* (Westport, CT: Praeger, 1998), pp. 48-50.

[34] Robin Luckham, "Military Withdrawal from Politics in Africa Revisited," in Kieh, Jr., and Agbese, Eds., *The Military and Politics in Africa*, p. 96.

[35] On Rawlings' various paths into power, see Onwumechili, *African Democratisation and Military Coups* p. 27.

[36] This doctrine was enunciated by President James Monroe in his 1823 State of the Union message; for relevant sections, consult Robert H. Holden and Eric Zolov, Eds., *Latin America and the United States : A Documentary History* (New York: Oxford University Press, 2000), pp. 11-14.

[37] Discussions of the state of federalism in Nigeria may be found in Rotimi T. Suberu, "Nigeria: Dilemmas of Federalism," in Ugo M. Amoretti and Nancy Bermeo, Eds., *Federalism and Territorial Cleavages* (Baltimore, Md. : Johns Hopkins University Press, 2004), pp. 327-354 and the same author's *Federalism and Ethnic Conflict in Nigeria* (Washington, DC: US Institute of Peace Press, 2001).

[38] Lovejoy, "Historical Setting," p. 68.

[39] Oyewole, *Historical Dictionary of Nigeria*, p. 145.

[40] Petrowealth has led to major corruption among Nigerian leaders, who may have stolen or misused $400 billion in government funds over the past

four decades; for a representative story, see Lydia Polgreen, "As Nigeria Tries to Fight Graft, a New Sordid Tale," *The New York Times* (November 29, 2005).

[41] Part of the growth of indigenous forms of English may be the challenge of translating thought into English; these challenges in the case of transforming Yoruba thought into English is described by the poet Niyi Osundare, *Thread in the Loom : Essays on African Literature and Culture* (Trenton, NJ : Africa World Press, 2002), pp. 115-131.

[42] On Nigerian English generally, consult Ayo Banjo, "The Sociolinguistics of English in Nigeria and the ICE Project," in Sidney Greenbaum, Ed., *Comparing English Worldwide : The International Corpus of English* (Oxford and New York: Clarendon Press and Oxford University Press, 1996), pp. 239-244; Ayo Bamgbose, "Standard Nigerian English: Issues of Identification," in Braj B. Kachru, *The Other Tongue: English Across Cultures* (Urbana, IL: University of Illinois Press, 1992), pp. 148-161.

[43] This interview took place on April 14, 1996.

[44] Ms. Phumzile Mlambo-Ngcuka has been South Africa's Deputy President since June 22, 2005.

CHAPTER 8

SHARIACRACY AND FEDERAL MODELS OF CHANGE: NIGERIA IN COMPARATIVE PERSPECTIVE

I n May 1999 a new President was sworn into office in Nigeria -- the first elected civilian President of Nigeria since the military coup of 1983. Retired General Olusegun Obasanjo was also the first *non-Muslim* to be popularly elected President nation-wide since Nigeria's independence.[1]

Nigeria has the largest concentration of Muslims on the African continent. It has more Muslims than any <u>Arab</u> country, including Egypt. [2] Approximately fifteen months after Olusegun Obasanjo became President, some predominantly Muslim states in the Nigerian federation started to take steps towards implementing the Sharia in their own states, although the country as a whole is constitutionally supposed to be a secular republic.[3] This has caused consternation among non-Muslim Nigerians. Indeed, in Kaduna state, Christian consternation exploded into inter-communal riots which cost hundreds of lives in the year 2000.[4] But the momentum for SHARIACRACY still continues.

Globalisation and Islamic Revivalism

Many different reasons have been advanced for the rise of Sharia advocacy and Sharia implementation in Northern Nigeria. One explanation is that the Nigerian federation is getting more decentralized, and part of the decentralization is taking the form of cultural self-determination. In Yorubaland this cultural self-determination is taking the form of Yoruba nationalism. In Igboland it is taking the form of new demands for confederation. In the Muslim North cultural self-determination is taking the form of *Shariacracy*.

Another explanation for the rise of Sharia militancy is to regard it as a political bargaining chip. As the North is losing political influence in the Nigerian federation, it is asserting new forms of autonomy in preparation for a new national compact among contending forces.[5]

What has not been discussed is whether the rise of Sharia militancy is itself a consequence of globalisation. One of the repercussions of globalisation worldwide has been to arouse cultural insecurity and uncertainty about identities. Indeed, the paradox of globalisation is that it both promotes enlargement of economic scale and stimulates fragmentation of ethnic and cultural scale.[6]

The enlargement of economic scale is illustrated by the rise of the European Union, and by the North American Free Trade Agreement (NAFTA). The fragmentation of cultural and ethnic scale is illustrated by the disintegration of the Soviet Union, the collapse of Czechoslovakia into two countries, the rise of Hindu fundamentalism in India and Islamic fundamentalism in Afghanistan, the collapse of Somalia after penetration by the Soviet Union and the United States, and the reactivation of genocidal behaviour among the Hutu and Tutsi in Rwanda and Burundi.

Since globalisation is a special scale of Westernisation, it has triggered off identity crises from Uzbekistan to Somalia, from Afghanistan to Northern Nigeria. Fragile ethnic identities and endangered cultures are forced into new forms of resistance. Resisting Westernisation becomes indistinguishable from resisting globalisation. In Nigeria the South is part of the vanguard of Westernisation and therefore the first to respond to globalisation. When, in addition, the South appears to be politically triumphant within Nigeria, alarm bells are sounded in parts of the North. This may not necessarily be Northern distrust of Yoruba or Igbo cultures. It may be Northern distrust of Westernisation. Is Southern Nigeria a Trojan horse for globalisation? And is globalisation in turn a Trojan horse for Westernisation?

The Sharia under this paradigm becomes a form of Northern resistance, not to Southern Nigeria, but to the forces of globalisation and to their Westernising consequences.[7] Even the policy of privatisation of public enterprises is probably an aspect of the new global zing ideology. Privatisation in Nigeria may either lead to new transnational corporations establishing their roots or to private Southern entrepreneurs outsmarting Northerners and deepening the economic divide between North and South. Again the Sharia may be a Northern gut response to these looming clouds of globalisation.

In Nigeria the Sharia is caught between the forces of federal democratisation and the forces of wider globalisation. What are the complexities of globalisation and the intricacies of democratic federalism?

Globalisation: Economic and Cultural

Two forms of globalisation have affected Nigeria in contradictory ways -- economic globalisation, on the one hand, and cultural globalisation, on the other. The forces of economic globalisation in the world as a whole have deepened the marginalisation of Nigeria. The forces of cultural globalisation, on the other hand, have substantially penetrated and assimilated much of Nigeria.

On attainment of independence the economic marginalisation of Nigeria was partly due to the fact that colonialism had created an elite of consumption rather than an elite of productivity. The post-colonial Nigerian elite was more adept at making money than at creating wealth. Money could be made in a network of capital transfers without generating genuine growth. The Nigerian elite had learnt the techniques of circulating money without a talent for creating new wealth.[8]

The colonial impact in Nigeria had generated urbanization without industrialization, had fostered Western consumption patterns without Western productive techniques, had cultivated among Nigerians Western tastes without Western skills, had initiated secularisation without the scientific spirit. The stage was set for the marginalisation of Nigeria in the era of globalisation.

Optimists had hoped that petroleum would enable Nigeria to join the more prosperous forces of globalisation. Following the dramatic rise of the Organization of Petroleum Exporting Countries in the 1970s, Nigeria became the fifth largest producer of petroleum in the world.[9] Yet the nature of the elite of consumption, and the shortage of relevant skills, plunged the Nigerian economy into mismanagement, corruption and debt. Long lines at petrol stations and recurrent shortages of fuel were the order of the day. Commercial activity was often disrupted by shortages of petroleum products like diesel, kerosene, cooking gas, and other commodities. The giant of Africa was in danger of becoming the midget of the world. Africa's Gulliver faced the threat of becoming the Lilliput of the globe.

On the other hand, cultural globalisation had indeed substantially co-opted Nigeria to its ranks. Southern Nigeria especially has demonstrated remarkable receptivity to the forces of cultural globalisation through Westernisation. Although Christianity arrived in India eighteen centuries before it arrived in what is today Nigeria, the population of Christians in India is still little more than two per cent (2.5 %) whereas the population of Christians in Nigeria is over thirty-five per cent.[10] In one century Christianity made more headway in Southern Nigeria than it has done in India in nearly two thousand years.

At least for a while, Nigeria has also been deeply receptive to Western education. By the beginning of the twenty-first century, Nigeria had exported proportionally more highly educated personnel to the United States than had any other country in the world. Of all the new immigrants to the United States, the Nigerians had the highest proportion of graduates.[11] The great majority of these immigrant Nigerians were Igbo, Yoruba and other southerners.

In addition to religion and education as forces of cultural globalisation, there has also been the impact of major European languages as international media of communication. In the case of Nigeria, the impact of the English language has been relatively profound. Nigeria has produced its own simplified version of English (Pidgin) as a grassroots lingua franca.[12] But standard English has made great strides -- producing such world-class literary figures as Chinua Achebe, Wole Soyinka, J.P. Clark and the late Christopher Okigbo. The great majority of Nigeria's great writers in the English language are Southerners -- complete with the Nobel Literary Laureate, Wole Soyinka. Once again Nigeria has shown great receptivity to cultural globalisation in a European idiom.

If in global terms Nigeria as a whole was economically on the periphery, northern Nigeria was the periphery of the periphery. The world economy had marginalised Nigeria as a country. The Nigerian economy had marginalised the North as a region. In spite of the fact that Northern soldiers had ruled Nigeria for so long since independence, the nation's economic elite was much larger in the south than in the north. The oil wealth and related industries were disproportionately located in the South. The Southern elite was, on the whole, more adept at making money than their northern counterparts.[13]

One of the triggers of the Shariacracy movement in some Northern states was Northern resentment of being the periphery of the periphery. When the North held political power, Northerners could more easily accept their economic marginality. But the Federal elections of 1999 shifted political power to the South without reducing the economic marginality of the North. The politics of Shariacracy were in part a protest against regional economic inequalities.[14]

But what is *Shariacracy?* We define it as *governance according to the norms, principles and rules laid down by Islamic law*. Under British colonial rule, the Sharia was implemented for Muslims in the domain of family law and certain areas of civil suit. But the *kadhis* (or Muslim judges and magistrates) were not normally authorized to administer the criminal side of Islamic law. In each British colony in Africa with a large Muslim population there was triple heritage of law -- indigenous, Islamic and British-derived. Criminal law tended to be British-derived with suitable imperial and colonial amendments.[15] However, issues like marriage, divorce, inheritance, succession and certain forms of property could be subject to either the Sharia or African customary law.

The Sharia is therefore nothing new in Northern Nigeria. What is new is <u>Shariacracy</u> -- the adoption of the Sharia as the foundation of governance and its expansion into the domain of the criminal justice system.

While Northern Nigerians have deeply minded being economically marginal, they have <u>NOT</u> minded being culturally authentic. Partly because of Islam and partly because of Lord Lugard's policy of Indirect Rule during the colonial period, the Hausa-Fulani have been far less receptive to Westernisation than the Southerners have been. To that extent Northern Nigeria had in any case remained more culturally authentic and less penetrated by the West even without the adoption of the Sharia law.[16]

However, the new globalisation in Southern Nigeria was bound to sound cultural alarm bells in the North. In the colonial era Lord Lugard had kept Christianity at bay in the North through the shield of Indirect Rule.[17] Post-colonial politicians in Northern states are seeking to keep globalisation at bay through the shield of the Sharia.

If modernization is a higher phase of Westernisation, and globalisation is a higher phase of modernization, the stage is now being set for new kinds of normative responses. Against economic marginalisation the Sharia is a form of passionate protest. Against encroaching globalisation the Sharia is cultural resistance to Westernisation. Northern Nigeria is engaged in both protest and resistance through the medium of the Sharia.

156

Ordinary people in Africa are often ignorant of Western-derived law; but if they are Muslims they have some prior familiarity with the Sharia. Courts of law in post-colonial African countries south of the Sahara use primarily the European imperial language for adjudication, argument, verdict, and sentencing. The legal concepts and principles invoked are in English, French, Portuguese or Latin, as the case may be. The defendant may be quite ignorant of the particular European language as he or she stands in the dock, and terms like 'accessory before the fact' or *mutates mutandis* are often beyond the comprehension of the average defendant or plaintiff in post-colonial Africa. Debates which go on between the lawyers in a Western-style courtroom in Africa are almost literally "double-Dutch" to the accused.

An Islamic court in sub-Saharan Africa, on the other hand, normally uses the language of the particular community within which the Court operates. An Islamic court in Zanzibar or in Mombasa, Kenya, is likely to use Kiswahili; while an Islamic Court in Northern Nigeria uses Hausa. The Qur'an and the written parts of the Sharia may indeed remain in Arabic, but the legal discourse in the Court is conducted mainly in the relevant African language.[18]

What is more, many of the basic phrases in the Sharia might already have entered the indigenous languages of African Muslims -- Arabic words like harem (forbidden), halal (permissible), riba (usury), zina (adultery), and hukumu (judgment) have already entered the Swahili language.[19] Many of such legal and moral terms drawn from the Sharia, have also been assimilated into Hausa. The gulf which separates the language of lawyers from the language of everyday life is much narrower in a post-colonial Muslim legal system than under a Westernised African judicial order.

Asymmetrical Federalism: Global Perspectives

If Nigeria is a secular federation, can some constituent states nevertheless be theocratic? Is national secularism compatible with official religions at the state-level?

This raises the issue of whether federations are viable if the constituent states are *asymmetrical* in their constitutional systems. Quebec in Canada has been demanding treatment as a distinct society. If Islamic law in Nigeria risks discriminating against non-Muslim Nigerians, language policy in Quebec risks discriminating against English-speaking Canadians. There is a built-in asymmetry in the

Canadian federation when one province can give the French language special status while the rest of the country is primarily English-speaking. The French language is the 'Sharia' of Quebec.[20]

Comparable asymmetry exists in the Indian Federation in which the de facto status of the Hindi language differs between Northern states and Southern states, although both Hindi and English are *de jure* national languages.

The United Kingdom virtually invented asymmetry as a constitutional order. Scotland has had its own law, its own currency and more recently its own regional assembly under Tony Blair in the 1990s. On the other hand, Northern Ireland has had a separate regional assembly long before either Wales or Scotland. As for England, it has no separate regional assembly distinct from the national parliament of the whole country. In short, the United Kingdom has never tried to have symmetrical constitutional arrangements for its main constituent regions (England, Scotland, Wales and Northern Ireland).[21]

For much of the nineteenth and twentieth centuries Scotland was the "Zamfara state" of the United Kingdom. Zamfara in Nigeria in the twentieth century had turned to Islamic law. Scotland much earlier had turned for guidance to Roman law, as developed by the jurists of France and Holland. The legal practices and judicial institutions of Scotland were very different from those of England at that time. The law of Scotland was not based on Roman law, but there was considerable infusion of Roman principles into it.

Like Zamfara, Scotland not only had a separate legal system from the rest of the country; like Zamfara Scotland also declared allegiance to a different religion. Zamfara in the twenty-first century had turned to Sunni Islam; Scotland continued its allegiance to a separate Church of Scotland (Presbyterian) in 1707. A separate Scottish church and a separate Scottish legal and judicial system have continued to the present day, although Scottish law has borrowed a good deal from English law in more recent times.[22]

Alongside the constitutional asymmetry, some degree of national integration was taking place among the constituent regions of the United Kingdom. The whole country was getting Anglicised and "Britishised" into a relatively coherent whole. Similarly, the decision of Zamfara, Kano and other Northern states in Nigeria to go Islamic need not be incompatible with the wider process of Nigerianisation and national integration.

A less enduring asymmetry was the ban on alcoholic drinks in the history of the United States. Initially prohibition of alcohol was by individual states. The first state law against alcohol was passed in Maine in 1850, and was soon followed by a wave of comparable legislation in other states. This was followed by two other waves of laws at various state levels.[23]

Meanwhile, a campaign for alcoholic prohibition at the Federal level had been gathering momentum. A constitutional amendment against alcohol needed a two-thirds majority in Congress and approval by three quarters of the states. Such a constitutional change was ratified on January 29, 1919, and went into effect on January 29, 1920, as the Eighteenth Amendment of the United States' constitution.[24]

Just as the Sharia in Nigeria can only work where there is popular support for it, the Eighteenth Amendment of the United States only worked where public opinion was genuinely for temperance and against alcohol. Prohibition at the federal level created resentment among those states which were not against alcoholic drinks, and in large cities in the United States where alcohol had long become a way of life.[25]

Bootlegging emerged as a new kind of crime -- the most dramatic embodiment of which was Al Capone and his bootlegging gang (illicit alcohol underground) operating from Chicago. Prohibition at the federal level created more problems than it solved. In less than fifteen years the United States was ready to repeal the Eighteenth Amendment. In February 1933 Congress adopted a resolution proposing a new constitutional amendment to that effect. On December 5, 1933, Utah cast the 36th ratifying vote in favour of the Twenty-first Amendment. At the federal level alcohol was legal again.[26]

A few states in the Union continued to be "dry states", and chose to maintain a statewide ban. But the disenchantment which the Federal-level prohibition had created adversely affected attitudes to temperance even in those states which had once led the way in favour of prohibition. It is arguable that prohibition at the state-level might have lasted much longer if the original asymmetry (some states for and some states against) had been respected and allowed to continue.

The Eighteenth Constitutional Amendment was a pursuit of national symmetry in American attitudes to alcohol. The Eighteenth Amendment sought a premature national moral consensus on alcohol -- and thereby hurt the cause of temperance in the country as a whole.

By 1966 virtually all the fifty states of the Union had legalized alcoholic drinks -- though some preferred that drinking be restricted to homes and private clubs rather than be served in public bars and saloons.

The most controversial elements of the Sharia are the *hudud,* Islamic punishments for criminal offenders. In a federation like Nigeria do different punishments for the same offence in different states violate the principle of "equal protection before the law"? Saudi Arabia has been known to put to death even a Princess on charges of adultery. Zamfara has not invoked the death penalty for adultery and fornication. But this Nigerian state has flogged an unmarried girl on the evidence of her pregnancy. [27] More famous perhaps was the death penalty imposed on a pregnant woman (Amina Lawal) on charges of adultery. Adultery can be a capital offence under Islamic Law. Appeals for clemency from the rest of the Muslim world probably saved Amina Lawal's life.[28]

Such punishments are too severe and ought to be reconsidered in the light of *ijtihad*. But this chapter focuses on the implications of having differing punishments within states for the same offence. Is such a situation a denial of "equal protection before the law"?

It is in the nature of federalism that some laws are state laws and some are federal enactments. Therefore some offences would be state offences and others federal felonies. The state offences are bound to differ from state to state.

But can there really be "equal protection before the law" when a citizen can be subject to the death penalty in one state and have a light sentence in another state for the same offence? In reality a similar asymmetry has been persistent in the United States. First, there is the fact that the death penalty has been abolished or ceased to be carried out in some American states and not in others. Texas is the leading executioner-state in the Union; Massachusetts has no death penalty at all. New York State had no capital punishment when Mario Cuomo was Governor, but has now reinstated the death penalty under Governor George Pataki.

Even more controversial are the following twin-questions: Can the death penalty be applied to mentally retarded offenders? Can it be carried out on young offenders whose crimes were committed when they were still minors? Some states have said "YES" to both questions -- "kill them!" Surprising as it may seem, the U.S. Supreme Court ruled in 1989 that it was perfectly constitutional to execute the mentally retarded or young offenders whose offences were committed when they were minors. In *Penry v. Lynaugh* (1989), the Court ruled that execution of a "mildly to moderately retarded" person did not violate the Eighth Amendment (cruel and unusual punishment); and in *Stanford v. Kentucky* (1989) the Court ruled that the Eighth Amendment did not prohibit the death penalty for a defendant who was 16 or 17 years old at the time of committing the crime. [29]

Twelve years later, in the year 2001, the issue of executing the mentally retarded was back before the U.S. Supreme Court with the case of a convicted killer whose mental capacity is that of a seven year old. The U.S. Supreme Court had previously said it was constitutional to execute this very offender, but new considerations brought the case back to the Court. In June 2002, the Court in Atkins v. Virginia held "it is a violation of the Eighth Amendment ban on cruel unusual punishment to execute death row inmates with mental retardation.[30] Behind it all is a nation still divided on the death penalty with some states upholding it and others rejecting it as 'cruel and unusual punishment.'

What all this means is that federalism is able to accommodate a lack of constitutional symmetry even when the areas of disagreement are about matters of life and death. The <u>hudud</u> in Nigeria and Sudan include matters of life and death. So does the debate about capital punishment in the United States.

Can God's Law be Reviewed?

To Nigerian Muslims the Sharia is an *alternative* paradigm of judicial order and law enforcement. Inherited colonial traditions of law enforcement and social responsibility are not working in the country as a whole.

One solution is to go back to ancestry. For Muslim Nigerians there are two ancient systems: African law and the Sharia. African customary law was unwritten and uncodified. Did it allow the judge too much discretion? The Sharia is ancient and firmly rooted in sacred scriptures. Is it allowing the judge too little discretion? Muslim Nigerians have preferred too little discretion rather than too much.

To Muslims, the Sharia is God's law. But it is God's law as interpreted by human beings/'man'. Here on earth there is no such thing as a law which is independent of human interpretation. God's law is infallible, but its human interpreters are not.

161

Africa was the first asylum of persecuted Islam—the pre-Hijjra hijra to Ethiopia of Islamized Arabs on the run from Mecca. Will Africa be the final asylum of the Sharia under persecution by materialism, secularism, Westernisation, globalisation and ungodliness everywhere else in the world?

Nascent Islam in the seventh century of the Christian era found refuge in the rising plateaus of Ethiopia. Will mature but harassed Islam in the twenty first century of the Christian era find asylum in the grazing fields of Muslim Nigeria?

This would be a great responsibility for Nigerian Muslims, for they would be mortals entrusted with immortal law. What is crucial is that human interpreters should not act as if they were in direct communication with Allah. Humans should always allow for their own fallibility in interpreting the Sharia.

For the Sharia to survive in Nigeria the door of *ijtihad*, or judicial review, would have to be reopened. Without saying so in so many words, the doors of *ijtihad* in Sunni Islam have in fact been closed for nearly a thousand years.[31] They were wide open during the days of the Prophet and the first four Caliphs. But the consolidation of the four Sunni Schools into *madhahib* effectively closed the doors of judicial review. [32] The question which now arises is whether Africa will eventually be the place which holds the key to the doors of *ijitihad*. And will Nigeria lead the way?

Will the Sharia survive the Governors who first initiated it in Northern Nigeria? Is the Sharia in Nigeria to stay? One scenario is that it will stay but not necessarily in the form in which it was first implemented. The doors of ijtihad may reopen through fresh *fatwa*, new legal interpretations of God's law.

Few public *ulamaa* today would openly proclaim that *slavery* is compatible with Islam, although slavery was tolerated in the Prophet's own time and long afterwards. Scholars like Taha Jaber Alalwani have given learned *fatwa* that many of the sayings of the Prophet, and some verses of the Quran, showed that Islam was in favour of emancipation. Islam was clearly in favour freeing individual slaves, but was Islam in favour of abolishing the institution of slavery?

Thirteen centuries before William Wilberforce and Abraham Lincoln, Islam was on the verge of evolving from being pro-emancipation of individual slaves to being pro-abolition of slavery. What interrupted this Islam's symphony of freedom was the historical accident that the Arabs went monarchical and royalist after the assassination of Caliph Ali Ibn Abi Talib. The royalization of the Arabs under the Umayyads and the Abbasids gave class and status among Muslims a new lease of life. Slavery became part of the interplay between servitude and privilege in the succeeding millennium of Muslim history. A new *ijtihad* against servitude, a new *fatwa* against slavery, had to await the <u>ulamaa</u> of the twentieth century.[33]

Similarly a new *ijtihad* is needed about the death penalty for adultery and amputation of the hand for stealing. These Islamic punishments were first introduced when societies had no police force, no forensic science, nor criminologists or psychiatrists about the causes of crime.

If all Muslim governments agreed today that amputating the hand of a thief is wrong, and the Prophet Muhammed had said, "My people will never agree on error", then the new Muslim consensus will outlaw amputation as punishment.

If the whole *ummah* finally agreed that the death penalty for fornication or adultery is no longer acceptable, that would mean that the *ummah* had reached consensus (*ijma*). And the Prophet had said "My people will not agree on error." Both *ijtihad* and *ijma* can be sources of fundamental legal review.[34]

Conclusion

The globalisation of the world economy has left Nigeria and much of the rest of Africa marginalised. Most Nigerians have been casualties of international capitalism rather than genuine partners or beneficiaries.

Cultural globalisation, on the other hand, has found ready receptivity in Nigeria. Large parts of the country were rapidly Christianised, and the English language developed a Nigerian dialect.

An earlier phase of cultural globalisation was Westernisation. Nigeria inherited a legal system based primarily on British law and the English judicial traditions. Moreover, the language of interpreting the Western-derived law and the Constitution was the imperial language, English.

If Nigeria as a whole was a periphery of the world economic system, Northern Nigeria was economically a periphery of the periphery. But this economic marginalisation of the North was for a while camouflaged by the fact that Northerners held political power. After General Olusegun Obasanjo was elected president in 1999, the political decline of the North exposed more mercilessly the North's economic marginality. The Shariacracy initiative by some Northern states is in part a protest against economic marginalisation, and in part a defence against unwanted cultural globalisation.

Nigeria is the only African country outside Arab Africa which has seriously debated an alternative to the Western constitutional and legal inheritance. In part, this is what the debate about Shariacracy is all about. It is an exploration of an alternative to the Western legacy. But Nigeria may need to use ijtihad as a process of reviewing the Sharia. After all, the Sharia is God's law as interpreted by fallible human beings.

Another problem posed by the Sharia debate is whether a federal system is able to support cultural self-determination of its constituent parts and still retain cohesion as a federation. Switzerland has conceded cultural autonomy to its constituent cantons, but in terms of *language* (German, French and Italian). [35] Initially, the Nigerian federation allowed for neither linguistic nor religious self-determination at the state level. What the Shariacracy debate has opened up is the possibility that religion, rather than language, could be the basis of cultural differentiation in an asymmetrical constitutional order.

Nigeria has the largest concentration of Muslims on the African continent. The population of Nigeria, as we indicated, encompasses more Muslims than the population of any Arab country, including Egypt. But can the Sharia be implemented at the state level without compromising secularism at the federal level? [36]

We have tried to demonstrate that in terms of theories of asymmetrical federalism, such a paradox of state theocracy combined with federal secularism is feasible. But it would only work if both political power and economic prosperity were more evenly distributed between North and South, and when globalisation in the wider world became more compatible with Nigeria's national well-being. No wonder there are voices sincerely pleading for the postponement of Shariacracy. In the name of Nigerian unity, should the Sharia be a dream deferred?

NOTES

[1] For a report, see *The Washington Post* (May 30, 2000), p. 1.

[2] Nearly 50 percent of the estimated 128 million Nigerians are estimated to be Muslims; see Arthur S. Banks and Thomas C. Muller, eds., *Political Handbook of the World, 1999* (Binghamton, NY: CSA Publications, 1999) p. 723, and *The World Guide 1999/2000* (Oxford, UK: New Internationalist Publications, 1999), p. 429.

[3] For a list of these states, consult *Africa Research Bulletin* 37,8 (September 22, 2000), p. 14077.

[4] See the reports in *The Guardian* (February 22, 2000), p. 1 and *Christian Science Monitor* (May 26, 2000), p. 1.

[5] An overview of the North-South and other cleavages bedeviling Nigeria may be found in *The Economist* (January 15, 2000), pp. 14-15; also see *The Economist* (July 8, 2000), p. 47. For longer analyses on earlier conflicts caused by the Sharia issue, see Toyin Falola, *Violence in Nigeria: The Crisis of Religious Politics and Secular Ideologies* (Rochester, NY: University of Rochester Press, 1998), especially pp. 77-113; Simeon O. Ilesanmi, *Religious Pluralism and the Nigerian State* (Athens, OH: Ohio University Center for International Studies, 1997), pp. 174-207; M. H. Kukah and Toyin Falola, *Religious Militancy and Self-Assertion: Islam and Politics in Nigeria* (Aldershot, UK, and Brookfield, VT: Avebury Press, 1996), pp. 117-139; and Pat A. T. Williams, "Religion, Violence, and Displacement in Nigeria," *Journal of Asian and African Studies*, 32, 1-2 (June 1997), pp. 33-49.

[6] Consult, relatedly Benjamin Barber, *Jihad Vs. McWorld*.(New York: Times Books, 1995).

[7] For an earlier example, consult Abdullah Mu'aza Saulawa, "Islam and its Anti-Colonial and Educational Contribution in West Africa and Northern Nigeria, 1800-1960," *Hamdard Islamicus* (1996), 19,1, pp. 69-79 and Falola, *Violence in Nigeria*, pp. 74-77.

[8] Much of the fruits of Nigerian development were stolen by the elite; see A. A. Nwankwo, *Nigeria: The Stolen Billions* (Enugu, Nigeria: Fourth Dimension Publishing, 1999).

[9] By the end of the 1990s, Nigeria produced about 931 million metric tons of oil, about 2.9 percent of world output; see John B. Ejobowah, "Who Owns the Oil: The Politics of Ethnicity in the Niger Delta of Nigeria, *Africa Today* 47

(Winter 2000), p. 37; also see Sarah Ahmed Khan, *Nigeria: The Political Economy of Oil* (Oxford: Oxford University Press for the Oxford Institute of Energy Studies, 1994).

[10] The figure for India is drawn from a report in *U. S. News & World Report* (January 25, 1999), p. 40, while the figure for Nigeria is drawn from Banks and Muller, *The Political Handbook of the World*, p. 723.

[11] Some interesting research on African immigrants to the United States is contained in Yanyi K. Djamba, "African Immigrants in the United States of America: Socio-Demographic Profile in Comparison to Native Blacks," *Journal of Asian and African Studies* 34, 2 (June 1999), p. 210-215.

[12] On Nigerian English, see Ayo Bamgbose, "Post-Imperial English in Nigeria, 1940-1990," in Joshua A. Fishman, Andrew Conrad and Alma Rubal-Lopez, eds., *Post-Imperial English: Status Change in Former British and American Colonies, 1940-1990* (Berlin and New York: Mouton de Gruyter, 1996) pp. 357-372; and on regional variations, consult V. O. Awonusi, "Regional Accents and Internal Variability in Nigerian English: A Historical Analysis," *English Studies* 67 (December 1986), pp. 555-560.

[13] See, for instance, Minabere Ibelema, "Nigeria: The Politics of Marginalisation," *Current History* 99, 637 (May 2000), p. 213.

[14] This resentment did have precedents in the 1970s and 1980s; see Roman Loimeier, *Islamic Reform and Political Change in Northern Nigeria* (Evanston, IL: Northwestern University Press, 1997), pp. 9-10.

[15] This was due to the British discomfort with some of the harsher aspects of Islamic criminal punishment; see Kukah and Falola, *Religious Militancy and Self-Assertion,* pp. 39-41.

[16] See Michael Crowder, "Lugard and Colonial Nigeria: Towards an Identity," *History Today* 36 (February 1986), pp. 23-29.

[17] Consult Pat Williams and Toyin Falola, *Religious Impact on the Nation State: The Nigerian Predicament* (Aldershot, UK and Brookfield, VT: Avebury Press, 1995), pp. 16-17.

[18] For an introduction to Islamic law, see, for example, R. Gleavy and E. Kermeli, eds., *Islamic Law: Theory and Practice* (London and New York: I. B. Tauris, 1997).

[19] Relatedly, consult Ali A. Mazrui and Pio Zirimu, "The Secularization of an Afro-Islamic Language: Church, State and Marketplace in the Spread of Kiswahili," in Ali A. Mazrui and Alamin A. Mazrui, *The Power of Babel: Language and Governance in the African Experience* (Oxford, Nairobi, Kampala, Cape Town, Chicago: James Currey, E.A.E.P, Fountain, David Philip, and the University of Chicago Press, 1998), pp. 169-171.

[20] Relatedly, for an interesting comparative work, see Amilcar A. Barretto, *Language, Elites, and the State: Nationalism in Puerto Rico and Quebec* (Westport, CT: Praeger, 1998).

[21] For an assessment of devolution in the United Kingdom, consult Jonathan Bradbury and James Mitchell, "Devolution: New Politics for Old?" *Parliamentary Affairs* (April 2001), pp. 257-275.

[22] A discussion on the origins and development of Scottish national consciousness and constitutional developments may be found in Robert McCreadie, "Scottish Identity and the Constitution," in Bernard Crick, ed., *National Identities: The Constitution of the United Kingdom* (Cambridge, MA and Oxford, UK: Blackwell Publishers, 1991), pp. 38-56.

[23] See K. Austin Kerr, *Organizing for Prohibition: A New History of the Anti-Saloon League* (New Haven and London: Yale University Press, 1985), p. 335.

[24] Consult Thomas M. Coffey, *The Long Thirst: Prohibition in America 1920-1933* (New York: W. W. Norton & Co., 1975) and Kerr, *Organizing for Prohibition*, p. 185.

[25] Kerr, Organizing for Prohibition, pp. 275-279.

[26] Coffey, *The Long Thirst*, p. 315.

[27] However, the three men who the woman said had coerced her into having sex went unpunished; see *The Guardian* (January 23, 2001), p. 16.

[28] See relatedly O. U. Kalu, "Safiyya and Adamah: Punishing Adultery with Sharia Stones in Twenty-first Century Nigeria," *African Affairs* (2003), Volume 102, No. 408, pp. 389-408. It should be noted that the sentences of stoning have never been carried out. Even in the most prominent case, that of Amina Lawal, the case against her was flawed and she may not have been in any danger of being executed at all, even under the Shariah. See the opinion piece by Helon Habila, "The Politics of Islamic Law: Shariah in Nigeria," *The International Herald Tribune*, (October 7, 2003).

[29] These and other significant Supreme Court death penalty cases are discussed in Barry Latzer, *Death Penalty Cases: Leading U. S. Supreme Court Cases on Capital Punishment* (Boston, Oxford, et al: Butterworth-Heinemann, 1998).

[30] The justices, in a 6-3 ruling that reversed a 1989 decision, said that imposing the death penalty on retarded criminals violated their constitutional protection against cruel and unusual punishment. For an analysis, see Thomas G. Walker, "Capital punishment and the Mentally Retarded: Atkins v. Virginia (2002)," in Gregg Ivers and Kevin T. McGuire, Eds., *Creating Constitutional Change : Clashes Over Power and Liberty in the Supreme Court* (Charlottesville, VA: University of Virginia Press, 2004), pp. 281-294.

[31] On *ijtihad*, see H. H. A. Rahman, "The Origin and Development of *Ijtihad* to Solve Complex Modern Legal Problems," *Bulletin of the Henry Martyn Institute of Islamic Studies* 17 (January-June 1998), pp. 7-21.

[32] Consult Frank E. Vogel, "The Closing of the Door of *Ijtihad* and the Application of the Law," *American Journal of Islamic Social Sciences* 10 (Fall 1993), pp. 396-401.

[33] For a discussion on Islam and slavery, consult John R. Willis, *Slaves and Slavery in Muslim Africa: Volume I: Islam and the Ideology of Slavery* (Totowa, NJ and London: Frank Cass, 1985).

[34] On *ijma*, see M. N. Khan, "*Ijma*: Third Source of Islamic Law," *Hamdard Islamicus* 22 (January 1999), pp. 84-86.

[35] Even the vaunted Swiss system is not a perfect model; consult, for instance, Clive Church, "Switzerland: A Paradigm in Evolution," *Parliamentary Affairs* 53, 1 (January 2000), pp. 96-113.

[36] Both religion and ethnicity are challenging aspects to developing a satisfactory Nigerian federal sytem; for an account of the development of various Nigerian federal systems and the challenges, see Martin Dent, "Nigeria: Federalism and Ethnic Rivalry," *Parliamentary Affairs* 53, 1 (January 2000), pp. 157-168.

CHAPTER 9

ISLAM IN WEST AFRICA AND THE UNITED STATES: A POLITICAL COMPARISON

Between Demography and Divinity

T he total population of West Africa as a whole is less than the population of the United States, but West Africa is closing the gap. The population of the Unites States is now approximately 280 million. The population of West Africa (partly depending upon where one draws the line) is in the region of 230 million.

The total population of Muslims in the United States has sometimes been estimated to be as high as the total population of the Republic of Niger, that is, about ten million. But it seems more likely that the Muslims of the United States are only seven million, although the number is growing all the time.[1]

Islam and Christianity in West Africa are rival religions, competing for the soul of Africa, as well as for influence and power. In the United States it is Muslims and Jews, rather than Muslims and Christians who are rivals. But the Judeo-Muslim rivalry in the United States is not for American religious souls; it is for American political minds.

Most American Christians feel closer to American Jews than they feel to American Muslims, but the Muslims are beginning to close the gap.

In domestic policies Bill Clinton was the most Muslim-friendly President in the history of the United States. And yet in the elections of the year 2000 the great majority of American Muslims voted for the Republican George W. Bush, rather than for Clinton's former Vice-President, Al Gore.[2] We shall return to this anomaly later, after we have examined more broadly the African context of political Islam.

Muslim empowerment in Africa is sometimes unexpected when it occurs. Nobody in Malawi expected that Dr. Kamuzu Hastings Banda, Elder of the Church of Scotland, who had ruled the country for so long with an iron hand, would one day be defeated in an election by a Muslim, Dr. Bakali Muluzi.[3]

In Sierra Leone prolonged rule by non-Muslims finally resulted in chaos and war. Out of the chaos the country turned for the first time to a Muslim President, Ahmed T. Kabbah. Unfortunately, the chaos and the war were too far-gone to be ended by a mere electoral change.[4]

My own country, Kenya, does not stand a chance of producing a Muslim President in the near future, although each of Kenya's immediate neighbours has had a Muslim head of state at some time or another. (Tanzania, Uganda, Somalia, Sudan and even Ethiopia). These are the five countries with which Kenya shares borders.

With planning and effective coalition building a *Muslim Vice-President* of Kenya is entirely in the cards. After all, nobody during the days of either Kofi Busia or Kwame Nkrumah expected Ghana to produce a Muslim Vice-President. And yet, there he is today, Alhaji Aliu Mahama, Vice-President of Ghana after the years of Jerry Rawlings.

In both Africa and the United States it is not enough for Muslims to be merely citizens; they must also be *engaged* in the affairs of their nation.[5] Nor is it enough for Muslims to be voters in elections; they should seek public office and run for elections.[6]

Some African countries, which are overwhelmingly Muslim, have sometimes permitted a non-Muslim to be their President. The percentage of Muslims in Senegal is 94% -- higher than the percentage of Muslims in Egypt. Yet Senegal had a Roman Catholic President for 20 years: Leopold Sedar Senghor. This relatively open African society, overwhelmingly Muslim, could have a Christian President without cries of "JIHAD" in the streets of Dakar at any stage over a period of twenty years from 1960 to 1980.[7]

The Muslim minority in Ghana is at least three times the size of the Christian minority in Senegal in percentage terms, and much more numerous in absolute numbers than Christians in Senegal. Recent estimates of Ghana's Muslim population are up to 27% of the 18.5 million.[8] If coalition building in Senegal could produce a Christian President in an overwhelmingly Muslim country, coalition building in Ghana should produce a Muslim President in the foreseeable future. The clock is ticking.

The Statue of Libertarianism?

For American Muslims, one paradox is that the Republicans are stronger on traditional family values and are more opposed to sexual libertarianism. This draws many Muslims (especially immigrant Asians) to the Republican Party.[9] Most Muslims share Republican concerns against abortion and gay rights.[10]

The second paradox concerns the legacy of the Clinton Administration. We have mentioned that, while the Clinton administration was more pro-Israel than any other U.S. administration since Lyndon Johnson, this same Clinton administration had domestically made more friendly gestures towards U.S. Muslims than any previous administration. The Clinton years were a measure of the growing American acceptance of Islam in fits and starts. President Clinton regularly sent greetings to Muslims during the fast of Ramadan from 1996 onwards.

We should also note how Hillary Clinton hosted a celebration of Idd el Fitr (the Festival of the End of Ramadan) in the White House in April 1996 and 1998. Vice President Al Gore visited a mosque in the fall 1995. And the first Muslim chaplain to serve the 10,000 Muslims in the US armed forces was sworn in under Clinton's watch.[11] A Muslim was also appointed for the first time to be Ambassador of the United States.

President Clinton received in the White House a delegation of Arab Americans to discuss wide-ranging issues, domestic and international. We should refer especially to the National Security Advisor, Anthony Lake, receiving a delegation of Muslims (including Ali A. Mazrui) in 1996 to discuss the ramifications of the Bosnian crisis. However, the administration of President George W. Bush humiliated a Muslim delegation in the White House at the beginning of his administration.[12] Will Bush eventually take risks with a more Muslim-friendly policy? Clinton had a Muslim Under-Secretary Siddiqui in his government; Bush had an Arab American Spencer Abraham as Secretary of Energy. But Abraham is a Christian.

The Clinton gestures towards Muslims were sufficiently high profile that a hostile article in the *Wall Street Journal* in March 1996 raised the spectre of "Friends of Hamas in the White House," alleging that some of President Clinton's Muslim guests were friends of "Arab terrorists," and supporters of the Palestinian movement. The critic in the *Wall Street Journal* (Steve Emerson) had a long record of hostility towards U.S. Muslims. His television programme on PBS entitled, Jihad in America (1994), alleged that almost all terrorist activities by Muslims worldwide were partially funded by U.S. Muslims. President Clinton's friendly gestures to Muslims probably infuriated this self-appointed crusader of Islamophobia.[13] Also infuriating to an Islamophobe was the decision of the United States' Post Office under Clinton to issue its first Islamic postal stamp [EID MUBARAK] which was released in September 2001.

The third paradox facing U.S. Muslims is that in foreign policy the Republicans in U.S. history – at least until recently -- have been greater friends of Muslims than have Democrats. In domestic policies – in most areas -- the Democrats are probably more friendly to Muslims than the Republicans.

The fourth paradox concerns the two Islams in America: African-American and immigrant. As a political tradition, African Americans and, therefore, African American Muslims, feel closer to Democrats than to Republicans. In the United States Western secularism has protected minority religious groups by insisting on separation of church and state. That is a major reason why the Jews in the United States have been among the greatest defenders of the separation of church and state.[14] Any breach of that principle could lead to the imposition of some practices of the religious majority, like forcing Jewish children to participate in Christian prayers at school.[15]

In discussing the role of American Muslims *qua* Muslims (heirs of the Hijrah), we have to look more closely at their moral concerns in relation to American culture. Curiously enough, American secularism is indeed good news for Muslims in America. The bad news is the expanding arena of American *libertarianism* which has resulted in greater divergence in values. Secularism in the political process does indeed help to protect minority religions from the potential intrusive power of the Christian Right. On the other hand, expanding American libertarianism in such fields as sexual mores alarms both the Christian Right and Muslim traditionalists in the United States. Libertanism is what has eroded what American values have in common with Islamic values.[16]

These moral concerns in turn have consequences on how American Muslims relate to the wider political divide between Republicans and Democrats in both foreign and domestic policies.

From the 1990s more and more American Muslims have been registering to vote and seeking to influence candidates in elections.[17]

On such social issues as family values and sexual mores, Muslims often find themselves more in tune with Republican rhetoric and concerns. On the need for a more strict separation of church and state, which helps to protect religious minorities, it is the more liberal Democrats who offer a better protection to Muslims. Let us look at these contradictions more closely.

The First Amendment of the U.S. Constitution permits religious minorities to practice their religions in relative peace. Of course, like all doctrines, secularism has its fanatics who sometimes seek to degrade the sacred rather than permitting it. But at its best a secular state is a refuge of safety for minority religions. It is in that sense that American secularism is a friend of Muslims living in the United States.

But while secularism is a divorce from formal religion, Muslims see libertarianism as a dilution of spirituality. Libertarianism makes America less and less Islamic. One can be without a formal religion and still be deeply spiritual in a humanistic sense. John Stuart Mill and Bertrand Russell were without formal religion, yet each had deeply held spiritual values. Albert Schweitzer, the Nobel Laureate for Peace, was at times an agnostic but he was deeply committed to the principle of reverence for life, even protecting the lives of insects in Africa.[18]

Religion has been declining in influence in the West since the days of the Renaissance and the Enlightenment. But it was mainly in the 20th century that spirituality in the West took a nose-dive. From an Islamic perspective, America has become not only less religious, but dangerously less spiritual. America has become not only more secular but also dangerously more libertarian.[19]

It is the libertarianism which is regarded as a danger to Muslims living in the Western hemisphere. There is the libertarian materialism of excessive *acquisitiveness* (greed), libertarian consumption (consumerism), the materialism of the *flesh* (excessive sexuality), the materialism of excessive *self-indulgence* (from alcoholism to drugs). These *four* forms of libertarianism could result in a *hedonistic* way of life, a pleasure-seeking career.

In both West Africa and the USA Islam might have arrived before Christianity. In East Africa we know for certain that Islam arrived a thousand years before Christianity.

In the Americas Islam might have arrived with explorers from ancient Mali a century and a half before Columbus. The explorers were led by Bakari II, of the same Dynasty as Mensa Musa of Mali.[20]

173

In West Africa Islam came initially with the Arabs and Berbers. It eventually helped to interact with African linguistic genius, and produce Hausa, one of the most remarkable indigenous African languages today.

The Contradictions of Nigeria

Nigeria is half the population of West Africa. In Nigeria Muslims have become politically weaker, but Islam has become politically stronger. Muslims have become politically weaker because they have lost control of the Federal Government, but the reactivation of the politics of the Sharia has made Islam stronger for the time being.

Nigerian Muslims have become more conscious of their religion, and Islamic ideas and precepts have become more firmly part of the national discourse and debate. Muslims in Nigeria have declined in power, but Islam in Nigeria has risen in vigour and visibility.[21] The political decline of <u>Muslims</u> may have a causal relationship with the political revival of Islam. The globalisation of the world economy has left Nigeria and much of the rest of Africa marginalised. Nigerians have been casualties of international capitalism rather than genuine partners.[22]

Cultural globalisation, on the other hand, has found ready receptivity in Nigeria. Large parts of the country were rapidly Christianised, and the English language developed a Nigerian dialect.[23]

An earlier phase of cultural globalisation was Westernisation. Nigeria inherited a legal system based primarily on British law and English jurisprudence. Moreover, the language of interpreting the Western-derived law and the Constitution was the imperial language, English.

As discussed earlier, if Nigeria as a whole was a periphery of the world economic system, Northern Nigeria was economically a periphery of the periphery.[24] But this economic marginalisation of the North was for a while camouflaged by the fact that Northerners held political power. After General Olusegun Obasanjo was elected president in 1999, the political decline of the North exposed more mercilessly the North's economic marginality. The Shariacracy initiative by some Northern states is in part a protest against economic marginalisation, and in part a defence against unwanted cultural globalisation.[25]

Nigeria is the only African country outside Arab Africa which has seriously debated an alternative to the Western constitutional and legal inheritance. In part, this is what the debate about Shariacracy is all about.[26] It is an exploration of an alternative to the Western legacy. But Nigeria may need to use ijtihad as a process of reviewing the Sharia.[27] After all, the Sharia is God's law as interpreted by fallible human beings.

Another problem posed by the Sharia debate is whether a federal system is able to support cultural self-determination of its constituent parts and still retain cohesion as a federation. Switzerland has conceded cultural autonomy to its constituent cantons, but in terms of languages (German, French and Italian). [28] Initially the Nigerian federation allowed for neither linguistic nor religious self-determination at the state level. What the Shariacracy debate has opened up is the possibility that religion, rather than language, could be the basis of cultural differentiation in an asymmetrical constitutional order.

Again Nigeria has the largest concentration of Muslims on the African continent. That population of Nigeria, as we indicated, encompasses more Muslims than the population of any Arab country, including Egypt.[29] But can the Sharia be implemented at the state level without compromising secularism at the federal level?[30]

We have tried to demonstrate that in terms of theories of asymmetrical federalism, such a paradox of state theocracy combined with federal secularism is feasible. But it would only work if both political power and economic prosperity were more evenly distributed between North and South, and when globalisation in the wider world became more compatible with Nigeria's national *well-being*. No wonder there are voices sincerely pleading for the postponement of Shariacracy. In the name of Nigerian unity, should the Sharia be a dream deferred?)
[31]

Conclusion

Islam has risen in Nigeria, even though Muslims have declined. What is more, Islam is more visible in Christian-ruled West Africa such as Ghana and the Ivory Coast.

In the United States the issue is not yet the rise of Muslims: it is their relative integration into mainstream America. The Clinton years saw remarkable progress in the integration of Muslims as part of

American pluralism. *Christians* and *Muslims* are rivals in Africa; *Jews* and *Muslims* are rivals in America. Neither in America nor in West Africa is there room for complacency. The struggle for inter-faith cordiality under the umbrella of good governance has to continue.

NOTES

[1] According to one study conducted by Professor Ihsan Bagby of Shaw University in Raleigh, North Carolina, 6-7 million is a reasonable number for those Americans who would consider themselves Muslim; reported by the Associated Press, Apr. 26, 2001.

[2] In the 2000 Presidential Elections, a Muslim Political Action Committee endorsed Bush; see the *Christian Science Monitor* (November 2, 2000), p. 18. The impact of 9/11, and changes in perceptions by U. S. Muslims led to an impact in the 2004 elections: In late September 2004, a poll conducted by Zogby International for Georgetown University's Muslims in the American Public Square found Muslims supporting the Kerry-Edwards ticket by a margin of 76% to 7% over Bush-Cheney. For a report, see the Associated Press report, "Muslims Could Prove Key in Choosing Next U.S. President," *USA Today* (posted October 9, 2004). <http://www.usatoday.com/news/politicselections/nation/president/2004-10-09-muslims-president_x.htm>. December 30, 2005

[3] The elections in Malawi occurred in 1994; for an analysis, see Deborah Kaspin, "The Politics of Ethnicity in Malawi's Democratic Transition," *Journal of Modern African Studies*, Volume 33, Number 4 (1995), pp 595-620.

[4] For a discussion of the descent into chaos in Sierra Leone, see Yusuf Bangura, "Strategic Policy Failure and State Fragmentation: Security, Peacekeeping, and Democratisation in Sierra Leone," in Ricardo R. Laremont, Ed., *The Causes of War and the Consequences of Peacekeeping in Africa*, (Portsmouth, NH : Heinemann, 2002), pp. 143-170.

[5] In the United States, groups and organizations established by Muslims in the United States to correct stereotypes and influence policy include the Council for American Islam Relations, based in Washington, D.C. and the Muslim Public Affairs Council: see "Muslims Learn to Pull Ropes in US", *Christian Science Monitor* (February 5, 1996) p. 10.

[6] After an initial period of hesitation in the post 9/11 era, more US Muslims have begun to resume participation in US elections as representatives; see Danna Harman, "More US Muslims Run for Office," *Christian Science Monitor*

(November 7, 2003). <http://www.csmonitor.com/2003/1107/p13s03uspo.html>, January 3, 2006.

[7]On the Senegalese political experience, consult Robert Fatton, *The Making of A Liberal Democracy: Senegal's Passive Revolution, 1975-1985* (Boulder, CO: Lynne Rienner, 1987).

[8]Indeed, figures in the *CIA World Factbook* (online at <http://www.odci.gov/cia/publications/factbook/>) put the Muslim population at about 30 percent of the 19.9 million Ghanaian population, while 24 percent is Christian.

[9]According to a survey of US Muslims in 2000, 30 percent are black, 33 percent South Asian, and 25 percent Arab (the survey did not include followers of the Nation of Islam); see *The Baltimore Sun* (April 27, 2001) p. 4.

[10]A poll by the American Muslim Council in 1999 showed that 53 percent of Muslims identified with the Democratic Party, while 47 percent identified with the Republican Party; see the *Denver Post* (December 18, 1999), p. 26.

[11]On the chaplains, see Jane I. Smith, *Islam in America* (New York: Columbia University Press, 1999), p. 159, and in 2001, the *New York Times* (October 7, 2001) reported that there were 14 Muslim chaplains – 8 in the Army, 3 in the Air Force, and 3 in the Navy (two of whom serve in the Marine Corps) serving an estimated 4,000 Muslims in the US military.

[12] At a meeting of US Muslims with the Office of Faith-Based and Community Initiatives, Secret Service agents removed an American citizen who was Muslim. See the report in the *New York Times*, (June 29, 2001), p. 14.

[13]Emerson's article appeared in the *Wall Street Journal* (13 Mar. 1996), p. 14.

[14]A principle of American liberalism is the separation of Church and State, and Jewish political activity has tended to be more liberal; see Lana Stein, "American Jews and the Their Liberal Political Behaviour," in Wilbur C. Rich, Ed., *The Politics of Minority Coalitions* (Westport, CT, and London: Praeger, 1996), p. 196.

[15]For some instances in the 1990s, see Frank S. Ravitch, *School Prayer and Discrimination: The Civil Rights of Religious Minorities and Dissenters* (Boston: Northeastern University Press, 1999), pp. 9-12. Relatedly, on the Jewish position on religion in public schools, see Jonathan D. Sarna and David G. Dalin, *Religion and State in the American Jewish Experience* (Notre Dame, IN: University of Notre Dame Press, 1997), pp. 239-240.

[16]See Smith, *Islam in America*, p. 127.

[17]See the *Christian Science Monitor* (November 2, 2000), p. 18.

[18]Consult David Kingsley, *Ecology and Religion: Ecological Spirituality in Cross-Cultural Perspective* (Englewood-Cliffs, NJ: Prentice-Hall, 1995), p. 123.

[19]See Kambiz Ghanea Bassiri, *Competing Visions of Islam in the United States: A Study of Los Angeles* (Westport, CT: Greenwood Press, 1997), pp. 44-45.

[20]See Ali A. Mazrui, *et al* "Trends in Philosophy and Science in Africa," *UNESCO General History of Africa, Vol. VIII*, (Paris, Berkeley, CA: UNESCO & University of California Press), pp. 660-661.

[21]A problematic of the introduction of the Sharia in the Nigerian case is the tendency to apply it to women accused of questionable cases of adultery; see the account by Richard Dowden, "Death by Stoning," *New York Times Magazine* (January 27, 2002), pp. 28-31. Relatedly, also see O. U. Kalu, "Safiyya and Adamah: Punishing Adultery with Sharia Stones in Twenty-first Century Nigeria," *African Affairs* (2003), Volume 102, No. 408, pp. 389-408. It should be noted that the sentences of stoning have never been carried out. Even in the most prominent case, that of Amina Lawal, the case against her was flawed and she may not have been in any danger of being executed at all, even under the Shariah. See Helon Habila, "The Politics of Islamic Law: Shariah in Nigeria," *The International Herald Tribune*, (October 7, 2003).

[22]This is in spite of Nigeria's considerable oil resources; in 200 Nigeria produced about 931 million metric tons of oil, about 2.9 percent of world output; see John B. Ejobowah, "Who Owns the Oil: The Politics of Ethnicity in the Niger Delta of Nigeria, *Africa Today* 47 (Winter 2000), p. 37; also see Sarah Ahmed Khan, *Nigeria: The Political Economy of Oil* (Oxford: Oxford University Press for the Oxford Institute of Energy Studies, 1994).

[23] On Nigerian English, see Ayo Bamgbose, "Post-Imperial English in Nigeria, 1940-1990," in Joshua A. Fishman, Andrew Conrad and Alma Rubal-Lopez, eds., *Post-Imperial English: Status Change in Former British and American Colonies, 1940-1990* (Berlin and New York: Mouton de Gruyter, 1996) pp. 357-372; and on regional variations, consult V. O. Awonusi, "Regional Accents and Internal Variability in Nigerian English: A Historical Analysis," *English Studies* 67 (December 1986), pp. 555-560.

[24] See, for instance, Minabere Ibelema, "Nigeria: The Politics of Marginalisation," *Current History* 99, 637 (May 2000), p. 213.

[25] This resentment did have precedents in the 1970s and 1980s; see Roman Loimeier, *Islamic Reform and Political Change in Northern Nigeria* (Evanston, IL: Northwestern University Press, 1997), pp. 9-10.

[26] Earlier conflicts caused by the Sharia issue are discussed in, among others, Toyin Falola, *Violence in Nigeria: The Crisis of Religious Politics and Secular Ideologies* (Rochester, NY: University of Rochester Press, 1998), especially pp. 77-113; Simeon O. Ilesanmi, *Religious Pluralism and the Nigerian State* (Athens, OH: Ohio University Center for International Studies, 1997), pp. 174-207; M. H. Kukah and Toyin Falola, *Religious Militancy and Self-Assertion: Islam and Politics in Nigeria* (Aldershot, UK, and Brookfield, VT: Avebury Press, 1996), pp. 117-139; and Pat A. T. Williams, "Religion, Violence, and Displacement in Nigeria," *Journal of Asian and African Studies*, 32, 1-2 (June 1997), pp. 33-49.

[27] On *ijtihad*, see H. H. A. Rahman, "The Origin and Development of *Ijtihad* to Solve Complex Modern Legal Problems," *Bulletin of the Henry Martyn Institute of Islamic Studies* 17 (January-June 1998), pp. 7-21 and also Frank E. Vogel, "The Closing of the Door of *Ijtihad* and the Application of the Law," *American Journal of Islamic Social Sciences* 10 (Fall 1993), pp. 396-401.

[28] Even the vaunted Swiss system is not perfect model; consult, for instance, Clive Church, "Switzerland: A Paradigm in Evolution," *Parliamentary Affairs* (January 2000), Volume 53, Number 1, pp..96-113.

[29] Nearly 50 percent of the estimated 128 million Nigerians in 1999 were estimated to be Muslims, and this percentage has not changed since appreciably; see Arthur S. Banks and Thomas C. Muller, eds., *Political Handbook of the World, 1999* (Binghamton, NY: CSA Publications, 1999) p. 723, and *The World Guide 1999/2000* (Oxford, UK: New Internationalist Publications, 1999), p. 429.

[30] Both religion and ethnicity are challenging aspects to developing a satisfactory Nigerian federal system; for an account of the development of various Nigerian federal systems and the challenges, see Martin Dent, "Nigeria: Federalism and Ethnic Rivalry," *Parliamentary Affairs* 53, 1 (January 2000), pp. 157-168.

[31] Of the twelve northern states in Nigeria, ten of them have introduced Sharia law; see Dowden, "Death by Stoning," p.28.

Section IV

SOUTH AFRICA AND THE MULTI-RACIAL CHALLENGE

CHAPTER 10

FROM THE HAITIAN REVOLUTION TO THE STRUGGLE AGAINST APARTHEID[1]

While 2004 marked the two hundredth anniversary of the Haitian revolution, it also marked the one hundredth anniversary of the Maji Maji war against the Germans in Tanganyika (now mainland Tanzania). The Maji Maji war was inspired by an East African version of voodoo. The warrior's immersion into water was supposed to provide a magical shield against German bullets. Those beliefs were successful in mobilizing the masses with next to no training or organization. In reality the African warriors' baptism was no match for German bullets. Thousands of Tanganyikans died before the warriors lost faith in the invincibility of water.[2]

The Maji Maji war lasted from 1904 to 1906, a much shorter period than the Haitian wars. Scholars have characterized the Maji Maji war as 'primary resistance,' meaning resisting colonisation before it was fully established. Secondary resistance is like the liberation movements in Zimbabwe and South Africa which were rebelling against colonial structures already entrenched.[3]

Since the bulk of the slave population in Haiti at the beginning of the nineteenth century was fresh from Africa, were they resisting against a new colonial subjugation (primary resistance) in their own experience? Or was it secondary resistance to a long-established imperial order? Should we judge the Haitian revolt by the newness of the victims (fresh from Africa) or by oldness of the slaving and colonial structures on the island?[4]

The Maji Maji war was brutally suppressed by the Germans. The Haitian revolution had a happier outcome, at least in the short run.

In addition to marking both 200th anniversary of the Haitian revolution and the 100th anniversary of the Maji Maji war, the year 2004 was also approximately the 50th anniversary of the Mau Mau war against the British in Kenya. Mau Mau, like Maji Maji, also invoked a version of East African voodoo. But Mau Mau, unlike Maji Maji, did not emphasize the protective qualities of baptism by water. Mau Mau invoked ritual use of *menstrual blood* and worked out elabourate oaths of allegiance for warriors stripped naked for the ceremonies.[5] The warriors fought bravely in spite of the awesome military odds against them.

Unlike Maji Maji, Mau Mau did defeat the British politically though not militarily. The Mau Mau warriors fought from 1952 to about 1960. They convinced the British that it was time to pull out of Kenya as an imperial power. The British colonial exit occurred in 1963, although they did not give up their colony in Kenya without a struggle and grievous violations of human rights.[6]

The Racial Legacies of Haiti and South Africa

The year 2004 also marked the tenth anniversary of the end of political apartheid in South Africa in 1994. What is the comparative meaning of South Africa in relation to Haiti? We purposely use the name 'Haiti' rather than the cold colonial name of St. Dominique.[7]

The following proposition is arguable. Haiti was the first Black rebellion against Whites which was successful enough to produce a Republic under Black rule. South Africa is the last Black rebellion against Whites which has been successful enough to produce a Republic under Black rule. Haiti set the precedent of 'revolt towards republic' under Black control. South Africa is hopefully the last chapter of Black militarised challenge to white racism. The two struggles have historically been symbolized by Toussaint L'Ouverture[8] of the Haitian revolution and Nelson Mandela of South Africa's liberation.

South Africa in 1994 and Haiti in 1804 had certain characteristics in common. South Africa in 1994 was the brightest jewel in Africa's crown. Haiti in the years preceding 1804 had been the brightest jewel in France's imperial crown. South Africa was Africa's vanguard of precious minerals – diamonds, gold, platinum and a variety of industrial minerals. South Africa led the rest of Africa in agricultural output and in industrial and social infrastructure.

As for Haiti in the years leading to 2004, it was widely regarded as the richest of all colonial territories in the world. In the 1780s, Haiti was supposed to account for

> . . .some 40 percent of France's foreign trade, its 7000... plantations were absorbing by the 1790s almost 10-15 percent of United States exports, and had important commercial links with the British and Spanish West Indies as well. On the coastal plains of this colony, little larger than Wales, was grown about two fifths of the world's sugar, while from its mountains interior came over half the world's coffee.[9]

If South Africa is today the first among equals among the well-endowed African countries Haiti was at the turn of the nineteenth century the first among equals among all the colonised territories of the world.

Given this background, how did Haiti descend from the brightest jewel in France's imperial crown to the poorest nation in the Western hemisphere? How did the first Black republic of the nineteenth century become among the most economically retarded of all republics in the world? The consequences for the health and well-being of the people are spelled out by a USAID Activity Data sheet:

> Haiti has the highest child mortality rate in the Western Hemisphere. One in eight children dies by age five, and a third are chronically malnourished. Maternal mortality is estimated at 1,000 per 100,000 live births. About 10% of Haiti's urban population are infected with HIV, and almost half the women of reproductive age currently have an untreated sexually transmitted infection (STI).[10]

In a multiracial society, healthy progress is reached either when the White elites are in control or when the Black majority has taken over. The worst scenario is when the mulattoes are in absolute power, poised against both the White minority and the Black majority. In the study of logic this is called the fallacy of the undistributed middle.

Haiti has been a casualty of the undistributed demographic middle. The mulattoes have been disproportionately powerful in postcolonial Haiti much more than the Coloureds in South Africa have ever been. But in both countries racial gradation has been a central engine of historical change.

Racial mixture as a category has been important in the history of both Haiti and South Africa. The so-called "miscegenation" may have a typology of four:

Descending Miscegenation: This means that children of mixed marriages descend to the status of the less privileged parent. This is the dominant model in the United States. If either parent is Black, the child is Black.

Ascending Miscegenation: Under this model, children of race mixture ascend to the status of the more privileged parent. In Israel, if the father is Jewish the child ascends to Jewish status regardless of who the mother is. In Sudan and Egypt, and indeed in the larger Arab world, if the father is Arab, the child is Arab, regardless of who the mother is.

Divergent Miscegenation: A child of racial mixture under this model belongs to a third group apart. This has been the dominant model in both Haiti and South Africa. In South Africa it produces a mixed category called *Coloureds*. In Haiti this category produced the *Mulattoes*.

Ambivalent Miscegenation: A child of racial mixture may move *up* or down racially, depending upon other variables like social class, level of education, or shade of skin colour. This is the dominant system of miscegenation in Brazil. But there are aspects of *Haiti's racial gradation, which* are also ambivalent. A darker skinned Mulatto may be categorized as "Black". A lighter skinned mulatto may ascend to *whiteness*.[11]

Haiti has often been described as the first slave rebellion in history to have successfully captured power. C.L.R. James comes close to that conclusion.[12] That is claiming too much for Haiti. Haiti was the first rebellion of *Black* slaves to have achieved control of a society, but not the first generally.

In Africa, there was a prior rebellion of slaves which succeeded in creating a whole new dynasty which lasted for centuries. The slaves were not black, but they did capture a major African state. The slaves were the Mamluks of Egypt who captured power and ruled Egypt as a dynasty from the year 1250 to 1517. Descendants of the Mamluks continued as a major political force from 1517 to 1798. The Arabic word Mamluk means the "owned one" or "slave".[13]

If the roots of the Haitian Revolution lie partly in the French revolution, do the roots of the French revolution reciprocally lie in Haiti as a country? It has been argued that the bourgeois revolution in France would not have taken place if the French bourgeoisie had not been enriched and emboldened by the huge profits from Haiti and from the accompanying slave trade. A revolution in Paris based on the Rights of Man was originally fuelled by the profits of enslavement and colonialism.

Haiti in World History

The Haitian Revolution is an epoch-making event in history not because of what it did for Haiti but because of what it did for world history. Haiti today is only marginally better off than it was two hundred years ago. So was the revolution worth it? Are there lessons for South Africa?

If we viewed the wider consequences of the Haitian Revolution, the revolution was worth it.[14] William Pitt's decision in England to abolish the slave trade in 1807 was probably partly influenced by events in Haiti and their significance for Britain's imperial rivalry with France. The use of the British navy on the high seas to enforce the ban on the slave trade was partly motivated by a British desire to weaken France in its economic and colonial ambitions.

Led by Toussaint L'Ouverture, the Haitian Revolution also dealt a major blow to Napoleon's dream to build an Atlantic empire for France. Napoleon decided to concentrate on his ambitions in Europe. He sold large tracts of land in North America to finance his European adventures.

In the midst of the Haitian Revolution France decided to sell Louisiana. The Louisiana Purchase was finalized in 1803. The purchase contributed to the Untied States expansion not only in itself but also by facilitating further American expansion to Texas and then westwards.[15]

Both the French Revolution of 1789 and the Haitian Revolution which followed fuelled slave revolts widely. More than *twenty* slave revolts in the Greater Caribbean flared up between 1789 and 1832. Particularly noticeable were the large-scale rebellions in Barbados in 1816, Demerara in 1823 and Jamaica in 1831. Those three, plus Haiti, were the largest slave uprisings in the history of the Americas.[16]

Temptations in some French circles to recolonise Haiti probably contributed to President James Monroe's decision to issue the Monroe Doctrine of 1823.[17] But both the British and the Americans were even more worried about any attempt by Spain to recolonise its former Empire in the Americas, and any new Spanish attempt to inherit Haiti.

The Haitian Revolution also had an impact on the debate about slavery in the United States. Racist opinion in the United States felt vindicated in their opposition to the emancipation of Blacks. On the other hand, American abolitionists regarded the Haitian revolution as a warning about the risks of continuing with slavery.

Sometimes a country of the world produces something which changes global history but does not do much for that country itself. The area of the world which today encompasses Israel and the Palestinian territories gave the world Jesus and his message of peace and love for thy neighbour, but that area has not itself benefited much from that Christian legacy. The land which gave the human race Jesus Christ is not itself *Christian*. The majority there are Jews and Muslims. The land which gave the world the messenger of love is today torn by hate and blood. Greater Palestine has given the world a glorious Gospel, but has not itself embraced it.

Similarly, Haiti gave the world a message of hope and freedom, a demonstration of how to rise from abject servitude to glorious self-determination. The Black race, especially, was inspired and emboldened by the Haitian Revolution. But, like the land which gave the world Jesus, Haiti has not itself benefited from its bequest to the human race.

From Port-au-Prince to Pretoria

Now that Haiti is entering its third century since the revolution, that agenda of hope and freedom should be re-addressed. In this third century Haiti should at last partake of what it gave to the world: that message of liberty and that confidence of self-upliftment.

What about South Africa? Now that the Republic is entering its second decade of democracy, South Africa needs to learn from the lessons of Haiti. As the *first* Black society to overthrow white oppression, Haiti rose triumphantly and then collapsed disastrously. As the *last* Black population to overthrow white oppression, South Africa has already risen triumphantly. Will it avoid the Haitian precedent of collapsing disastrously?

In spite of residual social and economic apartheid in South Africa, and in spite of the terrors of HIV/AIDS, the healing legacy of Nelson Mandela is likely to be more enduring than the revolutionary legacy of Toussaint L'Ouverture. But a successful South Africa should also rise to the challenge of healing Haiti in the aftermath of its own historic Francophone apartheid.

NOTES

[1] An earlier version of this paper was entitled "From Toussaint L'Ouverture To Nelson Mandela: The Haitian Revolution and Comparative Black Experience."

[2] Relatedly, consult John Iliffe, "The Organization of the Maji Maji Rebellion," and Patrick M. Redmond, " Maji Maji in Ungoni: A Reappraisal of Existing Historiography," in Gregory Maddox, Ed., *Conquest and Resistance to Colonialism in Africa* (New York: Garland, 1993), pp. 217-252.

[3] For discussions on these terms, see T. O. Ranger, "Connexions Between 'Primary Resistance' and Modern Nationalism in East and Central Africa, Parts I and II" *Journal of African History* (1968), Volume 9, pp. 437-453 and pp. 631-641.

[4] A fascinating comparative study of Haiti and the Dominican Republic may be found in Jared Diamond, *Collapse: How Societies Choose to Fail or Succeed* (New York: Viking Penguin, 2005), pp. 329-357.

[5] There were various oaths at different levels; for descriptions and analyses, consult Wunyabari Maloba, *Mau Mau and Kenya: An Analysis of a Peasant Revolt* (Bloomington, IN: Indiana University Press, 1993), pp. 102-109, and Marshall S Clough, *Mau Mau Memoirs : History, Memory, And Politics* (Boulder, CO: L. Rienner, 1998), pp. 98-99.

[6] Some recent analyses of the British struggle against Mau Mau may be found in Caroline Elkins, *Imperial Reckoning : The Untold Story of Britain's Gulag in Kenya* (New York: Henry Holt, 2005) and David Anderson, *Histories of the Hanged : The Dirty War in Kenya and the End of Empire* (New York: W. W. Norton, 2005).

[7] Haiti is the original Taino Indian name of the island of Hispaniola; see Diamond, *Collapse*, p. 335.

[8] For two portraits of Toussaint L'Ouverture, consult, for example, Wenda Parkinson, *"This Gilded African", Toussaint L'Ouverture* (London and New York: Quartet Books, 1980, 1978) and George F. Tyson, Jr., Ed., *Toussaint L'Ouverture* (Englewood Cliffs, NJ: Prentice-Hall, 1973].

[9] This quotation is from David Geggus, *Slavery, War, and Revolution: The British Occupation of Saint Domingue 1793–1798* (London: Clarendon Press, 1982), p. 6, cited in Franklin W. Knight, "The Haitian Revolution," *The American Historical Review* (February 2000), par. 11 <http://www.historycooperative.org/journals/ahr/105.1/ah000103.html> (1 Dec. 2005).

[10] USAID Activity Data Sheet , "Healthier Families of Desired Size, 521-003," at <http://www.usaid.gov/pubs/cbj2002/lac/ht/521-003.html> (1 Dec. 2005).

[11] These four models of "miscegenation" were first formulated in Ali A. Mazrui, *World Federation of Cultures: An African Perspective* (New York: Free Press of Glencoe, 1976).

[12] C. L. R. James, The Black Jacobins; Toussaint L'Ouverture and the San Domingo Revolution (New York, Vintage Books, 1963).

[13] On the Mamluks, see, for instance, Thomas Philipp and Ulrich Haarmann, Eds., *The Mamluks in Egyptian Politics and Society* (Cambridge and New York: Cambridge University Press, 1998) and Donald P. Little, *History and Historiography of the Mamlūks* (London: Variorum Reprints, 1986).

[14] Some of the effects of the Haitian revolution in the Atlantic area are described in David P. Geggus, Ed., *The Impact of the Haitian Revolution in the Atlantic World* (Columbia, SC: University of South Carolina Press, 2001).

[15] For some recent analyses of the significance of the Louisiana purchase, see, for example, Peter J. Kastor, *The Nation's Crucible : The Louisiana Purchase and the Creation of America* (New Haven, CT: Yale University Press, 2004) and Marie-Jeanne Rossignol, *The Nationalist Ferment:The Origins Of U.S. Foreign Policy, 1789-1812*, transl. Lillian A. Parrott, (Columbus, OH : Ohio State University Press, 2004).

[16] Knight, "The Haitian Revolution," par. 14.

[17] This doctrine was enunciated by President James Monroe in his 1823 State of the Union message; for relevant sections, consult Robert H. Holden and Eric Zolov, Eds., *Latin America and the United States : a Documentary History* (New York: Oxford University Press, 2000), pp. 11-14.

CHAPTER 11

SOUTH AFRICA FROM VICTIM TO VILLAIN? A PLAY IN FOUR ACTS[1]

T he story of South Africa in relation to the rest of the continent is <u>a play in four acts on the stage of history</u>. It is a play about South Africa's triumph, her emerging leadership, and the hazards of South Africa's new continental power.

Put in another way, South Africa's impact on Pan Africanism has included at least FOUR distinctive roles. These roles are what might be called "<u>the FOUR Vs of South Africa's destiny</u>:

- ♦ *V for <u>Victim</u>: South Africa as a victim and racial martyr*
- ♦ *V for <u>Victor</u>: South Africa's triumphant success in avoiding large-scale racial war, and establishing instead the most progressive democracy on the African continent*
- ♦ *V for <u>Vanguard</u>: South Africa in a continental leadership role, eager to open up new horizons*
- ♦ *V for <u>villain</u>: South Africa at risk of becoming a villain, with potential of evolving as a regional hegemon.*

The Play in Four Acts

Act I: The Victim

The tragic suffering of South Africa during the apartheid era was a resource for Pan-Africanism. The martyrdom of people of colour in South Africa generated passions among Black people worldwide.[2] Events like Sharpeville and the brutalities of Soweto struck a powerful code of sympathy.[3]

From 1948 to the 1990s, South Africa had evolved the most institutionalised form of racism in history. <u>South Africa's martyrs ranged from Mandela in prison[4] to Steve Biko in his grave.[5]</u>

Apartheid in South Africa also strengthened Trans-Saharan Pan Africanism and Afro-Arab relations. The idea that Whites and Blacks needed <u>separate homelands</u> was similar to the <u>Zionist</u> idea that Arabs and Jews needed separate homelands.[6]

Bantustans in South Africa were the equivalent of the Occupied Territories in Palestine – separate and brutally unequal.[7] Both Zionism and macro-apartheid were forms of ethnic cleansing. Africans and Arabs were brought together in the joint struggle, against the background of nuclear collabouration between Israel and apartheid South Africa.[8]

Act II: The Victor

Most of us expected a racial war before apartheid could be dislodged. But a great Faustian bargain was struck between Whites and Blacks. As I once formulated it in Cape Town, the Whites said to the Blacks: "You take the Crown and we will keep the Jewels." Blacks were to receive the political crown, while Whites kept the economic Jewels.[9] Since then there has been progress in political democratisation – but not yet progress in economic democratisation. Economic apartheid is still intact.[10] Is Black empowerment the answer?[11]

I prefer the term "economic democratisation" to "Black empowerment." Economic democratisation would seek not just racial equalization but also gender equity. Politically South Africa introduced the most liberal constitution and progressive system in Africa, if not in the Third World.[12] But full implementation has been slow.

Act III: The Vanguard

The triumph of South Africa created opportunities for the country to be a vanguard and pacesetter in the world. Perhaps it began with South Africa's voluntary disarmament – setting the precedent of giving up weapons of mass destruction.[13]

However, the motives of the West in pressuring Pretoria were dubious. In reality, the West believed that nuclear weapons were not for Africans, Muslims and children under sixteen. Nevertheless, South Africa's renunciation of nuclear weapons set a precedent of South Africa as a voice of global peace and justice.

Included in South Africa's peace policy is South Africa's support for the Palestinian cause, its opposition to the American war in Iraq, its efforts to find peaceful solutions to the problems of Congo, Burundi, and other African flashpoints. Both Mandela and Mbeki have tried to give Africa a voice on global issues.[14]

The vision of an AFRICAN RENAISSANCE is another potential vanguard role in quest of reactivating the creative energies of Africa.[15]

South Africa's vanguard role has included its role in the birth of The African Union – the most ambitious form of institutionalised Pan Africanism so far attempted. Also a vanguard role is South Africa as a midwife of NEPAD – a risky enterprise but probably worth attempting.[16]

Act IV: The Villain

South Africa has the requisite qualifications for becoming a regional super power or regional hegemon.

South Africa is the premier industrial state of Africa – perhaps the richest of the members of African Union. South Africa's immense capacity to invest in other African countries could be an engine of continental development – but it could also degenerate into intra-African colonisation.[17]

Lord Acton (1834-1902), a British aristocrat in the nineteenth century, formulated the dictum "Power tends to corrupt; absolute power corrupts absolutely."[18] This may even happen among former victims who are now newly empowered.

The Israelis have proven that even former victims of the Holocaust could commit their own crimes against humanity when they are in power. [19] Israelis have been narrowing the moral gap between themselves and the Nazis.

It was a liberal Israeli, Professor Yashayau Leibovitz, who coined the term "Judeo-Nazism".[20] The Jews, preeminent victims of history, have been learning how to victimize an almost defenceless people – and then complain if their victims try to fight back.

We are asked to believe that Israeli homicide bombers are morally superior to Palestinian suicide bombers. Marc Ellis, a Jewish theologian, has asked this question:

Could Palestinian suicide bombers be, at least for a population under occupation and closure and without an armed force that is comparable to the Israeli military, the equivalent to Israel's helicopter gunships? If it is morally right to condemn terrorism of the weak, does [Elie] Wiesel have the moral obligation to condemn other forms of terrorism, including terrorism carried out by the nation-state?[21]

If you fight by killing yourself is supposed to be a strategy which is morally worse than if you kill without harming yourself. If you fight by killing yourself is supposed to be more cowardly than if you fire a missile at a man in a wheel chair without hurting yourself.[22] South

Africa should learn from Israel that being former victims is no guarantee that you will not victimize those weaker than yourself. South Africa as a society of former martyrs should learn not to make martyrs of others.

Decades in Fours

The historic play in four acts has encompassed the distinctive roles South Africa has performed in Africa and World politics – as <u>victim</u>, as <u>victor</u>, as <u>vanguard</u>, and as <u>villain</u>, current or potential. These are roles which are indeed FOUR in number. The number of <u>FOUR</u> has also been significant as the fourth year of the decade of the 1990s – 1994, and the fourth year of the first decade of the twentieth century, 2004.

But in reality the destiny of Black people in history has been repeatedly shadowed by the fourth year of decade after decade. In 2004, we celebrated the first triumphant Black rebellion against White domination – the Haitian revolution of 1804. [23] In 2004, we also commemorated the first popular rebellion against German oppression long before Hitler and the resistance of the Allies– the Maji Maji war in Tanganyika which broke out in 1904.[24]

In 2004 we celebrated the fiftieth anniversary of the outbreak of the <u>Algerian </u>war of independence, fought against French colonialism and oppression. The Algerian revolution began in 1954.[25] The <u>Mau Mau War</u> in Kenya also gathered momentum in 1954 having been initiated two years earlier.[26]

2004 also marked the 30th anniversary of the collapse of the centuries old <u>Portuguese Empire</u>, following a coup in Lisbon, Portugal, in April 1974.[27] 1974 also witnessed the creeping revolution in <u>Ethiopia</u> against an imperial system which, according to tradition, had lasted three thousand years. Emperor Haile Selassie was overthrown.[28]

As for the African Diaspora, 2004 marked the fiftieth anniversary of the end of the pernicious legal doctrine of "<u>Separate but Equal</u>" in the United States. The US Supreme Court confronted the issue in the case of <u>BROWN vs. THE BOARD OF EDUCATION</u>, and the Supreme Court struck down the legal case for racial segregation in the United States forever.[29]

When South Africans decided to initiate their democracy in the fourth year of a decade (1994) they had no idea that the choice of the fourth year of the decade was so rich in Pan African significance and meaning.

South Africans knew about the four <u>gospels</u> of the New Testament (Mark, Matthew, Luke and John). South Africans knew that four was the usual number of legs for a throne. They knew that four was the usual number of legs of a bridal bed. Some South Africans counted four seasons in their year. Most mammals in their South African environment had four legs. South Africans themselves had four elongated limbs – two arms and two legs. What South Africans did not realize in the concluding decade of the twentieth century was that1994 was a year steeped in the quadruple heritage of the Black experience.

That is why South Africa's own role in the African experience has been a major historic play in <u>FOUR ACTS</u> – South Africa as victim, South Africa as victor, South Africa as vanguard and the dangerous possibility that the temptations of power would turn South Africa into a <u>villain</u> in spite of itself.

I would like to believe that South Africans will find the will and the resolve to be a vanguard of leadership without becoming a villain of power, to be former victims without becoming new violators, to be heirs to Mandela without becoming successors to Machiavelli.

NOTES

[1]This is a revised and updated version of a presentation at an international conference on "South Africa: Ten Years After Apartheid", hosted by the African Institute of South Africa at the Pretoria City Hall, Pretoria, South Africa, March 24-26, 2004. President Thabo Mbeki, the Head of State, attended the final session of the conference.

[2]Analyses of international reaction to the apartheid regime may be found in, for instance, Adrian Guelke, *Rethinking the Rise and Fall of Apartheid: South Africa and World* Politics (Houndmills, Basingstoke, Hampshire and New York: Palgrave MacMillan, 2005); Audie J. Klotz, *Norms in International Relations:The Struggle Against Apartheid* (Ithaca, NY: Cornell University Press, 1995); and Kenneth W. Grundy, *South Africa: Domestic Crisis and Global Challenge* (Boulder, CO: Westview Press, 1991). Also see, for historical accounts of the apartheid regime, Robert C. Cottrell, *South Africa: A State of Apartheid* (Philadephia, PA: Chelsea House, 2005); Nancy L. Clark and William H. Worger, *South Africa: The Rise and Fall of Apartheid* (Harlow, England and New York: Longman, 2004); and James Barber, *South Africa in the Twentieth Century : A Political History--In Search of a Nation State* (Oxford, UK and Malden, MA: Blackwell Publishers, 1999).

[3]For overviews of Sharpeville and Soweto, consult, for instance, Barber, *South Africa in the Twentieth Century*, pp. 164-165 and pp. 211-214 respectively.

[4] For Mandela's own account of his transition from prisoner to President, see his *Long Walk to Freedom: The Autobiography of Nelson Mandela* (Boston: Back Bay Books, 1995), and for a biography of this great leader, see Anthony Sampson, *Mandela : The Authorized Biography* (New York: Knopf, distributed by Random House, 1999).

[5]On Biko, see Barber, *South Africa in the Twentieth Century*, pp. 192-196.

[6] For comparisons and analyses of Zionism and apartheid, consult Daryl J. I. Glaser, "Zionism and Apartheid: A Moral Comparison," *Ethnic & Racial Studies* (May2003), Vol. 26 Number 3, pp. 403-21 and Ghazi-Walidi Falah, "Dynamics and Patterns of the Shrinking of Arab lands in Palestine," *Political Geography* (February 2003), Vol. 22, Number 2, pp. 179-209.

[7] This analogy is further explored in, for instance, Leila Farsakh, "Independence, Cantons, or Bantustans: Whither the Palestinian State? *Middle East Journal* (Spring 2005), Vol. 59, No. 2, pp. 230-245 and Jane Hunter, "Israel and the Bantustans," *Journal of Palestine Studies* (Spring 1986), Vol. 15, No. 3, pp. 53-89.

[8]Acounts of this nuclear collabouration between the two states who had very few friends in the international community in the 1960s and 1970s may be found in David Fischer, "South Africa," in Mitchell Reiss and Robert S. Litwak, Eds., *Nuclear Proliferation After the Cold War* (Washington, DC: Woodrow Wilson Center Press and The Johns Hopkins University Press, 1994), pp. 209-213; Joel Peters, *Israel and Africa: The Problematic Friendship* (London: British Academic Press, 1992), pp. 159-161; and Benjamin M. Joseph, *Besieged Bedfellows: Israel and the Land of Apartheid* (New York: Greenwood Press, 1988), pp. 57-71.

[9] Between 1995 and 2000 in the post-apartheid South Africa, according to one estimate, average income of black households fell by 19 percent while white household incomes rose by 15 percent; see Richard Morin, "Despite Deep Woes, Democracy Instills Hope," *Washington Post* (March 31, 2004).

[10]According to Morin:

> Despite aggressive affirmative action programs, whites still outnumber blacks among top managers by nearly 10 to 1, according to government employment statistics released in 2002. Even among middle managers, whites still outnumber blacks in a

country where blacks make up 79 percent of the population, whites are 9.6 percent, mixed race are 8.9 percent and Indian 2.5 percent.

Morin, "Despite Deep Woes, Democracy Instills Hope," *Washington Post* (March 31, 2004).

[11] For some perspectives on Black empowerment in South Africa, see Zakes Mda, "The Half-Revolution," *The New York Times* (April 27, 2004) and Allister Sparks, "What South Africa can Teach the Middle East," *The Washington Post* (April 18, 2004).

[12] For instance, South Africa's constitution is the first in the world to protect the rights of homosexuals, as Mark F. Massoud points out in his "The Evolution of Gay Rights in South Africa," *Peace Review* (September 2003), Volume 15, Number 3, p. 301, and recently South Africa took one more step towards joining a select group of countries -the Netherlands, Belgium, Spain and Canada – which currently allow same-sex marriages nationwide. See Craig Timberg, "S. Africa's Top Court Blesses Gay Marriage: Parliament Given One Year to Amend Law," *The Washington Post* (December 2, 2005).

[13] South Africa was the first state to give up nuclear weapons voluntarily and for accounts of the decision-making and rationale, see Joseph Cirincione, with Jon B. Wolfsthal and Miriam Rajkumar, Deadly arsenals : tracking weapons of mass destruction (Washington, DC: Carnegie Endowment for International Peace, 2005), Second Edition, p. 407; Helen E. Purkitt and Stephen F. Burgess, *South Africa's Weapons of Mass Destruction* (Bloomington, IN: Indiana University Press, 2005), pp. 119-145; and Fischer, "South Africa," in Reiss and Litwak, Eds., *Nuclear Proliferation After the Cold War*, pp. 216-227.

[14] For some assessments and descriptions of post-apartheid South African foreign policy, consult, for instance, James Barber, *Mandela's World : The International Dimension Of South Africa's Political Revolution 1990-99* (Oxford; Cape Town; Athens, OH: James Currey; David Philip; and Ohio University Press, 2004), pp. 147-201; Patrick Bond (with cartoons by Zapiro), *Talk Left, Walk Right : South Africa's Frustrated Global Reforms* (Scottsville, South Africa : University of KwaZulu-Natal Press, 2004); and Sharon LaFraniere, "After Reconciliation, Steering South Africa to a Reckoning," *The New York Times* (April 27, 2004).

[15] An assessment of Mbeki's "African Renaissance" idea may be found in Peter Vale and Sipho Maseko, "Thabo Mbeki, South Africa, and the Idea of An African Renaissance," in Sean Jacobs and Richard Calland, Eds., *Thabo Mbeki's World : The Politics And Ideology Of The South African President*

(Pietermaritzburg, SA; London; and New York: University of Natal Press and Zed Books, 2002), pp. 121-142. Some of the hopes and fears of Thabo Mbeki for Africa may also be found in his op-ed, "Building A Better Africa," *The Washington Post* (June 10, 2004).

16 On the African Union and its creation, consult Thomas K. Tieku, "Explaining The Clash And Accomodation Of Interests Of Major Actors In The Creation Of The African Union," *African Affairs* (Apr2004), Vol. 103, No. 411, pp. 249-267, and Corinne A. A. Packer and Donald Rukare, "The New African Union And Its Constitutive Act," *American Journal of International Law,"* (April 2002), Vol. 96 No. 2, pp. 365-379. Reports on NEPAD may be found in Vikram Sura, "NEPAD: Negotiating for Africa's Development," *UN Chronicle* (Mar-May 2003), Volume 40, Number 1, pp. 23-25, and K. Y. Amoako, "NEPAD: Making Individual Bests a Continental Norm," *UN Chronicle* (Mar-May 2003), Volume 40, Number 1, pp. 25-27.

17 For an early analysis, consult Robert Davies, "South Africa's Economic Relations with Africa: Current Patterns and Future Prospects," in Adebayo Adedeji, ed., *South Africa and Africa : Within Or Apart?* (London and Atlantic Highlands, NJ: Zed Books, in association with African Centre for Development and Strategic Studies (ACDESS), 1996), pp. 167-192.

18 The context of this famous quotation is described in Roland Hill, *Lord Acton* (New Haven and London: Yale University Press, 2000), pp. 296-300.

19 Some analysts have even termed the actions of the Israelis toward the Palestinians, especially during the 1948 Arab-Israeli war as "ethnic cleansing." See Ilan Pappe, *A History of Modern Palestine: One Land, Two People* (Cambridge and New York: Cambridge University Press, 2004), pp. 129-131 and pp. 136-141 and Meron Benvenisti, *Sacred Landscape : The Buried History of the Holy Land Since 1948* (Berkeley, CA: University of California Press, 2000), pp. 144-192. Relatedly, an interesting comparison between Israeli and Serbian practices may be found in Ron James, *Frontiers and Ghettos: State Violence in Serbia and Israel* (Berkeley, CA: University of California Press, 2003).

20 See Noam Chomsky, *The Fateful Triangle : The United States, Israel, and the Palestinians* (Boston: South End Press, 1983), p. 447.

21 Marc H. Ellis, *Israel And Palestine Out Of The Ashes : The Search For Jewish Identity in the Twenty-first Century* (London and Sterling, VA: Pluto Press, 2002), p. 69. Also see Saul Landau, *The Pre-Emptive Empire: A Guide to Bush's Kingdom* (London and Sterling, VA: Pluto Press, 2003), pp. 48-52.

[22] When political comedian Bill Maher suggested that fighting with missiles was in fact more cowardly than the 9/11 terrorists' actions, his comments drew a storm of protest; see Michael Kinsley, "Listening to Our Inner Ashcrofts," *The Washington Post* (January 4, 2002).

[23] C. L. R. James, The Black Jacobins; Toussaint L'Ouverture and the San Domingo Revolution (New York, Vintage Books, 1963).

[24] Consult John Iliffe, "The Organization of the Maji Maji Rebellion," and Patrick M. Redmond, " Maji Maji in Ungoni: A Reappraisal of Existing Historiography," in Gregory Maddox, Ed., *Conquest and Resistance to Colonialism in Africa* (New York: Garland, 1993), pp. 217-252.

[25] A description of this bloody war may be found in John E. Talbott, *The War Without a Name: France in Algeria, 1954-1962* (New York: Knopf, 1980).

[26] For accounts of this struggle, see Wunyabari Maloba, *Mau Mau and Kenya: An Analysis of a Peasant Revolt* (Bloomington, IN: Indiana University Press, 1993), pp. 102-109, and Marshall S Clough, *Mau Mau Memoirs : History, Memory, And Politics* (Boulder, CO: L. Rienner, 1998).

[27] Consult Stewart Lloyd-Jones and António Costa, Eds., *The Last Empire : Thirty Years of Portuguese Decolonisation* (Bristol, UK and Portland, OR : Intellect, 2003) and David Birmingham, *Portugal and Africa* (Houndmills, Basingstoke, Hampshire : Macmillan, 1999).

[28] Haile Selassie's overthrow is described in Paul B. Henze, *Layers of Time: A History of Ethiopia* (New York: St. Martin's Press, 2000), pp. 282-307. Consult also, on the military revolution that followed, Teferra Haile-Selassie, *The Ethiopian Revolution, 1974-1991: From a Monarchical Autocracy to a Military Oligarchy* (London and New York: Kegan Paul International; Distributed by Columbia University Press, 1997).

[29] For analyses of this decision and implications, consult, for example, the following: Charles J. Ogletree, Jr., *All Deliberate Speed: Reflections on the First Half Century of Brown v. Board of Education* (New York: W. W. Norton, 2004); Derrick Bell, *Silent Covenants: Brown v. Board of Education and the Unfulfilled Hopes for Racial Reform* (Oxford and New York: Oxford University Press, 2004); and Richard Kluger, *Simple Justice: The History of Brown v. Board of Education and Black America's Struggle for Equality* (New York: Vintage Books, 1977, 1975).

CHAPTER 12

SOUTH AFRICA AND COMPARATIVE DIASPORAS

The concept of Diaspora was invented by the Jews to refer to their own dispersal. Over time the term has been extended to other experiences of the global dispersal of people.[1] At this global level one distinction has almost never been made: the distinction between the Diaspora of the Victimized like that of the Jews or the Blacks, and the Diaspora of the Conquerors, like that of white settlers in Africa.

White South Africans have been the most important part of the European Diaspora in Africa. Diasporas have been created not just by the dispersal of Jews and Blacks, or Indians and Chinese. Diasporas have also been created by white gentiles, either on the run as persecuted Huguenots or exported as convicts to Australia.

The metaphor of 'tribe' has in the past been used to apply to Afrikaners as a coherent community in South Africa. The BBC once had a program on Afrikaners entitled 'The White Tribe of Africa.'[2] David Harrison wrote a book under that title.[3]

While the term 'white tribe' has thus been applied to Afrikaners long before now, the term 'white Diaspora' is only now being applied to the white presence in Southern Africa. A major reason why we seldom apply the term 'Diaspora' to white gentiles is that we tend to regard the idea of a Conquering Diaspora as a contradiction in terms.

The Jews and the Blacks got Diasporised as a result of being victimized in their ancestral homes; most Europeans (though not all) moved to Africa as conquerors rather than as victims in chains or victims on the run.

Among Black people, there are in turn two Diasporas, both of them of victim-experience. One is the Diaspora of enslavement and post-enslavement – like that of African Americans, Afro-Haitians, Afro-Brazilians and Afro-West Indians.[4]

The other Diaspora is the Diaspora of colonisation or of postcoloniality – like the exodus of Africans forced out or displaced by the consequences of colonialism, apartheid and their aftermath. These

198

are the Ali Mazruis, Chinua Achebes and Denis Brutuses of the second half of the twentieth century and beyond.

One consequence of the white Diaspora of conquest in South Africa is that it eventually contributed to the exodus of the victimized moving to other lands. Thousands of South Africans moved to other countries and other continents trying to escape the heat of apartheid.

By a strange destiny, the Diaspora of Conquerors among white folks was deepening the Diaspora of the Victimized among Black people. It was partly an exodus of Black activists seeking asylum abroad as part of the struggle against apartheid. Some were young South Africans (Black, Indian and mixed race) seeking better educational opportunities abroad than seemed accessible at home. Many were ordinary South Africans disgusted by racism and seeking an exit from it all.

Jewish South Africans were in an intermediate position. Their presence in South Africa was part of the wider Jewish Diaspora of the victimized. But because South African Jews were overwhelmingly of European extraction, the Jews became part of the Diaspora of Conquest.[5]

But many Jews were also ideologically *liberal* and nauseated by the obscenities of apartheid. Some were imprisoned and some departed to join the Diaspora of the Victimized abroad.

White South Africans on the run from apartheid had a wider range of destinations than Black South Africans. Many Euro-South Africans went to Europe, Australia, North America and a few were scattered in Black Africa, the West Indies and Latin America.

Black South Africans on the run from apartheid were disproportionately in neighbouring African countries, though many also found either educational opportunities or political asylum in the Western world. They became part of the Black Diaspora of post-coloniality. Pre-eminent among the preferred destinations for South Africans on the run was inevitably the United States. Here the Black Diaspora of post-coloniality converged with the Black Diaspora of post-enslavement.

In the heat of the contemporary debate about multiculturalism and diversity in the wider American society, one thing may so easily be overlooked: the increasing diversity within the African-American community itself. Never has the Black population in the United States been as diverse as it is today. The richness lies in a wider range of sub-ethnicity, a wider range of religious affiliation, a wider spectrum of ideology, and a more complex class structure. Are we facing a convergence of different Black Diasporas?

If Global Africa means people of African ancestry all over the world, the Black population of the United States is a microcosm of Global Africa. Today this Black population includes people from literally every Black country in the world: from every member of the African Union, every member of the Organization of American States, the Caribbean and from other parts of the Black world as well. If there is indeed a microcosm of global Africa, it is to be found within the shores of the United States of America - from Hutus to Haitians, from Baganda to Barbadians, from natives of Afro-Muscat to descendants of Afro-Mississippi. Black America is Global Africa in microcosm. The Black experience has a new dialectic of diversity.[6]

If the U.S.A. is the first universal nation in the world, South Africa may be developing into the first universal nation of Africa.[7] South Africa is also a microcosm of Global Africa. The demographic diversification of South Africa includes Black, Dutch, German, English; Malays from South East Asia; Indians from South Asia; religions include Christianity, Islam, Judaism, Hinduism, Sikhism, Confucianism, Buddhism and African religions. Multiple African national origins are involved.[8]

The geographic origins of the Black population in the United States have been diversified as a result of a number of factors. First, the immigration policies of the United States have been liberalized since the second half of the twentieth century as compared with the first half, thus admitting more Black immigrants.[9] Secondly, the racial situation within the United States has been desegregated enough to make the country more attractive to middle class Blacks from other lands. Thirdly, post-colonial problems in Africa and the Caribbean have created a brain drain to the Northern hemisphere, including the United States.[10]

Haiti has experienced the exodus not just of the intelligentsia but also of members of the poorest sectors of society, the Haitian boat people.[11] For a while, the problem of apartheid in South Africa also created a brain drain of refugees to Europe and North America. While many of these South Africans are now returning home, or planning to do so, a large proportion have become American citizens and will remain in the United States.

Partly because of the stimulus of new immigrants, and partly for other reasons, the religious landscape of Black America has also become more diverse. Haitians have not only strengthened Catholicism; some of them have also arrived with residual 'voodoo' culture of their own.[12] More ancestral traditional religions directly from Africa have become more legitimate in some African-American circles. Yoruba religious culture has been particularly influential. Religion too has its Diasporas.

Within the Protestant tradition there is also more diversity now in Black America than there was in the first half of the twentieth century. Immigrants from Africa and the Caribbean have enriched Protestant diversity in the country, ranging from Anglicans from Nigeria to followers of Simon Kimbangu from the Democratic Republic of the Congo.[13] South Africa had earlier versions of millenarian movements. In addition, African versions of the Eastern Orthodox tradition are now better represented in the United States. The Ethiopian Orthodox Church and the Coptic Church now have stronger leadership in the United States.

The Rastafari movement from the Caribbean has also been part of the American scene in the second half of the twentieth century. It is as much a cultural phenomenon as it is a religious one.[14]

The term Diaspora did indeed originate with the Jews. Black Jews are not a new phenomenon in the United States. Sometimes these are basically Old Testament Christians who have become more and more Abrahamic in the Old Testament sense. African-American Jews have sometimes had difficulty being recognized by Israel under the *Law of Return*. The Black Jews of Ethiopia (the so-called *Falasha*) were also slow in gaining full recognition in Israel, but most of the Ethiopian Jews were at last moved to Israel in the 1980s under Operation Moses and subsequent transfers.[15] A few Ethiopian Jews have migrated to the United States and become Americans.

Islam has wider pan-African implications. There are now virtually as many Muslims as Jews in the United States - but the Muslims are of course much less visible and much less influential than are the mainstream U.S. Jews.[16] Islam provides some direct African-American linkages with both Africa and the Middle East. But there are also areas of contrast between African-Americans and West Indians in relation to both Islam and indigenous African religion. Let us look at the sociology

201

of religion in the African Diaspora more closely. It inevitably intertwines with other Diasporas.

Black Religious Alternatives

Among Diaspora Africans of the Western hemisphere there are two routes toward re-Africanisation. One route is through Pan-Islam - the transition chosen by Elijah Muhammed and Malcolm X. The other is the route directly through Pan-Africanism, the transition chosen by Marcus Garvey and the Rastafari Movement. Ras (Prince) Tafari were the title and name of Haile Selassie before his coronation as Emperor of Ethiopia.

One question which arises is why Islam has made much more progress among North American Blacks than among Blacks in the West Indian Diaspora. The second question is why African traditional religion, or beliefs rooted in sacred Africanity, sometimes appears to be more visible in the Caribbean than among Africans of North America.

The transition from Africanity to Arab-ness among African Americans continues to be acceptable. Indeed, of all the religions associated with Asia, the one which is the most <u>Afro-Asian</u> is indeed Islam. The oldest surviving Islamic academic institutions are actually located in the African continent - including Al-Azhar University in Cairo which is over a thousand years old. The Muslim Academy of Timbuktu in what is today Mali is remembered by Pan-Africanists with pride.[17] Timbuktu was at its height under the Songhai empire (1325 to 1591) and the Mali empire (1100 to 1700) – overlapping periods.[18]

In Nigeria there are more Muslims than there are Muslims in any Arab country, including the largest Arab country in population, Egypt.[19] On the other hand, there are more Arabs in Africa as a whole than in Asia. Indeed, up to two thirds of the Arab world by population, and almost half the membership of the Arab League, lies in the African continent.[20] In that sense, Africa is an Afro-Arab continent.

Given then the tendency of the Black American paradigm to draw no sharp distinction between being Black and being "coloured", Islam's Africanness was not too diluted by its Arab origins. Elijah Muhammed, Malcolm X and Louis Farrakhan have sometimes equated Islamisation with Africanisation. North American Black Muslims have seen Mecca as a port of call on the way back to the African heritage, as well as a stage on the way back towards God.

Islam in the Caribbean, on the other hand, has been handicapped by two factors. Firstly, race consciousness in the Caribbean does not as readily equate Black with Brown as it has historically done in the United States. The Caribbean historical experience has been based on a racial hierarchy (different shades of stratification) rather than racial dichotomy (a polarized divide between white and "coloured"). Arabs in the Caribbean racial paradigm therefore tend to belong to a different pecking order from Africans. Indeed, Lebanese and Syrians in the West Indies are more likely to be counted as white rather than Black, especially if they are Christian. As a result, the Arab origins of Islam are less likely to be equated with Africanity, although there are exceptions, like the more radical nationalism of Afro-Trinidadian Islam led by Yasseen Abubaker.

Moreover, the Caribbean has a highly visible *East Indian Diaspora*, a large proportion of whom are Muslims. [21] In giving a lecture in Georgetown, Guyana, in the past, on the subject of 'Islam in Africa', the overwhelming majority of my audience were not Afro-Guyanese (eager to learn more about Africa) but Indo-Guyanese,(eager to learn more about Islam. Among most Blacks in Guyana and Trinidad, there is a tendency to see Islam neither as *African* nor as *Arab*, but as *Indian*. The result is a much slower pace of Islamic conversions among Caribbean Africans than among African-Americans. Fewer Caribbean Blacks are likely to see the Muslim holy city of Mecca as a spiritual port of call on the way back to the cultural womb of Africa. On the contrary, Mecca is more likely to be perceived as a stage of cultural refuelling on the way to the Indian sub-continent.

The Islamic option is regarded by African-Americans as a possible rival to the Christianity of the white man. From a racial perspective, parts of the Qur'an seem to be an improvement upon the white man's Old Testament. The Islamic civilisation once exercised dominion and power over European populations in Spain and later over Eastern Europe under the Ottomans. Historically Islamic culture refined what we now call 'Arabic numerals,' invented Algebra, developed the zero, pushed forward the frontiers of science, and built legendary constructions from Al-Hambra in Spain to the Taj Mahal in India.[22] Black America's paradigm of romantic gloriana is more comfortable with such a record of achievement than with the more subtle dignity of Yoruba, Igbo or Kikuyu traditional religion.

203

There is a related difference to bear in mind. Cultural nationalism in Black America often looks to ancient Egypt for inspiration - perceiving pharaonic Egypt as a <u>Black</u> civilisation. Caribbean Black nationalism has shown a tendency to look to Ethiopia. The Egyptian route to Black cultural validation again emphasizes complexity and gloriana. On the other hand, the Ethiopian route to Black cultural validation can be Biblical and austere. These are comparative Diasporas in search of ancestral reaffirmation.

The most influential Ethiopic movement in the African Diaspora has become the Rastafari movement, with its Jamaican roots. Named after Haile Selassie's older titled designation, the Jamaican movement evolved a distinctive way of life, often austere. Curiously enough, the movement's original deification of the Emperor of Ethiopia was more Egyptian than Abyssinian. The fusion of Emperor with Godhead was almost pharaonic. The ancient Kings of Egypt built the pyramids as alternative abodes. The divine monarchs did not really die when they ceased to breathe; they had merely moved to a new address. To die was, in fact, to change one's address and modify one's life-style. In this sense the original theology of the Rastafari movement was a fusion of Egyptianism and pre-Biblical Ethiopianism. The resulting life-style of the Rastas, on the other hand, has been closer to romantic simplicity than to romantic gloriana. In North America the Rasta style is still more likely to appeal to people of Caribbean origin than to long-standing African Americans with their grander paradigm of cultural pride.

Pan-Africanism and Pan-Islamism are still two alternative routes towards the African heritage. After all, Islam first arrived in the Americas and in South Africa in chains, for it was brought to the Western hemisphere by enslaved Africans and in South Africa through enslaved Malays. If Alex Haley is correct about his African ancestor, Kunta Kinte was a Muslim. So Haley assures us in <u>Roots</u>. In reality the Haley family under slavery was better able *to* preserve its African pride than to protect its Islamic identity. Slavery damaged both the legacy of African culture and the legacy of Islam among the imported Black captives. But for quite a while Islam in the Black Diaspora was destroyed more completely than was Africanity.

In South Africa, on the other hand, Islam among the ethnic Malays has survived strongly in spite of three hundred years of enslavement, racism and apartheid.

Pan-Africanism in the Post-Apartheid Era

In the new America since September 11, 2001, African American Muslims have sometimes undergone a transition from being members of a disadvantaged Black race to being members of a disadvantaged religious group. As Muslims they are part of a group which includes U.S. citizens of such diverse national origins as the Middle East, South Asia, South-East Asia, post-colonial Africa and parts of Europe.

As we have indicated, cultural Pan-Africanism among people of African descent has historically been inspired more by ancient Egypt in the North, and by Ethiopia in the East, than by South Africa in the South.

Black people have identified with the builders of the pyramids as a grand civilisation of Africa itself. Black people have also historically identified with Ethiopia as an African heritage which goes back to Biblical times and which had a Black imperial monarchy for thousands of years.

While ancient Egypt and traditional Ethiopia have been major inspirations of cultural Pan-Africanism, West Africa and Southern Africa have been fertile inspirations of political Pan-Africanism.

West Africa was one of the foundations of political Pan-Africanism partly because most Black people in the <u>Americas</u> are, or <u>believe</u> they are, of West African origin. In addition, West Africans joined Diaspora-led Pan-African movements earlier than did other continental Africans. Thirdly, West Africa produced Kwame Nkrumah and Sekou Toure, two of the most towering Pan-Africanists of the twentieth century. And, fourthly, West Africa produced Leopold Senghor, one of the founding fathers of Negritude, and Cheikh Anta Diop, Africa's greatest champion of Nilocentric Black Civilisation.

Until the 1990s, South Africa was a cause of political Pan-Africanism in others, but was not itself Pan-Africanist. The martyrdom of South Africa under apartheid aroused Black solidarity worldwide, and gave the newly independent African states a continuing basis of unification. But in spite of Steve Biko, South Africans themselves were not especially Pan-African.

There followed South Africa in the 1990s under Nelson Mandela. Mandela himself was also a great cause of Pan-Africanism in others. His martyrdom aroused the shared anger of much of the world, and especially the Black world. Mandela became a focus of Black solidarity.

205

But was Mandela a Pan-Africanist in the 1990s? Here comes a paradox. He was a globalist, on one side, and a South African patriot on the other. But in action, even as the first democratically elected President of South Africa, he was less of a Pan-Africanist than people like Kwame Nkrumah, Julius Nyerere and Moammar Qaddafy. Nelson Mandela has become the most globalist of all African political leaders. But when in power he concentrated less on Pan-African affairs than on South Africa, on one side, and world affairs, on the other.

By far, Thabo Mbeki has been more active in Pan-African affairs from Haiti to Harlem, from Kingston to Kinshasa, from Togo to Timbuktu. South Africa under Thabo Mbeki is among the leaders of the re-globalisation of Pan-Africanism. Pan-Africanism went global for the first time at the Manchester Congress of 1945 before it went local more recently. There are now tendencies towards its re-globalisation. Pan-Africanism has come full circle.

What is particularly appropriate is that South Africa is a new alliance between Black and Brown people, on the one hand, and the old European Diaspora of conquest, on the other. South Africans of all races may be reaching out to the wider world of Diasporas.

If ancient Egypt and imperial Ethiopia inspired *cultural* Pan-Africanism, and African Americans, West Indians and West Africans were the vanguard of *political* Pan-Africanism, South Africa is now accepting the torch as a vanguard of *global* Pan-Africanism. To paraphrase my television series, *The Africans: A Triple Heritage:*

We are a people of the day before yesterday and a people of the day after tomorrow. Today we are scattered so widely that the sun never sets on the descendants and Diasporas of Africa. The world has become our village and we plan to make it more human between now and the day after tomorrow.

NOTES

[1] For discussions on Diaspora, see André Levy and Alex Weingrod, Eds., *Homelands and Diasporas : Holy Lands and Other Places* (Stanford, CA: Stanford University Press, 2005); Erich S. Gruen, "Diaspora and Homeland," in Howard Wettstein, Ed., *Diasporas and Exiles: Varieties of Jewish Identity* (Berkeley, CA: University of California Press, 2002), pp. 18-46; as also Gabriel Sheffer, "Is the Jewish Diaspora Unique?" in Eliezer Ben-Rafael, Yosef Gorny, and Yaacov Ro'I,

Eds., *Contemporary Jewries: Convergence and Divergence* (Leiden and Boston, MA: Brill, 2003), pp. 23-44.

[2] David Dimbleby's documentary series, "The White Tribe of Africa", a history of the Afrikaner, won the Supreme Documentary Award of the Royal Television Society in 1979.

[3] David Harrison, *The White Tribe of Africa: South Africa in Perspective* (Berkeley, CA: University of California Press, 1982, 1981).

[4] Descriptions and analyses of the various African Diasporas may be found, for example, in the following: Joseph E. Harris, Ed. *Global Dimensions of the African Diaspora* (Washington, DC: Howard University Press, 2003), 2nd ed.; Shihan de Silva Jayasuriya and Richard Pankhurst, Eds., *The African Diaspora in the Indian Ocean* (Trenton, NJ: Africa World Press, 2003); Erna Brodber, *The Continent of Black Consciousness : On the History of the African Diaspora From Slavery to the Present Day* (London : New Beacon Books, 2003); John Hunwick and Eve T. Powell, *The African Diaspora in the Mediterranean Lands of Islam* (Princeton, NJ : Markus Wiener Publishers, 2002); Darlene Clark Hine and Jacqueline McLeod., Eds., *Crossing Boundaries: Comparative History of Black People in Diaspora* (Bloomington, IN: Indiana University Press, 1999); E.L. Bute, *The Black Handbook: The People, History and Politics of Africa and the African Diaspora* (London and Washington: Cassell, 1997); Alusine Jalloh and Stephen E. Maizlish, Eds., *The African Diaspora* (College Station, TX: Texas A&M University Press, 1996); Michael L. Coniff, *Africans in the Americas: A History of the Black Diaspora* (New York: St. Martin's Press, 1994); and Edward Scobie, *Global African Presence*, (Brooklyn, NY: A & B Books, 1994).

[5] On Jews in South Africa, see, for instance, Gideon Shimoni, *Community and Conscience: The Jews in Apartheid South Africa* (Hanover, NH and Glosberry: Brandeis University Press published by University Press of New England and David Philip, 2003) and Sergio DellaPergola and Allie A. Dubb, *South African Jewry: A Sociodemographic Profile* (Jerusalem : Institute of Contemporary Jewry, Hebrew University of Jerusalem, 1988).

[6] Even African Americans who have been in the US for generations can discover, with some confidence, their genetic match with African tribes and thus their geographic origins; see Amy Harmon, "Blacks Pin Hope on DNA to Fill Slavery's Gaps in Family Trees," *The New York Times* (July 25, 2005). Of course, it is to be noted that theories about a common African origin for humans have received increasing empirical support; see John Noble Wilford, "Homo Sapiens Gets a Lot Older in a New Analysis of Fossils," *The New York Times* (February 17, 2005).

[7] For an interesting comparison of diversity in the United States and South Africa, see Jacklyn Cock and Alison Bernstein, *Melting Pots & Rainbow Nations : Conversations About Difference in the United States and South Africa* (Urbana : University of Illinois Press, 2002).

[8] Some of the implications of this multicultural South Africa are analyzed in Kristin Henrard, *Minority Protection in Post-Apartheid South Africa : Human Rights, Minority Rights, and Self-Determination* (Westport, CT: Praeger 2002) and Wilmot James, Daria Caliguire, and Kerry Cullinan, Eds., *Now That We Are Free: Coloured Communities in a Democratic South Africa* (Boulder, CT: L. Rienner, 1996).

[9] The important law that changed these circumstances was the Immigration Reform and Control Act of 1965. Unlike previous immigration legislation, this Act did not have race as a category for immigration and naturalization decisions; a detailed analysis of this Act may be found in Cheryl Shanks, *Immigration and the Politics of American Sovereignty, 1890-1990* (Ann Arbor, MI: University of Michigan Press, 2001), pp. 144-186.

[10] A 2005 World Bank study pointed out that a quarter to almost half of the college educated citizens of African countries like Ghana, Mozambique, Kenya, Uganda lived abroad in an O.E.C.D. country - a fraction that rises to more than 80 percent for Haiti and Jamaica; for a report, see Celia W. Dugger, "Developing Lands Hit Hardest by 'Brain Drain'," *The New York Times* (October 25, 2005).

[11] It is instructive to note that while the population of Haiti is estimated at 10 million, more than a million live overseas (including in the United States); see Jared Diamond, *Collapse: How Societies Choose to Fail or Succeed* (New York: Viking Penguin, 2005), p. 338, p. 330. On the Haitian diaspora in the United States, consult Anthony V. Catanese, *Haitians: Migration and Diaspora* (Boulder, CO: Westview, 1998).

[12] On the interaction between Catholicism and voodoo in Haiti, see Leslie G. Desmangles, *The Faces of the Gods: Vodou and Roman Catholicism in Haiti* (Chapel Hill, NC: University of North Carolina Press, 1992). On the spread of voodoo in the Haitian diaspora, see Elizabeth McAlister, *Rara!: Vodou, Power, and Performance in Haiti and its Diaspora* (Berkeley, CA: University of California Press, 2002) and Barbara Browning, *Infectious Rhythm : Metaphors of Contagion and the Spread of African Culture* (New York: Routledge, 1998).

[13] For a report on the growth of African churches in New York City, for example, see Daniel J. Wakin, "Where Gospel Resounds in African Tongues,"

The New York Times (April 18, 2004). The Redeemed Christian Church of God, founded in Lagos, Nigeria, is building a North American headquarters in Greenville, Texas, causing some unease among its inhabitants; see Simon Romero "A Texas Town Nervously Awaits a New Neighbour," *The New York Times* (August 21, 2005). There have also been tensions between African denominations and their brethren in Western Christian denominations over US and UK-based denomination's stands on issues like homosexuality. For instance, the Anglican church of Nigeria has broken off relations with the US Episcopalian Church and the Canadian Anglican church as a protest as a result of actions such as the 2003 consecration in the United States of an openly gay bishop, V. Gene Robinson, and has also threatened to break off relations with the Church of England over similar issues. For a report, see Craig Timberg, "Nigerian Churches Tell West to Practice What It Preached on Gays," *The Washington Post* (October 24, 2005).

[14] On the Rastafarian movement, consult, for example, Leonard E. Barrett, Sr., *The Rastafarians* (Boston: Beacon Press, 1997).

[15] These subsequent operations were called Operation Joshua and Operation Solomon. For an account of Operation Solomon, see, for example, Stephen Spector, *Operation Solomon: The Daring Rescue of the Ethiopian Jews* (Oxford and New York: Oxford University Press, 2005).

[16] *The New York Times* put it in the following terms as far back as August 1995: Muslims now outnumber Episcopalians [Anglicans] 2-to-1. With six million adherents, Islam is expected to overtake Judaism as the largest non-Christian religion in the United States by the end of the decade. See Brooke James, "Amid Islam's Growth in the U.S., Muslims Face a Surge of Attacks", *The New York Times* (August 28, 1995), p. 1. A recent estimate puts the number of Jews in the US population at 6.06 million, amounting to about 2.2 percent of the US population, according to a table in *The Statistical Abstract of the United States* (Washington, DC: Bureau of the Census, January 2002), p. 56. Numbers of Muslims in the United States vary. According to one study conducted by Professor Ihsan Bagby of Shaw University in Raleigh, North Carolina (as part of a larger study of American congregations called "Faith Communities Today," coordinated by Hartford Seminary's Hartford Institute for Religious Research, there are approximately 6 million Muslims in the U.S. with over 2 million of these being regularly participating adult attenders at the more than 1,209 mosques/masjids in the United States. (The full report is available at <http://www.cair-net.org/mosquereport/>, April 19, 2004). The television program *Frontline* also points out that, "The estimated 5-7 million Muslims in the U.S. include both immigrants and those born in America. (three-quarters of whom are African Americans)." "Portraits of Ordinary Muslims: United

States" *Frontline,* PBS Television, May 9, 2002. Retrieved on May 1, 2004 from <http://www.pbs.org/wgbh/pages/frontline/shows/muslims/portraits/us.html>.

[17] The intellectual riches of Timbuktu are described in, among others, Alex Ulam, "Elusive Libraries of Timbuktu," *Archaeology* (Jul/Aug2004), Vol. 57 Issue 4, pp. 36-40; Brent D. Singleton, "African Bibliophiles: Books and Libraries in Medieval Timbuktu," *Libraries & Culture* (Winter2004), Vol. 39 Issue 1, pp. 1-12; "Timbuktu-City of Legends," at <http://news.bbc.co.uk/1/hi/world/africa/1911321.stm>, April 15, 2002); and Klaus-Friedrich Koch, "Fabulous Timbuktu," *Natural History* (May77), Vol. 86 Issue 5, pp.68-75.

[18] On the Mali empire, consult Edward William Bovill, *The Golden Trade of the Moors: West African kingdoms in the Fourteenth Century* (Princeton, NJ : M. Weiner Publishers, 1995), esp. pp. 85-90, and Nehemiah Levtzion, *Ancient Ghana and Mali* (New York, NY: African Pub. Co.,1973) and on the Songhai Empire, see Bovill, *The Golden Trade of the Moors,* pp.132-206.

[19] The estimation of the numbers of Muslims in Nigeria is somewhat controversial because of political issues over the census. According to an Associated Press report, "Muslim Mobs, Seeking Vengeance, Attack Christians in Nigeria," *New York Times* (May 13, 2004), "Many of Nigeria's 126 million people, [are] split almost evenly between Muslims and Christians. . ." However, another report estimates the percentage of Muslims in Nigeria at 75 percent; see <http://www.islamicweb.com/begin/population.htm>, May 28, 2004.

[20] According to the *World Factbook,* as of July 2001, the total estimated population of Algeria, Egypt, Libya, Morocco, Sudan and Tunisia was 182.9 million. These six African countries alone, which are part of the Arab League make up the majority of that organizations' widely reported total population of 281 million. These figures are compiled from the *CIA World Factbook, 2001,* available online at <http://www.odci.gov/cia/publications/factbook/>, and retrieved December 3, 2001. Current members of the Arab League may be accessed at <http://www.arableagueonline.org/>, December 3, 2001.

[21] As of July 2001, Trinidad and Tobago, and Guyana have populations of 1.16 million (40.3 % East Indian) and 697, 181 (49 % East Indian) respectively. The Muslim populations of Trinidad and Tobago and Guyana are 5.8 % and 9 % respectively. These figures are drawn from the *CIA World Factbook, 2001,* available online at <http://www.odci.gov/cia/publications/factbook/>, and retrieved May 1, 2004.

[22] For details on the Islamic contribution to scientific knowledge, consult C. M. Stanton, *Higher Learning in Islam: The Classical Period, A. D. 700 to 1300* (Savage, MD: Rowman and Littlefield, 1990), pp. 103-119.

CHAPTER 13

SOUTH AFRICA BETWEEN THE RENAISSANCE AND SEVEN PILLARS OF WISDOM

T E. Lawrence, better known as Lawrence of Arabia, once wrote a book entitled *Seven Pillars of Wisdom*.[1] He was echoing an earlier biblical formulation of such seven pillars.

Our concern in this chapter is an African reformulation. We need to address the Seven Pillars of the African Renaissance.

South Africa has done more than any other country to promote the concept of the African Renaissance. But Thabo Mbeki, now South Africa's President, had inherited the torch from earlier generations of thinkers.[2] In the 1930s, Nnamdi Azikiwe, who later became President of Nigeria, published a pamphlet entitled *Renascent Africa*. But in those early days of the twentieth century, when Africa was under colonial domination, the concept of an African Renaissance was a distant and remote dream.

In 1994 when South Africa was at last ready to embark on a democratic destiny, it made sense for South Africans to become the vanguard of a long delayed African revival. But we need to identify more explicitly the imperatives of that rejuvenation, and strengthen its seven pillars.

The first pillar of the African Renaissance grew directly out of the South African struggle against apartheid. This was the *imperative of liberation*. Kwame Nkrumah phrased it best when he said, "Seek ye first the political kingdom, and all else will be added unto you."

Nkrumah was right in the first phrase, "Seek yee first the political kingdom." Let us first pursue political freedom. But Nkrumah was grossly exaggerating when he said, "All else will be added unto you." The "all else" needed other imperatives.

Between Geography and Gender

South Africa attained political liberation in 1994, but she has not yet accomplished the *economic* liberation of the masses. The delay of economic emancipation was caused by the second pillar of the African Renaissance: *the imperative of accommodation.*

The pursuit of the political kingdom had to be moderated by the principle of accommodating competing and conflicting interests. What emerged out of the South African negotiations was a Faustian compromise. White South Africans said to Black South Africans, "You take the crown, we keep the jewels." The Blacks would at last capture the political kingdom, while white people would collectively retain control of the economic domain.

A related pillar of the Renaissance is *communication.* At its most literal sense, this is the domain of *words.* Like Canada, South Africa used to have a bilingual policy. While Canada has had English and French as the sole official languages, apartheid South Africa used to have Afrikaans and English. But English and French in Canada's policy were the mother tongues of the majority of Canadians. South Africa's bilingualism, on the other hand, marginalized the languages of the majority of the people. This third pillar of the African Renaissance consists of promoting communication in a manner that does not marginalize the linguistic heritage of the African peoples. South Africa took a major step when, after political apartheid, it adopted eleven official languages.

It is also reassuring that the new African Union is exploring ways of making two or more African languages official in this new continental organization. At the 2004 summit meeting in Ethiopia, the Heads of State listened for the first time to another Head of State addressing them in the Swahili language. It was a historic precedent, set by the President of Mozambique, Alberto Joachim Chissano.

It was also the fulfillment of a dream I had in 1973 when, at an International Congress of Africanists in Addis Ababa, I was asked to thank Emperor Haile Selassie after his address welcoming the guests.

I decided to begin by thanking him in Kiswahili. The choice of an African language was so unexpected that it caused consternation. The Emperor was turning his knob trying to find the relevant channel; the interpreters in their booths were in a state of linguistic paralysis. Having dramatically made my point that African international meetings should include the use of African languages, I then switched to the English language. The African Renaissance should include greater recognition of indigenous languages.

213

In addition to *liberation, accommodation and communication*, the African Renaissance demands expanding *participation*. Critical areas of participation include political participation and involvement in all areas of development.

The collapse of political apartheid opened the doors for fuller participation in politics by non-whites of South Africa. In the rest of Africa, political participation was often circumscribed by Africa's own Black dictators. But the good news of the 1990's included not only democratization in South Africa, but legalization of political parties in Black countries previously under single-party systems or previously under military rule. Africa is opening up, in spite of the deep instabilities of countries like Burundi, Rwanda and the Democratic Republic of the Congo.

Empowerment is often a higher degree of participation. The quest for Black economic empowerment seeks new economic opportunities for previously disadvantaged groups.

But as important as racial equality is the struggle for the greater empowerment of women. In the legislative process, Africa has previously experimented with *racial_reservation of seats*, as in apartheid South Africa, or the early years of independent Zimbabwe, or colonial constitutions like those of Kenya and Tanganyika in the 1950's. But now we should increasingly experiment with *gender reservation of seats*. One scenario is the following:

Phase I: Let us say 20% of legislative seats are reserved for women on a separate female electoral roll, while still allowing women to compete in the remaining 80% of seats. In this phase, both the voters and the candidates will be women.

Phase II: Still 20% of the legislative seats are reserved for women, but in this phase the voters would be both men and women. The candidates would, of course, remain female candidates.

Phase III: When women have become politically effective enough to no longer require the protection of reserved seats, all the 100% of the legislative seats can enter the arena of competitive campaigning entirely on the basis of merit and effectiveness.

The imperative of participation is democratically the most crucial among the pillars of the African Renaissance.

214

A fifth pillar of the African Renaissance is closely related to the second one. This new imperative of *reconciliation* is linked to the earlier imperative of *accommodation*. However, while accommodation need not be preceded by conflict, our concept of reconciliation in this text is an exercise in peace-making and conflict resolution. Accommodation is a quest for *compromise*, while reconciliation is a quest for *peace*. The negotiations to end the old cycle of apartheid was a combined quest for both peace (reconciliation) and compromise (accommodation). The African Renaissance should also seek to build upon those aspects of African culture which are oriented towards tolerance and forgiveness. This is often very basic to reconciliation.

The sixth pillar of African Renaissance is *conservation*, oriented towards protecting the ecology and environment. Planet Earth needs to be protected for both ethical and aesthetic reasons. The ethics may include ecological fairness to future generations or protectiveness towards the animal world.

The aesthetics of environmentalism rise to the level of appreciating the beauty of nature. African cultures are imbued with the ethics of environmentalism. Sometimes little hills are regarded as sacred; the baobab tree is recognized for its brooding majesty. Some African clans adopt such identity totems as the crocodile, the leopard, or the gazelle. A clansman of the gazelle does not kill it for food.

But strong as Africa is in the ethics of environmentalism, Africa is relatively weak in the aesthetics of environmentalism. Nowhere is this better illustrated than in the relative marginalization of flowers in African culture. It may be a particularly challenging task for the African Renaissance to reactivate the aesthetic environmentalism of Africa, and stimulate the flowering of the African heritage.

The Aesthetics of the Environment

The environmental movement of the twentieth century was only partly inspired by a concern for population growth, planetary survival, and an economic cost-benefit analysis. It was also inspired by the aesthetics of conservation. The concept of "endangered species" has been a call for deference of bio-diversity, rooted in the belief that a world with fewer species of animals and a smaller range of plants was a less beautiful world.

On this issue of natural beauty one question which has arisen is whether the love of flowers was culturally relative. Jack Goody, the distinguished Cambridge anthropologist, has strongly argued that although Africa is rich in plants, African culture is not fascinated by flowers.

> ...the peoples of Africa did not grow domestic flowers, nor yet did they make use of wild ones to any significant extent in worship, in gift giving or in the decoration of the body... But what is perhaps more surprising is that flowers, neither domesticated nor wild, play so little part in the domain of design or the creative arts.[3]

Jack Goody goes on to observe that African sculpture provides no striking floral designs. And even in African poetry, songs and proverbs, flowers are relatively absent unless there is a prior stimulus of Islam or some other external aesthetic.

George Bernard Shaw was once visited by a flower-loving aristocratic fan. The lady visitor observed that there were no flowers inside Shaw's home. "Mr. Shaw, I am surprised to see no flowers in your beautiful home. Don't you love flowers, Mr. Shaw?"

Bernard Shaw responded: "Indeed I do love flowers, dear lady. I also love children. But I do not go around chopping off their heads for display in my living room!" Shaw was asserting that a genuine love of flowers required our leaving them to prosper as plants in the soil. There is a way in which African attitudes to flowers is *organic* in the same sense.

Yet this does not explain the more limited use of the imagery of flowers in either African plastic art or African verbal arts. Where are the African poetic equivalents of William Wordsworth and his fascination with daffodils, or his sense of wonder about:

> *A violet by mossy stone*
> *Half hidden from the eye!*
> *Fair as a star when only one*
> *Is shining in the sky.*[4]

Shakespeare urges us not to attempt to beautify what is already naturally beautiful:

> *To gild refined gold, to paint the lily,*
> *To throw a perfume on the violet*
> *To smooth the ice, or add another hue*
> *Unto the rainbow...*
>
> *Is wasteful and ridiculous excess.*[5]

In African poetry and song is there an equivalent use of flowers as metaphors "to point a moral or adorn a tale"?

If it is true that African culture underutilizes flowers for either art or ritual, what are the underlying social and aesthetic reasons? One possible explanation would take us back to Bertrand Russell's assertion that "civilization was born out of the pursuit of luxury." It is possible to see civilization as a relentless quest for beauty. It is a sense of "civilization" which produced the Taj Mahal, the sunken churches of Lalibela, the Palace of Versailles, and the spectacular temples of Abu Simbel at Aswan built by Ramses II. Such splendor illustrates what Bertrand Russell regarded as "the pursuit of luxury".

Before European colonization were the cultures of equatorial Africa inadequately motivated to pursue luxury? Was that why there were so few indigenous palaces and monuments outside the Nile Valley?[6] Was the psychology of not constructing beautiful structures related to the psychology of inadequate attention to flowers?

Another possible explanation for the de-flowering of African cultures is that so many flowers on the Equator were potential fruit in the process of formation. A planted seed begins to germinate into a plant; the plant produces a bud; the bud blossoms into a flower, and the flower culminates into a fruit. Africa celebrates the end product [the fruit] rather than the intermediate stage (the flower). Africa may be poor in names for flowers. In most indigenous cultures there is no tropical equivalent of such range of names as, the lily, the violet, the tulip, the orchid, the daffodil. But African languages are fully competitive in names of *fruit: chungwa, chenzi, embe, bungo, kitoria, nazi, kanju, ndizi, kunazi, fenesi, buyu and many others*. More recent African loan words for fruit (usually borrowed from Arabic) include <u>nanasi</u> (pineapple) and *tufaha* (apple.)

Produce and Innovate

The seventh principle of the African Renaissance is the *twin imperative of production and innovation*. The principle of production would include the work-ethic and processes of production, distribution and exchange. The African Renaissance would seek to maximize efficiency and optimize returns. It would also seek African unity and economies of scale.

The innovative part of this imperative is caught in a different kind of African dilemma, the dilemma between continuity and change, between the heritage of ancestry and the potential of innovation.

African thinkers are in disagreement between *wisdom*, on one side, and *technical_skills*, on the other. Philosophers of *romantic gloriana* have emphasized the monumental structural achievements of Africa's past, from the pyramids of Egypt to the brooding majesty of Great Zimbabwe. Without necessarily realizing it, such gloriana thinkers seem to share part of Bertrand Russell's conviction that civilization is the pursuit of luxury. The obelisks of Ethiopia were a symbol of both civilization and creative luxury.

The greatest of Africa's post-colonial gloriana thinkers was Cheikh Anta Diop of Senegal, who emphasized ancient Egypt's pivotal role in the origins of world civilization as a whole. Diop saw the River Nile as the mother of the earliest human achievements.[7]

The other major African school of civilizational theory has emphasized not the grand monuments of Africa's structural achievements but the wisdom of being non-technical. In the words of the Black poet of Martinique, Aime Cesaire:

Hooray for those who never invented anything!
Hooray for those who never discovered anything;
Hooray for joy, hooray for love;
Hooray for the pain of incarnate tears...

Honor to those who have invented neither powder nor the compass;
Those who have tamed neither gas nor electricity;
Those who have explored neither the seas nor the skies...
My negritude [my Blackness] is neither a tower nor a cathedral;
It plunges into the deep red flesh of the soil.[8]

Western thought has a sub-field called the "philosophy of science". What this simplifying school of African thought represents is a philosophy of *unscience*. As Jean-Paul Sartre pointed out, this African reveling in not having invented either powder or the compass is a proud celebration of non-technicalness. It is a salute to the wisdom of closeness to nature.[9]

The greatest African thinker of this simplifying school was also Senegalese. The late Leopold Sedar Senghor, who was President of Senegal from 1960 to 1980, was a philosopher and a poet, as well as a statesman. Senghor argued that while Cartesian epistemology starts from the premise "I think, therefore I am", African epistemology starts from the vastly different source of self-awareness: "I *feel*, therefore I am." Senghor belonged to the philosophy of *unscience*, in contrast to his *gloriana* compatriot, Cheikh Anta Diop.[10]

As we seek to construct a Global Ethic based on seven pillars of wisdom, we need to listen to those two competing parental philosophies about the relationship between expertise, on one side, and genuine wisdom, on the other. We need also to listen to Africa's song of self-affirmation as captured in the following poetic prose:

> *We are a people of the day before yesterday and a people of the day*
> *after tomorrow. Long before slavery we lived in one huge village called*
> *Africa. And then strangers came into our midst and took many of us*
> *away, scattering us to all the corners of the earth. Before those*
> *strangers came, our village was the world; we knew no other. But*
> *we are now spread out so widely that the Sun never sets on the*
> *descendants of Africa. The world is now our village, and we plan*
>
> *to make it more human between now and the day after tomorrow."*[11]

Wisdom begins when we understand ourselves. Wisdom matures when we aspire to higher human standards. How we treat strangers in our midst is the ultimate humane standard. We need to respond to the ancient dialectic between continuity and change. We need also to learn from the guardianship of the African Renaissance, with its seven pillars: the pillars of liberation, accommodation, communication, participation, reconciliation, conservation and production linked to innovation.

NOTES

[1] T.E. Lawrence, *Seven Pillars of Wisdom* (London: Privately Printed 1926, and New York: Doubleday, 1935).

[2] For more on Mbeki's "African Renaissance," consult Peter Vale and Sipho Maseko, "Thabo Mbeki, South Africa, and the Idea of An African Renaissance," in Sean Jacobs and Richard Calland, Eds., *Thabo Mbeki's World : The Politics And Ideology Of The South African President* (Pietermaritzburg, SA; London; and New York: University of Natal Press and Zed Books, 2002), pp. 121-142. Some of the hopes and fears of Thabo Mbeki for Africa may also be found in his op-ed, "Building A Better Africa," *The Washington Post* (June 10, 2004).

[3] Jack Goody, *The Culture of Flowers* (Cambridge and New York: Cambridge University Press, 1993] pp. 12-13.

[4] William Wordsworth, "She Dwelt Among the Untrodden Ways," (1800), *The Poems: William Wordsworth* ed., John Hayden, Volume 1 (New Haven, CT: Yale University Press, 1981), p. 366.

[5] These lines are from Shakespeare's play, "King John," in Act IV, Scene II; see *The Works of William Shakespeare* (New York: Oxford University Press, Shakespeare Head Press Edition, 1934), p. 319.

[6] The few places that were the exception to some degree were some structures in Great Zimbabwe and Mali, among others; consult Innocent Pakirayi, *The Zimbabwe Culture; Origins and Decline of Southern Zambezian States* (Walnut Creek, CA; Lanham, MD; Oxford, UK: AltaMira Press, 2001) and A. J. Wills, *An Introduction to the History of Central Africa* (London: Oxford University Press, 1967, Second Edition), pp. 17-19.

[7] A bibliography of Diop's work may be found in Christopher Gray, *Conceptions of History in the Works of Cheik Anta Diop and Theophile Obenga* (London: Karnak House, 1989), pp. 109-113. Some major works that may be consulted include Cheik Anta Diop, *Civilization or Barbarism: An Authentic Anthropology* (Brooklyn, NY: Lawrence Hill Books, 1991) and *Precolonial Black Africa: A Comparative Study of the Political and Social Systems of Europe and Black Africa, From Antiquity to the Formation of Modern States* (Westport, CT: L. Hill, 1987).

[8] These lines are from his poem, "Journal of a Homecoming," (Cahier d'un retour au pays Natal); for commentary, see Gregson Davis, *Aimé Cesaire* (Cambridge, New York and Melbourne: Cambridge University Press, 1997), pp. 20-61.

[9] J. P. Sartre, "Introduction to African Poetry," in *Black Orpheus*, trans. S. W. Allen (Paris: Presence Africaine, 1963), pp. 41-43.

[10] For a bibliography on "negritude," consult Colette V. Michael, *Negritude: An Annotated Bibliography*, (West Cornwall, CT: Locust Hill Press, 1988). An English-language version of Senghor's thoughts on negritude may be found in his *The Foundations of "Africainite" or "Negritude" and "Arabite"* (Paris: Presence Africaine, 1971).See also Ali A. Mazrui and JF Ade Ajayi et al "Trends in Philosophy and Science in Africa", *Africa Since 1935* in Ali A. Mazrui and C.Wondjii, eds., *UNESCO General History of Africa* , Vol. VIII. (London: Heinemann Educational Books, 1993), pp. 633-677.

[11] This African song of reaffirmation is paraphrased from programme 9 of Ali A. Mazrui's television series, *The Africans: A Triple Heritage* (BBC/PBS and Nigeria's Television Authority, 1986).

CHAPTER 14

SOUTH AFRICA AND SIXTY YEARS OF PAN-AFRICANISM

The year 2005 has been celebrated as the 60th anniversary of the end of World War II. With additional moral relief, the year also marked the end of the Nazi Holocaust against the Jews, the Gypsies (Romany Rom) and others. Also celebrated was the aftermath of the invasion of Normandy by the Allies.

But one little event of 1945 has been singularly omitted: a small conference of immense historical significance for Pan-Africanism.[1] The event signified an important phase in Black history. Since then Black history has encompassed four stages of Pan-Africanism: global, continental, sub-continental, local. One of the ironies of the African experience is that Pan-Africanism went global before it went local.

This year (2005) marked the 60th anniversary since a globally oriented Pan-African Congress in Manchester, England, in 1945. In that year Pan-Africanism was global partly because World War II was just ending, and the world was searching for alternative visions for the future. 1945 was also the year of the formation of the United Nations Organization, destined to become the first truly global world institution. The League of Nations had been far short of representative of the human race. The U.S.A. and most of Africa were conspicuously absent from the League of Nations.

The Pan-African Congress of 1945 was in the shadow of momentous global events. This relatively obscure Pan-African Conference in Manchester included participants who would one day become global figures, including Kwame Nkrumah of the Gold Coast, Jomo Kenyatta of Kenya, W.E.B. DuBois of the United States, and George Padmore of the Caribbean. They were unknown at the time, but they grew into global dimensions.[2] There was also the Pan-African legacy of Jamaica's Marcus Garvey in the background at Manchester.[3]

In the 1950s and 1960s, Pan-Africanism moved from a *globo-centric* Black movement to an *Afro-centric* continental movement. As head of the newly independent Ghana, Kwame Nkrumah hosted the All-Africa

People's Conference in Accra in 1958, bringing together representatives of the people of Africa to Accra. Nkrumah also hosted a separate conference of the few African states which were already independent before 1960.[4]

In May 1963 Pan-Africanism went truly continental with the formation of the Organization of African Unity in Addis Ababa (O.A.U.).[5] 1963 was a good year for relations between Arab Africa and sub-Saharan Africa. Algeria had just become independent in 1962, and Gamal Abdel Nasser was becoming a truly global figure. But 1963 was a bad year for relations between Anglophone and Francophone Africa because of the assassination of Sylvanus Olympio in Francophone Togo, and the accusations that Anglophone Ghana might have been implicated in the assassination.[6]

Nevertheless, the O.A.U helped to heal the wound between Francophone and Anglophone Africa. The O.A.U. also helped to build on the emerging cordiality between Arab Africa and sub-Saharan Africa. It eventually became a quid pro quo.[7] African states supported the Arabs in their struggle against Israeli injustices against Palestinians. Arab states supported Africans in the struggle against the injustices of apartheid in South Africa.

There were, of course, Arab states that would have supported the struggle against apartheid regardless of what they had in return. And there were African states that would have supported the Palestinian struggle in its own right regardless of the *quid pro quo*.[8]

After this continental phase when Pan-Africanism was struggling for decolonisation and against racial minority rule, Pan-Africanism went *sub-continental* in form of sub-regional integration. The East African Community rose and fell.[9] The Economic Community of West African States [ECOWAS] was spread on the wings of West African solidarity. [10] With SADC, Southern Africa reached new levels of regional integration decades after the old days of the Pan-African movement of East, Central and Southern Africa (PAFMECSA).[11] North Africa tried to find a *modus vivendi* between Pan-Africanism and Pan-Arabism in the wake of the death of Gamal Abdel Nasser in 1970.[12]

Pan-Africanism was then challenged on the cultural front. The question had arisen as to whether Africa was a convergence of civilisations and not just a mixture of tribes and mini-states. Islam and the West converged with the ancestors of Africa.

Pan-Africanism and Cultural Legacies

Cultural nationalism in Black America often looks to ancient Egypt for inspiration - perceiving pharaonic Egypt as a Black civilisation. Caribbean Black nationalism has shown a tendency to look to Ethiopia. The Egyptian route to Black cultural validation again emphasizes complexity and gloriana. On the other hand, the Ethiopian route to Black cultural validation can be Biblical and austere. These are comparative Diasporas in search of ancestral reaffirmation.

The most influential Ethiopic movement in the African Diaspora has become the Rastafari movement, with its Jamaican roots. Named after Haile Selassie's older titled designation, the Jamaican movement evolved a distinctive way of life, often austere. Curiously enough, the movement's original deification of the Emperor of Ethiopia was more Egyptian than Abyssinian. The fusion of Emperor with God-head was almost pharaonic. The ancient Kings of Egypt built the pyramids as alternative abodes. The divine monarchs did not really die when they ceased to breathe; they had merely moved to a new address. To die was, in fact, to change one's address and modify one's life-style. In this sense the original theology of the Rastafari movement was a fusion of Egyptianism and pre-Biblical Ethiopianism. [13]

The resulting life-style of the Rastas, on the other hand, has been closer to romantic simplicity than to romantic gloriana. In North America the Rasta style is still more likely to appeal to the people of Caribbean origin than to long-standing African Americans with their grander paradigm of cultural pride.

Pan-Africanism and Pan-Islamism are two alternative routes towards the African heritage. After all, Islam first arrived in the Americas and in South Africa in chains - for it was brought to the Western hemisphere by enslaved Africans and in South Africa through enslaved Malays.[14] If Alex Haley is correct about his African ancestor, Kunta Kinte was a Muslim. So Haley assures us in *Roots*. In reality the Haley family under slavery was better able to preserve its African pride than to protect its Islamic identity. Slavery damaged both the legacy of African culture and the legacy of Islam among the imported Black captives. But for quite a while Islam in the Black Diaspora was destroyed more completely than was Africanity.

In South Africa, on the other hand, Islam among the ethnic Malays has survived strongly in spite of three hundred years of enslavement, racism and apartheid.

In the new America since September 11, 2001, African American Muslims have sometimes undergone a transition from being members of a disadvantaged Black race to being members of a disadvantaged religious group. As Muslims they are part of a group which includes U.S. citizens of such diverse national origins as the Middle East, South Asia, South-East Asia, post-colonial Africa and parts of Europe.

As we have indicated, cultural Pan-Africanism among people of African descent has historically been inspired more by ancient Egypt in the North, and by Ethiopia in the East, than by South Africa in the South.

Black people have identified with the builders of the pyramids as a grand civilisation of Africa itself. Black people have also historically identified with Ethiopia as an African heritage which goes back to Biblical times and which had a Black imperial monarchy for thousands of years.

While ancient Egypt and traditional Ethiopia have been major inspirations of <u>cultural</u> Pan-Africanism, West Africa and Southern Africa have been fertile inspirations of <u>political</u> Pan-Africanism.

West Africa was one of the foundations of political Pan-Africanism partly because most Black people in the *Americas* are, or *believe* they are, of West African origin. In addition, West Africans joined Diaspora-led Pan-African movements earlier than did other continental Africans. Thirdly, West Africa produced Kwame Nkrumah and Sékou Touré, two of the most towering Pan-Africanists of the twentieth century. And, fourthly, West Africa produced Leopold Senghor, one of the founding fathers of Negritude, and Cheikh Anta Diop, Africa's greatest champion of Nilocentric Black Civilisation.

Until the 1990s South Africa was a cause of political Pan-Africanism in others, but was not itself Pan-Africanist. The martyrdom of South Africa under apartheid aroused Black solidarity worldwide, and gave the newly independent African states a continuing basis of unification. But in spite of Steve Biko, South Africans themselves were not especially Pan-African.

There followed South Africa in the 1990s under Nelson Mandela. Mandela himself was also a great cause of Pan-Africanism in others. His martyrdom aroused the shared anger of much of the world, and especially the Black world. Mandela became a focus of Black solidarity.

But was Mandela a Pan-Africanist in the 1990s? Here comes a paradox. He was a globalist, on one side, and a South African patriot on the other. But in action he was less a Pan-Africanist than people like Kwame Nkrumah, Julius Nyerere and Moammar Qaddafy.

Nelson Mandela has become the most globalist of all African political leaders. But when in power he concentrated less on Pan-African affairs than on South Africa, on one side, and world affairs, on the other.[15]

Thabo Mbeki has been more active in Pan-African affairs – from Haiti to Harlem, from Kingston to Kinshasa, from Togo to Timbuktu. South Africa under Thabo Mbeki is among the leaders of the re-globalisation of Pan-Africanism.[16] Pan-Africanism went global at the Manchester Congress of 1945 before it went local more recently. There are now tendencies towards its re-globalisation. Pan-Africanism has come full circle.

What is particularly appropriate is that South Africa is a new alliance between Black and Brown people, on the one hand, and the old European Diaspora of conquest, on the other. South Africans of all races may be reaching out to the wider world of Diasporas.

If ancient Egypt and imperial Ethiopia inspired *cultural* Pan-Africanism, and African Americans, West Indians and West Africans were the vanguard of *political* Pan-Africanism, South Africa is now accepting the torch as a vanguard of *global* Pan-Africanism. The Pan-African Parliament in Cape Town is a start. So is the Diaspora preoccupation of South Africa's foreign policy.

Pan-Africanism and Global Africa

We have sought to demonstrate that Pan-Africanism started global from Manchester in 1945 and has since been struggling to go, first, continental; then sub-continental; then territorially local, then inter-civilisational within Africa, and then inter-gender within Africa. Political solidarity between men and women can be as Pan-African as solidarity between African states.

But what has been also happening more subtly is this new globalisation of Pan-Africanism. The dialogue of civilisations within Africa is one version of the re-globalisation of Pan-Africanism. Great civilisational challenges are occurring in Senegal, Nigeria, Egypt, Morocco, Libya, Tanzania and elsewhere. Are we heading for a dialogue of civilisations or conflict of cultures? Civilisational Ecumenicalism is best illustrated in Africa.

Cultures differ in hate retention. Armenians have been hating the Turks since the Armenian massacres in 1915-17. Africa has a short memory of hate. Nelson Mandela lost 27 of the best years of his life in prison. When he came out, he was prepared to have tea with the unrepentant widow of Hendrick Verwoerd, the architect of apartheid, begged white terrorists to stop their fasting unto death and thus laid the foundations of Black-White reconciliation.[17] Before Mandela, Jomo Kenyatta of Kenya was denounced by the British as "leader unto darkness and earth", but emerged from jail an Anglophile eager to consolidate good relations with the former imperial power.[18] Ian Smith unleashed a civil war on Rhodesia/Zimbabwe. He lived to sit in a Black dominated Parliament and to openly criticize the new Black government of the day.[19] Nigeria had a brutal civil war (1967-1970) but found the discipline to pardon the vanquished.[20]

African culture helps create the ecumenical spirit and religious tolerance in indigenous Africa. Africa had no religious wars before the coming of Islam and Christianity. African indigenous religions were therefore non-competitive with other religions.

Even imported religions are not divisive in Africa, unless they reinforce prior differentiations. Consider the following about Nigeria: Almost all Hausa are Muslim. Almost all Igbo are Christian. Thus, Islam reinforces Hausa identity while Christianity reinforces Igbo identity. The Yoruba are almost half Muslim, half Christian. In Nigeria, Yoruba Muslims and Christians are united by Yoruba nationalism.

Senegal is 94% Muslim, a higher percentage than the 92 percentage of Muslims in Egypt. Yet, this overwhelmingly Muslim country had a Roman Catholic President, not briefly, but for twenty years (1960-1980). Leopold Senghor was abused by the opposition for many political "sins", but not for his religion. He was called a lackey of the French and political hypocrite, but almost never *Kafir* (infidel).

Senghor was succeeded by Diouf, a Muslim, but the new First Lady of Senegal was another Roman Catholic. Contrast ecumenical Senegal with the United States. The American presidency has only once strayed away from the Protestant fraternity after 200 years of the secular state. Contrast this with Tanzania's religious rotation of the presidency: Christian Julius Nyerere, Muslim Ali Hassan Mwinyi, Christian Benjamin Mkapa, and the next President is likely to be a Muslim.

In Black America the link between the sacred and the secular lies in the bond between the pulpit and politics. Consider the semi-theocratic leadership of Rev. Martin Luther King, Jr., Rev. Jesse Jackson, Minister Malcolm X, Minister Elijah Muhammed, and Minister Louis Farrakhan.

Another pillar of Pan-African wisdom is *conservation*, oriented towards protecting the ecology and environment. Planet Earth needs to be protected for both ethical and aesthetic reasons. The ethics may include ecological fairness to future generations or protectiveness towards the animal world. This is Pan-Africanism across generations and perhaps across different species.

The aesthetics of environmentalism rise to the level of appreciating the beauty of nature. African cultures are strong on the ethics of environmentalism. As we indicated, little hills are sometimes regarded as sacred; the baobab tree is recognized for its brooding majesty. Some African clans do indeed adopt such identity totems as the crocodile, the leopard, the gazelle.[21] A clansman of the gazelle does not kill it for food. Here again is Pan-Africanism across different species.

What about globalisation of Africa in terms of its re-unification with its Diaspora? As illustrated by the Fifth Pan-African Congress in Manchester in 1945, the first wave of Africa's reunification with its Diaspora was led by Diaspora Africans like W.E.B. DuBois, Marcus Garvey, George Padmore and Sylvester Williams, culminating with that Manchester Congress of 1945. The *latest* wave of Africa's reunification with its Diaspora is being led by the Republic of South Africa, as we indicated.[22]

Racism in Black America and the Caribbean was once the stimulus of Pan-African solidarity in the direction of the Manchester Congress of 1945. Racism in Southern Africa has since been the stimulus of Pan-African solidarity in the direction of new African Union and the potential inclusion of the African Diaspora within it. Has the Manchester Congress now flowered into the Pan-African Parliament in Midrand, South Africa?

There was no Internet at Manchester in 1945. There were no Black broadcasters or African television personalities. Africa had few messengers for its message to the world. Today the re-globalisation of Pan-Africanism has a new technology of communication.

Africans of the world, unite!

You have nothing to lose but your pains!

NOTES

[1] Useful works on Pan-Africanism include Michael W. Williams, *Pan-Africanism : An Annotated Bibliography* (Pasadena, CA : Salem Press, 1992) and for an overview, see P. Olisanwuche Esedebe, *Pan-Africanism: The Idea And Movement, 1776-1991* (Washington, D.C. : Howard University, 1994 Edition), 2nd ed.

[2] Descriptions of this important conference may be found in Darryl C. Thomas, *The Theory and Practice of Third World Solidarity* (Westport, CT : Praeger, 2001), p. 155; Manning Marable, *Black Leadership* (New York : Columbia University Press, 1998), pp.94-95; and Esedebe, *Pan-Africanism*, pp. 138-146.

[3] Relatedly on Garvey, consult, for example, Tony Martin, *The Pan-African Connection : From Slavery to Garvey and Beyond* (Cambridge, MA: Schenkmann Pub. Co., 1983); John H. Clarke, ed., *Marcus Garvey and the Vision of Africa* (New York: Vintage Books, 1974); and Amy Jacques Garvey, *Garvey and Garveyism* (New York: Octagon Books, 1978, 1968).

[4] Nkrumah's case for unification of the continent is laid out in his *Africa Must Unite* (London and New York: Heinemann, 1963 and International Publishers, 1972); also consult D. Zizwe Poe, *Kwame Nkrumah's Contribution to Pan-Africanism: An Afrocentric* View (London and New York: Routledge, 2003) and Opoku Agyeman, *Nkrumah's Ghana and East Africa : Pan-Africanism and African interstate relations* (Rutherford : Fairleigh Dickinson University Press ; London ; Cranbury, NJ : Associated University Press, 1992).

[5] For some of the key documents of the OAU such as the original charter, rules of procedure and so on, see Gino J. Naldi, *Documents of the Organization of African Unity* (New York: Mansell, 1992).

[6] Relatedly, see J. Kirk Sale, "Togo: The Lesson for Africa," *The Nation* (February 16, 1963), Vol. 196, Issue 7.

[7] For assessments of the OAU, consult, for example, Klaas Van Walraven, *Dreams of Power : The Role of the Organization of African Unity in the Politics of Africa, 1963-1993* (Aldershot, Hants, England: Ashgate, 1999) and Yassin El-Ayouty, Ed., *The Organization of African Unity After Thirty Years* (Westport, CT: Praeger, 1994).

[8] One commentary on the role of the OAU in this regard is by Boutros Boutros-Ghali, "The OAU and Afro-Arab Relations," in El-Ayouty, Ed., *The Organization of African Unity After Thirty Years*, pp. 147-168.

[9] Relatedly, see Arthur Hazlewood, *Economic Integration : The East African Experience* (New York : St. Martin's Press,1975).

[10] For a description of the evolution of ECOWAS from a group formed for economic purposes to its current political and military activities, consult Emmanuel I. Udogu, "Economic Community of West African States: From an Economic Union to a Peacekeeping Mission," *The Review of Black Political Economy* (Spring 1999), Vol. 26, No. 4, pp. 57-74. For an analysis of one of the first peacekeeping actions, see Ademola Adeleke "The Politics and Diplomacy of Peacekeeping in West Africa: The ECOWAS Operation in Liberia," *The Journal of Modern African Studies*, Vol. 33, No. 4. (Dec., 1995), pp. 569-593.

[11] For assessments of SADC, see Mwesiga Baregu, "Economic and Military Security," in Mwesiga Baregu and Christopher Landsberg, Eds., *From Cape to Congo : Southern Africa's Evolving Security Challenges* (Boulder, CO: Lynne Rienner Publishers, 2003), pp. 19-30; and Naison Ngoma, "SADC: Towards A Security Community?" *African Security Review* (August 2003), Volume 12, Issue 3, pp. 17-28.

[12] Efforts have included the formation of the Arab Maghreb Union; consult Melani Cammett, "Defensive Integration and Defensive Integration and Late Developers: The Gulf Cooperation Council and the Arab Maghreb Union," *Global Governance* (Jul-Sep99), Volume 5, Issue 3, p379-402; and Robert A. Mortimer, "The Arab Maghreb Union: Myth and Reality," in Yahia H. Zoubir, Ed., *North Africa in Transition : State, Society, and Economic Transformation in the 1990s* (Gainesville, FL: University of Florida Press, 1999), pp. 177-194.

[13] On the Rastafarian movement, consult, for example, Leonard E. Barrett, Sr., *The Rastafarians* (Boston: Beacon Press, 1997).

[14] Historically, three waves of Muslims are recorded as coming to South Africa; exiles from South East Asia, slaves from other areas of Africa, and indentured labourers from the Indian subcontinent. See Charlotte A. Quinn and Frederick Quinn, *Pride, Faith, and Fear : Islam in Sub-Saharan Africa* (New York: Oxford University Press, 2003), pp. 127-135, and Mervyn Hiskett, *The Course of Islam in Africa* (Edinburgh: Edinburgh University Press, 1994), p. 174. Shamil Jeppie has questioned the ascribing of "Malay" identity to the first wave of exiles; see Jeppie, "Commemorations and Identities: The 1994 Tercentenary of Ilsma in South Africa," in Tamara Sonn, Ed., *Islam and the Question of Minorities* (Atlanta, GA: Scholars Press, 1996), pp. 78-79.

[15] Relatedly, consult, for instance, James Barber, *Mandela's World : The International Dimension Of South Africa's Political Revolution 1990-99* (Oxford;

Cape Town; Athens, OH: James Currey; David Philip; and Ohio University Press, 2004).

[16] See Gerrit Olivier, "Is Thabo Mbeki Africa's Saviour?" *International Affairs* (July 2003) Volume 79, Issue 4, pp. 815-828 and Rachel L. Swarns, "Awe and Unease as South Africa Stretches Out," *New York Times* (February 17, 2002).

[17] See Richard Morin, "A World Apart: A Decade After the Fall of Apartheid in South Africa, An Isolated White Community Clings to Its Past," *Washington Post* (March 31, 2004).

[18] Kenyatta even authored a related book; see Jomo Kenyatta, *Suffering Without Bitterness* (Nairobi and Chicago: East African Publishing House and Northwestern University Press, 1968).

[19] For an overview of the transition from the minority white rule to the majority black rule in Zimbabwe, consult Anthony Parsons, "From Southern Rhodesia to Zimbabwe, 1965-1985," *International Affairs* Vol. 9, No. 4, (November 1988), pp. 353-361.

[20] A bibliographical guide to the Biafra war may be found in Zdenek Cervenka, *The Nigerian War, 1967-70: History of The War, Selected Bibliography and Documents* (Frankfurt Am Main: Bernard & Graef, 1971).

[21] Bertus Haverkort, Katrien van t Hooft and Wim Hiemstra, Eds., *Ancient Roots, New Shoots : Endogenous Development in Practice* (Leusden, The Netherlands; London ; New York : : ETC/Compass in association with Zed Books and Palgrave, 2003), pp. 141-142.

[22] By virtue of its size, resources, and location, South Africa has always been a major player in Africa. For discussions of the centrality, importance and tensions of the post-apartheid South Africa in Africa, consult, for instance, Larry A. Swatuk and David R. Black, Eds., *Bridging The Rift : The New South Africa in Africa* (Boulder, CO: Westview Press, 1997) ;Adebayo Adedeji, Ed., *South Africa and Africa : Within Or Apart?* (London and Atlantic Highlands, NJ: Zed Books, in association with African Centre for Development and Strategic Studies (ACDESS), 1996) and Swarns, "Awe and Unease as South Africa Stretches Out," *New York Times* (February 17, 2002).

SECTION V

COMPARATIVE LEADERSHIP

CHAPTER 15

REFLECTIONS ON NNAMDI AZIKIWE

F or parts of Africa Nnamdi Azikiwe's life traversed the entire span of European colonial rule and beyond. As a senior politician of Africa's most populous country, Nnamdi Azikiwe was an important figure in the origins of such momentous African movements as modern nationalism, Pan-Africanism, the struggle for independence, the post-colonial struggle for stability, development and national integration, and the diplomacy of nonalignment in world affairs.[1]

He brought into politics the sportsmanship of his years as an athlete, the intellectual discipline of his training as a scholar, the verbal magic of his experience as a journalist, and the sense of theatre of his being a Nigerian.

Nnamdi Azikiwe has been not only a bridge between Nigerian and Pan-African political thought. He has also been a bridge between African thought and American ideas. While Kwame Nkrumah acknowledged Marcus Garvey and V.I. Lenin as the major ideological influences in his intellectual development, Nnamdi Azikiwe has had no Leninist fibre in him. Azikiwe has been a fusion of African nationalism and the best of American liberalism.

Both Nigeria and the United States struggled for independence from Great Britain. Both Nigeria and the United States were later engulfed in their own civil wars. In both cases the union was saved. Both Nigeria and the United States have remained economically liberal. Azikiwe has been part of the Nigerian story and part of the American dream transplanted to Nigeria.

Azikiwe's great dilemmas included the tension between ethnic claims and the claims of the nation; the tension between universalist ideologies and local concerns; and the tension between the plural society and cultural autonomy in Africa.

His period of office as Governor-General and later President of Nigeria included such events as the United Nations' intervention in the Congo from 1960 onwards; the French nuclear tests in the Sahara; the launching of the Organization of African Unity in 1963; the global rise of Kwame Nkrumah as President of Ghana; and Zik's own overthrow as President of Nigeria in 1966. The biography of a continent was captured in those momentous events.

But what kind of leader was this Nnamdi Azikiwe? How did he relate to the momentous times in which he worked and struggled? Let us take a closer took at Nnamdi Azikiwe in a comparative perspective.

Styles of Political Leadership

What was his style of leadership? In general, styles of leadership include the following:

MOBILISATION LEADERSHIP is a style seeking to engage the masses in popular political, economic or military participation; RECONCILIATION LEADERSHIP is committed to finding areas of compromise among contending groups; INTIMIDATORY LEADERSHIP tends to resort to the use of fear as a major instrument of soliciting support; BUREAUCRATIC or TECHNOCRATIC LEADERSHIP attempts high sensitivity to cost-effectiveness and considerations of efficiency. PATRIARCHAL LEADERSHIP seeks to invoke the father-figure credentials and the elder-tradition in ensuring allegiance and support. PERMISSIVE LEADERSHIP can go to the extreme of allowing widespread anarchy and misconduct.

In Nigerian history Shehu Shagari's administration was a case of permissive leadership (1979-1983). Yakubu Gowon (1967-1985) was in essence a reconciliation leader - waging a war in order to make real national peace possible. Muhammed Buhari (1983-1985) was a case of intimidatory leadership in the process of formation - Nigerians were losing their freedoms faster under Buhari than at any time since independence.

What about Murtala Muhammed (1975-1976)? Was he a mobilisation leader who never realized his potential? He did move against corruption in the six months before his assassination more than did any other Nigerian leader. The public was beginning to respond to him. Would he have mobilized the public?

The Sardauna of Sokoto, Sir Ahmadu Bello, did not hold a federal office but exercised power through Abubakar Tafawa Balewa as federal prime minister (1960-1966). The Sardauna was a patriarchal leader.

Ibrahim Babangida started off as a bureaucratic leader in search of cost-effectiveness and efficiency - but his regime deteriorated into the paradox of intimidatory permissiveness. Aguiyi Ironsi in 1966 could have either *mobilized* the Nigerian population in the enthusiasm of the

January coup or have attempted to *reconcile* the Nigerians as non-Igbo felt betrayed by the January 1966 coup. Unfortunately Ironsi had the skills *neither* of *mobilisation* nor of *reconciliation*. He paid with his life for that dual lapse.

Where does Azikiwe fit into this configuration of styles of leadership? In Eastern Nigeria Azikiwe was a mobilisation leader right up to independence. At the federal level Azikiwe was a reconciliation leader, for better or for worse. In other words, Zik was a *regional mobiliser* and a *federal reconciler*.

Even in his approach against British colonial rule he was against extra-constitutional methods, unlike Kwame Nkrumah. Zik's obsession with constitutional propriety was part of his national reconciliation style. When he was Chancellor of the University of Lagos he championed a system of government in which civilians and soldiers shared power, *diarchy*. It earned him widespread condemnation among intellectuals. And yet it is a dilemma which every African country continues to face: how to reconcile military realities with the ethics of representative government. In Zik's case it was part of his reconciliation style to recommend a straight power-sharing - a dual-sovereign, part military, part civilian.[2]

Has Egypt by the 1990s evolved the kind of *diarchy* that Zik dreamt about, with power-sharing between the military and civilians? Certainly as compared with 1952 when the Egyptian military first took over power, there is now much more power-sharing with civilians. But the military may still be too powerful in Egypt for equal partnership.

Between 'Tribe' and Continent

There was a time when Azikiwe briefly gave up on the principle of reconciliation. This was between 1967 and 1969 when he served as a diplomat-at-large for the secessionist Biafra war with the federal government of Nigeria.[3] During the colonial period Zik had been against using violence against the British. And yet between 1967 and 1969 he seemed to be in favour of Black Nigerians using weapons against each other over the fate of Biafra. What happened to Zik's ethic of strict constitutionalism? What had happened to his aversion to the use of violence for political ends? Where was his reconciliation style?

By 1969 Azikiwe recognized the historic contradictions of his position. He who had been for *strict non-violence against British colonial rule* was caught up in *a violent Biafran answer to the Federation of Nigeria*.

235

He risked being hated by both sides when he tried to sue for peace between Emeka Ojukwu and Yakubu Gowon from early 1969 onwards. The war finally came to end in 1970.[4]

There was one more attempt at federal reconciliation which Azikiwe wanted to make when the war was finally over: reintegration of the Igbo into the mainstream of Nigeria. Azikiwe's bid for the Nigerian presidency in the elections of 1979 and 1983 was, in part, to make the point that the Igbo were now active in the mainstream of Nigerian life - perhaps even more fundamentally than Jesse Jackson's bid for the Democratic presidential nomination had been an effort to make the point that African Americans were now active in the mainstream of American life. [5]

In the 1979 elections the former military leader of Biafra, Emeka Ojukwu, also made a bid for a seat on the Senate of the new Nigeria. Was Ojukwu also serving notice that the Igbo were back in the federal politics of Nigeria?

But Azikiwe's significance has not been merely in terms of the national politics of Nigeria, important as that national agenda is. Azikiwe was also involved quite early in Pan-African politics. His book *Renascent Africa* was, after all, published as far back as 1937.[6] He was conscious of the need for West African unity, and then the need for wider African and Black unity, and was in a sense one of the precursors of the philosophy of *non-alignment* well before the word was even coined.

He was aware of the interconnected nature of Nigeria's history with that of the rest of West Africa:

> From the earliest beginnings of our civil service, Sierra Leoneans helped to shape the course of our history. We cannot readily forget that as early as 1866...some parts of Nigeria were administered from Sierra Leone, which is an indication that, other things being equal West Africa needs a confederation.[7]

Although Azikiwe was later overshadowed by Kwame Nkrumah as the voice of Pan-Africanism *per excellence*, Zik started early in his Pan-African vision. After all, his book, *Liberia in World Politics* was published as far back as 1934.[8] As indicated, his *other* book, *Renascent Africa*, appeared three years later.

Zik heralded the origins of non-alignment in his speech to a Plenary Session of the British Peace Congress, London, October 23, 1949, when the Cold War was just getting under way:

It is very significant that in the last two world wars African peoples were inveigled into participating in the destruction of fellow human beings on the ground that Kaiserism and Hitlerism be destroyed in order that the world should be made safe for democracy - a political theory which seems to be an exclusive property of the good peoples of Europe and America, whose rulers appear to find war a profitable mission and enterprise.

Now the peoples of Africa are being told that it is necessary in the interest of peace and the preservation of Christianity, that they should be ready to fight the Soviet Union, which the war buglers allege is aiming at world domination...

We must search our hearts and accept some home truths. Someone has rightly said that 'Peace is indivisible'. One half of the world cannot enjoy peace while the other half lives in the throes of war...It is clear that imperialism is a perennial source of war.[9]

The historic Bandung Conference of 1955 is widely regarded as one of the milestones in the development of both nonalignment and the Afro-Asian movement. Curiously enough, Nigeria was not invited, while the Gold Coast (later Ghana) was. Zik had a word to say about the Bandung Conference, in a Presidential Address at the 6th Annual Convention of National Council of Nigeria and the Cameroons (NCNC) at Mapo Hall, Ibadan, May 5, 1955:

>...any decision made at Bandung on the future of this continent which does not take into account the fact that every sixth person in Africa is a Nigerian, is bound to be like a flower that 'is born to blush unseen and to waste its sweetness in the desert air.'....I appreciate that the conveners of this conference will make it clear that [the conference] was exploratory....But it is obvious that they blundered when they decided to invite one West African state-to-be [Gold Coast] and chose to ignore the other West African state-to-be [Nigeria]....Our time will come, and when it comes, as dawn follows dusk, we shall reserve ourselves the right to pick and choose our friends. In the meantime, we bear no malice towards any people, whether they hurt our feelings or not.[10]

Oratory in a Global Perspective

What exceptional resource did Zik use in his political career? It was important both for his style as a mobilisation leader in Eastern Nigeria and as a reconciliation leader in the national politics of Nigeria. Let us place Azikiwe the orator in a wider geographical and historical context.

The great mediating force between Africa's oral tradition and the new universe of the written word was indeed *oratory*, the art and craft of public speaking during the colonial period and the early years of independence.

Azikiwe was one of the pioneers in this new socio-cultural mediation - using a European language learnt through books (the written tradition) to mobilize the African masses through oratory (the oral tradition).

Did Azikiwe speak the English language like an Englishman? As Chinua Achebe would put it, "I hope not"! Like a true Anglophone African of the first half of the 20th century, Azikiwe loved to dazzle his compatriots with long unfamiliar English words - long Latinisms were, in Nigeria, known as long Zikisms.[11]

Unlettered peasants used to buy newspapers the next day, *holding them upside down*, fascinated by the utterances they could neither read nor understand.

This was the miracle of a cross-cultural transition. Why were Nigerian audiences fascinated by precisely those English words which they could least understand? More highly educated African intellectuals later called it a fascination with 'bombast.' This assumes that less educated Africans were simply enchanted by the *high-sounding* phrases. But was it the *high-sound* or the obscure meaning which enchanted us? Was it the *music* of the words (high sound) or the *mystery* of the words (obscurity) which enchanted the less educated?

Here too Zik was *of Africa*. This particular fascination with the *mystery* of unfamiliar words, as well as the music of those same words, was widespread in the African colonial Empire. At school in Mombasa, Kenya, in the 1940s we as little schoolboys used to memorize the following paragraph attributed to a highly admired black East African (Mbotela):

> If you wish to ascertain the precise meaning of a word, should you naturally avoid a disputation or articulating your supermentalities? Beware of psychological, philosophical pondorosity. Although I am **of** good solubrity, yet even in me there are a few symptoms which symbolize my verbosity.

Even today do I really know what all this means? The mystery persists.

A wider comparative approach to oratory and the Black experience may be in order here. Oratory has traditionally been divided into: legal (Aristotle called it forensic); *political* (Aristotle called it deliberative); *ceremonial* (Aristotle's epideictic); later a fourth category, **ecclesiastic** or religious oratory.

Was Abraham Lincoln's Gettysburg address *ceremonial* or political? Was Martin Luther King's "I have a Dream" speech ecclesiastical? Martin Luther King's address was made to a massive civil rights demonstration, in Washington DC, in 1963. His style was of the pulpit oratorical strategy.

What about oratory in the Jewish Diaspora? In 20th century America do Blacks produce more orators than Jews? How is this related to the silences of enslavement and the oratory of Nazism? The most politically significant Blacks of the second half of the 20th century have also been impressive orators: These include: Martin Luther King Jr., Malcolm X, Louis Farrakhan, Jesse Jackson and Andrew Young. Did enslavement produce not only *the blues* and spirituals in music, not only gospel and jazz, but also *oratory*?

In contrast the most politically famous US Jew of the second half of the 20th century is probably Henry Kissinger, who became Secretary of State. Kissinger has great *persuasive power*, but not so *great oratorical powers*. Are oratorical skills less valued in the Jewish experience after the Holocaust?

Yet Judaism is one of the earliest fountains of great oratory with examples like the early prophets like Jeremiah and Isaiah. In the Christian era great orators among the Christian founding fathers included the Apostle Paul, his evangelic colleagues and such later fathers as St. Augustine. Why have African Americans produced a disproportionate number of effective orators? Four 'P'-Factors are relevant:

- ♦ The Pulpit [Factor]: strong ecclesiastical tendency. The sermon on the mount.
- ♦ The Protest [Factor]: Blacks in deep grievance. Black rebellion against injustice.
- ♦ The Passion [Factor]: 'Emotion is Black, Reason is Greek.' Black Anger.
- ♦ The Pathos [Factor]: The Blues - Black Melancholy. The survival from the Middle Passage.

239

Is it worth comparing the Black experience with the experience of the Jews? Is there a psychic Jewish reluctance to re-enter the domain of mass hysteric oratory? Jewish oratory in America poses a number of questions:

- Is it more oratory of the *court room* than the *rally*?
- Is it more the rhetoric of the *chamber* than the *stadium*?
- Is Jewish passion more of the *written* word than of the *spoken*?
- Is the Talmudic tradition too *analytical* to be also *inspirational*?
- In the post Holocaust era is there a *Jewish distrust of oratory*?

After all, Germany's *genocide* began with Hitler's eloquence. Hitler rose to power partly because his oratory could articulate and manipulate the grievances of the German masses. Is that the reason for the Jewish distrust of mass oral skills?

When we return to Africa the golden age of African oratory still belongs to the generation which fought for independence: the great socio-cultural transition from the oral tradition to the new European languages of book-learning.

Julius K. Nyerere of Tanzania was himself to become a great orator in both English and Swahili, but he was once inspired by Mark Antony's speech in Shakespeare's Julius Caesar, 'I have come to bury Caesar, not praise him.'

In the play a single speech changed the course of history. Later Julius Nyerere translated Shakespeare's *Julius Caesar* into Swahili (published in 1963 by Oxford University Press).

In Uganda young Apollo Obote was a student in a school at Mwiri. He was so inspired by Lucifer's legitimation speech in John Milton's Paradise Lost that Apollo Obote adopted the name "Milton" as his own name. He was later to be known in history primarily as MILTON OBOTE. As a little boy Obote had particularly liked in Lucifer's legitimation speech the line:

"Better to reign in Hell than serve in Heaven"[12]

Lucifer (Satan before the fall) was in rebellion against what he regarded as God's vanity - constantly expecting obedience, prayers, and prostrate submission, from creatures He had Himself created. John Milton in the earlier sections of *Paradise Lost* does give Satan (Lucifer

240

before his disgrace) heroic proportions as a rebel against Divine Vanity. Satan's <u>speech</u> of legitimation was therefore heroic.

In Kenya Tom Mboya, who was assassinated in 1969 before he realized his full potential, became the most brilliant political orator that country had ever produced. In Senegal Léopold Senghor captured the music of the French language, if not in delivery certainly in composition. In Ghana Kwame Nkrumah was reaching out to the so-called 'verandah boys' and the masses chanted 'Lead, kindly light!".

But long before Julius Nyerere responded to Mark Antony's refrain, 'Was that ambition?', long before Milton Obote was inspired by the Miltonic line 'Better to reign in Hell than serve in Heaven,' certainly long before Tom Mboya briefly captured the imagination of the world from 1955 to 1969, perhaps even before Leopold Senghor became France's most eloquent voice in Africa, and even before Nkrumah was called upon to "Lead, kindly light," there was another African, tall, athletic, often brilliant, always patriotic.

Conclusion

Yes, Nnamdi Azikiwe was the great bridge-builder, but he was also *prophecy-incarnate*. When he was a gold medalist at Storer College way back in the *1920s* in one mile run, quarter mile race, and won other athletic awards, Nnamdi Azikiwe was prophecy incarnate about Africa's athletic prowess.

When he combined certificate in law, a qualification in journalism, a Masters in religion and philosophy, a Masters in anthropology, expertise in political science, Nnamdi Azikiwe was prophecy-incarnate signifying Africa's academic versatility when given half-a-chance.

And when he became Nigeria's greatest orator for a substantial part of the 20th century, Azikiwe was prophecy-incarnate signifying the transformation of the oral tradition into oratory in a critical period of historical transition.

His full name begins with the *first* letter of the alphabet, A -- Azikiwe. His abridged name begins with the *last* letter of the alphabet -- <u>Zik</u>. He traverses the whole span of the alphabet. He also traverses the whole space of Africa. He is the historical Azikiwe. He is Zik of Africa.

NOTES

[1] Relatedly, consult Agbafor Igwe, *Zik: The Philosopher of Our Time* (Enugu, Nigeria: Fourth Dimension Pub. Co. Ltd., 1992).

[2] For an overview of Zik's ideas on diarchy, see Igwe, *Zik: The Philosopher of Our Time*, pp. 136-141.

[3] On the Biafra War, consult Herbert Ekwe-Ekwe, *The Biafra War : Nigeria and the Aftermath*, Lewiston, N.Y., USA : E. Mellen Press, 1990); Peter Schwab, Ed. *Biafra* (New York, Facts on File, 1971); and Zdenek Cervenka, *The Nigerian War, 1967-1970. History of the War; Selected Bibliography and Documents* (Frankfurt: Bernard & Graefe, 1971).

[4]Consult also Ralph Uwechue, *Reflections on the Nigerian Civil War* (New York: Africana Publishing Corporation, 1971) -- with a foreword by Azikiwe.

[5]On Jackson's bid for the Presidency in 1988, see, for instance, Elizabeth O. Colton, *The Jackson Phenomenon : The Man, The Power, The Message* (New York: Doubleday, 1989) and Penn Kimball, *Keep Hope Alive! : Super Tuesday and Jesse Jackson's 1988 Campaign for the Presidency* (Washington, DC and Lanham, MD: Joint Center for Political and Economic Studies Press and National Book Network, 1992).

[6]For one edition, see Nnamdi Azikiwe, *Renascent Africa* (New York: Negro Universities Press, 1969).

[7]From Presidential Address at 6th Convention of NCNC, Mapo Hall, Ibadan, May 5, 1955. See Nnamdi Azikiwe, *Zik: Selected Speeches of Nnamdi Azikiwe* (Cambridge: The University Press, 1961) p. 66.

[8]Nnamdi Azikiwe, *Liberia in World Politics* (London: A. H. Stockwell, 1934).

[9]See Azikiwe, *Zik*, pp. 61, 62. See also Nnamdi Azikiwe, *My Odyssey: An Autobiography* (New York: Praeger Publishers, 1970). Consult also Nnamdi Azikiwe, *Liberia in World Politics* (Westport, Connecticut: Negro Universities Press, 1970; reprint of 1934 edition published in London).

[10]See, Azikiwe, *Zik*, pp. 63, 65.

[11]A late illustration may even include his Inaugural Address, November 16, 1960, as Governor-General of Nigeria entitled *Respect for Human Dignity* (Onitsha, Nigeria: Tabansi Bookshop)

[12] This is from John Milton, *Paradise Lost*. Book I, Line 261, retrieved <http://www.bartleby.com/100/173.13.html>. January 3, 2006.

CHAPTER 16

REFLECTIONS ON ARCHBISHOP DESMOND TUTU

A lmost exactly fifty years before Desmond Mpilo Tutu was elected Archbishop of Cape Town (the first black man to reach that status) a brown man in another part of the world had said, "It may be through the Negroes [meaning Black people] that the unadulterated message of non-violence will be delivered to the world."[1]

Tutu was elected Archbishop in March 1986. Mohandas Gandhi made the above prediction about 'Negroes' in March 1936. Gandhi was predicting that his torch would be passed to Black people. Does Desmond Mpilo Tutu represent the fulfilment of that Gandhian prediction?

As a moral figure of the twentieth and twenty-first centuries Desmond Tutu is a product of three ethical forces: Christianity, Gandhism and Africa's short memory of hate. Christianity was consciously learned and internalised by Desmond Tutu. Gandhism was a non-violent legacy of both India and South Africa. Africa's short memory of hate was part and parcel of Desmond Tutu's ancestral baggage as an African.[2]

This is Desmond Tutu's triple legacy as a moral activist from his days as a champion of international sanctions against apartheid to his equally historic role as Chair of the Truth and Reconciliation Commission which many have interpreted as a bargain to exchange truth for justice in post-apartheid South Africa.[3]

What is Tutu's triple legacy? *Christianity, Africanity and Gandhism,* though not necessarily in that order. Indeed, Tutu has been a less direct disciple of Gandhi than Martin Luther King was, but South Africa was a more direct theatre of action by Gandhi himself than Martin Luther King's motherland: the United States.

In the quest for the subjugation of the Black People, the white trader had often preceded the white conqueror. But in the struggle for the *liberation* of the Black People, the Black priest had often preceded the Black warrior.

In the history of imperialism and colonisation, European trading companies traversed the seas and traded with the natives long before European gunboats arrived for conquest. And even voyages of exploration like that of Christopher Columbus were initially in search of trading routes and economic opportunities rather than new worlds to conquer.

Much later came the phase of Black liberation. If in the history of Black subjugation the white trader preceded the white conqueror, in the history of Black liberation the Black priest often preceded the Black warrior. This is what brings us to the role of Archbishop Desmond Mpilo Tutu, the most famous African religious figure of the last one hundred years.

Born in October 1931, and educated in both South Africa and Great Britain, he started his career as a High School teacher before he decided to venture into the ministry of the Anglican Church. He became a deacon in 1960, and was ordained as a priest in 1961. The Christianisation of Desmond Tutu had reached a new plateau.

Desmond Tutu became Bishop of Lesotho in 1976 and General-Secretary of the South African Council of Churches in 1978. The internationalisation of his ministry contributed to the politicisation of his role. He began to speak out not only against apartheid (which he had been doing already) but also in favour of specific measures against it—such as the international boycott of South African coal in the 1970s.[4]

His troubles with the apartheid regime included experiencing harassments, arrests, fines, and deprivation of his passport on more than one occasion. On the other hand, both his international and his ecumenical credentials were growing. He met with the Pope at the Vatican, and in 1984, he was awarded the Nobel Prize for Peace. On April 4, 1986, he was elected Archbishop of Cape Town and was therefore head of the Anglican Church in South Africa, the first black man to hold such a post.

When in the struggle for liberation, the Black priest not only struggles for justice but also for political office, there is a risk of losing some of the moral fervour. This happened in the old Rhodesia, now Zimbabwe. Both the Reverend Ndabaningi Sithole and Bishop Abel Muzorewa not only tried to reach for a more just order, they also sought political office. Their moral fervour suffered as a result.

But neither the Reverend Martin Luther King Jr. nor Bishop Desmond Tutu sought political office. Their pursuit of justice remained a moral commitment without becoming political partiality.

Both Desmond Tutu and Martin Luther King Jr. lived in the historical shadow of a brown man, Mahatma Mohandas Gandhi. Desmond Tutu was less consciously a disciple of Gandhi but was nonetheless very conscious that Gandhi started his struggle against injustice in South Africa rather than India. Although Gandhi's ideas in South Africa were still youthful, he was developing them into a strategy of non-violent resistance. Both Desmond Tutu and Martin Luther King became a fusion of Christian love and Gandhian soul-force. As Martin Luther King put it:

Prior to reading Gandhi I had about concluded that the ethics of Jesus were only effective in individual relationships. The 'turn the other cheek' philosophy and the 'love your enemies' philosophy were only valid, I felt, when individuals were in conflict with other individuals... Gandhi was probably the first person in history to lift the love ethic of Jesus above mere interaction between individuals to a powerful and effective social force on a large scale....[5]

Both Tutu and King believed that *non-violence* should not be confused with *non-resistance*. Injustice had to be resisted. Desmond Tutu proclaimed in 1984, "We have warned consistently that unrest will be endemic in South Africa until its root cause is removed. And the root cause is apartheid--a vicious, immoral and totally evil...system."[6]

While Black leaders like Tutu and King would not forget Mahatma Gandhi, Mahatma Gandhi in turn could not forget Black people. During the lifetime of Mohandas Gandhi the term 'Negro' just meant 'Black person' without the pejorative connotations it acquired in the second half of the twentieth century. As far back as 1936 Mohandas Gandhi was beginning to be convinced, "It may be through the Negroes that the unadulterated message of nonviolence will be delivered to the world."[7]

Let us now pursue this Gandhian prediction in relation to Desmond Tutu's third legacy, Africa's short memory of hate.

Mahatma Gandhi's India gave birth to new principles of passive resistance and *satyagraha*. Yet, Gandhi himself said that it might be through the Black people that the unadulterated message of soul force and passive resistance might be realized. If Gandhi was right, this

245

would be one more illustration that the culture which gives birth to an ethic is not necessarily the culture which fulfils the ethic.

The Nobel Committee for Peace in Oslo seems to have shared some of Gandhi's optimism about the soul force of the Black people. Africans and people of African descent who have won the Nobel prize for Peace since the middle of the twentieth century have been Ralph Bunche (1950), Albert Luthuli (1960), Martin Luther King Jr. (1964), Anwar Sadat (1978) Desmond Tutu (1984), Nelson Mandela (1993) and Wangari Maathai (2004). Neither Mahatma Gandhi himself nor virtually any of his compatriots in India ever won the Nobel Prize for Peace. Was Mahatma Gandhi vindicated that the so-called 'Negro' was going to be the best exemplar of soul force? Was this a case of African culture being empirically more Gandhian than Indian culture? If we only looked at Desmond Tutu that proposition might prevail.

But in reality, Black people have been at least as violent as anything ever perpetrated by Indians. Desmond Tutu himself is on record for having protested about Black against Black violence. As indicated elsewhere in this book, what is distinctive about Africans is their short memory of hate.

In Kenya, Jomo Kenyatta was unjustly imprisoned by the British colonial authorities over charges of founding the Mau Mau movement. A British Governor denounced him as 'a leader into darkness and unto death.' And yet when Jomo Kenyatta was released he not only forgave the white settlers, but turned the whole country towards a basic pro-Western orientation to which it has remained committed ever since. Kenyatta even published a book entitled, *Suffering Without Bitterness.*[8] Desmond Tutu echoed similar sentiment with his own book, *Hope and Suffering* of 1983.[9]

Ian Smith, the white settler leader of Rhodesia, unilaterally declared independence in November 1 965 and unleashed a brutal civil war on the country. Thousands of people, mainly Black, died in Rhodesia as a result of policies pursued by Ian Smith. Yet, when the war ended in 1980, Ian Smith and his cohorts were not subjected to a firing squad or Nuremberg-style trial. On the contrary, Ian Smith was, for a while, himself a member of parliament in a Black-ruled Zimbabwe, busy criticizing the post-Smith Black leaders of Zimbabwe as incompetent and dishonest. Where else but in Africa could such tolerance occur? In post-independence Zimbabwe they have had a kind of *reconciliation*. But did they get the *truth* in exchange for the reconciliation?[10]

Across the border in South Africa, Desmond Tutu symbolized a different social contract. He believes that Reconciliation without the truth falls short of sincerity; the truth without reconciliation falls short of stability. Desmond Tutu's commission has symbolized both truth and reconciliation.

The Nigerian civil war (1967-1970) was the first most highly publicized civil conflict in post-colonial Africa.[11] As the war was coming to an end, many people feared that there would be a bloodbath in the defeated eastern region. The Vatican was worried that cities like Enugu and Onitsha, strongholds of Catholicism, would be monuments of devastation and bloodletting. Even Anglican Tutu himself was deeply concerned.

None of those expectations occurred. Nigerians, seldom among the most disciplined of Africans, discovered in 1970 some remarkable self-restraint. There were no triumphant reprisals against the vanquished Biafrans; there were no vengeful trials of 'traitors.' The war ended without reprisals against the vanquished. Tutu and his congregation thanked God in prayer for Nigeria.

We have also witnessed the phenomenon of Nelson Mandela. He lost twenty-seven of the best years of his life in prison under the laws of the apartheid regime. Yet, when he was released he not only emphasized the policy of reconciliation, he often went beyond the call of duty. On one occasion before he became President, white men were fasting unto death after being convicted of terrorist offences by their own white government. Nelson Mandela went out of his way to beg them to eat and thus spare their own lives. *On such issues Mandela and Tutu saw eye to eye.*

When Mandela became President in 1994 it was surely enough that his government would leave the architects of apartheid unmolested. Yet, Nelson Mandela went out of his way to pay a social call and have tea with the unrepentant widow of Hendrik F. Verwoerd, the supreme architect of the worst forms of apartheid, who shaped the whole racist order from 1958 to 1966. Mandela was having tea with the family of Verwoerd.[12] *Again Mandela and Tutu saw eye to eye on this issue of reconciliation.*

247

Was Mahatma Gandhi correct, after all, that his torch of soul force (satyagraha) might find its brightest manifestations among Black people?

In the history of civilisations there are occasions when the image in the mirror is more real that the object it reflects. Black Gandhians like Martin Luther King Jr., Desmond Tutu and, in a different sense, Nelson Mandela, have sometimes reflected Gandhian soul force more brightly than Gandhians in India. Part of the explanation lies in the soul of African culture itself with all its capacity for rapid forgiveness.

It is a positive modification of "The Picture of Dorian Gray." In Oscar Wilde's novel, the picture of Dorian Gray is a truer reflection of the man's decrepid body and lost soul than the man himself. The decomposition of Dorian's body and soul is transferred from Dorian himself to his picture. The picture is more real than the man.[13]

In the case of Gandhism, it is not the decomposition of the soul but its elevation which is transferred from India to the Black experience. In the last one hundred years both Indian culture and African culture have, in any case, been guilty of far less bloodletting than the West. Christian minimization of violence has been observed more by non-Christians than by ostensible Western followers of the Cross. But Black Christians like Desmond Tutu have kept the ultimate message of Love alive, aided by the converging legacies of African forgiveness and the Gandhian message of non-violence.

The mission continues into the challenges of the new millennium. Martin Luther King Jr. did not have to preside over a Truth and Reconciliation Commission to deal with the issues of slavery and lynching in the United States. But Desmond Tutu did have to preside over a Truth and Reconciliation Commission about apartheid and its brutalities in South Africa.[14]

Yet, in the final analysis, it was not only Desmond Tutu who was a product of Christianity, Gandhism and Africa's Short Memory of Hate. The triple legacy (Jesus, Gandhi and Africa) was also part of Martin Luther King's inheritance. Tutu and King are the Black World's most famous moral activists of the last hundred years.

NOTES

[1] This statement was reported in the *Harijan* (March 14, 1936); See Sudarshan Kapur, *Raising Up A Prophet: The African-American Encounter With Gandhi* (Boston: Beacon Press, 1992), pp. 89-90.

[2] For one biography of Archbishop Tutu, see Steven D. Gish, *Desmond Tutu: A Biography* (Westport, CT: Greenwood Press, 2004).

[3] Relatedly, consult Helena Cobban, *The Moral Architecture of World Peace : Nobel Laureates Discuss Our Global Future* (Charlottesville, VA: University of Virginia Press, 2000), pp. 128-150, and Michael Battle (foreword by Desmond Tutu), Reconciliation : the Ubuntu theology of Desmond Tutu (Cleveland, OH: Pilgrim Press, 1997).

[4] A collection of Archbishop Tutu's speeches may be found in Desmond Tutu (John Allen, Ed.,)*The Rainbow People of God : The Making of a Peaceful Revolution* (New York: Doubleday, 1994).

[5] Martin Luther King Jr., *Stride Towards Freedom: The Montgomery Story* (New York: Harper & Row), pp. 76-77.

[6] Bishop Desmond Tutu, "The Question of South Africa," Africa Report (January/ February 1985), Vol. 30, pp. 5052.

[7] Kapur, Raising Up A Prophet: The African-American Encounter With Gandhi, pp. 89-90, and Note 1 above.

[8] Jomo Kenyatta, *Suffering Without Bitterness* (Nairobi and Chicago: East African Publishing House and Northwestern University Press, 1968).

[9] Desmond Tutu; Mothobi Mutloatse, Comp.; John Webster, Ed., *Hope and Suffering : Sermons and Speeches* (Grand Rapids, MI: W.B. Eerdmans, 1984, 1983).

[10] On the transition from white rule to black rule in Zimbabwe, consult Anthony Parsons, "From Southern Rhodesia to Zimbabwe, 1965-1985," *International Affairs* Volume 9, Number 4, (November 1988), pp. 353-361; also see Victor De Waal, *The Politics of Reconciliation: Zimbabwe's First Decade* (London and Cape Town: Hurst and David Philip, 1981).

[11] Details and discussions on the Biafra War may be found in Herbert Ekwe-Ekwe, *The Biafra War : Nigeria and the Aftermath*, Lewiston, N.Y., USA : E. Mellen Press, 1990); Peter Schwab, Ed. *Biafra* (New York, Facts on File, 1971); and Zdenek Cervenka, *The Nigerian War, 1967-1970. History of the War; Selected Bibliography and Documents* (Frankfurt: Bernard & Graefe, 1971).

[12] Richard Morin, "A World Apart: A Decade After the Fall of Apartheid in South Africa, An Isolated White Community Clings to Its Past," *Washington Post* (March 31, 2004).

[13] For a modern edition, see Oscar Wilde, *The Picture of Dorian Gray* (New York: Modern Library, 1992).

[14] Discussions on the Truth and Reconciliation Commission may be found in, for example, Lyn S. Graybill, *Truth and Reconciliation in South Africa: Miracle or Model* (Boulder, CO: Lynne Rienner Publishers, 2002) and Deborah Posel and Graeme Simpson, Eds., *Commissioning the Past : Understanding South Africa's Truth and Reconciliation Commission* (Johannesburg : Witwatersrand University Press and distributed by Thorold's Africana Books, 2002).

CHAPTER 17

REFLECTIONS ON SHEHU SHAGARI

I n the early years of Nigeria's twenty-first century, former President Alhaji Shehu Shagari has become one of the figures working towards bridging regional gaps. In September 2005, *Africa News* reported that a group set up by the former President --- called the Shehu Shagari World Institute -- had set up four committees with a "view towards promoting unity between the zones"[North and South-south].[1] Would this have been possible if the President had been brought to trial and disgraced – or worse, executed like other African leaders? There was a vigorous debate in Nigeria on whether Shehu Shagari should be brought to trial. The same issue could be framed in a broader manner: should the former President have been pardoned and was there a case for political amnesty? Or would the price of forgiveness be too high?[2]

Particulars of the case notwithstanding, underlying the Shagari trial debate were two claims that were at once compelling and competitive, the rival claims of *national cohesion* on one side, which favours forgiveness, and *national discipline* on the other side, which favours punishment for wrong doing. Was there a risk to Nigeria's national unity if a former Head of State was publicly disgraced? Was there a risk to Nigeria's public morality if corruption and criminal negligence in high places went unpunished?

This was the fundamental dilemma facing those who had to decide what to do with Al-Haji Shehu Shagari. The imperative of national unity said, "Don't disgrace a former Head of State". The imperative of national discipline said, "Don't let wrong-doing go unpunished".

First, a rather basic distinction is to be noted between <u>explicit pardon</u> and <u>implicit pardon</u>. By definition an explicit pardon is formally conceded and pronounced. The culprit is forgiven, often by proclamation. An implicit pardon is a kind of tacit forgiveness: resuming a normal or friendly relationship without necessarily saying, "I forgive you".

President Shehu Shagari explicitly pardoned former Head of State Yakubu Gowon and later former Biafran leader Emeka Ojukwu.[3] This was formal forgiveness by proclamation.

On the other hand, most of Biafra's international diplomats were implicitly pardoned. These included Kenneth Dike, distinguished Ibo historian and first Nigerian Vice-Chancellor in history. Biafra's roving ambassadors also included Chinua Achebe, Anglophone Africa's most distinguished novelist. Such figures were forgiven implicitly after the Biafra war. Silent forgiveness was extended by the Federal system.

The Case for Pardoning Shagari

What was the case for pardoning Shagari instead of bringing him to trial? After all, his administration severely damaged Nigeria's economy and Nigeria's electoral system.[4] Would a pardon have been justified?

Regicide and High-Risk Leadership

Being Head of State or Head of Government in Nigeria has been a high-risk business in any case. Out of the six Heads of Government independent Nigeria had had before Shagari, three had been assassinated (Abubakar Tafawa Balewa, Johnson Agyi-Ironsi and Murtala Mohammed). Three out of six is a high casualty rate indeed, a high incidence of *"regicide"*-- (the killing of the king).[5] By contrast, unstable Uganda has so far not killed a single Head of State: Edward Mutesa, Milton Obote, Idi Amin, Yusuf Lule, Godfrey Binaisa, Paulo Muwanga, and Milton Obote.

Excessively victimizing Shagari would continue to make presidential service to Nigeria a notoriously high-risk enterprise.

Avoiding the Pendulum of Revenge

Trying and punishing a former Head of State is always potentially divisive at the national level, potentially damaging to the fabric of national cohesion. A *pendulum of revenge* could come into being: 'You hurt our man today; we shall hurt your man tomorrow.' The killing of Balewa and Ahmadu Bello in January 1966, for example, led to the killing of Ironsi and thousands of other Ibo a few months later.[6]

Dethronement but Not Decapitation

At the level of the Head of State, a military coup should perhaps limit itself to <u>dethronement</u> and <u>not destruction</u>. The coup d'etat should only depose the Head of State and not decapitate him. ("Off with his head.")

In British history this is the distinction between the removal of Charles I in 1649 (the King was beheaded) and the removal of James II in 1688 (the King was only deposed). Charles' beheading was part of the most violent period in English history: an actual civil war.

But the deposing of James II is regarded as political maturation; part of the evolution of the British institutions of peaceful political succession.

Lockean Dethronement and the Watergate Precedent

The fact that the Second Republic of Nigeria (1979 Constitution) was based on the U.S. political system makes it appropriate that Shagari should be deposed but not punished.

This is exactly what happened to Richard Nixon. Faced with the threat of impeachment, Nixon stepped down from the Presidency. The Watergate Drama had reached its climax. Theoretically, he could have been put on trial. After all, his assistants were being tried and punished: John Ehrlichman, H. R. Haldemann, John Dean, John Mitchell, and others, just like the punishment of Shagari's assistants.

Why should the King be pardoned when his Ministers were being punished? The answer is: "In order to protect national cohesion."

Forgiving White Tyrants and Punishing Black Ones

If Africa can extend implicit forgiveness to former white tyrants in Africa, why cannot Africa pardon Black tyrants?

Ian Smith, the dictator and killer in white-ruled Rhodesia, remained a free man in independent Zimbabwe under the rule of the socialist Robert Mugabe.[7] Indeed, Ian Smith and his white supporters were for a while far better off than Joshua Nkomo and his Black ZAPU supporters.

If independent Zimbabwe can forgive a white tyrant like Ian Smith, shouldn't Nigeria forgive Black failure, Shehu Shagari?

In Kenya, Kenyatta forgave his white tormentors: "Suffering without bitterness," as he put it.[8]

Sins: Commission Versus Omission

Was Shagari guilty only of helplessness? Or was he really guilty of malice? Was he guilty of *malpractice* or simply of *no-practice* at all?

253

In other words, was Shagari responsible for sins of *commission* or merely of *omission*? Was he himself corrupt or did he simply fail to stop corrupt practices by others?[9]

Sins of omission should be a matter of withdrawing confidence rather than penalizing. Such rulers should be subject to the passage of a vote of "no confidence" rather than passage of a jail sentence.

The maximum verdict should be dethronement of the incompetent King rather than executing him or incarcerating him.

Fitting the Pardon to the Crime

Ojukwu had once plunged the country into a civil war. Half a million to a million Nigerians died. And yet he **was** forgiven.

Were the sins of Shagari of the same order? In terms of loss of life, Shagari's hands are less blood stained than Ojukuwu's. Could Ojukwu be forgiven for the civil war, while Shagari gets punished for economic mismanagement?

The Case Against the Pardon

What are the arguments against pardoning Shagari?

Power is a Responsibility

Ultimate power is an ultimate responsibility and therefore accountable. We could not be sure if Shagari's sins were merely of omission unless he was put on trial. To try Shagari was not necessarily to find him guilty. It would have been only to ascertain if he <u>was</u> guilty.

No One Is Above the Law

It is important to establish the fact that nobody is above the law, not even the Head of State. If Shagari broke the law, he should be accountable. The feudal principle, "<u>The King can do no wrong</u>", is still alive today. Most African Presidents apply it to themselves. Louis XIV of France said, "<u>The State? I am the state.</u>" Richard Nixon, when interviewed by Frost, also argued that the President was above the law. But this idea should be challenged in Nigeria.

Political Freedom vs. Economic Anarchy

The Shagari years were, on the one hand, years of considerable political freedom in Nigeria. They were also years of unprecedented economic anarchy.[10]

Freedom of the press was so excessive that newspapers sometimes came close to inciting violence, which would be a journalistic offence in such countries as Britain.[11] In other words, press freedom in Nigeria was greater under Shagari than in most Western countries.

Freedom of public denunciation of rulers was also considerable, Nigeria's rulers were being condemned on campuses as 'pirates, looters and money-grabbing criminals.'

However, this remarkable openness of the Shagari years was accompanied by sheer economic chaos. Political freedom in the liberal sense was marred by economic anarchy.

The impact on Nigeria's resources was catastrophic. Billions of naira evaporated into thin air. The fact that the money-grabbing was occurring during a global oil glut made the offence of the Shagari Administration all the greater.[12]

In Search of a Philosophy of Punishment

Nigeria was looking for a viable philosophy of punishment. It wondered whether to adopt a policy based on one of the following principles:

Retributive Justice: Meaning that an offender must pay for an offence regardless of whether the punishment acts as a deterrent.

Punishment as a Deterrent: That is, is the punishment designed to dissuade and discourage others from similar violations.

Punishment as a Mode of Rehabilitation: Does the punishment help the offender to resume his or her place among law-abiding fellow citizens (Sweden is most advanced in seeking rehabilitation).

The emphasis under military rule in Nigeria was on either: (a) retributive justice or (b) punishment as a deterrent. There was little interest in rehabilitation for ordinary offenders. Should offending politicians enjoy greater rights of rehabilitation than other kinds of offenders? Should the Head of State be treated with greater compassion than those who obeyed his orders? What about the Vice-President? Should he be counted part of the Presidency and be forgiven? Or would that double-pardon violate elementary natural justice?

Punishment: Severity Versus. Certainty

In dealing with ordinary offenders, the Federal Military Government seemed to emphasize *severity* of punishment more than *certainty* of punishment as the deterrent. Hence the use of capital punishment for a wide variety of offences, from armed robbery to drug trafficking, from murder to petro-theft. Yet, most of the time certainty of punishment is a greater deterrent than severity of punishment. A situation where an offender stands a sixty percent chance of being arrested and convicted to a term of life imprisonment may be a greater deterrent than a situation in which he stands only a ten percent chance of being arrested and sentenced to death.

Offending African rulers may also have to face the dilemma between severe punishment (but uncertain) and certain punishment (but not necessarily severe). Since the regicide rate in Nigeria has been so high, Nigerian heads of government have suffered severity of retribution rather than certainty of retribution. With Shagari the balance could have been shifted towards less severity but more institutionalisation of penal accountability.

Conclusion

Africa has experienced a wide range of both forgiveness and vindictiveness since independence. Some pardons have been mere disguised acts of vindictiveness. Idi Amin in 1971 claimed to have forgiven all of Milton Obote's Ministers, but then quietly proceeded to kill one after another of the Ministers.

Mobutu Sese Seko was known to proclaim amnesty for a former minister in exile – and then to kill him on arrival back in Zaire. The most dramatic case was Mobutu's pardon of Pierre Mulele in 1968. Mobuto had Mulele executed on arrival.[13]

But there have also been genuine acts of amnesty. Post-colonial Africa's first military coup took place in *Egypt* in 1952. There was some discussion as to whether the corrupt King Farouk should have been executed, or at least interned. The new ruler of Egypt, *Gamal Abdel Nasser*, argued that a revolution which began in revenge would end in revenge. A political succession based on bloodletting would itself be succeeded by further bloodletting. Even as an act of self-preservation, Nasser was probably not eager to encourage murder of heads of state as a way to gain political office. So Farouk was permitted to spend his last years in exile.

Then there is the phenomenon of pardoning *dead* Heads of State. When Sir Edward Mutesa died in 1969, Milton Obote wanted to use the death as a basis of reconciliation with the Baganda. Unfortunately for Obote, the Baganda suspected Obote of being implicated in Mutesa's death. Subsequently, Idi Amin returned the body of Mutesa to Uganda for a state funeral as the country's first Head of State. All was forgiven between Amin and Mutesa, Amin who had once attacked King Mutesa's palace on behalf of President Obote n 1966.

Then there is the collective pardon, like that of the Ibo after Nigeria's civil war. The world expected an eruption of revenge, a new pogrom against the Ibo but more devastating than that of 1966. This unruly nation and undisciplined society, confronted with the supreme crisis of triumph in a civil war, nevertheless found the startling serenity for magnanimity in victory.

Let us place the Shagari case in this wider context of competing moral issues in Nigeria and Africa as a whole. There were indeed strong arguments for pardoning Shegari, just as there were strong arguments for trying and punishing him.

The ultimate underlying dilemma was between national conciliation and national discipline. Amnesty for political offenders and those who have abused power can be a contribution towards licking the wounds of the nation and achieving conciliation.

On the other hand, Nigeria sorely needed national discipline and restraint in the face of corruption and wild individualism. The high and mighty, when violating the law, may be punished as an example to others if the cost to national unity is not prohibitively high.

However, it should also be remembered that Africa needs not just methods of punishing bad presidential behaviour, but also methods of rewarding satisfactory presidential behaviour.

At the moment, most African presidents feel that power is a "zero-sum game". They must cling onto supreme power, or become victims or nonentities. We have yet to devise ways of making our former Heads of State continue to feel revered and honoured, like former U.S. Presidents are.

When Yakubu Gowon was overthrown in 1975, Nigeria seemed on the verge of inaugurating the Latin American style of military coups: give the fallen leader a chance to leave for exile with dignity. Gowon retained his rank and was guaranteed his pension.

But then came Murtala Mohammed's assassination in 1976 and all the ensuing suspicions and recriminations affected the fate of Gowon. The Latin Americanisation of Nigerian coups with exile was interrupted. Indeed, the process of voluntary exile came to a halt. Shagari's pardon of Gowon in 1982 helped to improve matters, though not completely as yet. Gowon became more and more of an elder statesman in Nigeria. Perhaps our former African leaders can become respected leaders who can be instrumental in uniting their countries and performing important international and national missions, as former US Presidents Jimmy Carter, George Bush, and Bill Clinton have done in areas such as elections, human rights promotion, tsunami and HIV/AIDS relief.

Of course, Nigeria is not the United States in terms of economic development, established democratic practices of political transitions. and access to peaceful means of resolving conflicts and tensions. Underlying tensions remain in Nigeria: the tension between the demands of conciliation and the imperatives of discipline, between the needs of national cohesion and the requirements of national self-restraint. In future cases like that of Shagari, the challenge before new African governments will be to find the sensitivity to recognize the choice of duties before it, the wisdom to identify which duty is the greater priority, and the courage to carry it through.

NOTES

[1] "Shagari Group Sets Up North S/South Unity Body," *Africa News* (September 21, 2005).

[2] Shagari, who celebrated his 80th birthday in 2005, was cleared of criminal charges; see "Nigeria Clears ex-President Shagari of Criminal Charges," *Jet* (April 7, 1986).

[3] See Shehu Shagari, *Beckoned to Serve: An Autobiography* (Ibadan, Nigeria: Heinemann Educational Books, 2001), p. 222, and David Williams, *President and Power in Nigeria : The Life of Shehu Shagari* (London and Totowa, NJ: Cass, 1982), pp. 190-91.

[4] See Toyin Falola, *The History of Nigeria* ((Westport, CT: Greenwood Press, 1999), pp.174-177.

[5] According to one analysis, this corresponds (but as is typical of the African colossus in the case of Nigeria, exceeded) to a general African pattern where deaths of incumbent heads of state in the case of coups peaked in the 1960s and declined or remained steady in subsequent decades; see George K. Kieh, Jr., "Military Engagement in Politics in Africa," in George Klay Kieh, Jr., and Pita Ogaba Agbese, Eds., *The Military and Politics in Africa : From Intervention to Democratic and Constitutional Control* (Aldershot, Hants, England ; Burlington, VT : Ashgate, 2004), p. 46.

[6] See A. Oyewole, *Historical Dictionary of Nigeria* (Metuchen, NJ: Scarecrow Press, 1987), pp. 143-144.

[7] Consult Anthony Parsons, "From Southern Rhodesia to Zimbabwe, 1965-1985," *International Affairs* Volume 9, Number 4, (November 1988), pp. 353-361; also see Victor De Waal, *The Politics of Reconciliation: Zimbabwe's First Decade* (London and Cape Town: Hurst and David Philip, 1981).

[8] This was the title of his book; see Jomo Kenyatta, *Suffering Without Bitterness* (Nairobi and Chicago: East African Publishing House and Northwestern University Press, 1968).

[9] As mentioned above, Shagari was cleared of criminal charges; "Nigeria Clears ex-President Shagari of Criminal Charges," *Jet* (April 7, 1986).

[10] On some of the ways in which this played out, consult Falola, *The History of Nigeria*, pp. 174-177.

[11] An overview of press freedom in Nigeria may be found in Adigun Agbaje, "Freedom of the Press and Party Politics in Nigeria: Precepts, Retrospect, and Prospects," *African Affairs* 89 (April 1990), pp. 205-226.

[12] For a detailed portrait of corruption in Nigeria, consult Arthur Agwuncha Nwankwo, *Nigeria: The Stolen Billions*, Vol. 1. (Enugu, Nigeria: Fourth Dimension Publishing, 1999).

[13] Ali A. Mazrui and Michael Tidy, *Nationalism and New States in Africa From About 1935 to the Present* (Nairobi: Heinemann, 1984), p. 218.

CHAPTER 18

REFLECTIONS ON NELSON MANDELA

As discussed elsewhere in this book, cultures differ in hate retention. Some cultures nurse their grievances for generations. Other cultures may be intensely hostile in the midst of a conflict, but as soon as the conflict has ended they display a readiness to forgive, even if not always to forget.

Armenians were butchered in large numbers by Ottoman Turks way back in 1915-1918. It has turned out that Armenian culture has a considerable proclivity towards hate retention. The story of the Armenian martyrdom of World War I has been transmitted with passion from generation to generation.[1] Armenians are still demanding justice from Turkey more than eighty years after the massacres.

The Irish also have long memories of grievance. Clashes occur in Northern Ireland every year concerning marches which commemorate "Orange conflicts" in the seventeenth century.[2] The Jews also have strong collective memories of the Holocaust and earlier outbursts of European anti-Semitism. But the Jews have been subtler in their troubled relationship with Germany than other offended parties.[3]

Nelson Mandela came from a culture which is illustrative of Africa's short memory of hate. That culture is far from being pacifist. Wars and inter-ethnic conflicts have been part of Africa's experience from before European colonisation, anti-colonialism and decades after independence. What is different about African cultures is their relatively low level of hate retention.

Mandela's life passed through stages. His early days as an African nationalist were characterized by a belief in non-violent resistance. In a sense he carried the torch of Albert Luthuli and Mahatma Gandhi. The Sharpeville Massacre of March 1960 was a major blow to his belief in passive resistance.[4] The African National Congress within which he had become one of the top leaders finally embraced the option of armed struggle and Mandela became the Commander-in-Chief.

When Mandela was finally sentenced to life imprisonment in 1964 after the Rivonia trial, some expected him to become more bitter than ever. Twenty-seven years later he emerged from prison as "truth and reconciliation" personified. The former Commander-in-Chief of armed struggle emerged in 1990 ready to hold the olive branch – magnanimous in triumph rather submissive in defeat.

But we need to place Nelson Mandela in the context of other African leaders as well. Post-colonial Africa had produced other leaders who had illustrated Africa's short memory of hate. Jomo Kenyatta was condemned by the British colonialists as "leader unto darkness and death"[5] and imprisoned in a remote part of Kenya. He emerged from imprisonment on the eve of independence and proclaimed "suffering without bitterness"[6] and proceeded to transform Kenya into a staunchly pro-Western country. A short memory of hate indeed!

Further South in Zimbabwe, Ian Smith unleashed a civil war when he unilaterally declared independence in November 1965. Yet, he lived to sit in a parliament of Black-ruled Zimbabwe, and was not subjected to postwar vendetta or trial.[7] Again, Africa's short memory of hate was manifest.

Nigeria waged one of the most highly publicized civil wars of post-colonial Africa, a brutal war that cost nearly a million lives. The Federal side under General Yakubu Gowon won the war, but was magnanimous towards the defeated Biafrans.[8] This was yet another manifestation of Africa's short memory of hate.

By the time Nelson Mandela was having afternoon tea with the unrepentant widow of the founder of apartheid, Mrs. Verwoerd, he had tough acts to follow in African magnanimity.[9] There were precedents of forgiveness which he followed and improved upon.

In comparing Mandela with other post-colonial African leaders there were other elements of style to be taken into account.

Post-colonial Africa produced five styles of political leadership. A *charismatic* leadership style depends mainly on the personal magnetism of the leader, and is best illustrated by Kwame Nkrumah of Ghana. *Mobilisational* style uses ideology and party organization to mobilize the masses, and is best exemplified by Julius K. Nyerere of Tanzania and Samora Machel of Mozambique. The *managerial* style uses skills of management and technocratic pragmatism, and this is illustrated by Thabo Mbeki of South Africa today and Felix Houphouet-Boigny of the Ivory Coast who died in 1993.

A *coercive* style of political leadership relies mainly on a regime of fear and demands for compliance and obedience. Most military regimes have been coercive in that sense, perhaps best personified by Idi Amin of Uganda. However, there have also been civilian regimes of coercion and fear like that of Hastings Banda of Malawi. Finally, there is a *conciliatory* style of political leadership, which is predisposed towards compromise and reconciliation. *Where does Nelson Mandela fit in?*

As a result of Mandela's record after he was released from prison in 1990, there is a temptation to think of him primarily as an example of conciliatory leadership. But in fact the younger Mandela was a powerful combination of charisma and mobilisation, rather than a conciliatory leader. The personal magnetism enabled him to rise rapidly in the African National Congress Youth League (NACYL). In 1952 he was elected National Volunteer-Chief, and proceeded to traverse the country trying to organize resistance as part of the ANC Campaign for the Defiance of Unjust Laws. For his role in the Defiance Campaign he was accused of violating the Suppression of Communism Act. He was convicted, but his record of strict non-violence at that stage earned him a suspended sentence and a confinement within the boundaries of the city of Johannesburg.[10]

But his role in the Defiance Campaign propelled him to the Presidency of the Youth League, the Presidency of the Transvaal region, and the Deputy Presidency of the African National Congress as a whole.

The ANC's initial policies still reflected the philosophies of non-violent resistance, which had been advocated earlier by Mohandas Gandhi (later Mahatma) and Albert Luthuli (the first African Nobel African Prize Laureate). The ANC's Programme of Action was inspired by the Youth League and envisaged a struggle based on civil disobedience, labour strikes and non-cooperation. Mandela was heavily involved in much of the planning, the organization and the implementation of such methods of struggle.

In anticipation of the possible banning of the ANC, Mandela accepted the awesome responsibility of preparing a master-plan for underground networking and secret lines of communication. But in most of the 1950s, Nelson Mandela as a mobilisation leader was averse to violence. He also helped to promote the *Freedom Charter* which had been adopted by the Congress of the People in 1955.

It was not until June 1961 that the African National Congress, after a long and agonizing reappraisal, reached the conclusion that violence could no longer to be ruled out against a coercive regime and racial intolerance. It was in that same year of 1961 that the *Umkhonte we Sizwe,* the armed wing of the ANC, was formed with Nelson Mandela as its Commander-in-Chief. Mandela as a charismatic leader, was now involved in <u>armed</u> mobilisation. As he put it at the Rivonia trial:

I and some colleagues came to the conclusion [in 1961] that as violence in this country was inevitable, it would be unrealistic and wrong for African leaders to continue preaching peace and non-violence at a time when the Government met our peaceful demands with force.

It was only when ... all channels of peaceful protest had been barred to us that the decision was made to embark on violent forms of political struggle, and to form *Unkhonto we Sizwe* ... The government had left us no other choice.[11]

Even after Mandela was eventually sentenced to life imprisonment and taken to the notorious maximum security fortress-cage on Robben Island, he continued to reaffirm the legitimacy of armed struggle. Later he was transferred to less isolated prisons in Cape Town [Pollsmor and Victor Vester prisons]. The apartheid regime offered him remission of sentence in exchange for renouncing violence. He turned the conditional offer down.[12]

And yet when he was finally released in February 1990, this most illustrious of all Africa's liberation fighters embarked on a mission of healing and forgiving. This former hero of mobilisational leadership became a paragon of the reconciliation style. Mandela became the greatest of all African examples of prolonged reconciliation and a short memory of hate.

Long may his legacy reign in the hearts of men and women, and long may reconciliation endure as a recurrent African achievement. And yet, there is a less known dimension of Nelson Mandala as the speaker of the word and the writer, perhaps an equally enduring legacy.

Nelson Mandela's initial impact on his own people in South Africa was through the spoken word. He gave political speeches and mobilized political activists through the spoken word. Over the years, he developed a competence in several languages relevant for South

African politics – including, of course, Afrikaans, the primary language of apartheid in the second half of the twentieth century.

Nelson Mandela also used the spoken word in his legal defence when he was placed in the docks by the apartheid regime against charges which ranged from communism to terrorism. The show-trial ultimately cost him twenty-seven years of his life, an innocent man languishing in racist prisons.

Much later in his post-apartheid reincarnation, Nelson Mandela also mobilized the spoken word in causes which ranged form denouncing the President of the United States for the unjust war in Iraq to criticizing President Thabo Mbeki of South Africa for pursuing what Mandela believed to be wrong policies about HIV-AIDS in the land. But he had earlier used the spoken word in negotiations with F.W. De Klerk to end apartheid.

Nelson Mandela has been seen as a bridge in a variety of senses. He has been a bridge between the architects of apartheid and the fighters for liberation. To the dismay of many fellow South Africans and the world at large, he had tea with the unrepentant widow of the supreme architect of apartheid, Mrs. Hendrick Verwoerd.[13] This is an ideological bridge. Nelson Mandela has also been seen as a bridge between white South Africans and non-white, regardless of ideology. This has been more specifically a racial bridge.[14]

By pursuing not only a secular but also an ecumenical strategy after apartheid, Nelson Mandela was also a bridge across the religious divide, including serving as a bridge between the Dutch Reform Church and other Christians, and a bridge between Christians on one side and Muslims, Hindus, Jews, Buddhists, secularists and followers of African indigenous religions, on the other.

Less clear-cut is whether Nelson Mandela has been a bridge between socialists and liberals, or even between communists and democrats. On these ideological nuances, Nelson Mandela has maintained a deliberate strategy of creative ambiguity.

But Mandela is not just a product and practitioner of the oral tradition. To the surprise of many people, Nelson Mandela is also a man of letters.

Africa, Mandela and the Centennial Muse

In July 2002 we assembled in Cape Town, South Africa, to celebrate Africa's 100 best books of the last one hundred years. Africa's <u>Nobel</u> Laureates in Literature were expected to be among the winners: Wole Soyinka, Nadine Gordimer and Naguib Mahfuz. At least one book of each literary Nobel laureate met Africa's own centennial standards.

What was not expected among the literary victors was someone whose Nobel Prize had been for *Peace*. This turned out to be Nelson Mandela. His book *Long March to Freedom*, written painfully while he was in prison under the apartheid regime, was chosen by the African literary jury among the one hundred best African books of the twentieth century. The Nobel Committee in Oslo had chosen Mandela in 1993 as a man of peace. The jury of Africa's 100 Books saluted Mandela in 2002 as a man of letters.

I was chosen to make the award presentation to Mandela at a glittering Gala Dinner celebration at the Cape Town Civic Center in South Africa. Other successful authors received their awards from Archbishop Desmond Tutu, another Nobel Laureate for Peace and a subject of discussion in another chapter of this book. Professor Njabulo Ndebele, Chair of Africa's Best Books Project and Vice-Chancellor of the University of Cape Town also played an active role in the occasion.

Nelson Mandela had, of course, excelled in many roles. He had excelled as a freedom fighter, as a prisoner of conscience, as a political and diplomatic negotiator, as Head of State and a statesman. In July 2002 we saluted Nelson Mandela as a *writer*.

Some scholars write history but do not make it themselves. Some statesmen make history but do not write it. But there have been people who both have recorded the annals of an age and contributed to the history of their own times. Outside Africa such a person included Winston Churchill, an interpreter of history and a maker of it. In Africa such a synthesis of activist-author includes our own Nelson Mandela. In July 2002 we honoured precisely that synthesis.

That July evening in Cape Town we celebrated a century of Africa's literary excellence. Of that century Nelson Mandela spent more than a quarter of it behind bars. There are prisoners who become more bitter in a cage. Mandela became more humane without losing his love for freedom. There have been prisoners in history who compromised their principles in order to get early release. Nelson Mandela repeatedly scorned the bribe of an early release if the cost was moral compromise.

If in the last half of the twentieth century there was one single statesman in the world who came closest to being *morally number one* among leaders of the human race, Nelson Mandela was probably such a person. Now in the twenty first century he has become the most distinguished and scathing critic of the American arrogance of power, the U.S. transition from Superpower to Super Empire.[15]

Mandela's love of books was enhanced rather than diminished in prison.[16] I personally discovered in an unusual way how Mandela had continued to read widely even in jail. It was the occasion when we first met. Mr. Mandela was attending his first summit meeting of the Organization of African Unity, but before he himself was Head of State. This was in Dakar, Senegal, in 1992.

I met Nelson Mandela in the corridor, one to one. I said, "Mr. Mandela, my name is Mazrui." He cut me short and completed my name, "Professor Ali Mazrui?"

Now why should Nelson Mandela in 1992 have heard my name at all when he had only recently been released after twenty-seven years in prison? After all, when he went to jail in the mid-1960s, I was a nonentity. The only explanation I could think of was that even in prison Mandela's reading was so wide-ranging that he even found time to read Ali Mazrui. I was flattered for myself, but more important, I was impressed by Nelson Mandela as a true lover of books.

In Dakar Mandela impressed me in his capacity as a *reader*. In Cape Town in 2002 we honoured him in his capacity as a *writer*. Although he had lost a quarter of the twentieth century behind bars, Mandela turned his bondage into a literary inspiration. His long walk to freedom was also a long march to literary excellence.

That dazzling evening in Cape Town reminded me of something else, relevant to Nobel-scale brilliance. U.S. President John F. Kennedy was entertaining 49 Nobel Laureates of different disciplines in the White House. Kennedy is reported to have said "I think this is the most extraordinary collection of talent, of human knowledge, that has ever been gathered together at the White House, with the possible exception of when Thomas Jefferson dined here –alone."[17] That night in Cape Town in 2002 I was confronting a concentration of literary brilliance of similar magnitude.

When in 1998 I proposed at a Book Fair in Zimbabwe that Africans selected Africa's own 100 greatest books of the last one hundred years, I had no idea that the proposal would fly. After all, my many proposals to Africa and the world over the years have had a mixed record. My most controversial proposal in my BBC Reith Lectures in 1979 was a recommendation that the Third World should pursue nuclear proliferation as a method of forcing the existing nuclear powers to agree to universal nuclear disarmament. My designated nuclear powers in Africa were post-apartheid South Africa, Egypt and Nigeria. In the end, my recommendation had no takers in Africa, though outside Africa, India and Pakistan became nuclear powers independently of any recommendation from me!! North Korea and perhaps Iran have recently been teasing and taunting the world with similar nuclear aspirations.

But if my proposal about bombs never took off, my recommendation about books has indeed reached fruition. I did manage to successfully persuade Africa to celebrate one hundred years of its own literary excellence. Perhaps the book is, in the final analysis, more powerful than the bomb. Mandela's book is an inspiration. A book can be a griot between covers, a sage in perpetual symbols, a creative moment captured for eternity.

The book, as a printed medium, has its rivals. There is literature in the oral tradition, on the radio, in magazines and their short stories, in drama on television, and now on the Internet. But there is a sense in which a book written behind bars is *scripture* in a special literary meaning.

Perhaps in the future Africa should select and honour the *ten* best books of each ten years. And when the century is complete, Africa should take another look and still identify the one hundred greatest works of that century. The choice at the end of the century may not be identical with the selection from decade to decade. After all, some decades may produce many more outstanding books than others. Even in this scenario, Mandela's book will always stand as a gospel of martyrdom.

What significance should I give that Project of 100 best books in my own life? Since my idea had come to fruition, was this the equivalent of my having completed one more book of my own? Or was it the equivalent of my having another child? My first five children are biological; is this sixth child literary?

I would like to believe that the fulfilment of such a big idea was the equivalent of having another child rather than completing another book. The event was momentous, had needed the crucial support of others, and had signified creativity at its best. Did it take the equivalent of a hundred best books to equal the excitement of having a child?

Since the idea of Africa's best books originated with me, my own works were disqualified from consideration. And it was considered inappropriate for me to serve on the jury. Instead I was given the honorific title of **"Founding Father"**!

I was honoured to present a literary prize to Nelson Mandela. Would it have been a greater honour if things were reversed: Mandela presented an award to me? In the final analysis what matters is that Mandela, this great prophet of the spoken word, was finally celebrated and saluted for his written word.

NOTES

[1] Readers interested in these massacres may consult Hamo B. Vasilian, ed., *The Armenian Genocide: A Comprehensive Bibliography And Library Resource Guide* (Glendale, VA: Armenian Reference Books Co., 1992).

[2] This is because of the commemoration by Protestants of their victory of the Orange Order against Catholics four centuries ago. On the origins of the Orange Order, see Marcus Tanner, *Ireland's Holy Wars : The Struggle for a Nation's Soul, 1500-2000* / Marcus Tanner (New Haven, CT : Yale University Press, 2001), pp. 189-292.

[3] For a historical relationship at the complex Jewish relationship with German culture, see Jacob Katz, "German Culture and the Jews," *Commentary* (February 1984), Volume 77, Number 2, pp. 54-59, and for a look at one example in the modern era, see Kim Chernin, "Is Wagner Good for the Jews?" *Tikkun* (February 2002) Volume 7, Issue 1, pp. 69-72.

[4] Anthony Sampson, *Mandela : The Authorized Biography* (New York: Knopf, distributed by Random House, 1999), p. 129-130. For a general overview of the Sharpeville massacre and consequences, see, for instance, James Barber, *South Africa in the Twentieth Century: A Political History--In Search of a Nation State* (Oxford, UK and Malden, MA: Blackwell Publishers, 1999), pp. 164-165.

[5] This was the appellation given to Kenyatta by British Governor Sir Patrick Renison, according to the Kenyan Ministry of External Affairs. <http://www.mfa.go.ke/kenyatta.html>. December 28, 2005.

[6] Jomo Kenyatta, *Suffering Without Bitterness* (Nairobi and Chicago: East African Publishing House and Northwestern University Press, 1968).

[7] Relatedly, see Anthony Parsons, "From Southern Rhodesia to Zimbabwe, 1965-1985," *International Affairs* (November 1988), Volume 9, Number 4, pp. 353-361; also see Victor De Waal, *The Politics of Reconciliation: Zimbabwe's First Decade* (London and Cape Town: Hurst and David Philip, 1981).

[8] On the Biafra war, Consult Herbert Ekwe-Ekwe, *The Biafra War : Nigeria and the Aftermath* (Lewiston, N.Y., USA : E. Mellen Press, 1990); Peter Schwab, Ed. *Biafra* (New York, Facts on File, 1971); and Zdenek Cervenka, *The Nigerian War, 1967-1970. History of the War; Selected Bibliography and Documents* (Frankfurt: Bernard & Graefe, 1971).

[9] On Mandela's meeting with Mrs. Verwoerd, see Sampson, *Mandela: The Authorized Biography*, p. 514.

[10] Sampson, Mandela : The Authorized Biography, pp. 68-71.

[11] The text of this quote is drawn from <http://www.anc.org.za/anzdocs/history/rivonia.html>. December 29, 2005.

[12] Mandela was repeatedly offered these conditional releases; relatedly, consult his *Long Walk to Freedom: The Autobiography of Nelson Mandela* (Boston: Back Bay Books, 1995), pp. 454-456.

[13] Sampson, Mandela: The Authorized Biography, p. 514.

[14] At Mandela's 87th birthday celebrations in 2005, former US President Bill Clinton remembered that "Mandela didn't merely speak of a multiracial society, he incorporated former apartheid leaders into his cabinet, he forgave the prosecutor who once tried to have him executed, he drank tea with the wife of the former South African president who kept him jailed. And in an enduring masterstroke still remembered keenly by white South Africans, he took to the field after the 1995 World Cup of rugby -- traditionally a sport of Afrikaners, the architects of apartheid – and donned a team jersey." Craig Timberg, "Clinton Brings Rhetorical Gifts to Mandela's Party," *The Washington Post* (July 20, 2005).

[15] For one instance of Mandela's scathing remarks about United States foreign policy and the Bush administration, see BBC News, "US threatens world peace, says Mandela," (September 11, 2002) at <http://news.bbc.co.uk/2/hi/africa/2251067.stm>. December 30, 2005.

[16]Sampson, Mandela: The Authorized Biography, p. 324.

[17]Kennedy's quip was reported in *Time* (May 11, 1962), p. 18.

CHAPTER 19

THE GENDER QUESTION AND CULTURE CHANGE:
NIGERIA, SOUTH AFRICA AND BEYOND

Nigeria probably leads Africa in economically independent women, but it does not lead Africa in politically empowered women. Uganda had a woman vice-president under Yoweri Museneni from the 1990s, but Uganda had a woman foreign minister even further back under the regime of the Idi Amin in the 1970s.[1]

Both Liberia and Kenya have had women presidential candidates who have campaigned hard for the ultimate political office. In 2001 Ellen Johnson Sirleaf in Liberia did lose to Charles Taylor and Charity Ngilu in Kenya did lose to Daniel arap Moi. But both women put a spirited fight and demonstrated substantial support. In the year 2005 Ellen Johnson-Sirleaf did at last win the Presidential election in Liberia.[2]

In the 1980s Winnie Mandela was the most famous African woman in the world. She was of course a South African.[3] Mrs. W. Sisulu was another high profile South African woman.

Before Rwanda and Burundi collapsed in the 1990s they were experimenting with women Prime Ministers.[4]

Nigeria for quite a while was at the modest level of having its highest-ranking woman as a minister for women's affairs. Nigeria has since moved up to have full female Ministers and a couple of Ministers of State. This may be significantly below the number of women ministers in a few other African countries.

On the other hand, Nigerian women are among the most economically independent in the whole of Africa. They are self-confident and assertive, and many of them know how to play the market.[5]

As for Nigerian women in scholarship and science, they compare well with others. It is true that Liberia had a woman president of a university long before Nigeria had a woman Vice-Chancellor, but the wider society in Liberia collapsed. And then Nigeria started catching up – first with a woman Vice-Chancellor at the University of Benin and later another female chief executive at the University of Abuja. Lagos State also started early with female academic leadership.

Nigerian educational institutions are in dire financial straits, but within these constraints there is optimism that Nigerian women will not be left too far behind Nigerian men in scholarship and, hopefully, in the sciences.

How does the gender divide relate to the digital divide? And what indeed is the digital divide? The digital divide arises out of either unequal access to the computer and the Internet or unequal skill in utilizing them. In a March-2000 lecture in Lagos, I raised the issue of whether there is a digital divide between different ethnic groups in Nigeria. Were certain ethnic groups in Southern Nigeria more computer literate than certain ones in the North? Were the reasons cultural or due to different degrees of economic access to computers?

On this occasion, I would like to relate the digital divide to gender rather than to ethnicity. Among Africans in the Diaspora there is strong evidence that African women are almost keeping pace with African men in computer literacy. At a conference at the Ohio State University at the beginning of June 2000 on the theme, "The Internet and Culture Change", about half of the paper presenters were African women, complete with computer demonstrations and illustrations operated by the women themselves.

All this is quite apart from the phenomenon of African-American women (as distinct from women directly from Africa). It is even clearer among African Americans that the women are keeping pace with the men in computer skills. Indeed, African American women may already be outstripping their men in those skills, as well as in education more generally.[6] Indeed, a high proportion of young Black males are in prison cells at the same time as females are in classrooms.[7] Women are getting computerized; men are getting convicted.[8] The gender divide is being widened by an inter-Black digital divide.

The agenda for the African Renaissance is wide and complex. But two critical reforms needed to transform Africa are a new policy on language favourable to indigenous languages and a new policy on gender more supportive of female empowerment. Nigeria has made a start on gender reform—but has not even begun serious consideration of a new post-colonial language policy.[9] The clock of history is ticking away. Time and tide wait for no policy-maker.

Nigeria will never become a first rank technological power until it scientificates the major indigenous languages, and perhaps technologise Pidgin as well. While a combination of French and English is called Franglaise, and while a combination of English and Swahili is called Swahinglish, the Pidgin of Nigeria may one day have to be re-named Nigenglish.

In indigenous African languages today, women are probably more proficient than men; in European languages men are probably more articulate than women in Africa as a whole.

In command of Pidgin English market women in Nigeria may have a special eloquence and skills of persuasion. The women of Bendal State, as well as the men, are famous for their Pidgin power, with a Bendal music of its own.

At the moment the elite of Nigeria think of Pidgin as a form of vulgarised and bastardised English. [10] However, it is worth remembering that the French language is descended from the vulgarised and bastardised Latin of Roman soldiers. Today the French language is widely regarded as the most beautiful in Europe.

Will Pidgin in Nigeria develop into Nigenglish and become a highly elegant medium of philosophical and literary discourse one day? The trend may have started already, especially among the women of the land.

But Nigeria does not only have a gender and digital divide. It also has a North-South divide, reinforced by a sectarian divide.[11] When twelve states in the Federation of Nigeria adopted Islamic law (the Sharia) as the law of the state, there were gender implications. The most notorious was the death penalty imposed on a pregnant woman (Amina Lawal) on charges of adultery. Adultery can be a capital offence under Islamic Law. Appeals for clemency from the rest of the Muslim world probably saved Amina Lawal's life. Northern Nigeria was to the right of the Islamic consensus (ijmaa) in the rest of the Muslim world. For most of the Muslim ummah, adultery was no longer a capital offence in this day and age.[12]

On the positive side of Northern Nigeria, the Sharia states had less alcoholism, less prostitution, less promiscuity, less narcotic drug abuse, and probably less HIV-AIDS, than did the other states of the Nigerian federation. Islam in Nigeria protects the sexual dignity of women better than the other traditions of Nigeria. But Islam in Nigeria is less protective of the social liberties of women than are the other traditions.

The Triple Custodial Role of Women

But what do the women of Nigeria have in common with the women of the rest of Africa, especially those of Southern Africa?

Through much of history mothers were the first teachers of both boys and girls – but women were often the last pupils. Mothers opened the doors of learning at the beginning of time, but women have had the gates of knowledge closed upon them for generations. The first classroom was the womb—the first nursery school was the cradle. Yet for a long time women were denied access to more formal classrooms of advanced institutions.

If we are dealing with generations of culture change rather than generations in biological ages, we should go back to ancient African myths of gender roles. Three custodial roles were culturally assigned to women

-women as custodians of fire
-women as custodians of water
-women as custodians of earth
Accompanying this third role was the doctrine of the dual fertility-
The fertility of the soil: Women as farmers
The fertility of the womb: Women as mothers.

As custodians of fire women all over Africa are in charge of rural energy supplies, such as firewood. As custodians of water, they are in charge of village water supplies and walk miles to rivers and lakes to fetch it. As custodians of earth, women are often the main cultivators of food crops. The history of economic racism in Southern Africa had distorted this triple custodial role of the African women.

Across generations, sons in Africa have respected their mothers more than have sons in the West. But husbands in Africa have respected their wives less then have husbands in the West.[13]

Vertical gender relations across generations in Africa are healthier than vertical gender relations in the United Sates. But horizontal gender relations in Africa between husband and wife, or between co-workers across gender, are less healthy than horizontal gender relations in the Western world today.

There are times when African men and African women mate across nationalities. These are different horizontal relations. I am a Kenyan married to a Nigerian. That is a Pan-African marriage. Kwame Nkrumah was a Ghanaian married to an Egyptian. That was a Pan-

African marriage. The second marriage of Nelson Mandela is to the former Mrs. Machel of Mozambique. That is a Pan African marriage. And the late lamented wife of Mr. Robert Mugabe, Mrs. Sally Mugabe, was Ghanaian, making it a Pan-African marriage.

The question arises whether Pan-Africa horizontal marriages like those I have mentioned stand a better chance of equality between the genders than marriages within the same ancestral African culture. This is a hypothesis rather a firm conclusion. Was Robert Mugabe's first marriage (Pan African) more egalitarian than his second marriage (intra-Zimbabwean)?

There is also a hypothesis that the first Mrs. Mugabe was a remarkable woman whose absence from the scene may partly explain the erosion of political restraint in the Zimbabwe regime since she died. Great men often need great women to help them find the right equilibrium. We wish the new First Lady of Zimbabwe great strength and influence in these turbulent times.

Gender and Land Reform

Zimbabwe's forceful acquisition of white farms probably used the wrong gender strategy. Instead of sending mainly male liberation veterans to forcefully take over white farms, Zimbabwe should have sent landless Zimbabwe women in large numbers as non-violent squatters on white farms.[14] Are there lessons here for South Africa?

Land hungry Black rural mothers of Zimbabwe campaigning for land redistribution from privileged white males would have grabbed the imagination of the world. Instead of the land grab appearing to be primarily a racial issue, it could have become primarily an issue of both racial and gender equity.

The suffragette movement in England in the nineteenth and early twentieth centuries was a movement for the right to vote. A black suffragette movement in Zimbabwe could have been a campaign for the right to cultivate. The women of Britain were struggling for redistribution of political power. The women of Zimbabwe could have been agitating for the redistribution of economic ownership.

White farms taken over by Black women could have been the Trojan horse for challenging the indigenous gender inequalities in land ownership in Southern Africa generally. Women all over Africa have extensive roles in agriculture but women have limited rights in land ownership.

There are three processes involved towards the betterment of the female condition in Southern Africa and beyond. The processes are the liberation of women, the centring of women and the empowerment of women. Women in Africa are more centred in the means of production than are women in Europe. Women in Africa have that triple custodial role – in agriculture, in water supply and in rural energy and firewood.

But although African women are more centred in the means of production than are their European sisters, women in Africa are still less liberated than women in Europe.

The third process is the empowerment of women. Uganda had a woman Foreign Minister before the United States had a woman Secretary of State. Liberia has a woman executive President long before the United States. Indeed, African countries have had women-vice presidents before Russia or the United States.

But on balance, female empowerment is still elusive in both Africa and the Western world. In Africa women may be central in agriculture, but they are not yet empowered on the land. Would a female land-grab in Zimbabwe have opened up a new chapter? Would it have been a major step towards female empowerment?

Three Forms of Sexism

There may be a case for affirmative action in favour of women – a kind of reverse discrimination in favour of women. In the past there was a different kind of reverse discrimination in favour of women – a form of benevolent sexism, rooted in ideas of masculine gallantry and protection of women. This ancient idea is captured in the principle of the Qur'an which declared "Al-Rijalu Quwaamuna al-nisaa". Men stand up for women and protect them.

And when the ocean liner, the Titanic, was sinking after hitting an iceberg in 1912, and there were not enough lifeboats on board, it was decided to give priority to women and children. This was benevolent sexism. Al-Rijalu Qawaamuna Al Nisaa. Among those who survived the disaster, women were disproportionate. Indeed, a few men disguised themselves as women in order to get onto the lifeboats.[15]

Virtually all societies put their military security and defence primarily in the hands of men. Almost no cultures conscript women in the army. They are exempt. Women may sometimes have a duty to die for their country, but almost never have a compulsory duty to kill for their country. In Southern Africa women did join armed liberation movements. Were they warriors or support staff?[16]

Al-Rijalu Qawaamuna Ala Nisaa

In addition to benevolent sexism, there is <u>benign sexism.</u> This is the form of sexism which is neither generous to women nor hostile – but emphasizes difference between genders without rank order. For example, men and women are normally expected to dress differently – but that does not involve superiority or inferiority.[17]

Men and women normally have gender specific first names. Joseph is almost never a woman; Jessica is almost never a man. Ngugi is almost never a woman, Ngina is almost never a man. Some African names are gender-neutral. But on the whole most personal names in most cultures are gender specific.

In most African cultures the duty of a father is to help bring up <u>good</u> children; the duty of a mother is to help bring up <u>happy</u> children. The father is the ultimate authority on family <u>discipline;</u> the mother is the ultimate authority on family love care and happiness. This particular division of labour between fathers of discipline and mothers of love can be benign, but it has its risks if the difference is carried too far.

The worst form of sexism is of course <u>malignant</u> and is the variety we try and fight against. This may involve sexual exploitation of women, political marginalisation, economic injustice towards women and military neutralization of women (keeping women out of the armed forces).

Africa-specific controversies about malignant sexism include debates about female circumcision or female genital surgery. Critics of the practice in the West call it female genital mutilation. I personally am a critic of the practice, but I prefer terms like female genital surgery or female genital cutting. The term "female genital mutilation" is judgmental rather than purely descriptive.[18]

I have no objection to the practice of polygamy (or poligyny), provided it is entirely with the consent of every partner – the consent of all the wives, as well as the consent of the husband of course. There are women who would rather share a man with another woman, rather than not have the man at all. There may be women who may not be married at all if they did not enter into polygamous relationships. Thus polygamy may continue to be legitimate in Africa – provided every partner freely <u>consents</u> to the union. Polyandry in most of Africa still lacks cultural legitimacy – just as same-sex marriages are yet to be legitimised in most of the world.

The Gender of War

How does the issue of gender relate to this era of counter terrorism? Here we must address generations of change in warfare. Old style warfare was highly masculine. Armies of men confronted each other on the battlefield. The macho factor was often at work as virility and valour were intertwined. In most societies throughout history the warriors were overwhelmingly <u>men.</u>

In the course of the 20th century three processes tended to increase the proportion of women in military matters. One was the change in the technology of war. Fighting involved more and more the pushing of buttons rather than the wielding of heavy weapons. Women as foot soldiers and infantry were still at a disadvantage. But technological sophistication made muscle power less and less relevant.

A second factor which has increased the role of women in the military from the twentieth century was the women's liberation movement worldwide. Both governments and the armed forces were under pressure for at least token participation of women in military matters. In Africa, Southern Africa led the way.

The third factor which has increased the role of women is the emergence of new forms of armed struggle, especially in developing countries. Guerrilla warfare, liberation wars and even the new strategies of suicide bombers have involved increasing participation by women in combat roles.[19] Women are warriors of liberation alongside men.

I am in favour of pursuing the ideal of androgynous armies in which there would be approximate parity between men and women in the armed forces. I support the ideal of such gender parity in the military because I believe if women were equals in decisions about war and peace, the world would have fewer wars. It is not sociologically accidental that women are underrepresented in hard-core prisons for crimes of violence every where in the world, as well as being underrepresented within the armed forces of almost all societies.

Women as a force for peace would only succeed if their participation in warfare went beyond obeying the orders of male generals and male field marshals. That is why the truly <u>significant</u> enlistment of women in the armed forces of the United States and Israel has not prevented those two countries from becoming the most internationally aggressive for the last fifty years. Since the 1950s, the

278

United States and Israel have engaged in more wars across national boundaries than almost any other states in the world.

The <u>American</u> and <u>Israeli</u> armed forces have a higher proportion of women than most other armies in the world. Yet the United States and Israel have militarily violated the territorial sovereignty of other countries more often than have any other countries with the possible exception of apartheid South Africa in the 1970s and 1980s.

The conclusion to be drawn is that it is not enough to have numerically more women in the armed forces, if women are to be a force for peace. Women must go beyond saluting male generals. There need to be greater parity in <u>command,</u> greater sharing of military authority.

In November 2002 in my hometown of Mombasa, in Kenya an Israeli hotel – The Paradise -- was bombed by suicide bombers. The bombers were definitely men. On the same day in Mombasa an attempt was made to shoot down an Israeli tourist plane.[20] This one failed. Again the presumption was that the shooters from the ground were men, but his presumption was based on probability rather than certainty.

There may be more and more women sacrificing themselves in Third World Liberation movements these days, but the chain of command is still heavily masculine.

A surface to air missile seems to have been used in an attempt to blow up the Israeli plane over Mombasa. The global media presented this as a wholly new threat to civilian aviation. In fact this attempt to shoot down a civilian plane was not new even in Africa. Sub-Saharan Africa had a 1978 precedent at the level of <u>national</u> terrorism. North Africa was accused of a similar 1988 destruction of a civilian airline at the level of <u>international</u> terrorism

The sub-Saharan precedent was the shooting down of a civilian government airliner by Zimbabwe liberation forces in 1978, in which about 50 people died. Among those who survived on the ground Joshua Nkomo's forces killed several of them. NEWSWEEK carried a photograph of Joshua Nkomo and Robert Mugabe raising their glasses. The caption of the photograph was <u>"We shot it down".</u> It was not clear whether the photograph was not an old one dug up by NEWSWEEK and taken long before the shooting down of the plane.[21]

But there is no doubt that Joshua Nkomo accepted "credit" for shooting down the plane, and he caused an uproar when he chuckled over the incident in a BBC interview. This was all part of anti-colonial terrorism at the national level of the politics of Southern Africa. Zimbabwe women participated in the liberation struggle, but had little role in decisions of such magnitude.

Less clear-cut was whether Libya was really responsible for the bombing of the Pan American flight 103 over Lockerbie, Scotland, in 1988. The fact that one Libyan (male) has been convicted by a Scottish court has still left many doubts about the nature of the evidence. But if Libya was indeed responsible for the bomb which destroyed pan American flight 103, it was North African participation in terrorism at the international level.[22] While Libyan women have served in the security forces, they have not shared ultimate military authority. Neither have women in either South Africa or Nigeria.

If women are potentially a force of peace, no long-term strategy of either counter-terrorism or counter-militarism will succeed without paying greater attention to the sexual sociology of war. In the final analysis a war on terrorism must include a campaign for the empowerment of women.

Conclusion

In peace and in war genuine modernity and genuine humaneness do require the empowerment of women. The human race has made a start—but there is still a long way to go before Afro-gender is reconciled to Afro-equity.

If Nigeria has led the way in the economic empowerment of women, and Liberia has since led Africa in the presidential empowerment of a woman, South Africa has been the vanguard in the legislative empowerment of women. Apart from the effort by the African National Congress to have a gender quota among legislative candidates, and apart from the high political profile of Winnie Mandela in post-apartheid South Africa, there has also been the remarkable record of a woman Speaker of the first democratic parliament of South Africa. Frene Ginwala presided over the first post-apartheid legislature of South Africa with remarkable leadership and discipline.

The quest for female empowerment continues from Lagos to Harare, from Monrovia to Pretoria, from Winnie Mandela to Ellen Johnson Sirleaf. The vanguard of change is at hand.

NOTES

[1] Dictator Idi Amin made Elizabeth of Toro Ambassador and then Foreign Minister of Uganda. He then tried to humiliate this proud African woman with allegations of sexual misconduct at a French airport. The lies were a disgrace to Idi Amin rather than to the Princess. She has described her life; see Elizabeth Nyabongo, *Elizabeth of Toro, The Odyssey of an African Princess: An Autobiography* (New York: Simon and Schuster, 1989).

[2] Ms. Johnson-Sirleaf was elected president in the midst of some controversy; see Lane Hartill, "President in Waiting Stays Cool in Liberia: Johnson-Sirleaf Unruffled by Fraud Claims," *The Washington Post* (November 14, 2005).

[3] For a general biography of Winnie Mandela, consult, for example, Emma Gilbey, *The Lady: The Life and Times of Winnie Mandela* (London: Cape, 1993).

[4] The new Rwanda has made impressive strides at least in the area of female participation in its Parliament. Women make up 48.8 percent of seats in the lower house of Parliament, a higher percentage than in the legislative bodies in countries like Sweden, Denmark, the Netherlands and Norway, known for their progressive policies. See Marc Lacey, "Women's Voices Rise as Rwanda Reinvents Itself," *The New York Times* (February 26, 2005).

[5] For instance, for a historical perspective on Igbo female participation in the economy, consult Gloria Chuku, *Igbo Women and Economic Transformation in Southeastern Nigeria, 1900-1960* (New York: Routledge, 2005). For more analyses, see Christiana E. E. Okojie "Women in the Rural Economy in Nigeria, in Parvin Ghorayshi and Claire Bélanger, Eds., *Women, Work, and Gender Relations in Developing Countries : A Global Perspective* (Westport, CT: Greenwood Press, 1996), pp. 57-74; essays by Onaiwu W. Ogbomo, "Esan Women Traders and Precolonial Economic Power," Toyin Falola, "Gender, Business, and Space Control: Yoruba Market Women and Power," Felix K. Ekechi, "Gender and Economic Power: The Case of Igbo Market Women of Eastern Nigeria," and Catherine VerEecke, "Muslim Women Traders of Northern Nigeria: Perspectives from the City of Yola," in Bessie House-Midamba and Felix K. Ekechi, Eds., *African Market Women and Economic Power : The Role of Women in African Economic Development* ((Westport, CT: Greenwood Press, 1995), pp. 1-80.

[6] The comparative underrepresentation of black men in higher education is startling, compared to black women and others in the same age group: Nationally, barely a quarter of the 1.9 million black men between 18 and 24 -- prime college-going years -- were in college in 2000, according to the American Council on Education's most recent report on minorities in higher education.

By comparison, 35 percent of black women in the same age group and 36 percent of all 18- to 24-year-olds were enrolled in higher education. Karen W. Arenson, "Colleges Struggle to Help Black Men Stay Enrolled," *The New York Times* (December 30, 2005).

[7] For instance, African Americans account for 12.3 percent of the US population, while accounting for 43.7 percent of the incarcerated population, according to a 2002 Human Rights Watch estimate; see Human Rights Watch Press Backgrounder, "Race and Incarceration in the United States,"(February 22, 2002)

[8] African-American men are more likely to end up in prison than earn a bachelor's degree or serve in the military, according to a recent analysis; see Becky Pettit and Bruce Western, "Mass Imprisonment and the Life Course: Race and Class Inequality in U.S. Incarceration," *American Sociological Review* (April 2004), Vol. 69, No. 2, pp. 151-169.

[9] Consult, for some related discussions, Unyierie Angela Idem, "Language and the National Question," in Abubakar Momoh and Said Adejumobi, Eds., *The National Question in Nigeria : Comparative Perspectives* (Aldershot, Hampshire, England and Burlington, VT: Ashgate, 2002), pp. 183-200, and F. Niyi Akinnaso, "The National Language Question and Minority Language Rights in Africa: A Nigerian Case Study," in Ronald Cohen, Goran Hyden, and Winston P. Nagan, Eds., *Human Rights and Governance in Africa* (Gainesville, FL: University Press of Florida, 1993), pp. 191-214.

[10] On Nigerian English generally, see Ayo Banjo, "The Sociolinguistics of English in Nigeria and the ICE Project," in Sidney Greenbaum, Ed., *Comparing English Worldwide : The International Corpus of English* (Oxford and New York: Clarendon Press and Oxford University Press, 1996), pp. 239-244; Ayo Bamgbose, "Post-Imperial English in Nigeria, 1940-1990," in Joshua A. Fishman, Andrew Conrad and Alma Rubal-Lopez, eds., *Post-Imperial English: Status Change in Former British and American Colonies, 1940-1990* (Berlin and New York: Mouton de Gruyter, 1996) pp. 357-372; Ayo Bamgbose, "Standard Nigerian English: Issues of Identification," in Braj B. Kachru, *The Other Tongue: English Across Cultures* (Urbana, IL: University of Illinois Press, 1992), pp. 148-161; and on regional variations, consult V. O. Awonusi, "Regional Accents and Internal Variability in Nigerian English: A Historical Analysis," *English Studies* 67 (December 1986), pp. 555-560.

[11] An overview of the North-South and other cleavages bedeviling Nigeria may be found in *The Economist* (January 15, 2000), pp. 14-15; also see *The Economist* (July 8, 2000), p. 47. For longer analyses on earlier conflicts caused by

the Sharia issue, see Toyin Falola, *Violence in Nigeria: The Crisis of Religious Politics and Secular Ideologies* (Rochester, NY: University of Rochester Press, 1998), especially pp. 77-113; Simeon O. Ilesanmi, *Religious Pluralism and the Nigerian State* (Athens, OH: Ohio University Center for International Studies, 1997), pp. 174-207; M. H. Kukah and Toyin Falola, *Religious Militancy and Self-Assertion: Islam and Politics in Nigeria* (Aldershot, UK, and Brookfield, VT: Avebury Press, 1996), pp. 117-139; and Pat A. T. Williams, "Religion, Violence, and Displacement in Nigeria," *Journal of Asian and African Studies*, 32, 1-2 (June 1997), pp. 33-49.

[12] See relatedly O. U. Kalu, "Safiyya and Adamah: Punishing Adultery with Sharia Stones in Twenty-first Century Nigeria," *African Affairs* (2003), Volume 102, No. 408, pp. 389-408. It should be noted that the sentences of stoning have never been carried out. Even in the most prominent case, that of Amina Lawal, the case against her was flawed and she may not have been in any danger of being executed at all, even under the Shariah. See the opinion piece by Helon Habila, "The Politics of Islamic Law: Shariah in Nigeria," *The International Herald Tribune*, (October 7, 2003).

[13] For instance, the large prevalence of wife-beating, and related attitudes, with special reference to Nigeria, was reported in a *New York Times* article. The article pointed out:

> One in three Nigerian women reported having been physically abused by a male partner, according to the latest study, conducted in 1993. The wife of the deputy governor of a northern Nigerian province told reporters last year that her husband beat her incessantly, in part because she watched television movies. One of President Olusegun Obasanjo's appointees to a national anticorruption commission was allegedly killed by her husband in 2000, two days after she asked the state police commissioner to protect her.

Sharon LaFraniere, "Entrenched Epidemic: Wife-Beatings in Africa," *The New York Times* (August 11, 2005).

[14] For a related report, see Michael Wines, "Zimbabwe Announces a New Plan to Seize Land," *The New York Times* (June 9, 2004).

[15] Relatedly, see Lisa C. Ikemoto, "Lessons From the Titanic," in Julia E. Hanigsberg and Sara Ruddick, eds., *Mother Troubles: Rethinking Contemporary Maternal Dilemmas* (Boston: Beacon Press, 1999), p. 157.

[16] For discussions on the South African case, consult Patricia T. Morris, "Women, Resistance, and the Use of Force in South Africa," in Ruth H. Howes

and Michael R. Stevenson, *Women and the Use of Military Force* (Boulder, CO: L. Rienner Publishers, 1993), pp. 185-206, and Barbara Harlow, *Barred: Women, Writing, and Political Detention* (Hanover, NH: Wesleyan University Press and University Press of New England, 1992), pp. 139-157.

[17] The differences are explored in Ruth Barnes and Joanne B. Eicher, Eds., *Dress and Gender: Making and Meaning in Cultural Contexts* (New York: Berg and St. Martin's Press, 1992).

[18] The controversy over this practice is explored in, for instance, Elizabeth Heger Boyle, *Female Genital Cutting : Cultural Conflict In The Global Community* (Baltimore, Md. : Johns Hopkins University Press, 2002); Ellen Gruenbaum, *The Female Circumcision Controversy : An Anthropological Perspective* (Philadelphia : University of Pennsylvania Press, 2001); and Bettina Shell-Duncan and Ylva Hernlund, Eds., *Female "Circumcision" In Africa : Culture, Controversy, And Change* (Boulder, Colo. : Lynne Rienner Publishers, 2000).

[19] Palestinian female suicide bombers have done so voluntarily; for a detailed analysis of the suicide bombers' psychology, see Suzanne Goldberg, "Special report: A mission to murder: inside the minds of the suicide bombers," *The Guardian* (London) (June 11, 2002), and for an extended discussion on female suicide bombers, see Mia Bloom, *Dying to Kill: The Allure of Suicide Terror* (New York: Columbia University Press, 2005), pp. 142-165.

[20] Beth Potter, "No Vacation From Terror's Reach," *U.S. News & World Report*, (December 9, 2002).

[21] See Richard Hull, "Rhodesia in Crisis," *Current History* (March 1979) Volume 76, Number 445, p. 107.

[22] Indeed, Libya has now taken responsibility for the Lockerbie bombing in an apparent bid to end sanctions; see *The Washington Post* (August 13, 2003), p. 17.

CHAPTER 20

DUAL BRAIN DRAIN: MIGRATION AND HIV-AIDS[1]

(With Amadu Jacky Kaba)

There are two interrelated theses which this paper seeks to demonstrate. Firstly, Africa entered the twenty-first century afflicted by two forms of brain drain – migrant brain drain and terminal brain drain. The migrant version is the usual skill exodus of Africans relocating to other societies and living there. The terminal brain drain is the emerging pandemic of HIV-AIDS and its devastating consequences among the younger generation of Africans.[2]

But this paper goes on to adopt as its two case studies the largest country in Southern Africa and the largest in West Africa. South Africa and Nigeria are afflicted by both forms of the brain drain – the loss of skilled human power to other societies (migrant) and the loss of younger citizens to HIV-AIDS (terminal). But the balance between the two forms of brain drain in South Africa and Nigeria is uneven. In Nigeria the migrant brain drain may be the highest from Sub-Saharan Africa. In South Africa it is the terminal brain drain which may be the highest in Africa. The skill exodus from Nigeria is disproportionate; the terminal brain drain in South Africa is exceptional.

While both Nigeria and South Africa have been losing a lot of their citizens through migration and fatal diseases, Nigeria has suffered less from HIV-AIDS than South Africa and more from export of skills than post-apartheid South Africa.[3] What are the forces at work in the two societies?

In order to explain the migrant brain drain one needs to identify the push-out factors in Nigeria and South Africa which have sent citizens out in search of alternative opportunities abroad. One also needs to identify the pull-in factors in the receiving countries which have served as magnets for incoming Nigerians and South Africans.

The push-out factors during the apartheid years in South Africa included rampant racist legislation, the structures of a police state, the threat of destabilization and the clouds of ethnic conflict. Many white liberals and victimized people of colour went into exile. This was quite apart from the African liberation fighters who were organized mainly in neighbouring countries to fight on behalf of the African National Congress and against the apartheid regime.

The push-out factors at work in post-colonial Nigeria included the civil war of 1967-1970 and its disruptive consequences, the role of the military in Nigerian politics, the tensions of north-south relations, the fluctuations of ethnic and sectarian politics, the ailing economy and the political conflicts of petro-corruption.

As for the host countries to which Nigerians have migrated, South Africa itself has been one of the magnets. The pull-in forces within post-apartheid South Africa have included the advantages of an industrialized economy, the dismantling of political apartheid, the liberties of an open society, and the best endowed research and academic institutions in sub-Saharan Africa.

But the bigger magnets for Nigeria's migrant brain drain have been in the Western world, especially countries of the European Union and the special attraction of the United States. Let us examine more closely the migrant brain drain in a comparative perspective before we return to the terminal brain drain in both Nigeria and South Africa.

Migrant Brain Drain to the Western World

The United States may have the largest number of educated Africans who live and work in Western nations. According to the U.S. Census Bureau, as of 2002 there were just over 1 million African immigrants residing in the United States.[4] According to the United States Census Bureau, as of the year 2000, there were an estimated 881,300 African immigrants in the United States. During that year, West African immigrants comprised 326,507 (37% of the total African immigrants), with Nigerians comprising 134,940 (41.3%), Ghana 65,572 (20.1%), and Sierra Leone 20,831 (6.4%) of the West African total. Southern African immigrants in the United States in 2000 comprised 66,496 (7.5% of all African immigrants in the United States), with South African immigrants comprising 63,558 (95.6%) of the Southern African total. There were 57,607 (6.5% of all African immigrants) African immigrants in the United States in 2000 whose origin was not classified. The 134,940 Nigerian immigrants in the United States in 2000 comprised 15.3% of all African immigrants.[5]

As a group, despite their relatively small population proportionally, the 700,000 African immigrants in the United States as of March 2000, were not only more highly educated than their compatriots in Africa, but they also have become one of the most highly educated groups within the entire United States, at a time when the people of Africa are at the bottom of the literacy ladder of the world. According to a 2001 U.S. Census Bureau report, 94.9% of these African immigrants age 25 and over have at least a high school diploma, compared with 87% of the American population. Furthermore, the proportion of the 700,000 Africans in the United States (as of March 2000) aged 25 and over with at least a bachelor's degree was 49.3%, substantially higher than the average for the general population of 25.6%, and other foreign born populations in the country such as Asians (44.9%).[6]

In a 2003 study of blacks in the United States, Logan and Deane said:

> Education attainment of Africans (14.5 years) is higher than Caribbean (12.8 years) and of African Americans (12.5 years) –Indeed, it is higher even than whites and Asians. This suggests that black Africans immigrate selectively to the U.S. based on their educational attainment or plans for higher education.[7]

Moreover, Egyptian and Nigerian immigrants in the United States are among the most highly educated groups. For example, according to a 1998 U.S. Census Bureau publication, of over 65 ancestry groups listed, in 1990, 60.4% and 52.9% of people of Egyptian and Nigerian descent aged 25 and over, had at least a bachelor's degree respectively. No other single group (English, German, Irish, Italian, Scottish, Dutch, etc.) had 50% bachelor's degree attainment rate. For master's degrees, 26.3% of Nigerians and 25.6% of Egyptians aged 25 and over held such degrees in 1990, with Egyptians third only behind Nigerians and Iranians (26%).[8] In a 2003 World Bank policy research paper Richard H. Adams, Jr. pointed out that in 2000, there were 90,620 Nigerian immigrants and 75,170 Egyptian immigrants aged 25 and older who had attained tertiary education in the United States. Adams also pointed out that in 2000, there were 361,773 Moroccan immigrants, and 91,019 Tunisian immigrants aged 25 and over who had attained tertiary education in OECD countries (p.26).[9]

How the West Benefits from Migrant Brain Drain

Many scholars and other commentators have argued that the brain drain from Africa not only benefits Western nations economically and socially, but it also has negative short and long-term consequences for the world's poorest continent.[10]

Writing about an effort to recruit 44 South African physicians to Canada, Crush notes that: "The estimated cost of training a South African doctor is $150,000. The Alberta [Canada] government spent a mere $1.2 million on the recruiting scheme, providing a $10.4 million net gain of medical expertise at South African expense."[11] Leslie notes that there were 1,700 South African trained doctors practicing in Canada alone.[12]

An estimated 100,000 expatriates from Western nations or the developed world are employed in Africa. It costs the continent $4 billion annually to pay the salaries of those foreign expatriates.[13] A World Markets Research Centre 2002 analysis pointed out:

Skilled workers emigrating from South Africa are estimated to have cost the country R67.8bn (US$7.8bn) in lost human capital since 1997 and this has retarded economic growth.... Currently there are no official statistics on the number of teachers who have left South Africa, but estimates put the figure at about 8,000.[14]

Nigerian analysts have started analysing their country's skill-transfer to countries like the United States. The best-educated ethnic group in the United States is probably the population of Nigerians living in America. It is estimated that sixty-four percent of Nigerians over eighteen years old living in the United States have one or more university degrees.

Half the members of major Nigerian associations in the United States probably have master's degrees and doctorates. If these figures are correct, this is skill transfer from Africa to America instead of the other way round.

When you compare the Nigerian presence in the United States in the year 2000 with what it was like when Nnamdi Azikiwe first arrived in America in the 1920s, the contrast is stark. When Zik set foot in America in 1924, the number of Nigerians in the U.S. was probably less than ten. By the end of the twentieth century the number of Nigerians in the United States had risen to a quarter of a million

Philip Emeagwali, the computer analyst from Lagos, may have been overstating the case, but even his hyperbole is at least worth considering. Philip Emeagwali says:

"One in three African university graduates live and work outside Africa. In effect, we are operating one-third of African universities to satisfy the manpower needs of Western nations. One-third of African education budget is a supplement for the American education budget. In effect, Africa is giving developmental assistance to the United States"[15]

Although Nigeria is less industrialized than South Africa, Nigeria is giving more development aid to the United States than South Africa is doing.

Earlier in the 1990s, a National Science Foundation Study indicated that out of the 345,000 scientists and engineers with PhDs involved in Research and Development (R and D) in the United States, 29% were foreign born.[16] Globalisation has continued to facilitate the brain drain. Nigeria and South Africa have been in the vanguard.

Comparative Pathologies and the Brain Drain

In the 1960s, South Africa was, by most medical metrics, the healthiest country in sub-Saharan Africa. It had the best doctor-patient ratio on the continent, some of the best trained nurses, and the most advanced preventive medicine system in Africa. For a brief period, South Africa even led in medical innovation when it accomplished the very first heart-transplant in the history of applied science. Christiaan Barnard of South Africa became a global medical superstar overnight.

Indeed, Christiaan Barnard's achievements symbolized how far ahead of other African countries South Africa's medicine was in the 1960s. As a resident surgeon at Groote Schuur Hospital in Cape Town (1953-1956), he discovered that intestinal atresia originated during pregnancy when the fetus received insufficient blood supply. His discovery gave rise to a surgical procedure to correct what used to be a fatal defect.

Christiaan Barnard's greater claim to global fame came in December 1967 when he led a team of 20 surgeons in an operation which replaced the incurable heart of Louis Washkansky with a heart obtained from a fatally injured accident victim. The operation was successful – although Mr. Washkansky lived for less than three weeks after the transplant.[17] By the late 1970s Barnard's patients managed to survive for several years after the heart transplants.

But while in the 1960s South Africa led the continent in quality of medicine, physical fitness and perhaps life expectancy, South Africa also led the continent in political pathologies within the same time-frame. The 1960s in South Africa witnessed deepening racial segregation, the massacre of unarmed Black protesters at Sharpeville in 1960, the ruthless displacement of Africans under the Group Areas Act, the forced withdrawal of South Africa from the [British] Commonwealth of Nations in 1961 as a result of Pretoria's racist policies. There was also the assassination of Prime Minister Hendrik Verwoerd by a fellow white man in 1966.

The 1960s were also the decade of the most historic of South Africa's political trials. Nelson Mandela was tried more than once, culminating in the Rivonia treason trial which opened in October 1963. Nelson Mandela was sentenced to life imprisonment the following year.[18]

Meanwhile, the pursuit of Bantu homelands and the implementation of Bantu education continued in full swing.

Then came the 1990s. A country which had once been the paragon of preventive medicine and an evolving model of physical fitness, was suddenly confronted with one of the most severe medical threats of the age. HIV-AIDS devastated significant parts of the population. The country which had led the world in heart transplant was now leading the world as a casualty of HIV-AIDS.

On the other hand, the 1990s also witnessed the political healing of South Africa as Nelson Mandela was released from prison, the African National Congress was legalized, the local communist movement tolerated and political apartheid dismantled. The racial pathologies of South Africa were healing at about the same time as the physical health of South Africa was worsening. Political apartheid was making its exit by the front door as HIV-AIDS was making its entry into South Africa from behind.

Nigeria's post-colonial experience revealed a different kind of paradox. The country became independent in 1960. A combination of political independence and the new wealth of petroleum converted Nigeria into the largest producer of Black intellectuals on the African continent. Petrowealth facilitated for a while both the establishment of more and more institutions of higher education within Nigeria, and facilitated extensive overseas education for children of the Nigerian elite.

The positive aspect of Nigeria's post-colonial experience has been this dramatic growth of the Black intelligentsia. The negative aspect has been the emergence of the political pathologies of ethnic conflict, religious sectarianism, the North-South regionalist divide, as well as a substantial breakdown of law and order.

A flourishing Nigerian intelligentsia produced Africa's leading historians like Kenneth Dikke and Jacob Ade Ajayi, Africa's literary giants like Chinua Achebe and Wole Soyinka, Africa's leading technologists like Bede Okigbo, and Africa's leading Islamic scholars in Northern Nigeria going all the way back to the legacy of Usman Dan Fodio and beyond.

Intellectually, Nigeria built upon the achievements of its past generations and produced Africa's largest intelligentsia. Yet the political pathologies of ethnic rivalry, sectarianism, and regionalist conflicts turned Nigeria into a political Intensive Care Unit. The diagnosis included a weak sense of nationhood among Nigerians and fragile capabilities of statehood in the country.

In time, South Africa began to have a terminal brain drain as it lost by HIV-AIDS more and more of its potentially talented people between the ages of 15 and 35. By the same token, Nigeria's clash between political pathology and intellectual enlargement resulted in large numbers of Nigerians leaving their country in search of better pastures abroad. Nigeria's exit of talent was disproportionately a case of migrant brain drain. South Africa's exit of talent from the 1990s was disproportionately a case of terminal brain drain.

Terminal Brain Drain Between Southern and West Africa

Throughout history, regions and continents of the world have had their share of the massive spread of deadly diseases in their populations, which caused the deaths of millions of people. For example, in the 14th century, the Black Death struck Europe and killed an estimated 50 million people or 60% of the total population.[19] In the 16th century, smallpox is said to have killed an estimated 18 million Native Americans in North America alone.[20] In the early 20th century, the flu killed tens of millions of people in Asia, the Americas, Australia and Europe.[21] It now appears that Africa is experiencing its share of such disease epidemics in the 21st century – HIV-AIDS.

291

There is a major difference between the diseases discussed above and HIV-AIDS. While those other diseases can at least be cured if one can afford the cost of medications, as of the first half of 2005, there is yet no cure for HIV-AIDS. The death in early January 2005 of the son of former South African President Nelson Mandela, Makgatho (aged 54), is an excellent example of the destructive force of HIV-AIDS at the highest level.[22] Also, former President of Zambia, Kenneth Kaunda is reported to have lost both his son and daughter-in-law to AIDS, leaving his grandchildren as orphans. Had the children of these two former presidents been infected with illnesses such as malaria or tuberculosis, there is a strong possibility that their families and friends would have spent any amount of money to save their lives.

Southern Africa (especially South Africa, Botswana and Zimbabwe), and countries such as Uganda, Kenya and Nigeria are being impacted severely by the HIV-AIDS brain drain. The disease now represents over two million of the estimated ten million annual deaths on the continent. According to a December 2002 report by the UNAIDS, of the 42 million people worldwide who were infected with the HIV-AIDS virus, 29.4 million (70%) were in sub-Saharan Africa. While the HIV adults prevalence rate for the world (for those age 15 to 49) was 1.2% during that year, it was 8.8% for sub-Saharan Africa.[23] A higher proportion of Africans with HIV-AIDS reside in Southern and Eastern Africa. Within the five regions of Africa, while the estimated HIV-AIDS prevalence rate (for adults aged 15 to 49) for all of Africa in 1999 was 8.8%, it was 10.18% for Eastern Africa, 5.40% for Middle Africa, 0.2% for Northern Africa, 3.5% for Western Africa, and 24.82% for Southern Africa. Of the estimated 2,204,200 Africans who died in 1999 of HIV-AIDS, Eastern Africa accounted for 1,219,970 (55%), 463,410 (21%) for Western Africa, 315,100 (14.3%) for Southern Africa, and 205,720 (9.3%) for Middle Africa.[24] No figures were provided for Northern Africa, partly because there has been no strong evidence yet showing large numbers of HIV-AIDS deaths in that region.[25]

The negative consequences of HIV-AIDS in Africa are now being felt all across the continent. According to one account, 11% of all children in Uganda and 9% in Zambia have been orphaned. Almost 15,000 teachers by the year 2010, and 27,000 teachers by the year 2020 will have died in Tanzania.[26] In Malawi, it is claimed that by 2009, 25% of nurses and other public health workers will die due largely to HIV-AIDS.[27]

Damage to the economy and polity is devastating. According to one report, HIV-AIDS has cut labour productivity in Africa by 50 percent. More than two out of three deaths among managers in Zambia have been due to AIDS, and an estimated 75% of deaths among the police force in Kenya are due to AIDS. A 1998 study notes that there was HIV rate of 50% in seven armies in central Africa.[28] Peter Piot, executive director of UNAIDS, was quoted as saying:

The devastating impact of HIV/AIDS is rolling back decades of development progress in Africa....Every element of African Society – from teachers to soldiers to farmers – is under attack by AIDS....[29]

There are now over 13 million orphans in Africa, primarily as a result of HIV-AIDS and 40% of all children eligible to attend elementary school are not enrolled because they are providing care for sick relatives. In 2002 more than one million children in Africa were reported to have lost their teachers to HIV-AIDS.[30]

South Africa and Botswana are two of Africa's most politically and economically stable countries. South Africa is losing citizens to HIV-AIDS, and this loss could directly or indirectly impact the entire continent. In 2001, an estimated 85.6% of South Africans aged 15 and above could read and write, 23.2 percentage points higher than the average for sub-Saharan Africa. The combined primary, secondary and tertiary gross enrolment ratio in 2000-2001 for South Africa was 78%, 34 percentage points higher than the sub-Saharan Africa average of 44 percent.[31] Of the 701,000 total deaths in South Africa in 2004, AIDS related deaths were 311,000 (44.4%). Of the total number of 1,126,000 orphans in 2004, 626,000 (56%) were AIDS orphans. More than 1.2 million people in South Africa have already died as a result of AIDS and just over five million are infected and 500,000 are sick with AIDS.[32]

As a result of the high rate of deaths of South Africans, predictions of increasing enrolments in secondary schools and colleges and universities have not happened. For example, there was a prediction that the number of secondary school graduates would increase from 89,000 in 1994 to 130,000 in 1998, but that prediction figure declined from 89,000 in 1994 to 69,000 in 1998. In higher education, in 1995, the total enrolment in universities and technikons was 569,000. By June 1999, it declined to 564,000.[33]

In terms of trade and economic development, South Africa (a nation of 45 million) today is a big investor in Africa. Since the mid-1990s, South Africa has become one of the largest investors in Africa.[34]

By the beginning of 2002, South African businesses were running Cameroon's railroad and were scheduled to run that of Madagascar. South African businesses were managing power plants in Mali and Zambia, and brewing local beers in Mozambique and Ghana. South African businesses were also the leading providers of cell phone service in Nigeria, Uganda and Cameroon. They also operate banks and supermarkets in Tanzania, Mozambique and Kenya.[35] South Africa has contributed substantially to the gradual peace and stability on the continent.[36]

Nigeria, Africa's most populous nation (137 million as of July 2004), has produced a substantial number of educated people scattered all across the world. Nigeria is one of the countries in Africa that has produced many talented individuals. That is due largely to its size. Karen MacGregor reported on college enrolments in Nigeria in *The Guardian* (U.K.) on July 12, 1993:

During civilian governments, universities had generally flourished: student numbers increased from 1,256 in 1960-61 to 60,000 in 1980 and a projected 200,000 during the early 1990s....the number of universities rose from one at independence in 1960 to 22; publishing outlets flowered, and Nigeria became one of the intellectual powerhouses in Africa.[37]

In 2001, an estimated 65.4% of Nigerians aged 15 and above could read and write. That is a high proportion because of Nigeria's large population, and higher than the 62.4% average for sub-Saharan Africa. The combined primary, secondary and tertiary gross enrolment ratio in 2000-2001 for Nigeria was 45%, one percentage point higher than the sub-Saharan Africa average of 44 percent. [38] That figure is very significant because of Nigeria's large population.

Although the HIV-AIDS prevalence rate (5.4% in 2003) in Nigeria is significantly lower than the average for Africa (7.6%), [39] the large population of the country makes it very important that the spread of the disease is reduced. As of 2001, the estimated number of people living with HIV-AIDS in Nigeria was 3.5 million.[40] That is a significant figure. Unlike South Africa and Botswana, the Nigerian government does not have sufficient resources to fight HIV-AIDS. For example, the estimated government revenues in Nigeria in 2000 were only $3.4 billion, and the government's expenditures for that year were only $3.6 billion, extremely low for a country with such a large population.[41] For comparative purposes, the city government of Washington, D.C., the

United States' capital, with 572,059 people had a budget of $4.686 billion in fiscal year 2000, $1.086 billion more than Nigeria's total expenditures in 2000.[42]

As the examples above have shown, Africa is experiencing a dual brain drain in the beginning of the 21st century. One could at least argue that the migration brain drain might be temporary, and examples show that those abroad tend to send remittances home to their families and friends. The terminal brain drain, on the other hand, takes the lives of Africans forever, after so much scarce resources have been spent to educate them only to lose them to HIV-AIDS and other diseases. As a result, this dual brain drain is sapping away most of the development gains in the continent in the past four decades.

Conclusion

There is a school of ethics in Western thought which is predicated on the pursuit of happiness and the avoidance of pain. The English Utilitarians – like John Stuart Mill and Jeremy Bentham – based their moral code on the vigilant pursuit of the greatest happiness of the greatest number. Actions were either right or wrong in proportion to whether they contributed to maximizing a pleasant life or minimizing a painful condition.

Africa's two versions of the Brain Drain are caught up in this Utilitarian contradiction. The migrant Brain Drain is usually motivated by the pursuit of greater happiness. The terminal Brain Drain is triggered by HIV-AIDS and is a relentless quest to minimize pain. Migrant Brain Drain is a sentence of personal relocation. Terminal Brain Drain is a sentence of death.

For our case studies in this essay we have chosen South Africa and Nigeria, the two most influential African countries between the River Niger and the Cape of Good Hope. On the more obvious side, we have noted that both South Africa and Nigeria have experienced considerable loss of human power because of the skill exodus (migrant Brain Drain) and HIV-AIDS (the terminal Brain Drain).

Less anticipated is the revelation that Nigeria has suffered more migrant drain and less terminal drain than South Africa. During the apartheid era, South Africa enjoyed higher levels of physical health and medical services than any other country south of the Sahara. But in that period South Africa suffered such exceptional <u>moral</u> pathologies as elaborate racial segregation and brutal authoritarianism. The health services were significantly advanced, but the body politic was both sick and sickening.

The post-apartheid era, on the other hand, has healed the body politic and race relations faster than almost anybody expected. But South Africa's physical health has been devastated by HIV-AIDS.

Nigeria's medical facilities have left much to be desired, both before and after independence. But the moral health of the body politic has worsened since independence – as ethnic and sectarian tensions have escalated, north-south relations deteriorated, law and order broken down, and petroleum has fuelled both corruption and instability.

These negative forces have precipitated the migrant Brain Drain from Nigeria on an exceptional scale. In the years ahead South Africa may continue to lose more of its citizens through HIV-AIDS than because of outward migration. With Nigeria the balance may be in reverse – hopefully more outward migrants than AIDS fatalities.

> *To everything there is a season,*
> *And a time to every purpose under the heaven.*
> *A time to be born, and a time to die...*
> *A time to weep, and a time to laugh;*
> *A time to mourn –*
> *A time to dance.*[43]

NOTES

[1] An earlier version of this paper, entitled "The Dual Brain Drain In Nigeria and South Africa: HIV-AIDS and the Skill Exodus," was presented at the annual meeting of the African Studies Association of the United States, held in Washington, D.C., November 17-20, 2005.

[2] One estimate puts the number of people infection worldwide at about 40 million – but Africa, with only 10 percent of the world's population, "suffers over half of its HIV infections." Nafi Diouf, "Nations Promote Awareness on AIDS Day," *The Washington Post* (December 2, 2005).

[3] But Nigeria cannot afford to be complacent about the HIV-AIDS threat. After South Africa and India, it has the largest number of people living with HIV. See Diouf, "Nations Promote Awareness on AIDS Day," *The Washington Post* (December 2, 2005), and for statistics, see <http://www.unaids.org/>.

[4] This figure is drawn from the United States Census Bureau, "American Community Survey Profile 2002," September 2, 2003, <http://www.census.gov/acs/www/products/Profiles/Single/2002/ACS/Tabular/010/01000U>, April 21, 2004. This chapter has greatly benefited from Amadu Jacky Kaba, "Africa's Migration and Terminal Brain Drain," *African Renaissance*, (London), (July-August 2005), Vol. 2, No. 4, pp. 112-118.

[5] United States Census Bureau. 2000. Census 2000 Summary File 3, Matrix PCT19. Washington, D.C.: Government Printing Office.

[6] United States Census Bureau, "Profile of the Foreign-Born Population in the United States: 2000," (December 2001), pp. 23-206. Washington, D.C.: Government Printing Office. This chapter is especially indebted to Amadu Jacky Kaba's statistical research on migration patterns.

[7] John R. Logan and Glenn Deane., February 17, 2003. "Black Diversity in Metropolitan America," Lewis Mumford Center for Comparative Urban and Regional Research, University at Albany. <http://mumford1.dyndns.org/cen2000/BlackWhite/BlackDiversity/Report/black-diversity01.htm>. April 12, 2004.

[8] U.S. Census Bureau, "Educational Attainment for Selected Ancestry Group, 1990," February 18, 1998. <http://www.census.gov/population/socdemo/ancestry/table_01.txt>, April 13, 2004.

[9] Richard H. Adams, Jr., June 2003. "International Migration, Remittances and the Brain Drain: A Study of 24 Labour-Exporting Countries," *World Bank Policy Research Working Paper 3069*. Washington, D.C: World Bank.

[10] Lindsay B. Lowell, "Some Developmental Effects of the International Migration of Highly Skilled Persons," *International Migration Papers # 46.* (Geneva, Switzerland: International Migration Branch, International Labour Office, 2001. A 2005 World Bank study pointed out that a quarter to almost half of the college educated citizens of African countries like Ghana, Mozambique, Kenya, Uganda lived abroad in an O.E.C.D. country; for a report, see Celia W. Dugger, "Developing Lands Hit Hardest by 'Brain Drain'," *The New York Times* (October 25, 2005).

[11] Jonathan Crush, "The Global Raiders: Nationalism, Globalisation and the South African Brain Drain," *Journal of International Affairs* (2002) Vol. 56, No. 1, p. 147.

[12] Colin Leslie, "Is it wrong to recruit MDs from poor nations?" *Medical Post* (March 18, 2003) Canada Vol. 39, Issue 11, p. 12.

[13] Konia T. Kollehlon and Edward E. Eule, "The Socioeconomic Attainment Patterns of African in the United States," *The International Migration Review* (2003), Vol. 37, No. 4, p. 1165.

[14] The World Markets Research Centre. "The Brain Drain — Africa's Achilles Heel," in "Africa In Focus 2002," <http://www.worldmarketsanalysis.com/InFocus2002/articles/africa_braindrain.html>, April 22, 2004

[15] Philip Emeagwali,. "Why Nigerians are not Returning Home,"*The News* (Lagos, Nigeria) 2000.

[16] National Science Foundation, "International Mobility of Scientists and Engineers to the United States - Brain Drain or Brain Circulation?" (November 10, 1998) <http://www.nsf.gov/statistics/issuebrf/sib98316.htm>. December 19, 2005.

[17] For accounts of Dr. Barnard's operations, see Marais Malan, Heart Transplant; The Story Of Barnard and the "Ultimate in Cardiac Surgery" (Johannesburg: Voortrekkerpers, 1968) and Peter Hawthorne, The Transplanted Heart; The Incredible Story of the Epic Heart Transplant Operations by Professor Christiaan Barnard and his Team (Chicago: Rand McNally, 1968).

[18] For historical accounts of South Africa, consult, for instance, Robert C. Cottrell, *South Africa: A State of Apartheid* (Philadephia, PA: Chelsea House, 2005); Nancy L. Clark and William H. Worger, *South Africa: The Rise and Fall of Apartheid* (Harlow, England and New York: Longman, 2004); and James Barber, *South Africa in the Twentieth Century : A Political History--In Search of a Nation State* (Oxford, UK and Malden, MA: Blackwell Publishers, 1999).

[19] Ole J. Benedictow, "The Black Death: The Greatest Catastrophe Ever," *History Today*, Volume 55, No. 3 (2005), p. 42.

[20] Roberts Leslie, "Disease and Death in the New World," *Science* (1989), Vol. 246, Issue 4935, p. 1245.

[21] Robert G. Webster, "A Molecular Whodunit," *Science* (2001), Vol. 293, p. 1773.

[22] BBC, "Mandela's Eldest Son Dies of AIDS," <http://news.bbc.co.uk/2/hi/africa/4151159.stm>. December 19, 2005.

[23] See UNAIDS, *AIDS Epidemic Update, December 2002* (Geneva, Switzerland: UNAIDS and WHO, 2002), pp. 3, 6.

[24] These figures were calculated by Dr. Kaba based on data in the 2001 CIA World Factbook. Can be accessed online at <http://www.cia.gov/cia/down load.html>.

[25] Updated statistics on the numbers and percentages of people with HIV-AIDS in Africa may be found at <http://www.unaids.org/EN/Geographical +Area/By+Region/sub-saharan+africa.asp>. December 20, 2005.

[26] K.Y Amoako,. "Economic Development and Reform Issues in Africa: Lessons for Ghana," September 21, 2000. Lecture Delivered at University of Ghana, Legon. <http://www.africaaction.org/docs00/eca0010a.htm>. April 23, 2004

[27] Celia W. Dugger,. "An Exodus of African Nurses Puts Infants and the Ill in Peril," *New York Times*, July 12 (2004), p.A-1.

[28] Richard A. Fredland "AIDS and Development: An Inverse Correlation?" *The Journal of Modern African Studies* (1998), Vol. 36, No. 4, 547-568.

[29] "HIV Horror: 28 Million Africans Infected," *Mail & Guardian*, South Africa (June 25, 2002). <http://www.mg.co.za/Content/13.jsp?0-5226>. June 25, 2002.

[30] Miriam R. Grant and Andrew D. Palmiere, "When Tea is a Luxury: The Economic Impact of HIV/AIDS in Bulawayo, Zimbabwe" *African Studies* (2003), Vol. 62, No. 2, p. 213

[31] United Nations Development Program. *Human Development Report.* (New York:Oxford University Press, 2003), pp. 239-240.

[32] Rob Dorrington, Debbie Bradshaw, Leigh Johnson, and Debbie Budlender, Debbie. "The Demographic Impact of HIV/AIDS in Africa," *National Indicators for 2004*. (Cape Town: Center for Actuarial Research, South African Medical Research Council and Actuarial Society of South Africa, 2004), pp. 10 and 17.

[33] D.S. Gilleland and J. P. Merisotis, "Funding South African higher education: Steering mechanisms to meet national goals," (Washington, D.C.: Institute for Higher Education Policy. 2000), p. 36.

[34] Jerome A. Singh, "Why AIDS in South Africa Threatens Stability and Economic Growth in Other Parts of Africa," *The Lancet* (2004) Vol. 364, No. 9449, p. 1920

[35] See Rachel L. Swarns, "Awe and Unease as South Africa Stretches Out," *New York Times* (February 17, 2002).

[36] Singh, "Why AIDS in South Africa Threatens Stability and Economic Growth in Other Parts of Africa," *The Lancet* (2004), p. 1920.

[37] Karen MacGregor, "Academic Repression: The Nigerian Brain Drain." *The Guardian* (U.K.) (July 12, 1993).

[38] United Nations Development Program. *Human Development Report.* p. 240.

[39] "HIV prevalence (% ages 15-49)" Table 8. Leading global health crisis and risks. UNDP World Human Development Report, 2004. <http://hdr.undp.org/statistics/data/indic/indic_69_1_1.html>. July 30, 2004.

[40] John W. Wright, Ed., *The New York Times Almanac.* (New York: Penguin Group, 2004), p.485.

[41] Wright, Ed., *The New York Times Almanac,* p. 633

[42] "FY 2001 Proposed Operating Budget: Overview" p.8. Government of the city of Washington, District of Columbia. <http://www..dc.gov./mayor/budget_2001/index.shtm>.

[43] These lines are based on *The Holy Bible: King James Version,* from The Book of Ecclesiastes, Chapter 3, Verses 1, 2, and 4.

CONCLUSION

FROM MURTALA MUHAMMED TO THABO MBEKI[1]

L et us explore the history of <u>political</u> leadership in Africa. Are there lessons to be drawn for <u>economic</u> leadership?

A Typology of Leadership

The history of political leadership in Africa has stood on eight pillars.[2] Were they eight styles of command or eight categories of commanders? At the time of independence there was a lot of discussion about <u>charismatic</u> leadership. This discourse was greatly influenced by the man who led the first Black African country to independence - Kwame Nkrumah of Ghana. He himself was a charismatic leader with considerable personal magnetism.[3] I first met him in New York in 1960 and fell under his spell. Nnamdi Azikiwe was also a charismatic personality, but his magnetism waned after the civil war in Nigeria (just as Winston Churchill's charisma waned after World War II for different reasons).[4] On the other hand, Nelson Mandela's charisma rose with the mystique of martyrdom across decades.[5]

I also happen to think that Idi Amin Dada of Uganda had a lot of charisma, which enabled him to survive in power for eight years until a foreign army (Tanzanian) forced him out.[6] Idi Amin (whom I knew well) was a brutal ruler who nevertheless captivated a substantial following, both at home and abroad. A more positive charismatic figure was Malcolm X (Malik El-Shabazz) of the African Diaspora. I met him in New York in 1961.

A <u>mobilisation</u> leader is another category. Nkrumah tried to use his charisma for mobilisation, but in reality Nkrumah was not a particularly successful mobilisation leader in Ghana after independence. On the other hand, Julius K. Nyerere in Tanzania was both charismatic and mobilisational. He succeeded in arousing the masses to many of his causes. Gamal Abdel Nasser in Egypt was also both charismatic and mobilisational from the Suez crisis in 1956 until his death in 1970. The

301

most impressive mobilisation leader in the history of Black America was first Marcus Garvey and secondly Martin Luther King Jr. Louis Farrakhan astonished the world by mobilizing the Million-Man march.[7] There is reason to believe that Steve Biko would have become a striking mobilisation leader. Nelson Mandela the <u>prisoner</u> was a greater mobiliser than Mandela the <u>President</u>.[8]

A <u>reconciliation</u> leader seeks areas of compromise and consensus from among disparate points of views. South Africa's Truth and Reconciliation strategy found a worthy leader in Bishop Tutu. Nigeria is a difficult country to govern. So far mobilisation has not worked for long. <u>Reconciliation</u> as a style of leadership is often essential. Both General Yakubu Gowon (who led the Federal side during the civil war) and General Abdulsalami Abubakar (who provided a transition between tyranny and redemocratisation) were reconciliation leaders. They attempted to find areas of compromise in widely divergent Nigerian points of view. Both Jesse Jackson and Jimmy Carter are reconciliation leaders in <u>world affairs</u>. Domestically Jesse Jackson has tried to be mobilisational but he promoted a rainbow coalition less spectacularly.[9]

A <u>housekeeping</u> style of political power is minimalist in sense of purpose. There is more governance and less genuine leadership, more verbosity and less vision. The Kenyan political elite since the late 1980s to 2002 has been at best a housekeeping elite – governing without leading, maintenance without movement.

As an African military head of state, Murtala Muhammed, was the best approximation to a <u>disciplinarian</u> leader that Nigeria has had. He initiated a campaign against corruption. He was assassinated within months of capturing power from Gowon. Muhammed Buhari was also a disciplinarian Nigerian head of state. But it is not certain that a disciplinarian style is what Nigeria's ethnic and sectarian realities can really sustain for very long.[10] But this option should at least be carefully considered. Was W.E.B. DuBois a disciplinarian leader - an austere "no-nonsense" figure?

A <u>patriarchal</u> system is one in which a father figure emerges, using the symbolism of the elder and the patriarch. Jomo Kenyatta was already about sixty years old when he emerged from a colonial prison in Kenya to assume the reins of power. He carried the title of <u>Mzee</u>, meaning both "the Elder" and "the Old Man". He ruled Kenya from 1963 until he died in 1978.[11] Félix Houphouët-Boigny of the Côte d'Ivoire was also a patriarchal leader who presided over the destiny of independent Côte d'Ivoire from

1960 until his death in 1993. Among 20th century American presidents Dwight Eisenhower was a patriarchal figure in this sense of "father-figure".

Nelson Mandela was both a reconciliation leader and a patriarchal figure. His long martyrdom in prison (1964-1990) and his advancing years gave him the credentials of the patriarch. His moral style in his old age was a search for legitimate compromises. The latter was a style of reconciliation. Was Nelson Mandela also a charismatic figure? Or, was he only a hero in history? That is a more open question.

Ibrahim Babangida played a patriarchal role in his transition program, but he was too young for such a role. Babangida's constitutional transition could have made him Nigeria's Charles de Gaulle, but the experiment collapsed when Moshood Abiola's election as president was not acknowledged by the military.

Has Africa really produced technocratic political leadership? The answer is yes - but rarely at the level of the presidency. Some vice-presidents have been technocrats or potential technocrats. Kenya has had a series of quasi-technocratic vice-presidents, some of whom got "debased" in office. They include Vice-Presidents Mwai Kibaki (distinguished economist), Josephat Karanja (former University Vice-Chancellor) and George Saitoti (former professor). Are Thabo Mbeki and Yoweri Museveni essentially technocratic leaders? Ghana's Jerry Rawlings was part disciplinarian and part technocratic. Ellen Johnson-Sirleaf in Liberia, the first woman president in Africa, is also a former World Bank economist.[12]

Personalistic political style in Africa is sometimes indistinguishable from monarchical political style in our sense. Both entail the personification of power. But the monarchical tendency goes further and sacralises authority while simultaneously seeking to create an aristocratic impact. Hastings Kamuzu Banda of Malawi was definitely a personalistic political leader, demanding unquestioning political allegiance. But was he also a pseudo-monarch, seeking to give his authority a semblance of sacredness? [13] Marcus Garvey in U.S. history combined mobilisation effectiveness with monarchical tendencies. Richard Nixon was an imperial president of the United States while he lasted. Robert Mugabe was a cross between mobilisation and reconciliation. He has increasingly become a personalistic leader. He once believed in changing people through persuasion and good example before using force. Has he now changed?[14]

More literally Jean-Bedel Bokassa of the Central African Republic tried to create a new monarchical and imperial dynasty, with himself as the first Emperor. He even renamed his country "the Central African Empire". He held an astonishingly lavish coronation that was supposed to be paradoxically Napoleonic.[15]

A new aspect of the monarchical tendency which is emerging is the dynastic trend in succession. Laurent Kabila in the Democratic Republic of the Congo has been succeeded by his son Josef Kabila. In Zanzibar Abeid Karume has produced a successor in his son. In Egypt Hosni Mubarak may be grooming his son to succeed him. In Kenya Raila Odinga is trying to follow the nyayo (footprints) of his famous father, Oginga Odinga. And in the United States, George W. Bush as President has succeeded George Herbert Walker Bush.

In addition to these nine types and styles of leadership there have been a number of pre-colonial cultural traditions which affected those types and styles. The most obvious was the elder tradition in pre-colonial African culture, which has probably conditioned the patriarchal style after independence. The reverence of Jomo Kenyatta as Mzee (the Elder) in Kenya was substantially the outcome of the precolonial elder tradition still alive and well. Nelson Mandela by the time of his release was also a heroic Mzee. Was Ronald Reagan held in affection by the American people partly because he was perceived as an elder?[16]

Also obvious as a continuing tradition from precolonial times was an older version of the monarchical tendency. Even African societies which were not themselves monarchical were influenced by the royal paradigm. Kwame Nkrumah attempted to create a monarchical tradition in independent Ghana by declaring himself life-president, by sacralising his authority with the title of Osagyefo (Redeemer), by surrounding himself with a class of ostentatious consumers passing themselves off as Ghana's new political aristocracy, and by increasingly regarding political opposition to the president as the equivalent of treason (a monarchical version of intolerance).[17]

Less obvious as a precolonial conditional factor was the sage tradition. This involved respect for wisdom and expertise. In the modern period the sage tradition was rapidly modernized to include the new products of western-style high schools, and later western-style colleges and universities. In Black America history W.E.B. Dubois was the supreme sage of the twentieth century.[18]

The sage tradition from the post-colonial period has sometimes resulted in promoting among Africans ostentatious display of Western learning.

Tapping on modernized versions of the sage tradition a number of founding fathers of independent Africa tried to become philosopher-kings. They attempted to philosophise about man and society and about Africa's place in the global scheme of things. Kwame Nkrumah wrote books and became the most prolific head of state anywhere in the world. Léopold Sédar Senghor of Senegal was a more original political philosopher and poet.[19]

Some leaders attempted to establish whole new ideologies. Julius K. Nyerere of Tanzania inaugurated ujamaa, intended to be indigenously authentic African socialism. Kenneth D. Kaunda of Zambia initiated what was called "humanism". Gamal Abdel Nasser of Egypt had previously written The Philosophy of the Revolution and subsequently attempted the implementation of "Arab socialism". Muammar Qaddafy of Libya has the Green Book championing the third way. Thabo Mkbeki is also in the sage tradition with the African Renaissance. He intellectually even challenged received wisdom on HIV/AIDS.

The modernized version of the Western tradition also popularised the use of honorary doctorates as regular titles of Heads of State. Thus the president of Uganda became "Dr. Milton Obote", the president of Zambia became "Dr. Kenneth Kaunda" - just as the president of Ghana before them had become "Dr. Kwame Nkrumah". These had been conferred as honorary doctorates, but they became regular titles used in referring to these heads of state. The sage tradition was attempting to realize itself in a modern veneer. African presidents were trying to become philosopher-kings. After his presidency, Yakubu Gowon of Nigeria took the more difficult route and studied for his PhD at Warwick University, England.

Finally, there was the precolonial warrior tradition, emphasizing skills of combat, self-defence and manhood.[20] Did this survive into the colonial period and onwards into independence? The Mau Mau fighters in colonial Kenya in the 1950s were greatly influenced by traditional warrior virtues, especially those of he Kikuyu. Even liberation fighters in Rhodesia/Zimbabwe two decades later, who were using much more modern weapons, were mainly recruited from the countryside and were deeply influenced by traditional concepts of the warrior.

But were African soldiers in regular African state armies part of the continuities of the warrior tradition? Were the Abdulsalami Abubakars fundamentally still old warriors? It largely depends upon how much of the old African cultural values are still part of their attitudes to combat, self-defence and manhood. The Warrior tradition is sometimes the <u>Shaka</u> syndrome – militarised political leadership, often intimidatory. The warrior tradition went wrong when personified in Idi Amin Dada of Uganda. Idi Amin was a warrior-soldier who was mis-cast as head of state in the modern world. He fluctuated between brute, buffoon and genuinely heroic figure. He courageously took on some of the most powerful forces in the world - and yet pitilessly victimized some of the most powerless individuals in his own country from 1971 to 1979.[21] In Idi Amin the warrior tradition had gone temporarily mad.

Nine types of political leadership and four precolonial traditions of political culture have helped to shape post-colonial Africa in the twentieth century. The question which now arises is whether the 21st century will either reveal totally new styles of leadership or create new combinations of the old styles and traditions and produce better results than Africa and its Diaspora have accomplished so far.

Here we must turn from <u>styles</u> of leadership to <u>goals</u> of leadership. We know that the twentieth century produced very effective leaders of liberation. Nationalists like Robert Mugabe of Zimbabwe and Sekou Toure of Guinea fought against great odds to gain us independence. There were many other brilliant liberation fighters all over the continent who helped Africa end its colonial bondage. Both imprisoned Nelson Mandela and imprisoned Jomo Kenyatta inspired liberation by their enforced absence from the scene. Martyrdom behind bars can inspire freedom fighters.

But leaders of <u>liberation</u> were not necessarily leaders of <u>development</u>. One African leader after another let Africa down in the struggle to improve the material well-being of the African people. Only a few African leaders since independence have demonstrated skills of development on the ground. Considering what a terribly damaged country he had inherited, Yoweri Museveni deserves some credit for bringing up Uganda from the depths of despair to being one of the main regional actors in the Great Lakes region. [22] It is to be hoped that the coming African Renaissance will produce more and more leaders skilled in the arts of development. In Black America Louis Farrakhan has been a leader of development as well as liberation. His effort to combat drugs and crime and promote economic self-reliance are cases in point.

In addition to leaders of <u>liberation</u> (like Mugabe, Sekou Toure, Samora Machel, Zik and Nkrumah), and leaders of development (like Yoweri Museveni, Louis Farrakhan, and Habib Bourguiba), has global Africa produced leaders of <u>democracy</u>? This is a much tougher agenda. The Diaspora has produced civil rights leaders. South Africa has the most liberal constitution in the world, and has ended political apartheid. But the wealth of the society is still maldistributed along racial lines. The mines, the best jobs, the best businesses, are still disproportionately owned by non-Black people. Leaders like Nelson Mandela and Thabo Mbeki have presided over substantial political democratisation, but they have also had to tolerate substantial economic injustice.

In Nigeria Abdulsalami Abubakar provided a smooth transition from the tyranny of Sani Abacha to a Nigerian return to democracy and civilian rule. In that democratic return Olusegun Obasanjo was elected the first Nigerian president of the new millennium. It was a very promising choice. After all, in 1979 Olusegun Obasanjo became the first African military ruler to hand over power voluntarily to a freely elected government. In 1979 Obasanjo had also been the first Nigerian military ruler to let political power slip from his own ethnic group without attempting to subvert the process.

However, Olusegun Obasanjo in the new millennium is still being tested. He is confronted with Shariacracy in some Northern states, with Yoruba nationalism in some Western states, and with demands for confederation among some of the Ibgo nationalists. In <u>style</u> will Obasanjo emerge as a gifted <u>reconciliation</u> leader? In normative Africanity is he a <u>warrior</u> or a <u>sage</u>? And in ultimate goals for Nigeria, does Olusegun Obasanjo stand a chance of emerging as a successful leader of genuine <u>democratisation</u>? It is conceivable that Obasanjo was more of a democrat when he was a military ruler than he has become as a civilian ruler. Was his re-election rigged?

We know that Africa has been served well by <u>leaders of liberation</u>. We are concerned that we have not produced enough <u>leaders of development</u>. In Nigeria and elsewhere we are also looking for leaders of democracy.

What about leaders of <u>Pan-Africanism</u> and wider transnational solidarity? Clearly this is a fourth goal on top of liberation, development and democracy. In 1966, soon after Nkrumah was overthrown from power, I described him as " a great African but not a great Ghanaian".[23] He subordinated the interests of Ghana to the wider Pan African crusade.

In the past two years South Africans who knew my assessment of Nkrumah have asked me whether I detected the same contradiction in Thabo Mbeki. Is Mbeki "a great African but not a great South African"? Has he put Africa ahead of his country?

Is globalisation bringing Africans closer together or pulling them farther apart? Let us first define "globalisation" itself. Some analysts have seen it mainly through the expanding world markets and deepening interdependence within the world economy. Other analysts have seen "globalisation" through the information superhighway and the Internet revolution. But it is possible to take an even more comprehensive view of globalisation - regarding it as consisting of all the forces which are leading the world towards a global village. Globalisation is thus the villagisation of the world.[24]

But for people of African ancestry is there a globalisation within the globalisation? Is there a globalisation of the black race within the globalisation of the world? I first coined the term "Global Africa" for the final episode in my television series The Africans: A Triple Heritage (BBC/PBS, 1986).[25] By it I meant the experience of people of African descent worldwide. Until the middle of the twentieth century "Global Africa" meant the people of Africa itself combined with the African Diaspora in the Americas, the Caribbean, Europe, and the Middle East. What has been happening in the twentieth century is a more extensive globalisation of Africa – making the African presence penetrating beyond the African world.[26]

Dimensions of Globalisation

Three senses have been paramount in analysis: Economic, informational and comprehensive. Economic globalisation began with the circumnavigation of the Cape of Good Hope by Vasco da Gama towards the end of the fifteenth century. That circumnavigation opened the prospect of trade and economic relations among the three continents of the ancient world – Europe, Africa and Asia. Before long the Americas were added as sources of raw materials, precious metals, and subsequently cash crops.

Southern Africa became in time a magnet for demographic globalisation – people from other continents found their way to Africa either willingly or by force in search of new opportunities.

Economic globalisation was the emergence of a global network of interlocking factors of production, and the growth of economic interdependence across vast distances.

In addition to economic globalisation, there is <u>informational</u> globalisation. This began with the printing machine from the fourteenth century onwards, enhanced by the birth of the Penny Press and newspapers in the nineteenth century, followed by the radio and the electronic revolution of the twentieth century. The computer and the Internet have finally provided us with the so-called Information Superhighway.

The third sense of globalisation is <u>comprehensive</u>. It means all the forces throughout history which have been leading the world towards a <u>global village</u>. These forces include <u>religion</u>, especially the global expansion of Christianity and Islam; <u>economy</u> which has grown from international trade to a global economy; thirdly, <u>empire</u>, especially the expansion of Europe as a colonizing power and the rise of the United States as a unique style of empire; and the fourth force of globalisation is <u>technology</u>. The technology of <u>production</u> has enhanced productivity, distribution and exchange; the technology of <u>communication</u> has created global aviation and initiated interplanetary exploration and a landing on the moon; and the technology of destruction has globalised patterns of military conflict, including the two World Wars of the twentieth century, the global Cold War while it lasted, and the newly emerging war against terrorism and the militarised revolt of the underprivileged groups against Western global hegemony.

In relations between races world wide, globalisation has initiated a process of convergence. Paradoxically, in relations between cultures and religions so far, globalisation is a force for divergence.

Racism has declined but far from ended in South Africa. What was inconceivable in the 1970s has now come to pass. Political apartheid has been dismantled, though economic apartheid is still alive and well. Progress has been made in racial convergence, but there is a lot more yet to be done. White leadership had said to the emerging Black leadership: "You take the political crown; we will keep the economic jewels."[27] That was the Faustian bargain at the beginning of the 1990s. South Africa's future is brighter than it looked in the 1980s, but there is no room for complacency.

In much of the rest of Africa globalisation is triggering off ethno-cultural and religious divergence rather than racial convergence. In the

Democratic Republic of Congo globalisation has unleashed an international scramble for the Congo's resources and the accompanying ethnic fragmentation and conflict. [28] The Congolese leadership is torn between ethnic ties and mineral temptations. Globalisation triggered the greed; and the greed triggered off ethnic rivalry.

Then there is the special case of Nigeria as an example of religious divergence. While South Africans are picking up the pieces to help reconcile their <u>racial</u> differences, Nigerians are fragmenting into new <u>religious</u> rivalries and <u>ethno-cultural </u>divergence.[29] South Africans are struggling towards mutual acceptance; Nigerians are retreating into mutual distancing.

The Sharia under this paradigm becomes a form of Northern resistance—not to Southern Nigeria, but to the forces of globalisation and to their Westernising consequences. [30] Even the policy of <u>privatisation</u> of public enterprises is probably an aspect of the new globalizing ideology. Privatisation in Nigeria may either lead to new transnational corporations establishing their roots or to private Southern entrepreneurs outsmarting Northerners and deepening the economic divide between North and South. Again the Sharia may be a Northern gut response to these looming clouds of globalisation.

In Nigeria the Sharia is caught between the forces of domestic democratisation and the forces of wider globalisation. On the one hand, Lord Lugard as a British Governor had helped to protect Islam in Northern Nigeria—and Islam had been an earlier form of cultural globalisation within a worldwide community of believers. On the other hand, the legacy of Lord Lugard had helped to heighten Hausa-Fulani identity, and was therefore a particularizing force. Both globalisation and Lugardisation in Northern Nigeria had therefore contributed to the rise of Shariacracy.[31]

Averting Marginalisation: Micro-Crusade

Both economic and informational globalisation have been marginalizing Africa so far. On the computer revolution, an African country of twenty million people may have fewer computers than a major U.S. university.[32] We may need to take a closer look at what Africa needs to do.

In terms of productivity what Africa needs in the short term are not Nobel Prize winners in micro-economics, but competent and responsible managers of both people and resources. The management of people requires the following skills:

- Capacity to <u>motivate</u> subordinates in the direction of optimum performance
- Capacity to define a realistic and productive <u>work-ethic</u> – which combines the dignity of labour with mental commitment.
- Capacity to inspire <u>pride</u> in the company or institution for which one is working,
- Capacity to inspire <u>faith and loyalty</u> towards the <u>leadership</u> of the company and the <u>agreed goals</u> of the enterprise.
- Capacity to separate <u>legitimate ambition</u> from <u>illegitimate greed</u> at all levels of the enterprise
- Readiness to prevent too wide a gap between the income of the lowest employee and of the highest. Some have suggested that the income of the highest paid executive in the company should never be more than twenty times the lowest productive member of the enterprise.

In such a situation one may have to decide whether a cleaner is, or is not, part of the productive sector of the enterprise.

- Capacity to recognize a minimum of <u>social justice</u> in the company or institution for the employees and their families and to strive for greater than minimum justice for all.

- Readiness to encourage in-service electronic training and the revamping of skills.
- These eight principles of management of people can be summarized as follows:
- The Work Ethic
- The Motivation to abide by it
- Pride in the effort
- Loyalty to its goals and the leadership
- <u>Yes</u> to ambition, <u>No</u> to greed
- No to overpaid executives, No to underpaid subordinates
- In search of corporate social justice
- In search of renewal of skills

In addition there are also Seven Principles of Management of <u>Resources</u> (as distinct from management of people):

311

1. Making <u>means</u> compatible with the <u>ends</u> being pursued
2. Using <u>past</u> experience to plan <u>future</u> strategies
3. Distinguishing between <u>short</u> term and <u>long</u> term goals
4. Balancing <u>economic</u> goals with <u>social</u> responsibilities
5. <u>Optimizing</u> benefits and <u>minimizing</u> costs (<u>Not</u> maximizing benefits but <u>optimising</u> them)
6. Balancing <u>industrial</u> claims against <u>environmental</u> well being
7. Redefining <u>profit</u> to include <u>non-monetary</u> gains, such as progress in empowering women. This balances the rational with the ethical.

To summarize the principles of management over resources:

- The balance between means and ends
- The balance between past experience and future planning
- The balance between economic goals and social responsibilities
- The balance between costs and benefits
- The balance between production and environment
- The balance between the <u>rational</u> and <u>ethical,</u> including the pursuit of affirmative action in favour of women and disadvantaged groups

These principles of management are crucial if Africa is to transcend the marginalizing consequences of globalisation. Critical to inspiring these principles of management at the micro-economic level is the political leadership of pivotal countries like Nigeria and South Africa. Murtala Muhammed did not last very long as leader in Nigeria. Thabo Mbeki has served for a longer period but it may be too early to assess if his leadership style has affected future South African generations of economic leaders.

NOTES

[1]This essay is indebted to Mazrui's earlier work on Political Leadership in Africa.

[2]For one analysis of comparative African leadership, see A. B. Assensoh, *African Political Leadership: Jomo Kenyatta, Kwame Nkrumah and Julius K. Nyerere* (Malabar, FL: Krieger, 1998).

[3] A Weberian discussion of Nkrumah as a charismatic leader may be found in E. O. Addo, *Kwame Nkrumah: A Case Study of Religion and Politics in Ghana* (Lanham, MD: University Press of America, 1997), especially pp. 22-23 and pp. 99-122.

[4] An autobiography of Zik may be found in Nnamdi Azikiwe, *My Odyssey: An Autobiography* (New York: Praeger Publishers, 1970) and also consult Agbafor Igwe, *Zik: The Philosopher of Our Time* (Enugu, Nigeria: Fourth Dimension Pub. Co. Ltd., 1992).

[5] For a biography of this great leader, see Anthony Sampson, *Mandela : The Authorized Biography* (New York: Knopf, distributed by Random House, 1999).

[6] For one description of the Tanzanian intervention in Uganda leading to the expulsion of Idi Amin, see Tony Avirgan and Martha Honey, *War in Uganda: The Legacy of Idi Amin* (Westport, CT: L. Hill, 1982).

[7] For historical overviews of African American leadership, consult V. B. Thompson, *Africans of the Diaspora: The Evolution of African Consciousness and Leadership in the Americas from Slavery to the 1920s*, (Trenton, NJ and Asmara, Eritrea: Africa World Press, 2000) and John Hope Franklin and August Meier, Eds., *Black Leaders of the 20th Century* (Chicago and Urbana, IL: University of Illinois Press, 1982).

[8] Mandela himself has described his transition from prisoner to President in his *Long Walk to Freedom: The Autobiography of Nelson Mandela* (Boston: Back Bay Books, 1995).

[9] The emergence of the Rainbow Coalition is detailed in Paulette Pierce, "The Roots of the Rainbow Coalition," *Black Scholar* 19, 2 (1988), pp. 2-16.

[10] These divisions make Nigeria difficult to govern; see Simeon O. Ilesanmi, *Religious Pluralism and the Nigerian State* (Athens, OH: Ohio University Center for International Studies, 1997) and Joseph A. Umoren, *Democracy and Ethnic Diversity In Nigeria* (Lanham, MD: University Press of America, 1996).

[11] For a biography, consult Jeremy Murray-Brown, *Kenyatta* (New York: E. P. Dutton, 1973, 1972).

[12] Ms. Johnson-Sirleaf was in fact elected president, although not without some controversy; see Lane Hartill, "President in Waiting Stays Cool in Liberia: Johnson-Sirleaf Unruffled by Fraud Claims," *The Washington Post* (November 14, 2005).

[13] Consult John Lloyd Lwanda, *Malawi under Kamuzu Banda: A Study in Promise, Power, And Paralysis (Malawi under Dr. Banda) (1961 to 1993)*(Bothwell, Scotland, Great Britain: Dudu Nsomba Publications, 1993).

[14] Robert Mugabe has resisted many attempts to introduce political reform and has thus earned widespread condemnation; see, for instance, Craig Timberg, "Mugabe Gains Expanded Powers: Zimbabwe's Parliament Votes to Restrict Travel, Limit Appeals on Land Seizures," *The Washington Post* (August 31, 2005), and Vaclav Havel, "Strangling Democracy," *The New York Times* (June 24, 2004).

[15] A portrait of this leader may be found in Brian Titley, *Dark Age: The Political Odyssey Of Emperor Bokassa*, (Montreal ; Buffalo : McGill-Queen's University Press, 1997).

[16] Even many young Americans who disagreed with Reagan policies saw him as a slightly misguided "avuncular" figure.

[17] On Nkrumah's tendencies toward authoritarianism, see Ali A. Mazrui, "Kwame Nkrumah: The Leninist Czar," *Transition* (Kampala), Volume 6, Number 26 (1966), pp. 9-17 and T. Peter Omari, *Kwame Nkrumah: The Anatomy of an African Dictatorship* (New York: Africana Publishing Corp., 1970), especially pp. 50-78; and for a general overview of Nkrumah's rule over Ghana, also consult Geoffrey Bing, *Reap the Whirlwind: An Account of Kwame Nkrumah's Ghana from 1950 to 1966* (London: MacGibbon & Kee, 1968).

[18] A guide to this towering figure in African American emancipation and intellectual thought may be found in Gerald Horne and Mary Young, Eds., *W.E.B. Du Bois : An Encyclopedia* (Westport, CT: Greenwood Press, 2000).

[19] For a biography of Senghor, see Janet G. Vaillant, *Black, French and African: A Life of Léopold Sédar Senghor* (Cambridge, MA: Harvard University Press, 1990).

[20] See Ali A. Mazrui, *The Warrior Tradition in Modern Africa* (Leiden : Brill, 1977).

[21] For some examples, see David Martin, *General Amin* (London: Faber, 1974), pp. 210-213 and p. 215.

[22] Relatedly, see Ondoga ori Amaza, *Museveni's Long March From Guerrilla To Statesman* (Kampala, Uganda : Fountain Publishers, 1998); the editorial in the *Washington Post* "A Strongman's Test," (April 17, 2005) on Museveni's accomplishments and challenges, especially in the political arena; and for a

critical look at Museveni, see Anne Mugisha, "Museveni's Machinations," *Journal of Democracy* (April 2004), Vol. 15, Issue 2, pp. 140-144.

[23]Mazrui, "Kwame Nkrumah: The Leninist Czar," *Transition* (Kampala), Volume 6, Number 26 (1966), pp. 9-17.

[24] See Marshall McLuhan and Bruce R. Powers, *The Global Village: Transformations in World Life and Media in the 21st Century* (New York: Oxford University Press, 1989, as also Mohammed A. Bamyeh, *The Ends of Globalisation* (Minneapolis: University of Minnesota Press, 2000); Mark Rupert, *Ideologies of Globalisation: Contending Visions of a New World Order* (London and New York: Routledge, 2000) and Colin Hays and David Marsh, eds. *Demystifying Globalisation* (New York: St. Martin's Press in association with Polsis, University of Birmingham, 2000).

[25]The companion volume is Ali A. Mazrui, *The Africans: A Triple Heritage* (London: BBC Publications, 1986).

[26]Treatments of these diasporas may be found in, for example, in the following: Joseph E. Harris, Ed. *Global Dimensions of the African Diaspora* (Washington, DC: Howard University Press, 2003), 2nd ed.; Shihan de Silva Jayasuriya and Richard Pankhurst, Eds., *The African Diaspora in the Indian Ocean* (Trenton, NJ: Africa World Press, 2003); Erna Brodber, *The Continent of Black Consciousness : On the History of the African Diaspora From Slavery to the Present Day* (London : New Beacon Books, 2003); John Hunwick and Eve T. Powell, *The African Diaspora in the Mediterranean Lands of Islam* (Princeton, NJ : Markus Wiener Publishers, 2002); Darlene Clark Hine and Jacqueline McLeod., Eds., *Crossing Boundaries: Comparative History of Black People in Diaspora* (Bloomington, IN: Indiana University Press, 1999); E.L. Bute, *The Black Handbook: The People, History and Politics of Africa and the African Diaspora* (London and Washington: Cassell, 1997); Alusine Jalloh and Stephen E. Maizlish, Eds., *The African Diaspora* (College Station, TX: Texas A&M University Press, 1996); Michael L. Coniff, *Africans in the Americas: A History of the Black Diaspora* (New York: St. Martin's Press, 1994); and Edward Scobie, *Global African Presence*, (Brooklyn, NY: A & B Books, 1994).

[27]Between 1995 and 2000 in the post-apartheid South Africa, average income of black households fell by 19 percent while white household incomes rose by 15 percent, and despite aggressive affirmative action programs, whites still outnumber blacks among top managers by nearly 10 to 1, according to government employment statistics released in 2002. Even among middle managers, whites still outnumber blacks in a country where blacks make up 79 percent of the population, whites are 9.6 percent, mixed race are 8.9 percent

315

and Indian 2.5 percent. See Richard Morin, "Despite Deep Woes, Democracy Instills Hope," *Washington Post* (March 31, 2004).

[28]This ethnic fragmentation and conflict has been exacerbated by external actors; see, for a guide to the parties involved, and their rationales, in the early Congo fighting, Francois Misser, "Who Helped Kabila," *New African* 354 (July/August 1997), pp. 9-10.

[29]Overviews of the North-South and other cleavages bedeviling Nigeria may be found in *The Economist* (January 15, 2000), pp. 14-15; also see *The Economist* (July 8, 2000), p. 47. Relatedly, consult Martin Dent, "Nigeria: Federalism and Ethnic Rivalry," *Parliamentary Affairs* (January 2000), Vol. 53, No. 1, pp. 157-168.

[30]For longer analyses on earlier conflicts caused by the Sharia issue, see Toyin Falola, *Violence in Nigeria: The Crisis of Religious Politics and Secular Ideologies* (Rochester, NY: University of Rochester Press, 1998), especially pp. 77-113; Ilesanmi, *Religious Pluralism and the Nigerian State* (Athens, OH: Ohio University Center for International Studies, 1997), pp. 174-207; M. H. Kukah and Toyin Falola, *Religious Militancy and Self-Assertion: Islam and Politics in Nigeria* (Aldershot, UK, and Brookfield, VT: Avebury Press, 1996), pp. 117-139; and Pat A. T. Williams, "Religion, Violence, and Displacement in Nigeria," *Journal of Asian and African Studies*(June 1997) Volume 32, Nos. 1-2, pp. 33-49.

[31]See relatedly, Pat Williams and Toyin Falola, *Religious Impact on the Nation State: The Nigerian Predicament* (Aldershot, UK and Brookfield, VT: Avebury Press, 1995), pp. 16-17 and Michael Crowder, "Lugard and Colonial Nigeria: Towards an Identity," *History Today* (February 1986), Vol. 36, pp. 23-29.

[32]For instance, the Congo in 2003 had 15,000 computers, according to one source. Statistics on the number of computers by country are available at the web-site of the International Telecommunications Union at <http://www.itu.int/ITU-D/ict/statistics/at_glance/Internet03.pdf> November 15, 2004.

BIBLIOGRAPHY

MAJOR CITED WORKS

Abrahams, Peter. *Path of Thunder*. New York: Harper, 1948.

Adams, Jr., Richard H. *International Migration, Remittances and the Brain Drain: A Study of 24 Labour-Exporting Countries*. World Bank Policy Research Working Paper 3069. Washington, D.C.: World Bank, June 2003.

Addo, E. O. *Kwame Nkrumah*: A Case Study of Religion and Politics in Ghana. Lanham, MD: University Press of America, 1997.

Adebajo, Adekeye. *Building Peace in West Africa: Liberia, Sierra Leone, and Guinea-Bissau*. Boulder, CO: Lynne Rienner, 2002.

Adeleke, Ademola. "The Politics and Diplomacy of Peacekeeping in West Africa: The ECOWAS Operation in Liberia." *The Journal of Modern African Studies*, 33.4, Dec. 1995: 569-593.

Adelman, J. "Iago's Alter Ego: Race as Projection in 'Othello'." *Shakespeare Quarterly* 48.2 (Summer 1997): 125-144.

Afigbo, Adiele E. "The Amalgamation: Myths, Howlers and Heresies," *The Amalgamation and its Enemies. An Interpretive History of Modern Nigeria*. Ed. Richard A. Olaniyan. East Lansing, MI: Michigan State University Press, 2003. 45-57.

Afigbo, Adiele E. *The Warrant Chiefs: Indirect Rule in Southeastern Nigeria, 1891-1929*. New York: Humanities Press, 1972.

Agbaje, Adigun. "Freedom of the Press and Party Politics in Nigeria: Precepts, Retrospect, and Prospects." *African Affairs* 89 (April 1990): 205-226.

Ager, Dennis. *Identity, Insecurity and Image: France and Language*. London: Multilingual Matters, 1997.

Agyeman, Opoku. *Nkrumah's Ghana and East Africa : Pan-Africanism and African Interstate relations*. Rutherford, London and Cranbury, NJ:

Fairleigh Dickinson University Press and Associated University Press, 1992.

Akenson, Donald H. *God's People: Covenant and Land in South Africa, Israel, and Ulster.* Ithaca and London: Cornell University Press, 1992.

Akinnaso, F. Niyi. "The National Language Question and Minority Language Rights in Africa: A Nigerian Case Study." *Human Rights and Governance in Africa.* Eds. Ronald Cohen, Goran Hyden, and Winston P. Nagan. Gainesville, FL: University Press of Florida, 1993.191-214.

Akinyemi, A. Bolaji, S. B. Falegan, and I. A. Aluko. *Readings and Documents on ECOWAS: Selected Papers and Discussions from the 1976 Economic Community of West African States Conference.* Lagos and Ibadan: Nigerian Institute of International Affairs: Macmillan, 1984.

Alao, Abiodun. *Sierra Leone: Tracing the Genesis of a Controversy.* London: Royal Institute of International Affairs, 1998.

Alden, Chris and Jean-Pascal Daloz, Eds. *Paris, Pretoria, and the African Continent: The International Relations of States and Societies in Transition.* Houndmills, Basingstoke, Hampshire and New York, NY: Macmillan Press; St Martin's Press, 1996.

Alden, Chris. "From Policy Autonomy to Policy Integration: The Evolution of France's Role in Africa." Alden and Daloz 1996,11-25.

Ali, Shaheen Sardar. *Gender and Human Rights in Islam and International Law: Equal Before Allah, Unequal Before Man?* The Hague and Boston: Kluwer Law International, 2000.

Allyn, David. *Make Love, Not War: The Sexual Revolution, An Unfettered History.* Boston: Little, Brown, 2000.

Amaza, Ondoga ori. *Museveni's Long March From Guerrilla To Statesman.* Kampala, Uganda: Fountain Publishers, 1998.

Amoako, K. Y. "NEPAD: Making Individual Bests a Continental Norm." *UN Chronicle* 40.1 (Mar-May 2003): 25-27.

---. "Economic Development and Reform Issues in Africa: Lessons for

Ghana," September 21, 2000. Lecture Delivered at University of Ghana, Legon. <http://www.africaaction.org/docs00/eca0010a.htm>. April 23, 2004

Amoretti, Ugo M. and Nancy Bermeo. Eds. *Federalism and Territorial Cleavages*. Baltimore, MD: Johns Hopkins University Press, 2004.

Amoroso, Bruno. *On Globalisation: Capitalism in the 21st Century*. Houndmills, Basingstoke and New York: MacMillan and St Martin's Press, 1998.

Anderson, David. *Histories of the Hanged : The Dirty War in Kenya and the End of Empire*. New York: W. W. Norton, 2005.

Assensoh, A. B. *African Political Leadership: Jomo Kenyatta, Kwame Nkrumah and Julius K Nyerere*. Malabar, FL: Krieger, 1998.

Atanda, J.A. *The New Oyo Empire: Indirect Rule and Change in Western Nigeria, 1894-1934*. London: Longman, 1973.

Avirgan,Tony and Martha Honey. *War in Uganda: The Legacy of Idi Amin*. Westport, CT: L. Hill, 1982.

Awonusi, Victor O. "Regional Accents and Internal Variability in Nigerian English: A Historical Analysis", *English Studies* 67 (Dec 1986): 550-560.

Azikiwe, Nnamdi. *Liberia in World Politics*. Westport, CT: Negro Universities Press 1970. Reprint of 1934 Edition, published in London by A. H. Stockwell.

---*My Odyssey: An Autobiography*. New York: Praeger Publishers, 1970.

---*Respect for Human Dignity: Inaugural Address, November 16, 1960*. Onitsha Union.

---*Zik: Selected Speeches of Nnamdi Azikiwe*. Cambridge: The University Press, 1961.

Bamgbose, Ayo. "Post-Imperial English in Nigeria, 1940-1990". *Post-Imperial English: Status Change in Former British and American Colonies, 1940-1990*. Eds. Joshua A Fishman, Andrew Conrad and Alma Rubal-Lopez. Berlin and New York: Mouton, De Gruyter, 1996.357-372

---"Standard Nigerian English : Issues of Identification." *The Other Tongue: English Across Cultures*. Ed. Braj B. Kachry. Urbana, IL: University of Illinois Press, 1992.148-161.

Bamyeh, Mohammed A. *The Ends of Globalisation*. Minneapolis: University of Minnesota Press, 2000.

Bangura, Yusuf. "Strategic Policy Failure and State Fragmentation: Security, Peacekeeping, and Democratisation in Sierra Leone." *The Causes of War and the Consequences of Peacekeeping in Africa*. Ed. Ricardo René Laremont. Portsmouth, NH: Heinemann, 2002. 143-170

Banjo, Ayo. "The Sociolinguistics of English in Nigeria and the ICE Project." *Comparing English Worldwide: The International Corpus of English*. Ed. Sidney Greenbaum. Oxford and New York: Clarendon Press and Oxford UP, 1996. 239-248.

Banks, Arthur S. Ed. *Political Handbook of the World 1993*. Binghamton, NY: CSA Publications, 1994.

Banks, Arthur S and Thomas C Muller. Eds. *Political Handbook of the World 1999*. Binghamton, NY: CSA Publications, 1999.

Barber, Benjamin. *Jihad Vs.McWorld: How Globalism and Tribalism are Reshaping the World*. New York: Times Books, 1995.

Barber, James. *Mandela's World : The International Dimension Of South Africa's Political Revolution 1990-99*. Oxford; Cape Town; Athens, OH: James Currey; David Philip; and Ohio University Press, 2004.

---. *South Africa in the Twentieth Century: A Political History--In Search of a Nation State*. Oxford, UK and Malden, MA: Blackwell Publishers, 1999.

Baregu, Mwesiga. "Economic and Military Security," in *From Cape to Congo : Southern Africa's Evolving Security Challenges*. Eds. Mwesiga Baregu and Christopher Landsberg. Boulder, CO: Lynne Rienner Publishers, 2003. 19-30

Barnes, Ruth and Joanne B. Eicher, Eds. *Dress and Gender: Making and Meaning in Cultural Contexts*. New York: Berg and St. Martin's Press, 1992.

Barrett, Leonard E., Sr., *The Rastafarians* Boston: Beacon Press, 1997.

Barretto, Amilcar A. *Language, Elites, and the State: Nationalism in Puerto Rico and Quebec*. Westport, CT: Praeger, 1998.

Bassiri, Kambiz Ghanea. *Competing Visions of Islam in the United States: A Study of Los Angeles*. Westport, CT: Greenwood Press, 1997.

Battle, Michael. *Reconciliation: The Ubuntu Ttheology of Desmond Tutu*. Cleveland, OH: Pilgrim Press, 1997.

Bayart, Jean-Francois. "End-Game South of the Sahara? France's Africa Policy." Alden and Daloz 1996, 26-41.

Beinart, William and Saul DuBow, Eds. *Segregation And Apartheid In Twentieth-Century South Africa*. London and New York: Routledge, 1995.

Bell, Derrick. *Silent Covenants: Brown v. Board of Education and the Unfulfilled Hopes for Racial Reform*. Oxford and New York: Oxford University Press, 2004.

Bemath, Abdul S. *The Mazruiana Collection*. New Delhi and Johannesburg: Sterling Publishers and Foundation for Global Dialogue, 1998.

Benedek, Wolfgang, et al. Eds. *The Human Rights of Women: International Instruments and African Experiences*. London and New York: Zed Books in association with World University Service and Palgrave, 2002.

Benedictow, Ole J. "The Black Death: The Greatest Catastrophe Ever." *History Today,*

55.3 (2005): 42-47.

Bennett, A LeRoy. *International Organizations: Principles and Issues*. Englewood Cliffs, NJ: Prentice Hall, 1991.

Benvenisti, Meron. *Sacred Landscape : The Buried History of the Holy Land Since 1948*. Berkeley, CA: University of California Press, 2000

Beshir, M. O. *The Southern Sudan: Background to Conflict*. New York and London: C Hurst and Company, 1968.

Bible, The Holy : King James Version. New York: Viking Studios, 1999.

Bing, Geoffrey. Reap the Whirlwind: An Account of Kwame Nkrumah's Ghana from 1950 to 1966. London: MacGibbon & Kee, 1968.

Birmingham, David. *Portugal and Africa.* Houndmills, Basingstoke, Hampshire : Macmillan, 1999.

Bloom, Mia. *Dying to Kill: The Allure of Suicide Terror.* New York: Columbia University Press, 2005.

Bond, Patrick (with cartoons by Zapiro). *Talk Left, Walk Right : South Africa's Frustrated Global Reforms.* Scottsville, South Africa : University of KwaZulu-Natal Press, 2004.

Bonner, Philip, et al, Eds. *Apartheid's Genesis, 1935-1962.* Braamfontein and Johannesburg, South Africa: Ravan Press and Wits University Press, 1993.

Bonner, Raymond. *At the Hand of Man: Peril and Hope for Africa's Wildlife.* New York: Knopf, 1993.

Boutros-Ghali, Boutros. "The OAU and Afro-Arab Relations." *The Organization of African Unity After Thirty Years.* Ed. Yassin El-Ayouty. Westport, CT: Praeger, 1994. 147-168.

Bovill, Edward William. *The Golden Trade of the Moors: West African kingdoms in the Fourteenth Century.* Princeton, NJ: M. Weiner Publishers, 1995

Boyle, Elizabeth Heger. *Female Genital Cutting : Cultural Conflict In The Global Community.* Baltimore, Md. : Johns Hopkins University Press, 2002.

Bradbury, Jonathan and James Mitchell. "Devolution: New Politics for Old?" *Parliamentary Affairs* (Apr. 2001): 257-275.

Brzezinski, Zbigniew. "A Plan for Europe." *Foreign Affairs* 74.1 (Jan/Feb 1995): 26-42.

Brodber, Erna. *The Continent of Black Consciousness: On the History of the African Diaspora From Slavery to the Present Day.* London: New Beacon Books, 2003.

Brouwer, Steve et al. *Exporting the American Gospel: Global Christian Fundamentalism.* New York: Routledge, 1996.

Browning, Barbara. *Infectious Rhythm : Metaphors of Contagion and the Spread of African Culture.* New York: Routledge, 1998.

Burke, Edmund. *Reflections on the French Revolution*. Para 171. The Harvard Classics 1909-1914. <http://www.bartleby.com/24/3/7.html>. December 5, 2005.

Bute, E.L. *The Black Handbook: The People, History and Politics of Africa and the African Diaspora*. London and Washington: Cassell, 1997.

Camaroff, John. Ed. with Brian William and Andrew Reed. *Mafeking Diary: A Black Man's View of a White Man's War, by Sol T. Plaatje*. Cambridge, UK; Athens, OH: Meridor Press in association with J. Currey and Ohio University Press, 1990.

Cammett, Melani. "Defensive Integration and Defensive Integration and Late Developers: The Gulf Cooperation Council and the Arab Maghreb Union." *Global Governance* 5.3 (Jul-Sep99): 379-402.

Cartelli, Thomas. "Shakespeare's Merchant, Marlowe's Jew: The Problem Of Cultural Difference." *Shakespeare Studies 20* (1988): 255-260.

Catanese, Anthony V. *Haitians: Migration and Diaspora*. Boulder, CO: Westview, 1998.

Cervenka, Zdenek. *The Nigerian War, 1967-1970: History of the War: Selected Bibliography and Documents*. Frankfurt a.M.: Bernard & Graefe, 1971.

Cesaire, Aimé. *Return to My Native Land*. Paris: Presence Africaine, 1939.

Chabal, Patrick. "The African Crisis: Context and Interpretation." *Postcolonial Identities in Africa*. Eds. Richard Werbner and Terence Ranger. London and Atlantic Highlands, NJ: Zed Books, 1996. 29-54.

Chazan, Naomi et al. *Politics and Society in Contemporary Africa*. Boulder, CO: Lynne Rienner, 1988.

Chernin, Kim. "Is Wagner Good for the Jews?" *Tikkun* 7.1 (February 2002): 69-72.

Chomsky, Noam. *The Fateful Triangle : The United States, Israel, and the Palestinians*. Boston: South End Press, 1983.

Chuku, Gloria. *Igbo Women and Economic Transformation in Southeastern Nigeria, 1900-1960*. New York: Routledge, 2005.

Church, Clive. "Switzerland: A Paradigm in Evolution." *Parliamentary Affairs* 53.1 (Jan. 2000): 96-113.

Cirincione, Joseph with Jon B. Wolfsthal and Miriam Rajkumar. *Deadly Arsenals: Tracking Weapons of Mass Destruction*. Washington, DC: Carnegie Endowment for International Peace, 2005, Second Edition.

Central Intelligence Agency, U.S.A. *World Factbook 2005*. <http://www.odci.gov/cia/publications/factbook/index.html>. October 11, 2005

Clark, Nancy L. and William H. Worger. *South Africa: The Rise and Fall of Apartheid*. Harlow, England and New York: Longman, 2004.

Clarke, John D. *Yakubu Gowon: Faith in a United Nigeria*. London and Totowa, NJ: F. Cass, 1987.

Clarke, John H. Ed. *Marcus Garvey and the Vision of Africa*. New York: Vintage Books, 1974.

Clough, Marshall S. *Mau Mau Memoirs: History, Memory, And Politics*. Boulder, CO: L. Rienner, 1998.

Cobban, Helena. *The Moral Architecture of World Peace : Nobel Laureates Discuss Our Global Future*. Charlottesville, VA: University of Virginia Press, 2000.

Cock, Jacklyn and Alison Bernstein. *Melting Pots & Rainbow Nations: Conversations About Difference in the United States and South Africa*. Urbana : University of Illinois Press, 2002.

Coffey, Thomas M. *The Long Thirst: Prohibition in America 1920-1933*. New York: W.W. Norton & Co., 1975.

Connah, Graham. *Forgotten Africa: An Introduction to its Archaeology*. London and New York: Routledge, 2004.

Coquery-Vidrovitch, Catherine. *African Women: A Modern History*. Trans. Beth Gillian. Boulder, CO: Westview Press, 1997.

Colton, Elizabeth O. *The Jackson Phenomenon: The Man, The Power, The Message*. New York: Doubleday, 1989.

Coniff, Michael L. *Africans in the Americas: A History of the Black Diaspora*. New York: St. Martin's Press, 1994.

Cottrell, Robert C. *South Africa: A State of Apartheid.* Philadephia, PA: Chelsea House, 2005.

Crocker, Chester A. "The Lessons of Somalia." *Foreign Affairs* 74.3 (May/June 1995): 2-8.

Crowder, Michael. "Lugard and Colonial Nigeria: Towards an Identity." *History Today* 36 (Feb 1986): 23-29.

Crystal, David. Ed. *The Cambridge Encyclopedia of Language.* Cambridge: Cambridge University Press, 1997.

Crush, Jonathan "The Global Raiders: Nationalism, Globalisation and the South African Brain Drain," *Journal of International Affairs* (2002) Vol. 56, No. 1, pp. 147-172.

Cumming, Gordon. *Aid to Africa: French and British policies from the Cold War to the New Millennium.* Aldershot, Hampshire, England and Burlington, VT: Ashgate, 2001.

Darkoh, Michael and Apollo Rwomire. Eds. *Human Impact on Environment and Sustainable Development in Africa.* Aldershot, Hampshire, England and Burlington, VT: Ashgate, 2003.

Robert Davies, "South Africa's Economic Relations with Africa: Current Patterns and Future Prospects." *South Africa and Africa: Within Or Apart?* Ed. Adebayo Adedeji. London and Atlantic Highlands, NJ: Zed Books, in association with African Centre for Development and Strategic Studies (ACDESS), 1996. 167-192.

Davis, Abraham L. and Barbara Luck Graham. *The Supreme Court, Race, and Civil Rights.* Thousand Oaks, CA: Sage Publications, 1995.

Davis, Gregson. *Aimé Cesaire.* Cambridge, New York and Melbourne: Cambridge University Press, 1997.

DellaPergola, Sergio and Allie A. Dubb. *South African Jewry: A Sociodemographic Profile.* Jerusalem : Institute of Contemporary Jewry, Hebrew University of Jerusalem, 1988.

Dent, Martin. "Nigeria: Federalism and Ethnic Rivalry." *Parliamentary Affairs* 53.1 (Jan 2000): 157-168.

Desmangles, Leslie G. *The Faces of the Gods: Vodou and Roman Catholicism in Haiti.* Chapel Hill, NC: University of North Carolina Press, 1992.

Diamond, Jared. *Collapse: How Societies Choose to Fail or Succeed.* New York: Viking Penguin, 2005.

Diop, Cheikh Anta. *Civilisation or Barbarism: An Authentic Anthropology.* Brooklyn, NY: Lawrence Hill Books, 1991.

---*Precolonial Black Africa: A Comparative Study of the Political and Social Systems of Europe and Black Africa, From Antiquity to the Formation of Modern States.* Westport, CT: l Hill., 1987.

Djamba, Yanyi K. "African Immigrants in the United States of America: Socio-demographic Profile in Comparison to Native Blacks." *Journal of Asian and African Studies,* 34.2 (June 1999): 210-215.

Dorrington, Rob., et al. *The Demographic Impact of HIV/AIDS in Africa, National Indicators for 2004.* Cape Town: Center for Actuarial Research, South African Medical Research Council and Actuarial Society of South Africa, 2004.

Drinkwater, John. *Abraham Lincoln.* Boston: Houghton and Mifflin, 1919. <http://www.gutenberg.org/files/11172/11172-h/11172-h.htm>. November 17, 2005).

Dubow, Saul. *Racial Segregation and the Origins of Apartheid in South Africa, 1919-36.* Houndmills, Basingstoke, Hampshire, New York, and Oxford: MacMillan with St. Anthony's College, 1989.

Durch, William J. Ed. *The Evolution of UN Peacekeeping: Case-studies and Comparative Analysis.* New York: St. Martin's Press, 1993.

Ejobowah, John B. "Who Owns the Oil: The Politics of Ethnicity in the Niger Delta of Nigeria." *Africa Today,* 47.1 (Winter 2000): 29-47.

Ekechi, Felix K. "Gender and Economic Power: The Case of Igbo Market Women of Eastern Nigeria." House-Midamba and Ekechi, 1995. 41-57.

Ekwe-Ekwe, Herbert. *The Biafra War: Nigeria and the Aftermath.* Lewiston, N.Y., USA: E. Mellen Press, 1990.

Elkins, Caroline. *Imperial Reckoning : The Untold Story of Britain's Gulag in Kenya.* New York: Henry Holt, 2005

Ellis, Marc H. *Israel And Palestine Out Of The Ashes : The Search For Jewish Identity in the Twenty-first Century*. London and Sterling, VA: Pluto Press, 2002.

El-Nawawy, Mohammed and Adel Iskandar. *Al-Jazeera : How The Free Arab News Network Scooped The World and Changed the Middle East*. Cambridge, MA : Westview Press, 2002.

Encyclopedia Britannica, Vol. 2 out of 30 volumes, 15th edition, 1974.

Esedebe, P. Olisanwuche. *Pan-Africanism: The Idea And Movement, 1776-1991*. Washington, D.C. : Howard University, 1994 Edition, 2nd ed.

Ezenwe, Uka. *ECOWAS and the Economic Integration of West Africa*. New York: St Martin's Press, 1983.

Falah, Ghazi-Walidi. "Dynamics and Patterns of the Shrinking of Arab lands in Palestine." *Political Geography* 22.2 (February 2003): 179-209.

Falola , Toyin, Ed., *Nigerian History, Politics and Affairs : The Collected Essays of   Adiele Afigbo* Trenton, NJ: Africa World Press, 2005).

--- *A History of Nigeria*. Westport, CT: Greenwood Press, 1999.

---*Violence in Nigeria: The Crisis of Religious Politics and Secular Ideologies*. Rochester, NY: University of Rochester Press, 1998.

---"Gender, Business, and Space Control: Yoruba Market Women and Power." House-Midamba and Ekechi, 1995. 23-40.

Falter, Rolf. "Belgium's Peculiar Way to Federalism." *Nationalism in Belgium : Shifting Identities, 1780-1995*. Eds. Kas Deprez and Louis Vos. Houndmills, Basingstoke, Hampshire and New York, NY: Macmillan Press & St. Martin's Press, 1998. 177-197.

Farsakh, Leila. "Independence, Cantons, or Bantustans: Whither the Palestinian State?" *Middle East Journal* 59.2 (Spring 2005): 230-245.

Fatton, Robert. *The Making of a Liberal Democracy: Senegal's Passive Revolution, 1975-1985*. Boulder, CO: Lynne Rienner, 1987.

First, Ruth. *The Barrel of a Gun: Political Power in Africa and the Coup*. London: Allen Lane, 1970.

Fischer, David. "South Africa," *Nuclear Proliferation After the Cold War*. Eds.Mitchell Reiss and Robert S. Litwak. Washington, DC: Woodrow Wilson Center Press and The Johns Hopkins University Press, 1994.207-230.

Fitzmaurice, John. *The Politics of Belgium: Crisis and Compromise in a Plural Society*. New York: St. Martin's Press, 1983.

Fleeman, J. D. Ed. *Samuel Johnson: The Complete English Poems*. New Haven and London: Yale University Press, 1971.

Franklin, John Hope and August Meier. Eds. *Black Leaders of the 20th Century*. Chicago and Urbana, IL: University of Illinois Press, 1982.

Friedman, Thomas L. *The Lexus and the Olive Tree*. New York: Farrar, Strauss, Giroux, 1999.

Fredland, Richard A. "AIDS and Development: An Inverse Correlation?" *The Journal of Modern African Studies* 36.4 (1998): 547-568.

Garvey, Amy Jacques. *Garvey and Garveyism*. New York: Octagon Books, 1978, 1968.

Gelb, Norman . "Thatcher Takes on the Commonwealth: Staving Off Sanctions," *New Leader* 69 (July 14/28, 1986): pp. 6-7.

Geggus, David P. Ed., *The Impact of the Haitian Revolution in the Atlantic World*. Columbia, SC: University of South Carolina Press, 2001.

---. *Slavery, War, and Revolution: The British Occupation of Saint Domingue 1793–1798*. London: Clarendon Press, 1982

Gilbey, Emma. The Lady: The Life and Times of Winnie Mandela. London: Cape, 1993.

Gilleland, D.S. and J. P. Merisotis, J. P. *Funding South African Higher Education: Steering Mechanisms to meet National Goals*. Institute for Higher Education Policy: Washington, D.C, 2000.

Gish, Steven D. *Desmond Tutu: A Biography*. Westport, CT: Greenwood Press, 2004.

Glaser, Daryl J. I. "Zionism and Apartheid: A Moral Comparison." *Ethnic & Racial Studies* 26.3 (May2003): 403-21

Gleavy, R. and E. Kermeli. Eds. *Islamic Law: Theory and Practice*. London and New York: I.B. Tauris, 1997.

Goldschmidt Jr., Arthur. *Modern Egypt: The Formation of a Nation State* Westport, CT: Westview Press, 1988.

Goody, Jack. *The Culture of Flowers*. Cambridge and New York: Cambridge University Press, 1993.

Goose, Stephen D. and Frank Smyth, "Arming Genocide in Rwanda." *Foreign Affairs* 73.5 (Sept/Oct 1994): 86-96.

Gordon, Vivian V. Comp. *Kemet and Other African Civilisations: Selected References.*   Chicago, IL: Third World Press, 1991.

Grant, Miriam R. and Andrew D. Palmiere. "When Tea is a Luxury: The Economic Impact of HIV/AIDS in Bulawayo, Zimbabwe" *African Studies,* 62.2 (2003): 213-241.

Gray, Christopher. *Conceptions of History in the Works of Cheik Anta Diop and Theophile Obenga*. London: Karnak House, 1989.

Graybill, Lyn S. *Truth and Reconciliation in South Africa: Miracle or Model?* Boulder, CO: Lynne Rienner Publishers, 2002.

Gruen, Erich S. "Diaspora and Homeland." *Diasporas and Exiles: Varieties of Jewish Identity* Ed. Howard Wettstein. Berkeley, CA: University of California Press, 2002. 18-46

Gruenbaum, Ellen. *The Female Circumcision Controversy: An Anthropological Perspective*. Philadelphia : University of Pennsylvania Press, 2001.

Grundy, Kenneth W. *South Africa: Domestic Crisis and Global Challenge*. Boulder, CO: Westview Press, 1991.

Guelke, Adrian. *Rethinking the Rise and Fall of Apartheid: South Africa and World Politics*. Houndmills, Basingstoke, Hampshire and New York: Palgrave MacMillan, 2005.

Haile-Selassie, Teferra. *The Ethiopian Revolution, 1974-1991: From a Monarchical Autocracy to a Military Oligarchy*. London and New

York: Kegan Paul International; Distributed by Columbia University Press, 1997.

Harris, Joseph E. Ed. *Global Dimensions of the African Diaspora*. Washington, DC: Howard University Press, 2003. 2nd ed.

Harrison, David. *The White Tribe of Africa: South Africa in Perspective*. Berkeley, CA: University of California Press, 1982, 1981.

Harlow, Barbara. *Barred: Women, Writing, and Political Detention*. Hanover, NH: Wesleyan University Press and University Press of New England, 1992.

Haverkort, Bertus et al. Eds. *Ancient Roots, New Shoots : Endogenous Development in Practice*. Leusden, The Netherlands; London ; New York : ETC/Compass in association with Zed Books and Palgrave, 2003.

Hawthorne, Peter. *The Transplanted Heart; The Incredible Story of the Epic Heart Transplant Operations by Professor Christiaan Barnard and his Team*. Chicago: Rand McNally, 1968.

Hays, Colin and David Marsh. Eds. *Demystifying Globalisation*. New York: St. Martin's Press in association with Polsis, University of Birmingham, 2000.

Hazlewood, Arthur. *Economic Integration: The East African Experience*. New York : St. Martin's Press,1975.

Henrard, Kristin. *Minority Protection in Post-Apartheid South Africa: Human Rights, Minority Rights, and Self-Determination*. Westport, CT: Praeger 2000.

Henze, Paul B. *Layers of Time: A History of Ethiopia*. New York: St. Martin's Press, 2000.

Hill, Roland. *Lord Acton*. New Haven and London: Yale University Press, 2000

Hine, Darlene Clark and Jacqueline McLeod. Eds. *Crossing Boundaries: Comparative History of Black People in Diaspora*. Bloomington, IN: Indiana University Press, 1999.

Hiskett, Mervyn. *The Course of Islam in Africa*. Edinburgh: Edinburgh University Press, 1994.

Holden, Robert H. and Eric Zolov. Eds. 2000. *Latin America and the United States: A Documentary History*. New York: Oxford University Press, 2000.

Hooghe, Lisbeth. "Belgium: Hollowing the Center."Amoretti and Bermeo 2004, 55-92.

House-Midamba, Bessie and Felix K. Ekechi. Eds. *African Market Women and Economic Power : The Role of Women in African Economic Development* Westport, CT: Greenwood Press, 1995.

Horne, Gerald and Mary Young. Eds. *W.E.B. Du Bois : An Encyclopedia*. Westport, CT: Greenwood Press, 2000.

Horrell, Muriel. *Laws Affecting Race Relations in South Africa*. Johannesburg, South Africa: South African Institute of Race Relations, 1978.

Hull, Richard. "Rhodesia in Crisis," *Current History* 76.445 (March 1979): 105-109,137-138.

Hunter, Jane. "Israel and the Bantustans." *Journal of Palestine Studies* 15.3 (Spring 1986): 53-89.

Hunwick, John and Eve T. Powell. *The African Diaspora in the Mediterranean Lands of Islam*. Princeton, NJ: Markus Wiener Publishers, 2002.

Ibelema, Minabere. "Nigeria: The Politics of Marginalisation." *Current History* 99.637 (May 2000): 211-214.

Ibrahim, Jibrin. *Democratic Transition in Anglophone West Africa*. Dakar, Senegal: CODESRIA, 2003.

Idem, Unyierie Angela. "Language and the National Question." *The National Question in Nigeria : Comparative Perspectives*. Eds. Abubakar Momoh and Said Adejumobi Aldershot, Hampshire, England and Burlington, VT: Ashgate, 2002. 183-200.

Igwe, Agbafor. *Zik: The Philosopher of Our Time*. Enugu, Nigeria: Fourth Dimension Pub. Co. Ltd., 1992.

Ikemoto, Lisa C. "Lessons From the Titanic," in *Mother Troubles: Rethinking Contemporary Maternal Dilemmas*. Eds. Julia E. Hanigsberg and Sara Ruddick. Boston: Beacon Press, 1999. 157-177

Ilesanmi, Simeon O. *Religious Pluralism and the Nigerian State*. Athens, OH: Ohio University Center for International Studies, 1997.

Iliffe, John. "The Organization of the Maji Maji Rebellion,"Maddox 1993. 217-234.

Inikori, Joseph E. and Stanley L. Engerman. Eds. *The Atlantic Slave Trade: Effects on Economies and Peoples in Africa, the Americas, and Europe*. Durham, NC: Duke University Press, 1992.

International Telecommunications Union. *World Telecommunication Indicators, 2004-2005*. <http://www.itu.int/ITU-D/ict/statistics/at_glance/Internet03.pdf> November 15, 2004.

Jackson, Robert H and Carl G Rosberg. "Why Africa's Weak States Persist: The Empirical and the Juridical in Statehood." *The State and Development in the Third World*. Ed. Atul Kohli. Princeton, NJ: Princeton University Press, 1986. 259-282.

Jalloh, Alusine and Stephen E. Maizlish. Eds. *The African Diaspora*. College Station, TX: Texas A&M University Press, 1996.

James, C. L. R. *The Black Jacobins; Toussaint L'Ouverture and the San Domingo Revolution*. New York, Vintage Books, 1963.

James, Ron. *Frontiers and Ghettos: State Violence in Serbia and Israel*. Berkeley, CA: University of California Press, 2003.

James, Wilmot et al. Eds. *Now That We Are Free: Coloured Communities in a Democratic South Africa* Boulder, CT: L. Rienner, 1996).

Jayasuriya, Shihan de Silva and Richard Pankhurst. Eds. *The African Diaspora in the Indian Ocean*. Trenton, NJ: Africa World Press, 2003.

Jennings, Judith. *The Business of Abolishing the British Slave Trade, 1783-1807*. London and Portland, OR: Frank Cass, 1997.

Jeppie, Shamil. "Commemorations and Identities: The 1994 Tercentenary of Ilsma in South Africa," *Islam and the Question of Minorities*. Ed. Tamara Sonn. Atlanta, GA: Scholars Press, 1996. 73-92.

Johnson, Chalmers. *Blowback: The Costs and Consequences of American Empire*. New York: Henry Holt, 2001, 1st Owl Books ed.

Johnson, R. W. "Sekou Touré and the Guinean Revolution." *African Affairs* 69. 277 (October 1970): 350-365.

Johnston, Douglas. "The Churches and Apartheid in South Africa." *Religion, The Missing Dimension of Statecraft*. Ed. Douglas Johnston and Cynthia Sampson. New York: Oxford University Press, 1994.177-207.

Joseph, Benjamin M. *Besieged Bedfellows: Israel and the Land of Apartheid*. New York: Greenwood Press, 1988.

Judd, Denis and Keith Judd. *The Boer War*. London: John Murray, 2002.

July, Robert W. and Peter Benson. Eds. *African Cultural and Intellectual Leaders and the Development of the New African Nations*. New York and Ibadan: Rockefeller Foundation and Ibadan University Press, 1982.

Kaba, Amadu Jacky. "Africa's Migration and Terminal Brain Drain". *African Renaissance*, 2.4 (July-Aug. 2005): 112-118.

Kalu, Kelechi Amike. *Economic Development and Nigerian Foreign Policy*. Lewiston, NY: Edwin Mellen Press, 2000.

Kalu, O. U. "Safiyya and Adamah: Punishing Adultery with Sharia Stones in Twenty-first Century Nigeria." *African Affairs* 102.408 (2003): 389-408.

Kapur, Sudarshan. *Raising Up A Prophet: The African-American Encounter With Gandhi*. Boston: Beacon Press, 1992

Karatnycky, Adrian. "Freedom in the World 2005: Civic Power and Electoral Politics." <http://www.freedomhouse.org/research/freeworld/2005/essay20 05.pdf>. December 4, 2005.

Kaspin, K. Deborah. "The Politics of Ethnicity in Malawi's Democratic Transition", *Journal of Modern African Studies* 33.4 (1995): 595-620.

Kastor, Peter J. *The Nation's Crucible : The Louisiana Purchase and the Creation of America*. New Haven, CT: Yale University Press, 2004.

Katz, Jacob. "German Culture and the Jews." *Commentary* 77.2 (February 1984): 54-59.

Kelly, G. A. *Lost Soldiers: The French Army and Empire in Crisis, 1947-1962.* Cambridge, MA: MIT Press, 1965.

Kenyatta, Jomo. *Suffering Without Bitterness.* Nairobi and Chicago: East African Publishing House and Northwestern University Press, 1968.

"Jomo Kenyatta." Kenyan Ministry of External Affairs. <http://www.mfa.go.ke/kenyatta.html>. December 28, 2005.

Kerr, K. Austin. *Organizing for Prohibition: A New History of the Anti-Saloon League.* New Haven and London: Yale University Press, 1985.

Khaleel, Ibrahim. "The Hausa." *Ethnic and Cultural Diversity in Nigeria.* Okehie-Offoha and Sadiku, 1996. 37-62.

Khan, M. N. "Ijma: Third Source of Islamic Law." *Hamdard Islamicus* (11 Jan 1999): 84-86.

Khan, Sarah Ahmed. *Nigeria: The Political Economy of Oil.* Oxford: Oxford University Press for the Oxford Institute of Energy Studies, 1994.

Kieh, George Klay , Jr. "Military Engagement in Politics in Africa," Kieh and Ogbese 37-46.

Kieh, George Klay , Jr. and Pita Ogaba Agbese. Eds. *The Military and Politics in Africa: From Intervention to Democratic and Constitutional Control.* Aldershot, Hants, England: Burlington, VT: Ashgate, 2004.

Kimball, Penn. *Keep Hope Alive! : Super Tuesday and Jesse Jackson's 1988 Campaign for the Presidency.* Washington, DC and Lanham, MD: Joint Center for Political and Economic Studies Press and National Book Network, 1992.

King, Martin Luther, Jr. *Stride Towards Freedom: The Montgomery Story.* New York: Harper & Row, 1958.

Kingsley, David. *Ecology and Religion: Ecological Spirituality in Cross-Cultural Perspective.* Englewood Cliffs, NJ: Prentice Hall, 1995.

Kirk-Greene, A. H. M. Comp. and Ed. *Lugard and the Amalgamation of Nigeria: A Documentary record; being a reprint of the 'Report' by Sir F.D.Lugard on the amalgamation of Northern and Southern Nigeria and administration 1912-1919; together with supplementary*

unpublished amalgamation reports, and other relevant documents.
London: Cass, 1968.

Klotz, Audie J. *Norms in International Relations: The Struggle Against Apartheid.* Ithaca, NY: Cornell University Press, 1995.

Koch, Klaus-Friedrich. "Fabulous Timbuktu." *Natural History* 86.5 (May77): 68-75.

Kluger, Richard. *Simple Justice: The History of Brown v. Board of Education and Black America's Struggle for Equality.* New York: Vintage Books, 1977, 1975.

Knight, Franklin W. "The Haitian Revolution," *The American Historical Review* (February 2000), par. 11 <http://www.historycooperative.org/journals/ahr/105.1/ah000103.html> 1 Dec. 2005).

Kollehlon, Konia T. and Edward E. Eule. "The Socioeconomic Attainment Patterns of African in the United States." *The International Migration Review* 37.4 (2003): 1163-1190.

Kukah, M. H. and Toyin Falola. *Religious Militancy and Self-Assertion: Islam and Politics in Nigeria.* Aldershot, UK and Brookfield, VT: Avebury Press, 1996.

Kuperus, Tracy. *State, Civil Society and Apartheid in South Africa: An Examination of Dutch Reformed Church-State Relations.* New York: St. Martin's Press, 1999.

Kouassi, Edmond Kwam. "Africa and the United Nations since 1945." Mazrui and Wondji, 1993. 829-904.

Landau, Saul. *The Pre-Emptive Empire: A Guide to Bush's Kingdom.* London and Sterling, VA: Pluto Press, 2003.

Latzer, Barry. Ed. *Death Penalty Cases: Leading U.S. Supreme Court Cases on Capital Punishment.* Boston, MA: Butterworth-Heinemann, 1998.

Lawrence, T.E. *Seven Pillars of Wisdom.* London: Privately Printed 1926, and New York: Doubleday, 1935.

Lemarchand, René, Ed. *The Green and the Black: Qadhafi's Policies in Africa.* Bloomington, IN: Indiana University Press, 1988.

Leopold Sédar Senghor. <http://www.au-senegal.com/decouvrir_en/senghor.htm>. March 15, 2004.

Levtzion, Nehemiah. *Ancient Ghana and Mali.* New York, NY: African Pub. Co.,1973.

Levy, André and Alex Weingrod. Eds. *Homelands and Diasporas: Holy Lands and Other Places.* Stanford, CA: Stanford University Press, 2005);

Little, Donald P. *History and Historiography of the Mamlūks.* London: Variorum Reprints, 1986.

Lloyd-Jones Stewart and António Costa. Eds. *The Last Empire : Thirty Years of Portuguese Decolonisation.* Bristol, UK and Portland, OR : Intellect, 2003.

Logan, John R and Glenn Deane. "Black Diversity in Metropolitan America." Lewis Mumford Center for Comparative Urban and Regional Research, University at Albany, SUNY. <http://mum ford1.dyndns.org/cen2000/BlackWhite/BlackDiversity/Report/bla ckdiversity01.htm>.April 12, 2004 .Also at: <http://mumford.al bany.edu/census/report.html>. Revised Aug. 15, 2003.

Loimeier, Roman. *Islamic Reform and Political Change in Northern Nigeria.* Evanston, IL: Northwestern University Press, 1997.

Lovejoy, Paul E. *Transformations in Slavery: A History of Slavery in Africa.* Cambridge and New York: Cambridge University Press, 2000.

Lovejoy, Paul E. (1992). "Historical setting," *Nigeria: a Country Study.* Ed. Helen Metz. Washington, DC: U. S. G. P. O., Library of Congress, Federal Research Division, 1992: 1-83.

Lowell, Lindsay B. *Some Developmental Effects of the International Migration of Highly Skilled Persons,* International Migration Papers #46, International Migration Branch, International Labour Office. Geneva, Switzerland: ILO, 2001.

Luckham, Robin. "Military Withdrawal from Politics in Africa Revisited." Kieh and Ogbese 91-108.

Ludlow, N. Piers. *Dealing With Britain: The Six and the First UK Application to the EEC.* Cambridge and New York: Cambridge University Press, 1997.

Lwanda, John Lloyd. *Malawi under Kamuzu Banda: A Study in Promise, Power, And Paralysis (Malawi under Dr. Banda) (1961 to 1993).* Bothwell, Scotland, Great Britain: Dudu Nsomba Publications, 1993.

Lyons, Gene M. and Michael Mastanutono. Eds. *Beyond Westphalia? State Sovereignty and International Intervention.* Baltimore, MD: Johns Hopkins University Press, 1995.

Maddox, Gregory. Ed. *Conquest and Resistance to Colonialism in Africa.* New York: Garland, 1993.

Malan, Marais. *Heart Transplant; The Story Of Barnard and the "Ultimate in Cardiac Surgery."* Johannesburg: Voortrekkerpers, 1968.

Maloba, Wunyabari. *Mau Mau and Kenya: An Analysis of a Peasant Revolt.* Bloomington, IN: Indiana University Press, 1993.

Mandela, Nelson. *Long Walk to Freedom: The Autobiography of Nelson Mandela.* Boston: Back Bay Books, 1995.

Mansergh, Nicholas. *The Commonwealth Experience, Volumes I and II.* Toronto and Buffalo, NY: University of Toronto Press, 1983.

Marable, Manning. *Black Leadership.* New York : Columbia University Press, 1998.

Martin, David. *General Amin.* London: Faber, 1974.

Martin, Tony. *The Pan-African Connection: From Slavery to Garvey and Beyond.* Cambridge, MA: Schenkmann Pub. Co., 1983.

Massoud, Mark F. "The Evolution of Gay Rights in South Africa." *Peace Review* 15.3 (September 2003): 301-309.

Mazrui, Ali A. "Brain Drain between Counter-terrorism and Globalisation." *African Issues*, 30.1 (2002): 86-87.

---"Afro-Renaissance." *International Politik* (Bonn) 51.9 (1996): 11-18

---"The United Nations and Four Ethical Revolutions of the Twentieth Century." Presented at an international conference to mark the 50th anniversary of the United Nations, sponsored by La Trobe University, Victoria, Australia, July 2-6, 1995.

--- "Global Apartheid? Race and Religion in the New World Order." *Beyond the Cold War: New Dimensions in International Relations.*

Eds. Geir Lundestad and Odd Arne Westad. Stockholm: Scandinavian University Press, 1993. 85-98.

---*The Africans: A Triple Heritage.* London: BBC Publications, 1986.

---"Through the Prism of the Humanities: Eurafrican Lessons from Shakespeare, Shaka, Puccini, and Senghor," *African Cultural and Intellectual Leaders and the Development of the New African Nations.* Eds. Robert W. July and Peter Benson. New York and Ibadan: Rockefeller Foundation and Ibadan University Press, 1982. 197-220.

---"Boxer Muhammed Ali and Soldier Idi Amin as International Political Symbols: The Bioeconomics of Sport and War," *Comparative Studies in Society and History* 19. 2 (April 1977):189-215.

--- *The Warrior Tradition in Modern Africa.* Leiden: Brill, 1977.

---*World Federation of Cultures : An African Perspective.* New York: Free Press of Glencoe, 1976.

---"Kwame Nkrumah: The Leninist Czar." *Transition* (Kampala)6.26 (1966): 9-17.

Mazrui, Ali A. and Alamin M. Mazrui, *The Power of Babel: Language and Governance in the African Experience.* Oxford, Nairobi, Kampala, Cape Town, Chicago: James Currey, E.A.E.P, Fountain, David Philip, and the University of Chicago Press, 1998.

Mazrui, Ali A. et al. "Trends in Philosophy and Science in Africa." Mazrui and Wondji, 1993. 633-677.

Mazrui, Ali A. and C. Wondji. Eds. *UNESCO General History of Africa, Vol. VIII: Africa Since 1935.* London: Heinemann Educational Books, 1993.

Mazrui, Ali A. and Pio Zirimu. "The Secularization of an Afro-Islamic Language: Church, State and Marketplace in the Spread of Kiswahili." *Journal of Islamic Studies* 1.1 (1990): 23-35; also Mazrui and Mazrui 1998, 169-171.

Mazrui, Ali A. and Michael Tidy. *Nationalism and New States in Africa From About 1935 to the Present.* Nairobi: Heinemann, 1984.

McAlister, Elizabeth. *Rara!: Vodou, Power, and Performance in Haiti and its Diaspora*. Berkeley, CA: University of California Press, 2002.

McCreadie, Robert. "Scottish Identity and the Constitution." *National Identities: The Constitution of the United Kingdom*. Ed. Bernard Crick. Cambridge, MA and Oxford, UK: Blackwell Publishers, 1991: 38-56.

McLuhan, Marshall and Bruce R. Powers. *The Global Village: Transformations in World Life and Media in the 21st Century*. New York: Oxford University Press, 1989.

McRoberts, Kenneth. *Misconceiving Canada: The Struggle for National Unity*. Toronto, New York, and Oxford: Oxford University Press, 1997.

Michael, Colette V. *Négritude: An Annotated Bibliography*. West Cornwall, CT: Locust Hill Press, 1988.

Miles, Hugh. *Al-Jazeera: The Inside Story of the Arab News Channel that is Challenging the West*. New York: Grove Press, 2005.

Milton, John *Paradise Lost*. <http://www.bartleby.com/100/173.13.html>. January 3, 2006

Moors, Annelies. *Women, Property, and Islam: Palestinian Experience, 1920-1990*. New York: Cambridge University Press, 1995.

Morris, Patricia T. "Women, Resistance, and the Use of Force in South Africa." *Women and the Use of Military Force*. Eds. Ruth H. Howes and Michael R. Stevenson. Boulder, CO: L. Rienner Publishers, 1993. 185-206

Mortimer, Robert A. "The Arab Maghreb Union: Myth and Reality." *North Africa in Transition : State, Society, and Economic Transformation in the 1990s*. Ed. Yahia H. Zoubir. Gainesville, FL: University of Florida Press, 1999. 177-194.

---"ECOMOG, Liberia, and Regional Security in West Africa," *Africa in the New International Order: Rethinking State Sovereignty and Regional Security*. Eds. Edmond J. Keller and Donald Rothchild. Boulder, CO: Lynne Rienner, 1996: 149-164.

Mowat, Barbara and Paul Werstine. Eds. *Othello*. New York and London: Washington Square Press, Pocket Books, 1993.

Mugisha, Anne ."Museveni's Machinations." *Journal of Democracy* 15.2 (April 2004): 140-144.

Murphy, Alexander B. *Regional Dynamics and Cultural Differentiation in Belgium: A Study in Cultural Political Geography.* Chicago: University of Chicago Committee on Geographical Studies, 1988.

Murray-Brown, Jeremy. *Kenyatta.* New York: E. P. Dutton, 1973, 1972.

Na'Allah, Abdul-Rasheed. Ed. *Ogoni's Agonies : Ken Saro-Wiwa and the Crisis in Nigeria.* Trenton, NJ: Africa World Press, 1998.

Naldi, Gino J. *Documents of the Organization of African Unity.* New York: Mansell, 1992.

National Science Foundation, "International Mobility of Scientists and Engineers to the United States - Brain Drain or Brain Circulation?" (November 10, 1998) <http://www.nsf.gov/statistics/issuebrf/sib98316.htm>. December 19, 2005.

Neill, M. "Unproper Beds: Race, Adultery and the Hideous in 'Othello'." *Shakespeare Quarterly* 40.4 (Winter 1989): 383-412.

Ngoma, Naison. "SADC: Towards A Security Community?" *African Security Review* 12.3 (August 2003): 17-28.

Nkrumah, Kwame. *Africa Must Unite* London and New York: Heinemann, 1963 and International Publishers, 1972.

Nmehielle, Vincent O. (2004). "Sharia Law in the Northern States of Nigeria: To Implement or Not to Implement, the Constitutionality is the Question." *Human Rights Quarterly* 26.3 (Aug 2004): 730-759.

Nwachuku, C. B. and Aja Akpuru-Ajo. "The Igbo in the Political Economy of Nigeria," *The Igbo and the Tradition of Politics.* Eds. U. D. Anyanwu and J.C. U. Aguwa. Enugu, Nigeria: Fourth Dimension Publishing,1993:188-198.

Nwankwo, Arthur A. *Nigeria: The Stolen Billions.* Enugu, Nigeria: Fourth Dimension Publishing, 1999.

Nwigwe, Henry E. *Nigeria – The Fall of the First Republic.* London: Motorchild Press, 1972.

Nwokedi, Emeka. "France, the New World Order, and the Francophone West African States: Towards a Reconceptualization of Privileged Relations," Alden and Daloz, 1996. 195-217.

Nyabongo, Elizabeth. Elizabeth of Toro, The Odyssey of an African Princess: An Autobiography. New York: Simon and Schuster, 1989.

Ogletree, Charles J.,Jr. *All Deliberate Speed: Reflections on the First Half Century of Brown v. Board of Education.* New York: W. W. Norton, 2004.

Ogbomo, Onaiwu W. "Esan Women Traders and Precolonial Economic Power." House-Midamba and Ekechi, 1995. 1-21.

Okehie-Offoha, Marcellina Ulunma and Matthew N.O. Sadiku. *Ethnic and Cultural Diversity In Nigeria.* Trenton, NJ: Africa World Press, 1996.

Okojie, Christiana E. E. "Women in the Rural Economy in Nigeria." *Women, Work, and Gender Relations in Developing Countries : A Global Perspective.* Eds. Parvin Ghorayshi and Claire Bélanger. Westport, CT: Greenwood Press, 1996. 57-74.

Olaniyan, Richard A. Ed. *The Amalgamation and its Enemies: an Interpretive History of Modern Nigeria.* Ile-Ife, Nigeria: Obafemi Awolowo University Press, 2003.

Olivier, Gerrit. "Is Thabo Mbeki Africa's Saviour?" *International Affairs* 79.4 (July 2003): 815-828.

Omari, T. Peter. *Kwame Nkrumah: The Anatomy of an African Dictatorship.* New York: Africana Publishing Corp., 1970.

Onwumechili, Chuka. *African Democratisation and Military Coups.* Westport, CT: Praeger, 1998.

Ostler, Nicholas. *Empires of the Word : A Language History of the World.* New York: HarperCollins, 2005.

Osundare, Niyi. *Thread in the Loom: Essays on African Literature and Culture.* Trenton, NJ: Africa World Press, 2002.

Oyewole, A. *Historical Dictionary of Nigeria.* Metuchen, NJ: Scarecrow Press, 1987.

Packer, Corinne A. A. and Donald Rukare. "The New African Union And Its Constitutive Act." *American Journal of International Law* 96.2 (April 2002): 365-379.

Pakirayi, Innocent. *The Zimbabwe Culture: Origins and Decline of Southern Zambezian States.* Walnut Creek, CA: Lanham, MD; Oxford, UK: AltaMira Press, 2001.

Palmer, Alan Warwick. *Dictionary of the British Empire and Commonwealth.* London: Murray, 1996.

Paludan, Philip S. *A People's Contest: the Union and Civil War, 1861-1865.* Lawrence, KS: University of Kansas Press, 1996, Second Edition.

Pankhurst, Richard. *The Ethiopians: A History.* Oxford, UK and Malden, MA: Blackwell Publishers, 2001.

Ilan Pappe, *A History of Modern Palestine: One Land, Two People* Cambridge and New York: Cambridge University Press, 2004

Parenti, Michael. *Against Empire.* San Francisco, CA: City Lights Books, 1995.

Parkinson, Wenda. *"This Gilded African", Toussaint L'Ouverture.* London and New York: Quartet Books, 1980, 1978.

Parsons, Anthony. "From Southern Rhodesia to Zimbabwe, 1965-1985." *International Affairs* 9.4 (November 1988): 353-361.

Perret, Marion D. "Shakespeare's Jew: Preconception and Performance." *Shakespeare Studies* 20 (1988): 261-268.

Pettit, Becky and Bruce Western. "Mass Imprisonment and the Life Course: Race and Class Inequality in U.S. Incarceration." *American Sociological Review* 69.2 (April 2004): 151-169.

Perham, Dame Margery F. *Lugard*, 2 volumes. London: Collins, 1956-60.

Peters, Joel. *Israel and Africa: The Problematic Friendship.* London: British Academic Press, 1992.

Pfaff, William. "A New Colonialism? Europe Must Go Back into Africa," *Foreign Affairs* 74.1 (Jan/Feb 1995): 2-6.

Philipp, Thomas and Ulrich Haarmann. Eds. *The Mamluks in Egyptian Politics and Society.* Cambridge and New York: Cambridge University Press, 1998

Pierce, Paulette. "The Roots of the Rainbow Coalition." *Black Scholar*, 19.2 (1988): 2-16.

Poe, D. Zizwe. *Kwame Nkrumah's Contribution to Pan-Africanism: An Afrocentric View*. London and New York: Routledge, 2003.

Porter, Dale H. *The Abolition of the Slave Trade in England, 1784-1807*. Hamden, CT: Archon Books, 1970.

"Portraits of Ordinary Muslims: United States" *Frontline*, PBS Television, May 9, 2002. <http://www.pbs.org/wgbh/pages/frontline/shows/muslims/port raits/us.html>.May 1, 2004.

Posel, Deborah and Graeme Simpson. Eds. *Commissioning the Past : Understanding South Africa's Truth and Reconciliation Commission*. Johannesburg : Witwatersrand University Press and distributed by Thorold's Africana Books, 2002.

Prozesky, Martin. Ed. *Christianity Amidst Apartheid: Selected Perspectives on the Church in South Africa*. New York : St. Martin's Press, 1990.

Purkitt, Helen E. and Stephen F. Burgess. *South Africa's Weapons of Mass Destruction*. Bloomington, IN: Indiana University Press, 2005.

Quinn, Charlotte A. and Frederick Quinn. *Pride, Faith, and Fear : Islam in Sub-Saharan Africa*. New York: Oxford University Press, 2003),

Rahman, H. H. A. "The Origin and Development of *Ijtihad* to Solve Complex Modern Legal Problems." *Bulletin of the Henry Martyn Institute of Islamic Studies* 17 (1998): 7-21.

Ranger, T. O. "Connexions Between 'Primary Resistance' and Modern Nationalism in East and Central Africa, Parts I and II." *Journal of African History* 9 (1968): 437-453, 631-641.

Ratcliffe, Susan. Ed. *The Oxford Dictionary of Quotations*. Oxford: Oxford UP, 1994.

Ravitch, Frank S. *School Prayer and Discrimination: The Civil Rights of Religious Minorities and Dissenters*. Boston: Northeastern University Press, 1999.

Redmond, Patrick M. "Maji Maji in Ungoni: A Reappraisal of Existing Historiography." Maddox 1993. 235-252.

Rosenau, James N. *The United Nations in a Turbulent World*. Boulder, CO and London: Lynne Rienner Publishers, 1992.

Rosenthal, Eric. "Early Shakespeare Productions in South Africa." *English Studies in Africa* 17.2 (Sept. 1964): 202-216.

Rossignol, Marie-Jeanne. *The Nationalist Ferment:The Origins Of U.S. Foreign Policy, 1789-1812*. Transl. Lillian A. Parrott. Columbus, OH : Ohio State University Press, 2004.

Rostow, W. W. *The Economics of Take-Off Into Sustained Growth*. New York: St. Martin's Press, 1963, 1964.

Ruggie, John Gerard. "Wandering the Void: Charting the UN's New Strategic Role." *Foreign Affairs* Vol. 72.5 (Nov/Dec 1993): 26-31.

Rupert, Mark. *Ideologies of Globalisation: Contending Visions of a New World Order* London and New York: Routledge, 2000

Sadiku, Matthew. (1996). "The Yoruba." Okehie-Offoha and Sadiku, 1996. 125-147.

Sampson, Anthony. *Mandela : The Authorized Biography* New York: Knopf, distributed by Random House, 1999.

Sarna, Jonathan D. and David G. Dalin. *Religion and State in the American Jewish Experience*. Notre Dame: University of Notre Dame Press, 1997.

Sartre, Jean-Paul. "Black Orpheus." *Race*. Ed. Robert Bernasconi. Malden, MA: Blackwell Publishers, 2001. 115-142.

---. "Introduction to African Poetry", *Black Orpheus, transl.* Allen, S.W. Paris: Presence Africaine, 1963. 41-43.

Saulawa, Abdullah Mu'aza. "Islam and its Anti-Colonial and Educational Contribution in West Africa and Northern Nigeria, 1800-1960." *Hamdard Islamicus*, 19.1(1996): 69-79.

Schaeffer, Robert K. *Understanding Globalisation: The Social Consequences of Political, Economic, and Environmental Change*. Lanham, MD: Rowman and Littlefield Publishers, 1997.

Schwab, Peter. Ed. *Biafra*. New York : Facts on File, 1971.

Scobie, Edward. *Global African Presence*. Brooklyn, NY: A & B Books, 1994.

Senghor, Leopold Sédar. *The Foundations of "Africanité" or "Negritude" and "Arabité"*. Paris: Presence Africaine, 1971.

Shagari, Shehu. *Beckoned to Serve: An Autobiography*. Ibadan, Nigeria: Heinemann Educational Books, 2001.

Shakespeare, William. *King John, The Works of William Shakespeare*. New York: Oxford University Press, Shakespeare Head Press Edition, 1934.

Shanks, Cheryl. *Immigration and the Politics of American Sovereignty, 1890-1990*. Ann Arbor, MI: University of Michigan Press, 2001.

Sheffer, Gabriel. "Is the Jewish Diaspora Unique?" *Contemporary Jewries: Convergence and Divergence*. Eds. Eliezer Ben-Rafael, Yosef Gorny, and Yaacov Ro'i, Leiden and Boston, MA: Brill, 2003), pp. 23-44.

Shell-Duncan, Bettina and Ylva Hernlund, Eds. *Female "Circumcision" In Africa : Culture, Controversy, And Change*. Boulder, CO: Lynne Rienner Publishers, 2000.

Shimoni, Gideon. *Community and Conscience: The Jews in Apartheid South Africa*. Hanover, NH and Glosberry: Brandeis University Press published by University Press of New England and David Philip, 2003.

Simes, Dimitri K. "America's Imperial Dilemma," *Foreign Affairs* 82.6 (November-December 2003): 91-102.

Singleton, Brent D. "African Bibliophiles: Books and Libraries in Medieval Timbuktu," *Libraries & Culture* (Winter2004), Vol. 39 Issue 1, pp. 1-12;

Smith, Jane I. *Islam in America*. New York: Columbia UP, 1999.

Snyder, Susan. "Othello: A Modern Perspective." *Othello*. Eds. Barbara Mowat and Paul Werstine. New York and London: Washington Square Press, Pocket Books, 1993.

Spector, Stephen. *Operation Solomon: The Daring Rescue of the Ethiopian Jews*. Oxford and New York: Oxford University Press, 2005.

Stanton, C. M. *Higher Learning in Islam: The Classical Period, A. D. 700 to 1300*. Savage, MD: Rowman and Littlefield, 1990

The Statistical Abstract of the United States. Washington, DC: Bureau of the Census, January 2002.

Stein, Lana. "American Jews and Their Liberal Political Behaviour." *The Politics of Minority Coalitions.* Ed. Wilbur C. Rich. Westport, CT and London: Praeger, 1996. 193-200.

Stearns, Peter N. *Gender in World History.* London and New York: Routledge, 2000.

Suberu, Rotimi T. *Federalism and Ethnic Conflict in Nigeria.* Washington, DC : US Institute of Peace Press, 2001.

Suberu, Rotimi T. "Nigeria: Dilemmas of Federalism". Amoretti and Bermeo, 2004. 327-354.

Sura, Vikram. "NEPAD: Negotiating for Africa's Development." *UN Chronicle* 40.1 (Mar-May 2003): 23-25.

Suret-Canale, Jean. *French Colonialism in Tropical Africa, 1900-1945.* London: C. Hurst, 1971.

Swatuk, Larry A. "Review Essay: Dead-End to Development? Post-Cold War Africa in the New International Division of Labour." *African Studies Review* 38.1(April 1995): 103-117.

Swatuk, Larry A. and David R. Black. Eds. *Bridging The Rift: The New South Africa in Africa.* Boulder, CO: Westview Press, 1997.

Talbott, John E. *The War Without a Name: France in Algeria, 1954-1962.* New York: Knopf, 1980.

Tanner, Marcus. *Ireland's Holy Wars : The Struggle for a Nation's Soul, 1500-2000.* New Haven, CT : Yale University Press, 2001),

The World Guide 1999/2000. Montevideo: Third World Institute, 1999.

Thomas, Darryl C. *The Theory and Practice of Third World Solidarity.* Westport, CT: Praeger, 2001.

Thompson, V. B. *Africans of the Diaspora: The Evolution of African Consciousness and Leadership in the Americas from Slavery to the 1920s.* Trenton, NJ and Asmara, Eritrea: Africa World Press, 2000.

Tibenderana, Peter K. "The Emirs and the Spread of Western Education in Northern Nigeria, 1910-1946." *Journal of African History* 24.4 (1983): 517-534.

Tieku, Thomas K. "Explaining The Clash And Accomodation Of Interests Of Major Actors In The Creation Of The African Union." *African Affairs* 103.411 (Apr 2004): 249-267.

"Timbuktu-City of Legends, " at <http://news.bbc.co.uk/1/hi/world/africa/1911321.stm> (April 15, 2002)

Titley, Brian. *Dark Age: The Political Odyssey of Emperor Bokassa.* Montreal; Buffalo: McGill-Queen's UP, 1997.

Touval, Saadia. "Why the UN Fails."*Foreign Affairs* 73.5 (Sept/Oct 1994): 44-57.

Tutu, Desmond. *The Rainbow People of God: The Making of a Peaceful Revolution.* Ed. John Allen. New York: Doubleday, 1994.

---"The Question of South Africa," Africa Report 30 (January/ February 1985): 50-52.

---*Hope and Suffering : Sermons and Speeches.* Comp. Mothobi Mutloatse, Ed. John Webster. Grand Rapids, MI: W.B. Eerdmans, 1984, 1983.

Tyson, George F. Jr. Ed. *Toussaint L'Ouverture.* Englewood Cliffs, NJ: Prentice-Hall, 1973.

United Nations (UN). *World Urbanization Prospects: The 2003 Revision Database.* New York: Department of Social and Economic Affairs. Population Division. 2004.

UNAIDS, *AIDS Epidemic Update, December 2002.* Geneva, Switzerland: UNAIDS and WHO, 2002..

United Nations Development Program. *Human development Report, 2000.* New York:Oxford University Press, 2000.

United Nations Development Program. *Human development Report 2003.* New York:Oxford University Press,2003.

UNDP World Human Development Report, 2004. <http://hdr.un dp.org/statistics/data/indic/indic_69_1_1.html>. July 30, 2004.

United States Agency for International Development Activity Data Sheet , "Healthier Families of Desired Size, 521-003." <http://www.usaid.gov/pubs/cbj2002/lac/ht/521-003.html> 1 Dec. 2005.

United States Census Bureau. *Profile of the Foreign-Born Population in the United States: 2000.* Washington, DC: U.S.G.P.O., 2000.

---"American Community Survey Profile 2002," September 2, 2003, <http://www.census.gov/acs/www/products/Profiles/Single/2002 /ACS/Tabular/010/01000U> April 21, 2004.

---*Educational Attainment for selected Ancestry group, 1990. 1998*, Feb. 18. <http://www.census.gov/population/socdemo/ancestry/table_01.t xt>.April 13, 2004.

--- *Census 2000 Summary File 3, Matrix PCT19*. Washington, DC: Government Printing Office, 2000.

Udogu, Emmanuel I. "Economic Community of West African States: From an Economic Union to a Peacekeeping Mission." *The Review of Black Political Economy*, 26.4 (Spring 1999): 57-74.

Ulam, Alex. "Elusive Libraries of Timbuktu." *Archaeology* 57.4 (Jul/Aug2004): 36-40

Umoren, Joseph A. *Democracy and Ethnic Diversity in Nigeria*. Lanham, MD: UP of America, 1996.

Unterhalter, Elaine. *Forced Removal : The Division, Segregation and Control of the People of South Africa*. London: International Defence and Aid Fund for Southern Africa, 1987.

Uwechue, Ralph. *Reflections on the Nigerian Civil War*. New York: Africana PubL. Corp, 1971.

Vaillant, Janet G. *Black, French and African: A Life of Leopold Sédar Senghor*. Cambridge, MA: Harvard UP, 1990.

Vale, Peter and Sipho Maseko, "Thabo Mbeki, South Africa, and the Idea of An African Renaissance," *Thabo Mbeki's World : The Politics And Ideology Of The South African President*. Eds. Sean Jacobs and Richard Calland. Pietermaritzburg, SA; London; and New York: University of Natal Press and Zed Books, 2002), pp. 121-142.

Vasilian, Hamo B. Ed. *The Armenian Genocide: A Comprehensive Bibliography And Library Resource Guide*. Glendale,VA: Armenian Reference Books Co., 1992.

Vaughan, Olufemi. *Nigerian Chiefs: Traditional Power in Modern Politics, 1890s-1990s*. Rochester, NY: University of Rochester Press, 2000.

VerEecke, Catherine. "Muslim Women Traders of Northern Nigeria: Perspectives from the City of Yola." House-Midamba and Ekechi, 1995. 59-79.

Vogel, Frank E. (1993). "The Closing of the Door of Ijtihad and the Application of the Law." *American Journal of Islamic Social Sciences* 10 (Fall1993): 396-401.

Waal, Victor De. *The Politics of Reconciliation: Zimbabwe's First Decade.* London and Cape Town: Hurst and David Philip, 1981.

Wai, Dunstan M. *The African-Arab Conflict in the Sudan.* New York and London: Africana Publishing Co, 1981.

Waldau, Paul. *The Specter of Speciesism: Buddhist and Christian Views of Animals.* Oxford and New York: Oxford University Press, 2002.

Walker, Thomas G. "Capital punishment and the Mentally Retarded: Atkins v. Virginia (2002)." *Creating Constitutional Change : Clashes Over Power and Liberty in the Supreme Court.* Eds. Gregg Ivers and Kevin T. McGuire. Charlottesville, VA: University of Virginia Press, 2004), pp. 281-294.

Walraven, Klaas Van. *Dreams of Power : The Role of the Organization of African Unity in the Politics of Africa, 1963-1993.* Aldershot, Hants, England: Ashgate, 1999

Wardhaugh, Ronald. *Languages in Competition : Dominance, Diversity, and Decline.* Oxford, UK; New York; and London, England: B. Blackwell and A. Deutsch, 1987.

Waswo, Anne. *Modern Japanese Society, 1848-1994.* Oxford: Oxford University Press, 1996.

Weiss, Thomas George et al. *The United Nations and Changing World Politics.* Boulder, CO: Westview Press, 1994.

Werbner, Richard and Terence Ranger. Eds. *Postcolonial Identities in Africa.* London and Atlantic Highlands, NJ: Zed Books, 1996.

Werlin, Herbert H. "Ghana and South Korea: Explaining Development Disparities." *Journal of African and Asian Studies* 29.3-4 (July/October 1994): 205-225.

Westwood, J. N. *Endurance and Endeavor: Russian History, 1812-1992.* Oxford: Oxford University Press, 1993.

White Jr., Lynn. "The Historical Roots of Our Ecologic Crisis." *Pollution and the Death of Man: The Christian View of Ecology.* Ed. Francis A. Schaeffer. Wheaton, IL: Tyndale Publishing House, 1970. 97-115.

Wilde, Oscar. *The Picture of Dorian Gray.* New York: Modern Library, 1992).

Williams, David. *President and Power in Nigeria: The Life of Shehu Shagari.* London and Totowa, NJ: Cass, 1982

Williams, Michael W. *Pan-Africanism : An Annotated Bibliography* Pasadena, CA : Salem Press, 1992

Williams, Pat A.T. (1997). "Religion, Violence, and Displacement in Nigeria." *Journal of Asian and African Studies*, 32.1-2 (June 1997): 33-49.

Williams, Pat A.T. and Toyin Falola. (1995). *Religious Impact on the Nation State: The Nigerian Predicament* . Aldershot, UK and Brookfield, VT: Avebury Press, 1995.

Willis, John R. *Slaves and Slavery in Muslim Africa, Volume I: Islam and the Ideology of Slavery.* Totowa, NJ and London: Frank Cass, 1985.

Wills, A. J. *An Introduction to the History of Central Africa.* London: Oxford University Press, 1967, Second Edition.

Wolpe, Harold. *Race, Class, and the Apartheid State.* London: Currey, 1988.

Wordsworth, William. "She Dwelt Among the Untrodden Ways," *The Poems: William Wordsworth.* Ed. John Hayden. New Haven, CT: Yale UP, 1981.

World Bank. *Sub-Saharan Africa: From Crisis to Sustainable Development.* Washington D.C.: The World Bank, 1989.

The World Guide 1999/2000 Oxford, UK: New Internationalist Publications, 1999.

The World Markets Research Centre. "The Brain Drain — Africa's Achilles Heel," in "Africa In Focus 2002," <http://www.world marketsanalysis.com/InFocus2002/articles/africa_braindrain.html >. April 22, 2004

Wright, John W. Ed., *The New York Times Almanac.* New York: Penguin Group, 2004

INDEX

Ordering this book and other books by Adonis & Abbey Publishers

Wholesale inquiries in the UK and Europe:
Gardners Books Ltd
+44 1323 521777: email: custcare@gardners.com

Wholesale enquiries in USA and Canada
Ingram Book Company (ordering)
+1 800 937 8000 website: www.ingrambookgroup.com

*Online Retail Distribution: All leading online book sellers including www.amazon.co.uk, www.amazon.com, www.barnesandnoble.com

*Shop Retail: Ask any good bookshop or contact our office:
http//:www.Adonis-abbey.com

Phone: +44 (0) 207 793 8893

Printed in the United States
120453LV00003B/7/A

9 781905 068296